The Royals and The Roaches

The Royals and The Roaches

◆

Living Abroad with the Government

Patricia L. Hughes

To Ruth and Clem,
I hope you
enjoy my memories.
Family ~ the best
of the Royals.

Pat

iUniverse, Inc.

New York Lincoln Shanghai

The Royals and The Roaches
Living Abroad with the Government

iUniverse, Inc.

For information address:
iUniverse, Inc.
2021 Pine Lake Road, Suite 100
Lincoln, NE 68512
www.iuniverse.com

ISBN: 0-595-31496-1

Printed in the United States of America

I dedicate this book to my husband in gratitude for his support and without whom there would be no book

To our children, Alexander and Katherine, who shared the royal experiences and repelled a few roaches along with us

To my mother for encouraging me to write and to our parents for saving my letters throughout the years, thus providing me with a diary

To our friends and colleagues around the world who have shared their stories and their friendship.

I am grateful to my son-in-law, Jeffery Honea, for his enthusiastic help and advice.

Thank you to Francesca Kelly whose editing was invaluable.

Contents

CHAPTER 1   THE ROYALS 1
An Introduction

CHAPTER 2   IN THE BEGINNING 6

CHAPTER 3   JOINING UP 19

CHAPTER 4   FRANKFURTERS AND APFELWOI 30

CHAPTER 5   THE ROACHES 44

CHAPTER 6   GUAJIROS AND OIL WELLS 52

CHAPTER 7   THE PERILS OF PACKING 78

CHAPTER 8   THE RHINE AND THE ROCK 93

CHAPTER 9   LAUGHING IN A FOREIGN LANGUAGE 116

CHAPTER 10   THE MERMAID AND THE MAGIC 132

CHAPTER 11   HOME IS WHERE? .164

CHAPTER 12   DUTCH TREATS 179

CHAPTER 13   SAFEGUARDS AND SAFEKEEPING 200

CHAPTER 14   OLD TESTAMENT AND NEW TRIALS 218

CHAPTER 15   THE OTHER ROACHES 247

CHAPTER 16   MR. AMBASSADOR 267

CHAPTER 17   ARABIA FELIX 272

REFERENCES 301
GLOSSARY 303

1

THE ROYALS

✦

An Introduction

I was sorry I was wearing a hat. The day was much too warm—and so was the black and white suit I had on. Queen Elizabeth, elegantly dressed in beige lace and satin with a matching hat and gloves, didn't even glisten. The rest of us were sweating.

The year was 1991. We were having tea in the green and blossom-laden gardens of the British Embassy in Washington, DC. Queen Elizabeth and Prince Philip were visiting the United States and the May garden party was to celebrate the cooperation between the British and American governments during the recent war in the Gulf.

My husband Arthur, a career Foreign Service Officer, was assigned to the Office of the Secretary of Defense. Through his work Art had had a close and continuing association with the British Embassy and its military officers throughout Desert Shield and Desert Storm. When the invitation arrived, ostensibly from the British ambassador, but "commanded by the Queen…" I was delighted that the address read "Mr. *and* Mrs. Hughes." I immediately went shopping and bought a hat.

What a disappointment it was when Art found out that he would be out of the country on the day of the party. He knew I would attend—with or without him—so he suggested that perhaps our daughter could go in his place. Katherine has just finished a semester's work at Columbia University in New York and she planned to be home for a visit that week.

We were aware that security would be extremely tight and no one would be allowed in the embassy gardens without an invitation. Would it be presumptuous to ask? Or just plain bad manners? I dithered for days until finally Art prodded me into calling the British Embassy. When I reached the office in charge of the momentous event, a pleasant voice replied to my request: "Why, yes, we would be happy to have your daughter attend. We'll prepare another invitation—with pleasure."

The pleasure was surely ours! Kathy and I dressed that day in our spring finest—as did all the guests. Knowing the Queen would wear a hat, the majority of women did likewise. Everyone was concerned with making a good impression and behaving properly in the company of royalty. Kathy in her spring-fresh white long-sleeved dress was almost giddy with excitement—she was young and impressionable.

As we approached the British Embassy, a young man coming out the gate greeted us with a big smile and enthused, "The shrubberies are fantastic!" At least we thought he said "shrubberies" and we were puzzled. After we entered the garden and looked around, however, we realized that he had said "strawberries." And they *were* fantastic! Bright red, plump and fresh, mounded high in enormous silver bowls with whipped cream nearby to spoon over. I had never before seen such a quantity of beautiful berries in one place—but then there were also several hundred guests in one place.

In addition to the fruit, tiny tea sandwiches and sweets were arranged elegantly on flower-festooned tables shaded by canopies. Huge silver urns dispensed hot tea into delicate china cups. Since the day was unusually warm for mid-May, many of the guests eventually drifted toward the tables where iced tea sparkled in crystal pitchers. Waiters served it in tall glasses adding pretty bunches of fresh mint.

The Queen of England and the Duke of Edinburgh, together at first and then separately, circulated among the guests stopping here or there to greet someone and to comment on their visit to the United States. Most guests—following the dictates of protocol—stood in groups and waited for one or the other royal to approach. Her Majesty strolled regally, smiling and speaking softly.

American royals abounded at the Queen's garden party: Vice President Daniel Quayle and Marilyn Quayle, actress Jane Fonda, journalist Barbara Walters, Senators Ted Kennedy and John Warner. Angela Lansbury was charming as she talked and laughed with one of her fans—a little girl who was breathlessly excited to meet the great actress. We recognized many other senators, congressmen, ambassadors and international dignitaries—and shook hands with a few.

But what I will remember most about that day is the sheer elegance of the event, the understated quality of the décor and service and the organizational expertise that was so evident. And the Queen. I wasn't as young as Kathy, but I was still impressionable.

Another of Her Majesty's millinery became known as "The Talking Hat." Although I have it on good authority that she had a splendid sense of humor, I doubt that the monarch was amused by the exaggeration of the story. The hat incident occurred on the grounds of the White House during her arrival ceremony. When Queen Elizabeth stepped up to the podium to respond to President George H.W. Bush's welcoming remarks, the microphones obscured her face. Because of her short stature and the height of the lectern, all that the audience, including television viewers, could see was a hat that appeared to perch on top of the microphones. When she spoke, the disembodied voice seemed to come from the hat!

A faceless photograph of the Queen appeared in the newspapers. All of Washington tittered that day about "The Talking Hat," while government functionaries got scoldings from all sides. Later, an investigating journalist reported that there had been a step stool for Her Majesty to stand on—but no one had pulled it out for her.

America has not had a monarch since 1776, but make no mistake, we *do* have our royals. They live in the White House, walk on the moon, enforce the law, lead protest marches, write poetry, put out fires, design buildings, serve in the military, paint murals and win Olympic medals. We look upon our entertainers as royalty: the orchestra conductors, movie stars, singers, quarterbacks, ballerinas, guitarists, thespians and novelists. Americans may not revere their royals in the British manner, but we treat them with a great deal of attention and awe.

A few months after eating strawberries in the presence of Queen Elizabeth, I had tea at the White House with the First Lady—the embodiment of an American royal. I can best describe Barbara Bush with two words: warm and genuine.

I first met her in Denmark and again in the Netherlands. She immediately impressed me because she looked in my eyes when she spoke to me. I observed her interaction with others and continued to see the same eye contact. She didn't look over your shoulder to see who else was around. Politicians do that—so do diplomats. While they're speaking to one person, their eyes are roving the room looking for the next handshake. But not so with Mrs. Bush.

In the Yellow Room of the White House she greeted us with her warm smile and expressive eyes. We were a group of wives who were participating in the State Department's ambassadorial seminar with our husbands. When the training course was in session (two or three times a year) and the First Lady was in town, she invited the women to tea. Her husband had been our ambassador to China and later to the United Nations and both of the Bushes had an affinity with Foreign Service people. Having served in an embassy abroad, they understood what diplomatic life entailed.

"Have I met you before?" Mrs. Bush said to another woman and me as we sat down with our teacups. I recalled to her where and when we had met, not really expecting her to remember.

"Oh, yes. Now who was your ambassador in Denmark?" When I told her his name, she responded, "Oh my!" rolling her eyes. "That was quite a situation!" (And indeed it was.) She told me about a return trip to Denmark and we reminisced a few minutes about Danish government people we both knew.

Mrs. Bush turned then to Ann whom she remembered from a recent trip to Zaire. "Do you remember about the holey old sweater?" The suggestion set them both laughing and they had to share the story with the rest of us.

One evening in Kinshasa President Bush found himself without a wrap and the night air was chilly. Unbeknownst to Barbara, Ann opened a nearby closet and grabbed the closest thing at hand. It happened to be an old ratty sweater full of holes that belonged to her husband, the ambassador.

A little later Barbara noticed what the President was wearing and, feeling slightly embarrassed, she remarked to her hostess, "I don't know why George is wearing that awful old sweater."

When she found out that the sweater belonged to the ambassador, not her husband, she was mortified to have maligned the old but favorite sweater.

The conversation turned to the guests' upcoming assignments, the different countries, new languages and the changes that would come in our lives due to our husbands' ambassadorial appointments. Each of us except Ann would be an ambassador's wife for the first time.

"I will tell you about another trip," Mrs. Bush began. She and the President were in a foreign country and she was scheduled to make a particular visit out in the countryside. There had been a lot of rain and her advisers told her to wear "comfortable" shoes. Being a practical woman she dressed in a plain cotton dress and canvas shoes.

She arrived—to be greeted by the local women wearing "silks and stilts" as she described them. In honor of her visit the ladies had worn their finest dresses and high-heeled fancy shoes. "Even if you would like to think otherwise, it *does* matter what you wear. Everyone will be looking at you."

As we were saying goodbye to the First Lady at the end of our allotted hour—she was hosting a group of ballet dancers next—she gave us some thoughtful advice.

"Keep a diary," she said. "You'll enjoy doing it and—someday you may want to write your memoirs."

2

IN THE BEGINNING

Our adventures began with the U.S. Army when Art was posted to Fulda, Germany in 1963. There and then we discovered the allure of traveling, the enthusiasm for learning about other cultures, the excitement of new experiences, and the fascination of being on the outskirts of "danger." Fulda was a mere 15 kilometers from what was then the East German border.

Art had passed the Foreign Service exam and planned a career as a diplomat, but first he wanted to fulfill his obligation to the Armed Forces. After completing his course work toward a graduate degree at the University of Nebraska he entered the military. He went first to Fort Benning, Georgia for basic training, then Fort Holibird in Maryland. He left for Germany in the spring. I stayed in Lincoln with our baby, Alexander, to finish my last months at the university.

The day after graduation my parents took Alexander and me to the airport in Omaha. We would spend two nights in New York with college friends before going on to Europe. I had never flown before. I was 22 years old, armed with a Bachelor of Science degree in secondary education and, figuratively speaking, "fresh off the farm." I was excited and not a little nervous. My dad gave me detailed instructions about what to do if anything untoward happened or if we missed our connection. It happened and we did.

The flight was late arriving in Chicago and we raced through O'Hare airport hoping to be in time for our connecting flight. Alex, two weeks short of his first birthday, was not yet walking. Running and carrying a child was not an easy feat—but I had help. Next to us on the plane from Omaha had been a good-looking middle-aged gentleman who kindly offered to carry my raincoat and the heavy diaper bag. We arrived breathless at the gate only to receive the bad news: the plane to New York was full—they had overbooked the flight.

My friendly seat partner with the shock of white hair was still with us. By this time he was no longer a stranger and I didn't hesitate a second when he offered to make the ticketing arrangements so I could concentrate on Alex. When the man rejoined us a little while later, he had our new tickets—and also a surprise for me. The airline had given each delayed passenger an "apology bonus:" twenty-three dollars and some cents—cash! Fresh out of school and living on an army salary in 1963, I thought it was a great deal of money.

"You need to inform your friends in New York that you'll be delayed," my fellow traveler reminded me. "The airline will pay for the call." That had been my dad's advice, but I had forgotten.

During the flight to New York my new friend again sat next to us. After he finished his meal he took a tired and cranky Alex on his lap and lulled him to sleep. While I ate and enjoyed the short intermission, we exchanged names and he told me that he and his wife had grown up in Nebraska. After we landed he helped me retrieve the luggage and together we went to meet Dave and Anne.

I repeatedly thanked the man for his help and good humor—but he cut short my profusion of gratitude with a nonchalant wave of his hand. He grinned and then pulled a card from his pocket. "Tell your husband you were in good hands." The card read "Colonel Barney Oldfield, USAF (Ret.)"

The name was somehow familiar. Race car driver? No, this man was too young. I found out that this Barney Oldfield was a renowned World War II veteran, a journalist and public relations expert in the European Theater of Operations. He was an officer in both the air force and the army—the only man to claim that distinction—and he is featured in the United States Air Force Museum as one of its "Celebrities in Uniform." I was in good hands indeed!

In his book, *Never a Shot in Anger*, Colonel Oldfield relates amusing anecdotes from the war years and tells of shepherding the war correspondents who were assigned to his care. He proudly gives credit to the "noncombatant word merchants." The list of his subsequent accomplishments is lengthy and awe-inspiring. He and his wife Vada, one of the original WAACs, have established numerous memorials and foundations that award educational scholarships—"the best game in town," he says.

When I wrote my parents from Germany that I had met Colonel Oldfield, they told me about the hometown connection. Vada was the sister of a long-time friend of my parents. After I decided to write this book, I inquired about the colonel through my mother, asking if her friend might have some biographical data. When my phone rang a week later, I recognized the voice immediately. "Is this the young woman I befriended on an airplane thirty years ago?"

I answered that it was closer to thirty-four years and, yes, I was the woman but I was no longer young. "I remember our plane ride as if it were yesterday—and I am still in your debt," I told him.

In a subsequent letter Colonel Oldfield commented, "I have been watching myself lately. Women have become so militant." He said he would probably not risk such a thing today—referring to the help he gave me in 1963. Recently a young woman had reacted scornfully when he held a door open for her. I can't imagine how anyone could refuse the attentions of this kind man.

The flight was long. We didn't jet over to Europe; we flew in an old-fashioned prop plane. The Icelandic Airlines aircraft was small and full and there was no Colonel Oldfield to help us out. There was also no in-flight movie. Our entertainment during the twenty-plus hours consisted of a few small toys that I had managed to stuff into the diaper bag alongside the usual necessities. A refueling stop in Gander, Newfoundland, was a godsend, the only opportunity to rest my weary arms and let Alex crawl around on the airport floor—a very dirty floor—but I didn't care a whit. He needed to move!

As the airplane approached Luxembourg where Art would meet us, we hit some turbulence. The nasty weather not only delayed our arrival but also bounced us around sufficiently to make many passengers airsick, including me. When at last we deplaned, I spotted Art waiting behind a fence that separated the passengers from the greeters. He wore a big smile and was obviously happy to see us. I, on the other hand, feeling extremely nauseous and wanting only to lay my head down in a cool, quiet place, uttered something akin to "horse pucky." I thrust Alex over the fence at his father and announced I was never going to fly again!

It was not the warm, loving greeting Art had anticipated. And Alex, who had not seen his daddy for three months and wanted nothing to do with this strange man, began to kick and bellow drawing everyone's eyes and ears in our direction. Ahh—the happy family together again!

Thus began our adventures abroad. During the next fourteen months we explored many areas of Germany and we visited France with my parents. We traveled to Spain and Italy where we camped out in a tent that leaked when it rained. We learned a great deal about Germans and about Europeans in general. We experienced for the first time the absence of our extended family; we relished foods that we had never eaten before; we walked and gawked a great deal—and we grew up.

We lived on the upper floor of a small house in Heimbach, a village outside Fulda in the same direction as Downs Barracks, home of the 14th Armored Cavalry. The house was owned jointly by a German couple who would be married—when the house was completed. They both had jobs and they contracted out the work on the house at a pace they could afford. During our stay the basement was completed, front sidewalks were put in, the hallways were wallpapered and railings were added to the stairways between floors. But there was no stucco on the outside walls to cover the concrete blocks. At $70.00 for a month's rent, we couldn't expect perfection.

When I found out we didn't have a telephone—and it would be impossible to acquire one—I was horrified. I soon became accustomed to its absence, however, and eventually wrote home that I didn't miss it. I wonder if I would say the same thing today. There were only two telephones in the entire village and in case of an emergency—like the day Alex locked me outside on the balcony—we felt reassured knowing that one of those phones was in the house directly across the street from us.

We also didn't have a clothes dryer—that would have been an extravagant expense. On nice days we hung wet clothes out on the balcony. In the winter, we hung them in the half-finished, cold but dry basement. Our antique wringer-style washing machine was a serious challenge. I frequently got articles of clothing caught in the wringer. After they were stretched back and forth a few times they took on odd shapes. One day I caught my blouse in the wringer—while I was wearing it. Buttons broke, snaps and zippers smashed and bits and pieces of these plugged up the hose so Art often had to upend the machine and "go fish."

Air conditioning was a rare phenomenon in Germany back then so we didn't have that either. Even today, home air conditioners are much less common in Europe than in the United States. On warm days we kept the windows open, inviting in the flies, bees, wasps and all manner of flying things—but there were no roaches. Window screens were unheard of, but we were fortunate that the mosquitoes weren't too numerous that year.

There were no built-in kitchen cupboards; dishes and food went into free-standing cabinets. We didn't have closets—anywhere. We hung our clothes in wardrobes, which took up a great deal of space. Art managed to "requisition" a funny-looking piece of furniture for Alex's room. It was formerly a display case for selling newspapers and magazines. It worked admirably for storing toys and small articles of clothing.

We had flash heaters in the kitchen and bathroom that heated the water as it ran through. We also had a "telephone shower." This was a hose attached to the bathtub faucet and at the end of it was a gizmo that resembled a telephone receiver. One simply held it and used it like a shower. It was also handy for rinsing out the tub.

Art had entered the army as a second lieutenant, having completed ROTC (Reserved Officers Training Corps) at the university. His office was located in a large old-fashioned house in the city of Fulda, and the unit was part of the 541st Military Intelligence Detachment headquartered in Frankfurt. Part of his job was translating German to English including the local newspapers on which he briefed his boss. His most interesting work, however, was observation reporting from the East-West German border.

Unlike our landlords, we were less than financially secure when we married—we had college loans to repay. Consequently, "flight status" seemed a good way to augment our income. This meant that several times a month Art would make observation flights along the border, sometimes by helicopter but more often in a light scout airplane. Armed with binoculars, he watched for any East German troop activity or unusual occurrences. Unfortunately, his stomach—taking its cue from the middle ear, according to scientists—revolted when in the air, especially in a small vehicle that moved rapidly and not at all smoothly up, down and sideways. After his first trip in an L19 Bird Dog, his face matched his fatigues—it was a complimentary green color. I had never seen him so sick, not even on Christmas day when he drank too much artillery punch.

After he had recovered that day and was able to speak once again, he told me that when he began to feel sick, he leaned out the window of the small propeller plane to throw up. Unfortunately, the prop wash threw the vomit back in the window all over him. But Art was always a fast learner. On his next trip up in the blue he used his fatigue hat to upchuck in.

Finally, one day I had to ask him: "Is it worth it?"

I wasn't surprised by his reply. "For $110 a month in flight pay I can buy a lot of new fatigue hats!" And he continued to do observation flights.

A defection to the East one night caused a great deal of disturbance and anxiety. A captain from a nearby unit fled across the border driving a U.S. Army vehicle. The officer fit the unfortunate profile: he was in debt, unhappy, foolish, and the quality of his life was in serious decline. The rest of that night Art and the other officers pursued the question "What did he *know?*" and agonized over "How could he *do* this? He was one of *ours!*"

During the aftermath of the defection the officers, NCOs, and the troops were called in for a command performance: a lecture during which high-ranking officers instructed their men on the hazards of certain life styles. Types of behavior they should avoid were borrowing money from another soldier, excessive drinking, and womanizing. The truth was that the lieutenant who was second in command of Art's unit was guilty of all of the above and the men knew it. That particular training session was met with disdain and a good deal of snickering—especially since it was the detachment commander who was loaning money to the lieutenant.

There were also several defectors who came across the border in *our* direction causing a lot of excitement on post—but spouses weren't told about those cases.

(Several years later, the East Germans pushed out the unfortunate defector. They had wrung from him all the information he had and he was no longer useful. The ex-captain returned to the West where he was court-martialed for misappropriation of government property and for going AWOL.)

Since we didn't have a telephone, there were times when a driver had to be dispatched out to Heimbach to notify Art that he was needed on duty. I woke up one night to find Art pulling on combat boots over his fatigue pants. When he saw that my eyes had opened he said, "Can you quickly fix me something to eat?"

"Of course," I replied, "but where are you going?" He said there was an alert and the battalion was going out on maneuvers. I knew that such exercises were planned to test preparedness and units were notified at the last minute—so how did Art know?

"I could hear the tanks revving up," he told me.

Art was dressed, fed, watered, and ready by the time the army jeep pulled up out front. By then, I could hear the tanks, too—scores of them, lumbering over the roads and away to the "field."

Among our many lessons about army life and military procedures was a basic concept that we learned quickly: a "request" by a superior officer translated into a command. And an invitation from a superior officer meant a command performance.

The captain invited the entire unit to his home for dinner one evening. Although it was a pleasant enough evening, none of us wanted to be there and no one really liked the captain. Immediately after dinner, one of the sergeants popped up and circled the room offering antacids from the little roll he always carried. Unfortunately, that was the only bit of humor we experienced during the long evening and none of us dared laugh. The captain's wife was (naturally) offended. The look on her face brought conversation to a dead halt.

When we lived in Nebraska, the milkman came to our door. That wasn't possible in Fulda, but to compensate for that lack, our beer and soft drinks were delivered. The hefty gray-haired deliveryman in his leather apron carried the heavy cases of bottles upstairs—huffing and puffing all the way—and took away

the empties. The beer came in half-liter and liter-sized bottles with old-style porcelain and rubber snap-on tops.

The bread wagon came down our street every day except Sunday, its horn
honking raucously to get the attention of the housewives in the neighborhood.
When Alex and I went out to investigate the first time, I was taken aback at seeing the rolls and loaves of bread tossed willy-nilly into the back of the little station wagon—unwrapped! Some of the bread was still warm and we discovered
how remarkably delicious bread tasted with its fresh crunchy crust that hadn't yet
been encased in plastic.

The knife-sharpener paid regular visits to Heimbach. He rang a little bell as he
came along the street riding a bicycle and pulling a small cart with his equipment
attached. He also sharpened scissors and attempted to hone my pinking shears
but with less success. The man always wore *Lederhosen*, heavy thigh-length
leather pants, even during the warm weeks of summer. Perched on his head was a
wonderful felt hat with a feather in it.

We learned early on that we had to supply our own bags when we went shopping. Most shopkeepers didn't provide plastic or paper sacks. In the open air
markets particularly, nothing came wrapped. If we forgot our bag, however, the
vendor would kindly wrap our carrots or apples in a piece of old newspaper.

We soon made a wise investment: we purchased an *Einkaufsnet*. Every German *Hausfrau* carried one—a small square "bag" made of strong, elasticized net-
ting that could be tucked easily into one's handbag or pocket to be always
available. This little marvel could stretch to several times its original size and hold
all the ingredients for a meal: meat, potatoes, vegetables or whatever one needed.
Most Germans shopped every morning and bought only what they would use
that day.

Estelle tells a story about a friend of hers. The woman, new to Germany, went
into a meat market for the first time and asked to buy a piece of calf's liver. The
butcher handed her the meat—dripping red and unwrapped! Her skill in the
German language was limited but she managed to stammer out the word for
paper. Obligingly, the meat man put the liver on a little square of waxed paper,
handed it to her, and turned to the next customer. Estelle's friend had to hold the
liver very gingerly all the way home on the bus.

Gisela and Ernst, our first German friends, didn't own a refrigerator when we
met them. Since Gisela shopped every day they didn't need cold storage, and they
had no use for a freezer. Like most Germans they didn't like ice in drinks of any
kind. Even after they bought their first refrigerator—a small half-size appli-
ance—a few years later, Ernst kept the beer and wine in the cellar where the bot-

tles would stay just "cool." When he came to our home he thought the beer was much too cold. He would wrap both hands around his glass in an attempt to warm up the contents.

The doorbell rang one morning and when I opened the front door I thought I had died and passed over! Standing in front of me was a man dressed all in black: high-collared doubled-breasted black suit, heavy tall boots, and a black stovepipe hat, Abraham Lincoln-style. My mouth hung open preventing any coherent speech. My ears, however, were picking up the sound of a foreign language—but it could have been Swahili for all I understood. As I continued to stare, I realized that the fancy suit and tall hat were dusty and there were dark smudges on the man's face. The stranger, frustrated by my lack of communication, finally muttered the English word "chimney." Suddenly the data computed—I realized that here on my doorstop was a real live CHIMNEY SWEEP!

I looked around him then and saw his tools lying in the yard: long and short brushes, brooms, and coils of cable that he snaked through the chimneys and flues to clean out the soot. Legend tells us that a chimney sweep brings good luck. I was a happy camper the rest of the day!

A band of Gypsies had encamped on the edge of town. The colorful clothing the Roma wore always intrigued me as well as the energy they displayed. The women in their bright headbands and scarves would knock on doors in our neighborhood and ask for old clothes. Sometimes the men went out selling something or other from house to house. When the gypsies and other sales people rang our bell, they often asked me, "Is your mother at home?" I could truthfully say "no," which usually sent them on their way. Back then it was one of the advantages of being young and petite.

I wore a size five shoe and in all of Fulda I found only one pair of shoes that fit and they were made in Italy. I found it impossible to buy clothes for myself because the local stores stocked only fashions to fit the more "full-bodied" frame of the natives.

When Americans commemorated the thirtieth anniversary of the assassination of President John F. Kennedy in 1993, one of the reminders presented on television and in magazines was the oft-repeated question, "What were you doing when…" or "Where were you when the President was shot?" We were in Fulda.

The November afternoon was cold and dark as we gathered on the parade ground at Downs Barracks for a memorial service for the President. Fog and mist enveloped us as if nature were also in sorrow. Shock and grief blemished the faces of the mourners as soldiers fired the 21-gun salute—each round deafening. During the salute I stooped down next to Alex, seventeen months old, who was sitting in a stroller. His eyes were wide as he looked up at me and tears were falling down his little pink cheeks. He had to have been frightened by the tremendous noise but perhaps he sensed the solemnity of the situation because he didn't make a sound. After the service Art picked up one of the huge shell casings that had dropped to the ground. We keep it still today as a remembrance.

For a long time after the assassination, local people who recognized us as Americans approached Art and me on the street and said how sorry they were about our President.

The exchange rate was kind to us when we were in Fulda and throughout the 1960's—four German marks to the dollar. We were trying to be frugal so we watched every penny and every *Pfennig*. In December, I wrote to my parents that our Christmas tree, a table model, cost the equivalent of eighty-eight cents. I told them I felt a bit guilty because I had also purchased—for eighty-eight cents—an evergreen holiday decoration with an Advent candle. It was beautiful, but much too extravagant.

My grandmother sent us a Valentine card and inside were two one-dollar bills and a note: "Art, take Pat out for a nice Valentine dinner." And he did. A delicious meal in a local restaurant cost just $1.00 per person, although that didn't include a beverage.

We located a young woman in the village who was willing to baby-sit for us and we ate out occasionally with our army friends. We particularly liked the specialties at one little *Gasthaus* down the road: "*Zigeuner Schnitzel*" and "*Goulasch Suppe*." The first was a veal cutlet smothered in a spicy sauce of tomatoes, onions, bell peppers—and pickles. The second was a hearty beef soup flavored with sweet paprika. We subsequently savored many a bowl of this soup on ski holidays both in Germany and Austria. I doubt that either of these dishes is native to Germany, but we still find them on menus throughout the country.

An old monastery reposed on top of a mountain called Kreuzberg, an hour or so from Fulda. The inhabitants brewed beer, made special cheeses and baked a variety of breads for their own consumption and to sell to visitors. One Sunday after enjoying the magnificent view and touring the monastery grounds, we went inside for a mug of beer and a bite to eat. I had taken along a container of milk for Alex and he drank it down quickly. The fresh air and long walk had made us all thirsty.

Not surprisingly, we became engaged in conversation with some of the friendly Germans who sat near us. Typically, there were no individual tables—people sat on benches at long communal tables. Alex soon began to fuss and wanted more milk, which we didn't have. We told our new acquaintances that it was time to say good-bye and we began putting on our coats.

"Your little boy is thirsty," a woman spoke up. "Give him a drink of beer—it's good for him!" I was a bit disconcerted by that statement but Art wasn't. He immediately gave Alex a few sips from his beer mug. Our son seemed satisfied so we stayed a little while longer. Alex napped soundly in the car on the way home. I was to learn that giving children a bit of wine or beer was not the slightest bit unusual in Europe.

It didn't take long to discover that Germans loved a good *Fest*, a party, a festival, a parade, a celebration for whatever purpose. *Fests* in Germany were crowded noisy affairs inside a great hall, a tent, an auditorium or outside in the open air during the summer. We participated in many a weekend celebration, arm in arm with complete strangers singing wonderful songs in German and eating wurst with *Brötchen*—a delicious crusty hard roll you can find only in Germany. The local people were always pleased when foreigners joined in their activities and unabashedly enjoyed the fun. We loved going to local events and learning about German customs.

The thought of *Brötchen* congers up warm happy memories of Sharon and Herm, army buddies also from the Midwest. Sharon claimed she had never liked beer in the U.S. but after arriving in Germany she gave up her afternoon coffee for a "beer and *Brötchen*" break. She blamed the latter for having gained a few pounds.

We, in turn, introduced our German friends to American customs such as taking homemade cookies and sweets to neighbors and friends during the Christmas season. When we invited them for drinks we served savories or salted snacks like nuts and potato chips and dip that they had not eaten before. They generally offered cookies and chocolates with alcoholic drinks, which likewise seemed strange to us.

The best part about our time in Fulda was getting to know the people. At a shooting competition Art had the good fortune to meet Ernst and Rudi, lawyers with the district attorney's office. After I arrived we met their wives, Gisela and Gerta, and a great friendship developed among us. Their custom was to invite friends to their homes after dinner to spend the evening and later on they served a snack. The "snack" was akin to a meal—a hearty late supper that perpetuated our growing admiration for German food.

Most German women did their own cooking and didn't resort to bags and boxes of pre-prepared shortcuts. Baking was another matter, however. Bakeries and *Konditorei* were numerous and prices were reasonable so they usually purchased their desserts, decorated cakes and fancy pastries. Gerta and Gisela thought I was a kitchen wizard when I served them a homemade peach pie.

Germans were much more formal in their relationships than Americans. We called each other "Herr Matzke" and "Frau Hughes" for over a year. It wasn't until shortly before I left Fulda that our friendship was considered well enough established to permit more familiarity. And only after we had become better acquainted did we invite each other for dinner.

The first time they came to our home I opened the door—and there in front of me were two beautiful bunches of flowers, genuine fresh flowers! I was so excited by the unexpected honor, I gaped. We learned that Germans always brought flowers when they came to dinner, especially for the first time, and the men presented them. An endearing custom that we followed from then on. Unfortunately, the situation proved embarrassing that evening. I didn't have a vase to put the flowers in—we simply didn't own one. We did have an empty quart jar, however, which I quickly covered in shiny aluminum foil. Somehow I managed to squeeze all the flowers into the one jar. We bought our first vase the next week.

Our new friends gradually introduced us to their friends and before long they invited us to become members of a bowling club called *Dobbelte Neun,* which means "double nine." The club was limited to 18 members—hence the name. At the end of the year the best bowler got the *Kette,* a splendid chunky metal chain to wear around the neck. The game used nine pins and was similar to American duckpins. We felt very privileged to join, along with an army friend, Les, and his German fiancee, Birgid.

We had such fun with the group twice a month! They were friendly jolly people who always made us feel welcome. Besides Ernst and Gisela and Rudi and Gerta, there were Ottmar and Marianne, Bernhard and Edel, Erik and Erica, Ernst and Annalise. Some spoke English, most did not, but we were always able to communicate. My German was quite sparse then, but Art managed for both of us.

A great deal of joshing and bantering and laughing went on during bowling evenings—and also a lot of toasting. Only the slightest excuse would prompt someone to buy a round of schnapps and make a toast: to Rudi's new car, to the

Marvitz' departure for a ski trip, to the Weber's return from their vacation and to many other less notable events. But we also raised our glasses to important things like a raise in salary, a new baby—and Art's promotion to 1st Lieutenant.

Those fun-loving friends of ours, by the way, did *not* drink and drive—usually they walked. In the winter those who lived a bit far from the bowling alley shared a car and designated a driver.

Bowling was not the only club activity. Members went on outings and sightseeing adventures together. One such trip was a visit to the Will Brewery, owned by a relative of Ottmar. The men dressed in suits or sport coats and of course ties, typical for that decade. The women wore suits or afternoon dresses. It was winter and I wore the only pair of dress shoes that I owned—black suede high-heeled pumps—that were also typical of the times.

We toured every square inch of the brewery including the cold dank cellars where the floors were wet with spilled beer, water from cleaning and all manner of whatever. My suede pumps never recovered. The older, more experienced ladies had worn "sensible" shoes, but I was a novice at brewery touring.

Every year the group spent a weekend in and around the town of Maikammer, where the main event was a wine tasting, a traditional, very organized activity. The *Weinprobe* lasted all afternoon. We sampled the wines slowly and we ate small pieces of plain rye bread to freshen the palate between selections of wine. As the tasting progressed, the room became warmer and smokier, the voices louder and the jokes bawdier. Afterwards, we cleared our heads with a brisk walk out in the cool fresh air, then rejoined in the evening for dinner and games.

We ate wonderful food during our outings—although maybe the food tasted so good because of the companionship and because we were enjoying ourselves so thoroughly. The German word *Gemütlichkeit* comes to mind. Though the term is not easily translated into English, it connotes the spirit, the atmosphere and the warm feeling that made those gatherings so special.

Art and I first tasted *Saumagen* at the inn in Maikammer. Helmut Kohl featured this dish, literally sow's stomach, in his best-selling cookbook published when he was Chancellor. The formed and sliced meat tastes considerably better than it sounds. We also enjoyed *Quark* for breakfast. Similar to ricotta or pureed cottage cheese, *Quark* is eaten with rye bread and heavily adorned with sweet paprika. Breakfast also included cold cuts and soft-boiled eggs.

My thirteen months in Fulda passed by all too quickly. I treasure the photograph Art took of our German friends who came to say *auf Wiedersehen* to Alex and me that last day. Ernst and Gisela and Rudi and Gerta drove to the airport in

Frankfurt, two hours away, where we had dinner together before Art took us to our plane. He would follow a few weeks later after he separated from the army.

I remember how happy and excited I was while I was packing to go home to the U.S.—and how sad and reluctant I felt when I said good-bye to our friends. I didn't know then that I would be seeing them a year later. I *did* know that our experiences and life in Fulda would help prepare us for the Foreign Service—if Art achieved his goal.

3

JOINING UP

THE BECKONING CALL

We felt as if we had won the lottery when THE CALL came from the State Department. The caller said Art was to be appointed to the Foreign Service—subject to approval by Congress—and we were to arrive in Washington, DC by the first of April.

It was winter, 1965, and we had been back home in Lincoln, Nebraska for only a few months. After Art left the army he returned to graduate school and began work on his master's thesis. He was a graduate assistant in the history department and, in addition, he earned a small income from the Army Reserves. I was working part-time at the university also, teaching secondary-level correspondence courses in Spanish and government. We took Alex to a baby-sitter where he had two children to play with and we paid the mother $1.00 a day, the usual rate at that time.

We phoned our families with the wonderful news of Art's appointment, then called everyone else we knew to share the glad tidings. I was giddy with excitement. I remember rolling down the car window as we waited at a traffic light the next day. An acquaintance had pulled up in the next lane and I shouted over to him: "We're going to Washington!" He responded, but his level of enthusiasm was considerably lower than mine.

Our parents and siblings were as happy for us as only families can be. I didn't realize then how difficult it must have been for our parents, knowing they would be separated from us and from their grandchildren for several years at a time. But we were in our mid-20s, setting out on a grand adventure and they cheered us on.

"Will you wear a uniform?" several people asked Art. A few of his close friends knew about the Foreign Service, mostly because of what he had told them when he took the exam a few years earlier. The majority of our friends, however, knew nothing about the State Department or the diplomatic corps—which was exactly what I knew before I met Art. The Foreign Service was not a hot topic in the Midwest.

Our friend, Wesley, told us this story. He was on home leave from an early assignment with the United States Information Service when he went to the Motor Vehicle Administration in Toledo, Ohio, to renew his driver's license. The employee behind the counter looked over his application with a furrowed brow.

"Hmmm." Pointing to the line that asked for the applicant's occupation she inquired, "Foreign Service Officer—is that like a policeman?"

Wes grinned. "No, it 's like a diplomat." When he received his new license, the line for occupation read "diplomat worker."

What Art had told me about the State Department's career diplomats had mostly to do with the job: what they did on a day to day basis and what their major responsibilities were. The more important aspects (from my point of view) came from a book. Early in our marriage Art brought home from the library *Living in State,* which was published in 1959. Through the author, Beatrice Russell, I learned about the Foreign Service—not just about the work, but about the *life.* I have to admit I was daunted at first, but intrigued and willing to give it a go.

What is the Foreign Service? What does a diplomat do?

The play *Sheer Madness,* a comedy that had a long run at The Kennedy Center in Washington, DC attempts to answer the second question. A hairdresser asks his pompous middle-aged client, "What does your husband do?"

"Do?" she responds with a wide-eyed look. "He's a diplomat; he doesn't *do* anything!"

The truth is, a Foreign Service Officer is a well-rounded individual personally, and a well-trained diplomat professionally. Anyone interested in a Foreign Service career must first pass a lengthy written exam that is usually offered just once a year. Successful candidates must then pass a series of oral examinations. Only about one percent of the initial candidates become career officers. We like to think that this selection process is what makes the service elite. Although the number of people accepted each year varies, depending on the need and the government's budget, the total number of officers averaged approximately four thousand from the 1970's through the 1990's.

After thirty-three years in the Foreign Service, I read the Russell book again. Although I appreciated it the first time, I enjoyed it more the second—my perspective had changed. But little has changed in diplomatic goals. Mrs. Russell wrote in 1959: "The prime objective of a United States mission abroad, large or small, is to represent the United States in its contacts with foreign nations, and in this capacity to win friends and influence people to the American point of view." (Someone else put it this way: "Diplomacy means letting someone else get your way.")

The methods used in achieving this objective, however, have changed considerably with the advent of computers, facsimiles, E-mail, and all manner of modern communications including secure telephone systems. Still, nothing has taken the place of face-to-face dialogue between diplomats.

There is a premise regarding personal objectives that has remained the same over the years: as a Foreign Service Officer you won't become wealthy, but you'll be richly rewarded—figuratively speaking, at least.

I pondered for ten years before I began to write this book. Since I hadn't kept a diary, I wasn't certain I could rely solely on my memory. But when I discovered that our parents had saved most of my letters, principally those in which I described life at post and our experiences in different cultures, there was no more hesitation. As I reread the letters—material abounded as memories popped out from every page.

Having decided to tell my story, I set about reading books written by other Foreign Service wives, including one by a spouse from the British service. I was interested in their experiences but also I hoped that my memory would be further prodded into discovering some long forgotten stories. In that objective I was happily successful. An unexpected bonus was finding out that even though the posts were varied and the time periods different, the authors and I shared many similar experiences. I could identify with their enjoyment and empathize with their difficulties.

The memoirs I read spanned almost fifty years, from the 1940's through the 1980's. The Russell book confirmed how much more difficult it was to live abroad in earlier decades than when we started out in the mid-1960's. And what someone may have considered a deprivation in the 1960's or 70's is unknown today. While local conditions in many third world countries may have remained primitive and difficult, the State Department strives to make the work and the life at post as attractive and worry-free as possible.

Foreign Service support systems were improving by the time we joined and since then training opportunities for spouses have increased. Today a family arrives at its new post well trained, prepared for almost anything, and armed with all sorts of information about the host country. And the support continues at post, where other programs are offered to help families adjust to their new surroundings.

"Glazed eyes" was a phrase used in one variation or another in nearly all the women's books. Art and I have found it aptly descriptive. When we returned home after Fulda and again after our first FS assignment, we were consumed with enthusiasm about our travels and *unique* experiences. We launched into long narrative descriptions of our life overseas, expecting our hometown friends and our relatives to be enthralled. At some point, we belatedly realized that our listeners' eyes had glazed over. The timing varied from person to person, but I'm talking about mere minutes.

"How did you like living in Venezuela?" That was the only question directed my way when I returned to my hometown after almost three years. I had looked forward to having dinner with my old friends and telling them about my experiences. After reminiscing about school days, however, the conversation turned to an earnest discussion of home building and remodeling. Where to buy carpet, which company should lay tile and color choices for drapes. I had no suggestions.

A few friends were interested in our experiences, however. I told Sally and Tom about Art traveling to Vienna with President Jimmy Carter in the late 70's for the signing of the second Strategic Arms Limitation Treaty [which was never ratified by Congress.] Sally, impressed with Art's career, brought up the subject of the SALT II during a high school reunion lunch. There was a second's hesitation in the women's conversation—and then talking resumed. "…Betty didn't show up for bridge yesterday…"

In later years we learned to curb our eagerness and we became more adept at gauging the interest of our listeners before we recounted our exciting adventures. Even now during conversations with Foreign Service friends, I have noticed a certain glassy look to their eyes if my story telling becomes too detailed. These colleagues have their own tales to tell.

From the books I read and from conversations with other diplomatic wives, I have concluded that there is a consensus about what one needs in order to enjoy and survive the Foreign Service. Maybe in this order—and maybe not—one must have: sturdy feet, stamina, thick skin, a sense of humor and a strong stomach.

I think "intestinal fortitude" sums it up nicely!

CAPITAL TRAINING

We packed up our meager belongings and sent them with a moving company to Washington, DC and we three drove out in our little red Volkswagen Beetle. Several pint jars of peaches nestled under my seat wrapped in layers of newspaper. Art's mother and I had canned the peaches in her kitchen the previous fall and I refused to leave them behind.

Because pennies really did count in those days, we had asked Army friends, Jim and Loy, if we could stay a few days in Baltimore with them. In spite of the commute, it was cheaper than a hotel. Besides, we were eager to see them again; we had shared the house in Heimbach, Germany. For several days Art drove back and forth to Washington, an hour each way, making his initial contacts at the State Department and hunting for an apartment.

With the latter accomplished, we repacked the suitcases and started off for our new home. As we came out of the Harbor Tunnel outside Baltimore we were startled to see a policeman waving a flag in our direction and signaling us to pull over.

"We received an urgent message for you," the officer said. "You are to call this number immediately" and he handed Art a piece of paper. We both recognized the phone number as that of our friends whom we had just left. Art found a pay phone and when he came back to the car he looked less than happy.

"Loy said we left the diaper pail there. I suppose we need it?"

Of course we needed it! There were more dirty diapers soaking in the pail than there were clean ones in the suitcase—we couldn't afford to buy new ones. Back to Baltimore we went to retrieve the dirty diapers and on to Washington to locate a Laundromat.

To the diaper novices, I would like to impart some historical information. Way back in the 1960's we used cloth diapers. After we took one off the baby, we rinsed it in the toilet and put it in the bucket to soak in a disinfectant solution. When the bucket, which had a lid, was full, we rinsed, washed, and again rinsed the diapers in a washing machine. We then dried them by whatever means we had and folded them. Simple as that. Disposable diapers and "pull-ups" were science fiction.

Though Art and I had visited Washington, DC briefly when we were younger, we were thrilled to be living in the nation's capital and our enthusiasm was limitless. We moved into our little furnished "walk-up" apartment across the river in Arlington, Virginia near the Department's training facilities. We had *arrived*!

Every Foreign Service Officer remembers his or her A-100 class, usually with warm affection, and often with humor. A-100 is the basic course that every candidate must take to learn the diplomatic ropes and spouses are invited to participate in many of the sessions. We had a great class: thirty-one aspiring officers including three women. Many of the men were married, a few had children, and we all became fast friends. Most of us were in our twenties; we were squeaky-clean, clear-eyed, and energized to serve our country proudly.

Together we planned weekend activities and went sightseeing. Art and I participated in anything that was free but drew the line when it came to nightlife because we had a small child. We didn't know any teenagers we could ask to baby-sit and the grandparents were twelve hundred miles away. During the day, however, trainees could use a nursery at Fort Meyer for a small fee. The location was convenient and Alex liked having other children to play with when I went to class.

Mrs. Dean Rusk, wife of the Secretary of State, was very supportive of Foreign Service families. She encouraged government funding of language classes and other training for spouses. Of course, more training for spouses led to an expanded need for child-care and Mrs. Rusk was helpful in that area also. These issues still plague the Department.

Immediately after our arrival in Washington, I received a letter from the director of the Foreign Service Institute inviting me to enroll in the two-week Overseas Assignment Course, better known as "wives' orientation." The letter is pasted in an old scrapbook along with other mementos.

"May I welcome you, as I have welcomed your husband, to the new and challenging career you both will share. Our country, when it enlists your husband as a Foreign Service Officer, includes you as well. You and he are now and will continue to be a team working together."

The letter continues: "Your primary job as a wife will always be, of course, to maintain a happy home and to be sure that your husband and children are fit and happy, ready for their work. Now, as a Foreign Service wife, you have an additional role. As a member of our American official family your life will be dedicated to serving your country in the most effective way. Your days and years will be spent accumulating experience and knowledge that will help you do each job as it comes along effectively, cheerfully and responsibly. At the Foreign Service Institute we have many resources to help you…."

I recently showed the letter to my daughter, a sociologist, and she was appalled—at first—but she understood when she saw the date. The scope of that message is unacceptable to modern educated women, but then that kind of letter would never be written today.

In 1965 I was far from offended—I was totally enthusiastic about being a team member in the official family. When spouses were invited to attend sessions of the A-100 class with our husbands, we were welcomed and admired, stroked and petted (figuratively). The moderators and speakers continued to remind us that the government considered married couples to be teams. "Two for the price of one" was not only acceptable, it was taken for granted.

Canadian Ambassador Sidney Freifeld had this to say in his memoirs published in 1990: "…while a foreign service career has many attractions, you and your wife…should not contemplate entry unless you are prepared to accept the ethos of service that it entails." Freifeld's thirty-year career began after the end of World War II.

The wives' orientation was informative, instructive, worthwhile and fun although there were occasional moments when I thought it was "high-schoolish." The first half of the course was devoted to American life and included lectures on our history and culture. In the second week the sessions dealt with learning about and fitting into a foreign community. The course officially had started only three years earlier with the blessings and encouragement of LadyBird Johnson, whose husband was then the Vice President. A great deal of research, thought and preparation by many women went into the project and over the ensuing years the course has changed, evolved, expanded and improved.

A few years ago I sat next to the ambassador from Ireland at an elegant dinner party. Several wineglasses sparkled at each place setting and the meal continued through six courses. Just before dessert the ambassador gestured around the table and announced with a smile, "There are three professional hazards of a diplomat: alcohol, cholesterol and protocol."

Instructions to the wives, back in 1965, on the do's and don'ts of protocol have remained indelibly etched in my memory. Although protocol is still taken very seriously, the hat and gloves regimen has slipped away along with the engraved calling cards. The following Rules of Behavior (my term) were reinforced many times along the way.

1. When invited to the residence of the Chief of Mission, remember you are there to work. Always arrive at least fifteen minutes early.

2. Never leave a function before the Chief of Mission departs (or his wife if it is a women's affair.)

3. Before going out to post, write a letter introducing yourself to the Chief of Mission's wife. Ask if you can bring her anything from the States.

4. At official functions, you have duties: circulate.

5. Remember that wherever you go, whatever you do, you are a representative of your country. Behave accordingly.

I didn't find any of the above decrees out of line then and I still consider them as guidelines for today.

There is another dictum that I remember, but fortunately it is one of those that *has* changed. Our course leaders impressed upon us the necessity of paying calls on our "superiors:" namely, the wives of our husbands' bosses. As soon as we arrived at post we were obligated to make an appointment to call on the wife of the Chief of Mission. After that visit was completed—and we were instructed not to stay longer than one-half hour—we were to make arrangements to visit the wife of our husbands' immediate supervisor. Though these calls are occasionally still made today, out of courtesy, the obligation of making them was canceled definitively in 1972.

Terms like "senior wives" and "superiors" are no longer politically or diplomatically correct. An ambassador's wife today isn't likely to refer to other women as "my wives" or "my girls" as she may have done some years before. And, the useful but misleading description "dependent spouse" may be on the way out.

State Department regulations concerning foreign-born spouses have also changed dramatically. Previously, when a Foreign Service Officer married someone from another country, the officer was not allowed to be abroad on assignment until the spouse became an American citizen.

One of the men in our A-100 class had married a Canadian who was not overly happy about changing her citizenship to accommodate the requirements of her husband's new career. Nevertheless, she complied. The day Eva was sworn in as an American citizen the other wives had a surprise luncheon for her to say congratulations—we considered it a happy occasion. Eva, on the other hand, was less than elated. She was born and reared in Canada and she felt offended when, at the end of the ceremony, the official said: "Welcome to the land of the free!"

Art was on a city bus one day with a couple of friends from the class. One of them looked up at the advertisements that were posted and he began to laugh.

"Have You Chosen the Right Career?" read the ad. A photo of a happily grinning bus driver looked out at them. Underneath, the ad quoted a happy salary that was more than the starting paycheck of a Foreign Service Officer.

Foreign Service Requisite: a sense of humor.

Living expenses in the Washington area were higher than what we were accustomed to, particularly for those of us from the Midwest. Although the government paid our moving and transportation costs, we now had to think of purchases we would need to make before leaving for our first assignment.

During the seminar for spouses, for instance, our leaders pointed out that we should order engraved calling cards and personalized note paper. "Informals" were a must. They were also a large outlay of cash for Art and me. We complied, however, but only after being assured by the merchant that our engraving plates would be kept at the shop for years to come, and future orders would cost considerably less. And that proved to be true until the company that had our plates went out of business while we were out of the country. Today, fortunately, printed cards and notes are quite acceptable.

Since we anticipated a busy social life at post, additional clothing was essential. Many of the class members had to buy their first tuxedos. Fortunately, Art already had his. He was a member of the University Singers when he was an undergraduate and they wore black tie for performances. That same tux served him for the next fifteen years.

One of my new friends was commiserating with me one day about the strain on our budgets. I commented that I, nevertheless, needed at least one new dress. I didn't think my present wardrobe would be adequate for our new post and, besides, the Junior Foreign Service Officers' Club was sponsoring a traditional Independence Day Reception and it was to be a fancy affair. I really wanted a new dress!

Susan suggested that we shop for fabric and she would make it for me. That was an offer I couldn't and didn't refuse. We chose a lovely brocaded material in shades of gold and she made a gorgeous dress with a matching jacket. She was an excellent seamstress and a more than generous friend who wouldn't accept any payment for her good deed. I'll not forget her—or that dress!

When the six-week A-100 course was completed, the Senate confirmed the appointments of all the candidates and they became true-life Foreign Service Officers. According to the news clipping in my scrapbook, the names were entered into the Congressional Record on May 10, 1965.

The culmination of the training process was notifying the class members of their assignments. All of us were excited...and nervous. Somehow, it seemed our entire future was wrapped up in this very first posting. Each officer had submitted a "wish list" and hoped to be assigned to one of the cities on his list. It was like waiting to hear which colleges would accept you—but multiplied ten-fold.

When the moderator read from his list, "Arthur Hughes—Frankfurt" we were elated, ecstatic…and relieved. We had wanted to return to Germany. After a few weeks of language training we would leave in July. Another beginning, another journey.

An A-100 class tradition was a competition for the questionable distinction of being assigned to the WORST POST. Worst in this case meant the country with the least desirable living conditions and/or the most difficult political situation. After all the assignments were announced, our class agreed there was a tie. The prize would be shared by the officers going to Belize (British Honduras) and Somalia. (I wonder if the same conclusion would be reached today?)

The last item on the class agenda was a celebration. We gathered at a Spanish restaurant to mark the successful completion of the course and to wish each other well as we began our new careers. None of the new officers had been assigned to the same post, except those few who would remain in Washington, so we didn't expect to see each other for a long while.

Art and I ignored our budget and hired a baby-sitter; we didn't want to miss this last gathering of the 66th A-100 class. Nevertheless, our frugal mind-set pestered us as we read the menu and we both ordered the least expensive meal available. During dinner several bottles of wine circulated, but we declined.

It was a grand evening full of energetic conversations, pronouncements of career aspirations, and promises of saving the world for democracy. But the euphoria faded, for us, when the dinner check came. A group at the other end of our table decided that the bill should be split up equally, as that would be the "simple solution." My mouth went dry—as if I had just eaten wood shavings. I glanced sideways at Art hoping he would object but he remained mute. He looked like a condemned man when he paid our share of the bill. On the way home we wondered how we had managed to eat cheaply and pay dearly! We still had a lot to learn, it seemed.

The Fourth of July reception was held on the eighth floor of the State Department in the beautiful John Quincy Adams Room. Decorated with furnishings and drapes of the period, it was, and still is, an elegant salon. The party was a grand affair, especially impressive for those of us who were new to the diplomatic field. (And I had a new dress to wear.)

During the evening I excused myself from our group on the terrace and I went in search of the ladies' room. On my way back, I went rushing around a corner and plowed into the sturdy frame of a tall, elegantly attired gentleman nearly bowling us both over. As I looked up at his familiar face and tried to sputter apologies, he calmly looked at me, smiled and said, "Excuse *me*." He was the Secretary of State, Dean Rusk. And thus I literally ran into my first Royal.

4

FRANKFURTERS AND APFELWOI

Germany proved to be a magnet for us. When we were drawn back the second time, we were holding diplomatic passports along with high expectations—and we were not disappointed.

We moved into an apartment in "HiCog," an area several city blocks square. The High Commission for Germany—thus the name—originally constructed the buildings to house occupation forces in Frankfurt. Now they were home to military and Foreign Service people. Germans referred to the area as the *Amerikanische Seidlung,* the American settlement. Most of us called our neighborhood, simply, "the *Siedlung.*" A commissary, PX, and small medical dispensary were nearby.

As soon as we arrived we explored our spacious two-bedroom apartment, which was downright posh after the tiny third floor walk-up in Arlington. Suddenly, in the process of opening the suitcases, Art said, "Let's go to Fulda!"

Les, our friend from army days, was getting married the next day to Birgid, a Fulda native. We wanted to be there for the wedding, but we hadn't promised them—or ourselves—that we would make it. We had been concerned about making all our plane connections and we didn't know how tired we would be or how three-year-old Alex would tolerate the trans-Atlantic flight. As it turned out, jet lag hadn't hit us yet. We must have had a sudden adrenaline fix, because off we went.

We arrived in Fulda just in time to join the *Polterabend,* a fun, raucous gathering in honor of the bride and groom. Similar to a "shivaree," it takes place the night before the wedding. What a grand reunion we had! Our friends from the Dobbelte Neun bowling club were all together and suddenly we were speaking German again. We had left Fulda barely a year ago.

After a beautiful wedding and a glorious weekend, we trained back to Frankfurt to rest and unpack. Art's new job—new career!—would begin in earnest on Monday morning.

It soon became clear why the American Consulate General in Frankfurt was and still is a good starting place for new officers. This large post offers the entire range of consular services. A junior officer has the opportunity to rotate among the various sections (administration, personnel, visas, citizenship, general services), learning and practicing every aspect of consular work. Although the trainee may learn the same basic duties in a small post, the larger consulate has numerous officers and their collective years of experience can be valuable to new officers.

As the first months passed by, our social life became increasingly active and we met people of many nationalities as well as Germans. The apartments across the street from us housed other foreign diplomats and we soon numbered Argentineans, Finns and Austrians among our friends.

The new American Consul General arrived in Frankfurt shortly after we did. We had met James Johnstone and his wife, Dixie, in Washington and we knew we would like them. The fact that Mr. Johnstone turned out to be a great boss boded well for the future, we thought. Besides, they were warm and friendly, fun people who made everyone around them feel comfortable.

While Art was learning about his role as a vice consul, he discovered that "escort service" was one of his duties. Perhaps I should explain. This escorting involved meeting a "visiting fireman" (someone from the State Department) or a dignitary at the airport and accompanying him or her to appointments and meetings, shepherding the visitor here and there and where-ever, and maybe even going shopping. Among the more notable of Art's charges whom he enjoyed assisting were Robert Kennedy, Attorney General; Lawrence O'Brien, Postmaster General; and Eleanor Lansing Dulles, a grand lady whom we would meet again in Bonn.

Art was also the control officer for several senators and congressmen. One of our least illustrious government servants handed my husband a stack of several hundred post-cards and told him to mail them. The senator emphasized that he wanted his constituents to know that "he was thinking of them while he was overseas." But there were no stamps on the post-cards.

It took some pestering before Art was able to convince the pompous visitor that the cards would not be mailed until the latter paid for the postage. The senator finally complied, but Art was annoyed by this time. His job description did not include licking hundreds of stamps for an ungrateful and unpleasant traveler. (In 1966 self-adhesive stamps were a thing of the future.) Art ran the post-cards through the postage meter at the consulate and sent them through the APO (Army Post Office). Never mind that the postmark was American and not German as the visitor had expected. The senator, by the way, was forced to withdraw from a later election campaign after he was charged with corruption.

In August, we knew that I was pregnant and we were delighted. Since we had access to excellent medical services, Frankfurt would be an ideal place to have another child. My pregnancy went well through the sixth month and we decided to get away for a weekend. We probably wouldn't have another opportunity to travel until after the baby was born in late February. Our Fulda friends had planned an outing in the countryside of Bavaria, near Bad Bruckenau, and we went to join them.

My contractions started that Saturday night. Art and the others were enjoying the evening's revelry; someone had organized party games and I could hear howls of laughter. I had gone up to our room in the *Gasthaus* soon after dinner because I felt unusually tired and my back ached. When the pains began, I couldn't believe I was actually in labor—it was much too early. I tried not to think about the fact that Alex was born six weeks early. When Art came upstairs to get his camera, I told him the bad news. The contractions worsened.

Art immediately went in search of a telephone and discovered that the only one on the premises was in the manager's office—and it was locked tight. At a small country inn in the 1960's, there were no telephones in the rooms. One of our group, however, located the innkeeper's cottage on the grounds and rousted the man out of bed. Once the office was unlocked, Art tried to call the U.S. Army post in Grafenwehr but he couldn't reach anyone. While another friend called the nearest hospital, Les and Birgid took off with great speed in their little Porsche and headed for the post.

The local ambulance from a small hospital in Bad Bruckenau arrived first. Les, Birgid, and the U.S. Army ambulance pulled up just as the German medics were carrying me out on a stretcher. I remember watching the eerie reflection of a revolving blue light on the rain-soaked windows as I lay inside the strange vehicle.

At the hospital the doctor gave me a medication to slow the labor process—I was already dilating. He then recommended that we go immediately to Schweinfurt where the hospital was larger and had more facilities.

"We can be of no help here," the doctor told my husband. In his limited English he complained of the lack of medical facilities in the small towns. He said, "All the money goes to the cities."

The doctor located a trained midwife to ride in the ambulance with us to Schweinfurt. For some reason we forgot my shoes, which were parked beside the bed—never to be seen again.

Before we left Bad Bruckenau Art communicated with the (American) 97th General Hospital in Frankfurt. He arranged for a helicopter to stand ready to transport an incubator to Schweinfurt if it were needed. Thankfully, we didn't need the incubator. During the next twenty-four hours my contractions came less frequently and the pain lessened. The baby was safe—we hoped. I spent a long week in the Schweinfurt hospital, not allowed to get up for any reason. (So it didn't matter that my shoes were missing.)

As I began to feel better, I found that the most difficult and disquieting aspect of my hospital stay was my inability to communicate. Although I could converse with my German friends on a basic but ungrammatical level, I certainly didn't have the German vocabulary needed for this particular situation. Out of necessity I learned a great number of German words by the end of that week: labor, pain, contraction, ache, stomach, back, bowels and other "medical" terms.

The most unsettling communication problem was a consequence of my being in the maternity ward where the other women had given birth. A sweet friendly nun came by each day for a cheery visit. She would pat my tummy and then remark in German, "No baby yet today? Well, don't worry, *Schatz*, maybe tomorrow!" I understood the words and her intent, but I didn't know how to reply, "No, I don't *want* to have my baby for three more months!"

I'm still amused when I remember the "egg timer." Actually it was an old-fashioned stethoscope shaped like an hourglass. Bending over me the doctor would move the instrument from place to place over my protruding stomach, putting his ear to the upturned part to listen to the baby's heart beat. Evidently it worked, but it looked like an egg timer to me!

The drive between Schweinfurt and Frankfurt took almost two hours, but Art made the trip as often as he could. Ann and Chuck and other generous friends from the consulate took turns caring for Alex. When I was transferred to the hospital in Frankfurt, Art came for me in the biggest vehicle the consulate had and he brought a driver—just in case. He also brought pillows and a blanket and I lay prone all the way to the 97th General. Several more days went by before I was allowed to go home.

There was a happy ending to this saga. After three months of almost complete bed-rest (no stairs, no laundry, no cleaning, no sex, no fun) our daughter Katherine was born. She was healthy and beautiful and two weeks overdue!

I met a friendly young woman at the hospital whose baby was born the same week as ours. We saw each other periodically during the following year and always chatted about our families. She complained one day that her children woke up much too early—they never slept past five a.m. It was summer, so I suggested putting up heavy dark drapes to keep out the early sun.

"I've done that," she fretted. "I've tried everything!"

Finally, I asked her what time she put the little ones to bed.

"At five o'clock," she replied. "That way, my husband and I can have a quiet dinner and long evening together." I knew better than to try to change the woman's mind or her habits, but I did tell her frankly that she shouldn't expect her children to sleep longer than twelve hours!

Frankfurt, a trade and commercial center, was a popular gathering place for American companies and business groups. Since one of the objectives of a U.S. mission abroad is to further our country's interests, the consulate general (CONGEN) sponsored numerous teas, cocktail parties, and receptions for the visitors, giving them the opportunity to meet German business people as well as representatives of other American companies. These events were usually held at the residence of the consul general and, to insiders, they were known as "work parties." Junior officers were invited on a rotating basis and that included us.

"Two for the price of one" was etched into my brain by that time. I went to each event prepared to be helpful, diplomatic and charming. A guest list was sometimes provided so we could look it over before the party. In fact, occasionally a copy was in my hands as early as noon on the day of the event! When all was well with our children and there were no major household crises, I assiduously studied those lists.

My efforts proved to be worthwhile, at least on one occasion. That time the guest list was long and time was short, so I wrote down the names of several companies that would be represented that evening and noted their home states. Then I picked out one name from each business and tried to remember it.

At the reception, I introduced myself to a friendly-looking gentleman and he told me his name. I promptly said, "You must be with Telltale Dyes of Texas. Welcome." His mouth gaped and, obviously pleased, he wanted to know how I knew his business and where it was located.

I don't remember how I answered him. Pure luck had put me in his path. Nevertheless, studying guest lists was a worthwhile practice. In addition to the obvious reason, it helped me to overcome some of my shyness when walking into a room filled with strangers.

I remember another work party at the Johnstone's. As I was moving from one group of guests toward another, I stopped to say a brief hello to two consulate women whom I knew slightly. They were leaning against the back of a sofa, drinks in hand, having a chat. At that moment Mr. Johnstone caught my eye and motioned me in his direction. I was quite taken aback by his request.

"Do you want to tell those young ladies to move their fannies away from the sofa and circulate? If you don't want to, I will." I didn't—but I did. In my best diplomatic tone I told the women that the consul general wanted them to move about.

Later, by way of apology I thought, Mr. Johnstone said to Art and me that he didn't believe the government owed food and drink to its "employees" who didn't earn it. He was quite right and, by having me appeal to the women, he saved them some embarrassment.

As the years went by and the running total of work parties mounted, I sometimes resented being "invited to work." On occasion I tired of being a body with a mouth. But I never could ignore that feeling of obligation and duty. Art always said that it was my decision whether or not to accept an invitation—but if I accepted, I worked.

One of Art's rotational jobs was staff aid to the consul general for six months. A consequence of the assignment was serving as secretary to the consular corps. During that period, we were invited to more than the usual number of diplomatic dinners, receptions and other functions. As we met more and more people I began to hope that sometimes we were invited because they liked us and not just because Art was an American official. (A concern that would crop up many times during the following years.)

When President Johnson made his six-nation "Mission of Peace" trip during the Vietnam war, my husband went to New Zealand as part of the advance team. Two junior officers from posts in Germany were chosen for the special assignment and it was a distinct honor for Art. And he met the President of the United States—his first royal. When he came home I was excited to hear about the President and I asked him what had impressed him the most.

"Johnson's pure energy," he replied. He also told me that the cabin crew on Air Force One had instructions to have bean soup available for the President at all times. Art's chief duty for two weeks was writing, in advance, thank you letters to the New Zealanders who were involved with the President's visit.

Among our most pleasant job-related activities were casual evenings spent with groups of German students. Some were our age; others were younger; all were interested in using and improving their English and discussing common interests. Over coffee and cake our conversations usually focused on foreign affairs, international relations and politics. The get-togethers gave the students a better understanding of what Americans were all about—and we profited from the reverse.

Reimer was Art's German instructor but mostly he was a musician. He played clarinet in the "Barrellhouse Jazz Band," which produced some great rousing music. The first time he and Beatte invited us to their apartment, we told them we needed to book a baby-sitter before we could be sure of coming. That surprised them. Beatte said that when they wanted to go out for the evening, they waited until their little one was asleep in his crib—and they left. I was never sure how customary the practice was since we knew few other couples with small children.

The memory of one particular evening plagued me for a long time. Reimer and Beatte invited us for a dinner of fresh mushrooms. That sounded odd to us but we were always enthusiastic about spending time with Germans and learning more about their culture. It turned out that Reimer was a mushroom connoisseur. He had studied fungi extensively and went out with like-minded enthusiasts to pick wild varieties in the nearby forests. He had several books about mushrooms and enjoyed telling us about numerous species that could be found around Frankfurt.

A mushroom with reddish-orange spots on its cap was one of the most dangerous. I never understood why it was considered the "lucky" mushroom. Its attractive likeness was used in decorations, especially at Christmas time, but it was deadly.

Our meal that evening was superb: two kinds of fresh wild mushrooms, sautéed in butter and herbs, accompanied by boiled potatoes. Prior to coming to Germany my only experience with mushrooms had been with the button variety that came out of a can. I didn't like them at all. But Reimer's mushrooms were delicious.

After we ate we sat relaxing together, further discussing wild fungi—a totally novel subject for Art and me. Reimer showed us pictures and talked about distinguishing the edible from the poisonous varieties. We read about the symptoms of mushroom poisoning including the worst: instant death.

A few hours after going to bed that night, I woke up with horrendous cramps and nausea. I spent the rest of the night writhing on the bathroom floor. Pictures of deadly mushrooms flashed repeatedly through my feverish mind. I was certain I had been poisoned and only wished to die quickly and not suffer the 48-hour decline we had read about. I was still alive the following morning, however, and by evening it was clear that my fate didn't include death by fungus. At least not then. But several years passed by before I ate wild mushrooms again!

We found a wonderful woman to baby-sit for us. Frau Schwabe was a stocky German with a round happy face who believed in lots of fresh air for the children. She took them outside whenever she came—cold weather, snow, even rain didn't deter her. In the baby buggy, then the stroller, then on her own tiny feet, Kathy went walking through the *Siedlung* with Frau Schwabe. Sometimes, they strolled over to the nursery school to fetch Alex home for lunch. While the children napped, she did laundry and light housework—she wasn't one to be idle. And in the evenings, her teenage daughter Gabi often baby-sat. What treasures they were!

The exchange rate was favorable while we were in Frankfurt, but we continued to watch our budget. Somewhere down the line, we wanted to buy a house in Washington.

Art decided that a good way to save a few *Deutsche Mark* was to trim Alex's hair himself. This worked well initially—until the infamous haircut that included clipping off the bottom of Alex's earlobe! He only cut off a tiny bit, but the scissors were razor sharp, and the wound bled profusely. I think it hurt Art almost as much as Alex. It wasn't surprising that our son didn't want to have his hair cut again for a long time.

We often went sightseeing around the city, taking Alex and Kathy with us. The huge Frankfurt zoo was a family favorite and so was the Palmengarten, a tropical botanical garden. We liked to stroll there, all dressed up, on a Sunday afternoon.

We visited the birthplace of Goethe; the Frankfurt Cathedral, where emperors were crowned a few centuries ago; and of course, the Eschenheimer Turm, a medieval tower. We toured the Henninger tower, a modern brewery silo, and one evening Art and I had dinner in its spectacular revolving restaurant way up on top.

Across the Main River is an area called Sachsenhausen. We spent many a fun evening there with friends, drinking *Apfelwoi* (hard cider) in various pubs called *Kneipen*. As I write this, my mouth begins to water at the thought of *Handkäse mit Musik*, a remarkable cheese covered with chopped onions one could find only in Sachenhausen. We surmised that the name, "cheese with music," probably had to do with the fact that this unusual dish produced bodily effects similar to those from beans!

I wasn't fond of the cider, but I didn't want to admit it since it was the local specialty. One evening when our friends were visiting from Fulda, Ernst joked that *Apfelwoi* tasted like gasoline. From then on, I felt justified in drinking something else with my *Handkäse*.

One autumn we went with Nancy, Art's younger sister, and consulate friends, Sue and Harry, to the Oktoberfest in Munich where we met up with Ernest and Gisela and her sister. We marveled at the waitresses who carried several hefty liter beer mugs—full!—at one time. Some of the women were hefty themselves. We also drove to Bingen and Rudesheim for the fall wine festivals where we sampled wine from small souvenir glasses. On another of our sightseeing ventures we rode a steamer down the Rhine River and passed by the famous Lorelei.

Gastronomic memories of those trips are still with us: *Bratwurst* and *Brötchen*, long white crunchy radishes, herring with onions and rye bread, fat salty pretzels, and whole juicy dill pickles. Many photographs in our album show Nancy and me with our mouths open, about to bite into another taste treat.

The "Burning of the Castle" was a fantastic spectacle that we witnessed in Heidelberg. The castle actually was not on fire but to the uninitiated it looked that way, as it was supposed to. Flares and torches were lit around the perimeter of the massive structure and in several nooks and crannies of the building itself. Once I was convinced that the castle really was *not* burning, I appreciated what a beautiful sight it was, silhouetted by the flames. A torchlight parade preceded the "burning" with both children and adults dressed in traditional costumes of the era and area. Afterwards, an impressive fireworks display lit up the night sky. The colored sparks reflected magically in the adjacent river.

Our first visit to Berlin was a memorable trip. The free and convenient transportation definitely made getting there half the fun—to use a well-tuned expression. We took the troop train to the East and back, traveling at night in a sleeping compartment. Some of the U.S. Army trains were designated for transporting troops to and from Berlin. When there was space, military and other government personnel were allowed to use the trains for pleasure trips.

The American officials gave stern instructions before we boarded and warnings were posted all over the train. DO NOT take photos from the train. DO NOT open the window curtains when stopped at a station. DO NOT look out the windows when the train is stopped. DO NOT lean out the windows.

I had difficulty sleeping; I woke up every time the train groaned. People used to joke that the troop trains had square wheels. Actually the wheels weren't to blame—the tracks needed work. Especially those in the eastern zone. The unusual experience of sharing a sleeping car with strangers also added to my wakefulness. Our children weren't with us and the compartment had four bunks.

"We were up early and eager to see our first Russian." Young and naive, I wrote that sentence to my parents after our trip. I wonder if my friend Natasha from Moscow would have said something similar about Americans in 1966. Berlin had been the capital of Germany until World War II. Now the Allied powers (The United States, France, Great Britain and Russia) were administering this great historic city. The Russian sector isolated itself from the others with barbed wire and fences. And the Berlin Wall had gone up only a few years before our visit.

The train had to stop for clearance at Potsdam, just outside Berlin. East German guards were not allowed to board the troop trains but the Russians could. We waited and listened. That morning the Russian soldiers did not board the train and we traveled on into the city.

Regulations required us to go to the American Mission for a briefing before we crossed into the Communist sector. Although our embassy had moved to Bonn after the war, the United States maintained a mission in West Berlin to administer the occupation. The briefing included a geography lesson of the city and directions to East Berlin—and more importantly, how to get back—using the underground train. Our instructions were to hold tightly to our passports when showing them to the border controllers. Under no circumstances should we surrender them. The American official told us what to expect, what to avoid, and what to do in case of an "incident." I found the latter rather unsettling.

I wrote home: "The Russians certainly were clever to grab the most historic part of the old city for their domain." The old opera house, famous museums, and the beautiful tree-lined avenue Unter den Linden were in the Soviet sector. At a war memorial that honored the dead and "victims of fascism," we watched a solemn changing of the guards, complete with goose step. As we were looking at the Brandenburg Gate from the east and Art was taking pictures, we saw two very young Russian soldiers taking photos, being tourists just like us.

We spent less than three hours in East Berlin but they were fascinating hours. Getting in and out took almost as long as being there—we passed through three control stations going each way. We had hoped to take a bus tour that included the Soviet sector, but the State Department prohibited it for a valid reason. East German control officers often stamped visitors' passports at the checkpoints. Since our government didn't recognize East Germany and followed occupation rights, we dealt only with the Soviets.

In the western sectors we saw the famous sights we had heard of and read about. The church ruins on a grand avenue called the Kurfurstendam remained stark and blackened as a remembrance of the war. We took photographs at Checkpoint Charlie and other allied control stations. But the most remarkable and the saddest sight in all of Berlin was the WALL. It looked just like the pictures I had seen in newspapers and magazines, with barbed wire and pointed glass shards sticking out of the top. It was ugly! And what an eerie feeling to see the guards on the other side, standing watch, pointing their guns at us.

The citizens of West Berlin were overwhelmingly middle-aged and elderly. Most of the young had left the city before the wall made leaving difficult—and later impossible.

There were several gimmicks designed to encourage young people to stay in Berlin. When a young couple married, for instance, they were given a substantial loan for eleven years. If they had three children during that time, the loan was forgiven. Taxes were lower in Berlin than in other parts of Germany and, most unusual, the young men were not drafted into the military.

In front of our apartment building in Frankfurt one day, I happened to notice a man in a brown suit carrying an attaché case. I said "Good morning" in the German way and he responded politely. After that, I saw the thin elderly gentleman several times in our neighborhood, always in the brown suit.

Months later as I went around to the back to put a bag of trash in the dumpster, I saw him there—with his hands in the trash bin. I was so surprised I backed away and he didn't see me. I realized then that he was searching the bins for edible food that he put into his attaché case. His brown suit, now that I saw it more closely, was frayed and worn. But he had dignity and he walked with a straight back. I continued to greet him whenever we met—but only in front of the building.

A sad and shocking thing happened in December of 1966. Art brought home an unusual amount of mail one evening and we were delighted. Mail was always eagerly awaited—especially at holiday time. But two letters brought tragic news: a friend's plane had been shot down over Vietnam. A captain in the U.S. Air Force, Monte had been flying an F-105 Thunderjet and leading a strike mission north of Hanoi. He was listed as missing in action. After the children were in bed, I sat in our bedroom answering mail and begging for more information about Monte's status. Art was lying on the sofa in the living room with the television on.

"Pat!" he suddenly shouted, "Come in here! Hurry!"

I flew into the other room to find Art pale as snow, staring at the TV. He told me what he had seen and we both were stunned. A German program had aired a clip obtained from a Vietnamese news service. The film showed a smoldering heap of ruins that once was an American airplane. In front of the debris was a North Vietnamese soldier holding high a helmet on which was stenciled "Moorberg," the last name of our friend. Nineteen years later Monte's remains were brought home for burial at Arlington National Cemetery.

One piece of mail that Christmas gave us a smile. A printed card with a holiday motif arrived at our door. It said: "A merry (sic) Christmas and a Happy New Year." And at the bottom were the smaller words: "wish you also for this year, the seven garbage men of your area." That lovely greeting earned them a holiday tip.

A crew of Foreign Service inspectors came to Frankfurt while we were there to check out the consulate general. Such inspections take place periodically at every post around the world by a team consisting of present and retired officers as well as people from outside the service. The group was welcomed, fed, and entertained in several different homes during their stay. Not only did they examine the interior workings of the Consulate, but they also wanted to meet and chat with the personnel outside the office. (Today, inspectors discourage personal socializing during their visits.)

I began to feel nervous at a buffet dinner when I observed the visitors individually seeking out the spouses for a bit of private chitchat. What if I said something stupid? What if one of the inspectors didn't like me? I found out later that what they were interested in was post morale.

Until 1972 a Foreign Service Officer's efficiency report could—and often did—include comments about his wife. I say wife because I didn't know any male spouses then. "She is an excellent hostess and shows a great deal of leadership in local women's organizations. She is an asset to her husband's career." That, of course, would have been a very positive report. Something like winning the Miss Congeniality contest.

Another supervisor might have written: "The officer's spouse does not participate in official social events nor does she entertain in their home. She makes no contribution to her husband's diplomatic career nor does she enhance post morale."

Sound like the Dark Ages? The truth is—spouses were "rated." That now-disallowed practice certainly encouraged (in most cases) a good return on the "two for the price of one" package deal. Fortunately for *my* morale, I got A's and B's. I was never convinced, however, that my grades made an iota of difference when it came to Art's promotions, nor did the opposite seem possible.

The Arab-Israeli Six-Day War began shortly before we left Frankfurt. It was June 1967, and the American government was evacuating dependents and non-essential personnel from our missions in the Middle East. The CONGEN received word one morning that evacuees from Beirut would arrive in Frankfurt in approximately twelve hours.

Ted, the General Services Officer, set up a telephone committee and the word spread rapidly: "Get the servants' quarters ready for guests."

Mops, brooms, and cleaning supplies sped up to the fourth floor of the apartments in the hands of women and teenagers. We all went to work and hurriedly but thoroughly cleaned the single rooms that were assigned, one each, to the apartment dwellers as maids' rooms. Most had not been inhabited for some time, judging by the thickness of the dust and dirt. Paint was sorely needed but scrubbing had to suffice.

Flowers were blooming around the *Siedlung* and a hastily organized committee scrounged all the available blossoms and arranged them in vases. My group rounded up magazines and paperbacks and distributed them among the rooms in our building. The kids collected toys in big boxes that we positioned in each stairwell to be used by whichever families needed them.

When the rooms were clean, we made up the beds and laid out fresh towels that the Housing Office delivered. Then we cooked. Some of us combined our supplies to save a trip to the commissary. We made extra food since we had no idea how many people would arrive. It was a tremendous community effort—the kind of neighborliness that gives you an extra pitty-pat in your heart.

"Taking out the trash is too much at home," the GSO said as he applauded the teenagers, "but when there is an emergency—watch 'em pitch in!"

We were disappointed when none of the evacuees came to use the fresh and spotless rooms in our building. Fifty families arrived, however, and they were temporarily "at home" in other areas of HiCog.

A family wedding was the grand finale to our two years in Frankfurt. Nancy, Art's younger sister, had come to visit us; she stayed, took a job with the military and met Dan, a lieutenant in the U.S. Army. They relinquished some of their independence and were married on the Fourth of July—a date that was assigned to them. In Germany a church marriage has no legal status; the couple must be married in a civil ceremony. Dan applied to the legal powers in Frankfurt and after a long wait, a letter arrived designating the date, time and place. The setting was the Town Hall, an historic medieval building called the *Römer*, in the center of the city. The structure was built on the site of a Roman settlement, hence the name: "the place of the Romans."

The wedding ceremony consisted of little more than signing documents. Nancy laughed when she realized that all the papers were in German. "Do you think I should sign?" she facetiously asked her brother.

The gentleman who officiated was sensitive and kind and there was definitely a twinkle in his eye. He knew that procedures in a foreign country as well as marriage in general were new and flustering experiences.

After the nuptials and the picture-taking outside in the lovely summer sunshine, we had a reception for the bridal pair at our apartment. It was an exciting day for all of us, including Alex and Kathy. We nearly had to get a bank loan for the case of champagne we bought. It was a good investment, though, since Dan and Nancy later joined us in the Foreign Service.

We left Frankfurt the first of August 1967, and sailed home on the grand ship SS United States. Once our bodies got in sync with the rocking of the boat, we were able to relax, gorge ourselves with luscious food, enjoy the entertainment, and revel in a few days of pure vacation with our children.

I had a warm weepy feeling when we approached New York Harbor and saw the Statue of Liberty. It was early morning, but already the sun was attempting to burn off the misty haze. We had dressed and packed early so we could take Alex and Kathy up on deck to see the sights. There SHE was—boldly holding her torch aloft—welcoming us home. What a glorious sight!

We were excited about returning to Nebraska after two years, seeing our families, and showing off our kids. Kathy was almost seventeen months old and hadn't yet met her grandparents. We looked forward to taking off our training wheels for a while before we rolled back into Washington for Spanish classes. Medellin, Colombia, was to be our next post.

5

THE ROACHES

Growing up in the Midwest I didn't have much experience with cockroaches. I had heard of them from people who lived in the southern part of the United States but they politely called them "water bugs." When someone did say the word *cockroach* it was a whisper with the hand loosely covering the mouth in case of an eavesdropper. You certainly wouldn't tell anyone if you had cockroaches in your home!

Except a close relative, a sister perhaps. Carol and her husband, Delm, lived in an apartment in the humid clime of Baltimore, Maryland during their army days in the early 1960's. My sister was not amused when she discovered her first battalion of roaches. She couldn't bear to swat bugs or step on them; that was too messy. And she didn't have any bug spray—they had just moved in and hadn't anticipated the need for Raid. The solution, then, was to cover up the roaches so she couldn't see them and, ergo, she wouldn't be afraid of them.

When Delm arrived home from work, the counter top, kitchen table and all other horizontal surfaces including the floor were dotted with upended glasses, coffee cups, bowls and even sauce pans. After my brother-in-law discovered what was wriggling underneath all of that kitchenware, he and Carol had a serious discussion about alternate means of disposing of bugs. One method involved a simple rolled-up newspaper.

When Art and I were first married, we lived in a small basement apartment where the floors were covered with smooth linoleum. At night when it was dark and otherwise quiet I often heard a tiny clicking sound coming from under our bed. Finally, but reluctantly, I decided to investigate. I grabbed the flashlight that we kept nearby and hung my torso over the edge of the bed. I directed the beam underneath—and discovered what I had expected and feared: "water bugs." (So, I thought maybe only apartments have roaches.)

During the next thirty or so years we would become further acquainted with cockroaches—the genuine articles—not water bugs. Following are a few examples of those cockroaches we met—or at least witnessed. And I will also tell you about another kind of sickening bug. Later in the book, you will meet the symbolic roaches.

In 1968 we were posted to Maracaibo, Venezuela, where every day was cockroach Christmas—and we didn't live in an apartment. The roaches were not only huge (two inches-plus and bulbous) but they could also fly!

One evening my husband was lying on the sofa with his arms outstretched holding the newspaper. A large, very determined cockroach flew in through the window and plowed into the newspaper, knocking it completely out of Art's hands. There were no screens on the windows, just louvers that kept out the birds and the bats, but not the bugs.

There was also ample space under the doors to let in all manner of things, not only roaches but lizards. For a quick fix we put a strip of wide masking tape along the bottom of the doors. Small insects tended to get stuck on the tape and we would find them there still squirming when we opened the doors in the morning. Not a pleasant sight. But Art soon acquired some weather stripping, which he screwed to the bottoms of our doors. Thereafter at night and during part of each day when we turned on the air conditioning and closed the doors and windows, the cockroaches had to wait outside.

In Israel in the 1980's we again suffered the presence of giant flying cockroaches. In areas of the world where the temperatures seldom, if ever, fall below freezing, the ugly creatures multiply rapidly and if the climate is humid, so much the better—for them. Our homes in Tel Aviv fortunately had screens on some of the windows and those deterred a few vermin. We made sure that all holes and spaces around plumbing pipes were plugged up. We took every precaution we knew of to discourage cockroaches and other bugs, including scorpions.

Roach hotels and baits were available locally but when I saw the size of the tiny traps I was convinced that those enormous cockroaches couldn't possibly get in there to reach the poison. We resorted to using chemicals, frequently spraying around doors, in corners, and along baseboards. Since we didn't have small children or pets, that seemed to be the best thing we could do.

One day, however, I was revolted to see a huge cockroach emerge from where I didn't even know there was a space! I thought I was hallucinating. I wished I were hallucinating. After that, I laid in a large supply of roach traps. Maybe the manufacturers knew what they were doing after all.

After living in Tel Aviv for a while, some people tried to give the impression that they were inured to the ugly pests. After all, "everyone" had them. Nevertheless, they certainly got "everyone's" attention. During one of our dinner parties we were sitting in the living room having coffee and there were several lively conversations going on. I caught a movement out of the corner of my eye and saw to my horror not one, but two out-sized cockroaches crawling up the wall behind the sofa. I attempted to be nonchalant with the guest who was talking to me but evidently I was not successful because his eyes strayed in the direction I had looked and the conversation began to flounder.

A large portion of white wall framed between aqua drapes had become a stage for the two bugs. They circled and then traversed the space like peacocks in mating season. Other conversations around the room broke off briefly and then resumed while eyes darted back and forth. Only the people sitting on the sofa with their backs to the wall were oblivious to the theatrics. After what seemed like a very long time, but probably wasn't, the roaches tired of their performance and scurried off to play somewhere else.

Relating Roach Reports was a form of entertainment among my circle of friends. Not that we didn't also enjoy conversations on a higher plain, but somehow the recounting of these stories gave the narrator an outlet for the shock, surprise, horror, or simply frustration she had suffered. One friend, for example, spent an unusually long time in the bathtub one evening. She had spotted a roach on the bathroom floor and there was no way she would get out of the tub with bare feet until *it* left the room or otherwise disappeared.

The Bug in the Bed story became familiar to us all—with different variations and different participants. The narrator was shocked awake by something crawling on her leg or arm or somewhere. When this happened, you had to jump up, turn on all the lights, awaken the bed partner and search through every inch of the bed linens. If you found the culprit, it was hard to get back to sleep after squashing it. If you didn't find anything, it was even harder to get back to sleep because you wondered what and where *it* was.

My daughter and I had a prize-winning story although this was not the kind of contest one sets out to win. Kathy had just arrived home from college to spend the summer with us. Robert, our cook, prepared her favorite Alsatian dish, *tarte aux oignon* or *Zwiebel Kuchen* (onion tart to Americans.) After dinner Robert tightly covered the leftover tart with two layers of plastic wrap and left it on the kitchen counter in case we might want another piece during the evening.

A short while later, Kathy went into the kitchen and I heard her shriek. It was definitely an "I saw a cockroach" shriek and not a "help—I'm bleeding" scream so I didn't panic. When I reached the kitchen she was jumping up and down pointing to the onion tart. Under the plastic covering two cockroaches were running busily in circles!

Kathy suddenly stopped jumping and barked, "Let's nuke 'em!" It was a clever idea. I grabbed two hot pads for protection, even though the dish wasn't even warm. I gingerly picked it up—Kathy threw open the door of the microwave oven—I shoved the tart in and slammed the door. My daughter gleefully turned the oven to high power for two minutes. Through the frosted-glass door, we could still see movement. She set the dial for three more minutes. When all was still I carefully opened the door.

A roach bolted from the far corner of the microwave and ran down behind the counter-top! As we stared in utter disbelief, the other seemingly dead cockroach escaped from the wrappings over the tart and headed for the floor. Wasn't that carrying "survival of the fittest" a bit too far?

Yemen hosted big ugly cockroaches as well, but they weren't as pervasive in our home in Sanaa as in the other two posts. I came across a big brown roach in the front hallway one day and since I had nothing to swat it with, I had to step on it—I couldn't let it escape! Our staff was gone that day and because it was time for lunch, I quickly changed my shoes, washed my hands and promptly forgot about it.

In the afternoon I remembered the incident and went back to the hallway prepared to clean up a squashed bug. But it had disappeared. There was no sign of it—not even a drop—the floor was clean. After that, I worried about what else was living in our house that ate dead roaches!

There are other kinds of bugs that are much, much smaller, but equally as annoying and frustrating as roaches. And these can be painful. "Montezuma's revenge" is a malady caused by one of these tiny bugs. Tourists who have been to Mexico will be familiar with it. Other travelers may have had a passing acquaintance with "Tehran tummy," "Ramses' revolt," "Delhi belly," or the "Tagoosa-gallops." However euphemistically the bugs are named, they all produce the same results: diarrhea and stomach cramps and sometimes vomiting.

The nasty creatures can cool off a honeymoon, shorten a vacation, and literally cramp your style. Fortunately, most of these microorganisms pass in and out of the body in a few hours or, at worst, a few days, leaving only a bad memory. And yes, fellow citizens, these bugs can also be found lurking in America, but they are much less prevalent than in other parts of the world.

The worst of these invisible bugs are the parasitic bacteria, which like to hang around a while making one's life miserable. Like cockroaches, they have to be killed and this requires chemicals—in the form of medication. It is often difficult to determine exactly what kind of bug is making you sick and therefore what specific medicine is needed. Trial and error can be mighty unpleasant in these cases. A greatly modified diet is required while the eradication is taking place.

Alex was only seven our first Christmas in Venezuela when we went to a holiday dinner at the home of friends, Jan and Hal, along with several other families and their children. Later that night Alex became extremely ill and by morning he had a high fever. We gave him aspirin and lots of liquids but he couldn't keep anything in his stomach. When the pediatrician returned our call, he said, "…lots of fluids, and if the child isn't better by tomorrow, take him to the hospital." That seemed a bit drastic. No one else at the dinner had become ill so we assumed he had "the flu"—and we assumed wrong. We were very naïve.

Alex was not better by the next morning. After many fruitless telephone calls in an effort to make an appointment (it was the holidays), we finally spoke with a doctor who told us, "Get that child to the hospital now!"

We did—and Alex was immediately hooked up to an IV. It had been only 28 hours since he had become ill, but he was dehydrated. We learned a hard lesson that day. Children dehydrate quickly with these illnesses. The hospital laboratory was not able to determine the specific bug and the doctors would only say "gastroenteritis." Our sick little boy remained in the hospital almost a week which is tough on a child—and his parents.

One afternoon when we visited him I was shocked when I spotted something red and wet in the wastebasket. I was relieved when Alex told me, "It's Jell-O, Mommy. I won't eat any more Jell-O!" He was feeling better.

Tap water in Maracaibo was not drinkable so we boiled it at home. When we went out, we drank only what came out of sealed bottles: mineral water, soft drinks, or beer and certainly nothing with ice cubes in it. It was possible to buy large bottles of water (like water coolers in an office) that would be delivered on a regular basis, but I didn't trust it.

Several families who boiled their water at home nevertheless allowed their children to purchase "snow cones" (made with shaved ice and flavored syrup) from street vendors. These were the same children who suffered periodically from "amoebas," a generic term. Parasites were common in Venezuela and at that time the preferred treatment for repeat, long-term bouts was arsenic.

Egypt, home of "Ramses' revolt," is a historic wonderland but a dietary dilemma. Before our first visit in 1986 we read guidebooks and conferred with colleagues and friends who had been there. We paid close heed to all the warnings: don't drink the water, don't drink anything with ice in it, don't eat any uncooked vegetables, watch out for little sprigs of parsley, don't eat fruit unless you can wash it and peel it yourself. Worthwhile advice that we strictly followed.

We were a group of ten, all more or less family, and only two of us managed to get through the week without a bout of diarrhea (or two or three). The following trip the score for three of us was "two well, one ill." Later Art and I accompanied his brother and sister-in-law to Cairo and Luxor and improved our record to "three and one." The one, Brother Dave, continued to be ill and needed medication after he went home to Nebraska. The foregoing family score-sheet is to give you an idea of the odds.

Friends with the Egyptian embassy in Washington invited Art and me to their home for dinner. During the evening our hostess was entertaining us with stories about life in their previous post, Moscow. She said that her husband had had a choice between two posts and they had decided to go to Russia instead of India because they were concerned about stomach bugs in India! Everything is relative.

The microscopic bugs of Yemen proved to be the most vile and persistent for us. Art contracted food poisoning at an American oil camp in the desert. The only men in the group who didn't become ill were two who didn't eat the dessert—a tasty chocolate concoction that was infected with staphylococcus. Laboratory tests and sleuthing proved that the bacteria resulted from improper handling of the dairy products used in the dessert. Art's hosts for the visit were mortified that their kitchen had poisoned eighteen people—including the American ambassador! A chef or two were out job-hunting after that incident.

Art was a long way from home when he became ill. He had to endure a trip in a small plane to get back to Sanaa. When he arrived, I thought he hadn't looked so sick since the observation flights near Fulda thirty years earlier. We were fortunate to have a Health Unit at the embassy with an American doctor and two nurses who took wonderful care of all of us. Dr. John watched over Art while he suffered through fever, pain and diarrhea for over a week. He lost twelve pounds and was weak as a new puppy for a long while.

Not to be outdone, a few months later I ingested a nasty little bug that put me to bed for even longer. When the doctor saw that I was slow in recovering, he coaxed me out of my bedroom for a "bit of fresh air" and then lured me next door to the Health Unit. The nurses immediately put me on a bed and hooked me up to an intravenous rehydrating solution. And there I remained all day, relaxed, coddled, and on the road to recovery. I thought.

Unfortunately, the pesky microorganism continued to harass me with bouts of stomach pain and diarrhea for three months. Hattie, our capable laboratory technician, did all the usual tests, repeatedly, but was unable to identify the parasite. The nurses, Fatima and BJ, supplied me with various medications and soothing antidotes but to no avail. Finally, I had to be med-evaced to London. After several days and more tests and regimens than I care to remember, the laboratory at the Princess Grace Hospital found the culprit: yersinia. A rather intriguing moniker for such an ugly bug, I thought. It took another ten days and a debilitating medication before I was finally on the mend.

Foreign Service Requisite: a strong stomach.

The water in Yemen, as in Venezuela, was not potable and many of the food crops nourished by that water contained bacteria. In addition, there was the problem of unsanitary handling of foodstuffs in markets, grocery stores, and restaurants. Simply put: lack of personal hygiene resulted in unclean hands.

We expatriates washed our fresh fruits and vegetables in sterilized water to which we added a few drops of chlorine bleach or iodine. Except Katarzyna, our friend from Poland. Her theory was that our bodies needed to become accustomed to the local bugs. She insisted that her family never had stomach ailments.

Doris, the German Ambassador's wife, was of the opposite opinion—quite the opposite. She used sterilized water to wash and rinse her dishes! She refused to buy local bread because she had observed the baker's unhygienic practice of handling the dirty money and also the fresh bread with the same (assuredly unclean) hands. Yemeni money was extremely dirty.

Don and Debbie solved the bread problem: before slicing it they rotated the loaf over a gas flame on their stove to fire away any bacteria.

One Yemeni practice gave me a strong feeling of foreboding and an uncomfortable flutter in my stomach: serving tea in wet glasses or cups. This generally indicated that the receptacles were merely "rinsed" after use and there was no way of knowing if they were rinsed in clean water. One could hardly ask to inspect the host's kitchen.

The tea ceremony in Yemen was almost as significant as in Japan. Although the ritual wasn't ceremonious, it was an important part of Yemeni hospitality. To refuse a glass of tea would be considered impolite. There was one comforting thought: if you saw steam arising from the just-poured tea then probably the water had been boiled, hopefully obliterating any bacteria.

On a few occasions when we were out in the countryside in a tent or a hut, I saw that there were only three or four glasses for the tea. Those few were passed around the group and recycled time and again. A disconcerting practice when the others in the group were strangers.

To my chagrin I observed this same practice after dinner at the home of an Arab Ambassador in Washington—six cups rotated among fifteen or so guests. (And we were not out in the countryside!)

6

GUAJIROS AND OIL WELLS

"There's been a change in plans," said the caller from the State Department. (Whose plans were they, I wondered.) It was August 1967. We were back from Frankfurt, visiting my parents in Nebraska and showing off our children—according to *our* plans.

When Art hung up the phone, he reported that we were not going to Medellin, Colombia—our assignment had been changed to Maracaibo. We looked at each other and almost simultaneously asked, "Where's Maracaibo?"

"In Venezuela?" Art was uncertain. My dad, always the education enthusiast, quickly located his atlas and confirmed that Venezuela was indeed our next post.

"I think Maracaibo is an oil town." As Art dredged up another piece of information from somewhere in his memory bank, I tried to erase from mine all the things we had just learned about Colombia from the Department of State Post Report.

After our home leave we returned to base camp, Washington, DC. We rented yet another small apartment, studied Spanish, and shopped for a houseful of furniture—our first. In less than five months we were packing up—again.

We felt like traveling royalty during our trip to Venezuela. We left winter behind and sailed to Caracas on a gorgeous Grace Lines' ship—relaxing, dining lavishly, dancing, and overdosing on sunshine. The crewmembers pampered all four of us. After a hectic time of studying, frantic buying, and packing, we were happy to vacation on the seas once more. Art discovered smoked salmon and ate it every day, sometimes for breakfast. I indulged in desserts and the incomparable flavors of exotic tropical fruits. The children ate whatever and whenever they wanted.

On our way from the dock to the airport outside Caracas, I happened to look up and I saw a huge white bird swooping over us—it was a beautiful stork.

"That's a good luck omen," the taxi driver told us. And it was. We didn't have another baby, but we had incredibly good luck during the next two and a half years: happy times, wonderful friends, and worthwhile work.

At Grano del Oro Airport in Maracaibo the employees of the consulate were there to meet us. There were eight, I think, including the Consul, John King, and his wife, Laura. No one was minding the shop; John had closed the consulate for the afternoon. We had a splendid welcome and I clung tightly to those homey feelings of hospitality as we walked across the scorching tarmac. It was January, but everything was dry and dusty, dingy and dirty. As I looked around me I wondered: what are we *doing* here?

Inside the airport, several people in shabby clothes pushed each other about and vied for the job of carrying our bags to earn a few coins. At every turn there were beggars—and some were small children. This was our introduction to Maracaibo.

We spent our first weeks at the attractive Hotel del Lago in a *casita*, a small detached bungalow equipped with cooking facilities, dishes and linens. The grounds were beautifully landscaped and I immediately fell in love with the palm trees. Our daily pleasure was a luxurious swim in the huge pool. From there we could look out at Lake Maracaibo and see oil wells in the distance.

The first morning when I walked out to explore, a long fat green iguana waddled across the sidewalk in front of me. I nearly fainted. I had to go back inside gasping and sputtering. After I calmed down, I gave myself a little talking-to. "Self," I advised, "Don't be silly! This is the way it is and this is the way it's going to be. This is Venezuela, lizards and all." That seemed to work—temporarily—but I did a lot more heavy breathing at the first sight of a giant cockroach. As I saw more and more of the vile creatures, I again wondered: what are we *doing* here? But I soon came to love Maracaibo—in spite of the "water-bugs," mosquitoes, reptiles, rats and rabid dogs.

As we changed continents, we moved from one culture to another. The differences between Germany and Venezuela were countless: the climate, the people, and the language were the most obvious. On a personal level, our life style changed in many ways. We hired a servant for the first time; our first-born started school; and I went out to work. The consulate was small and the scope of Art's work was different than in Frankfurt. And we saw poverty everywhere.

Rita was our first live-in maid. In Maracaibo—and other parts of the world as I later learned—female domestic servants were called maids. I had always pictured a maid in a starched black uniform with a lacy white apron and cap. She would answer the door and the telephone, serve you iced tea on a silver tray, and prepare your perfumed bubble bath. That was not the case in Maracaibo. The maid was a cleaning woman, a baby-sitter, a gardener and sometimes a cook. Rita was all of those things, except the last. She was also dependable, speedy and usually happy. She had a pretty smile and a quick laugh that accentuated the spaces where several teeth were missing.

Initially, Art and I had decided that we didn't need full-time help, but a part-time baby-sitter would be ideal. Ideal yes—available no. There *was* no part-time daily help and we had to follow the "When in Rome…" doctrine. We also learned from others that having someone in the house while we were away helped to discourage burglars.

The majority of maids came from Colombia where the average income was even lower than in Venezuela. Many women left families across the border and sent money home each month. There couldn't have been much to send; starting salaries were only about $50.00 a month. On the other hand, domestics received uniforms from their employers and room and board. They had few expenses unless they were supporting a family.

We taught Alex some basic words and phrases in Spanish so he could begin to communicate with Rita. Young children have few inhibitions and it wasn't long before the two were conversing. In the fall he began Spanish classes at school. Kathy, at age two, picked up the language automatically. I can still remember her singing the Spanish version of "Itsy-Bitsy Spider" that she learned at a bilingual Montessori school.

Alex always had a keen interest in his dad's tools and repair kits—a prophetic interest, it seems now. He still likes to tinker. He was especially fascinated with a coil of solder that he got into one evening when we were out. After playing with it, experimenting, and twisting it out of shape, he couldn't get it back in its tube. His dad always told him, "Put things back in their places." But the solder wouldn't fit!

So he hid it and left a note in its place. He wrote—in Spanish—something like this: "I took your solder. It wasn't your son Alex." He didn't know the Spanish word for solder so he wrote it in English. He signed the note: "*El Bandito.*"

Maracaibo was hot and humid year round although December through February were sometimes as "cool" as the low 80's (Fahrenheit). Those were the only months during which we dared to entertain outside in the evening. Even then, the pesky mosquitoes were often spoilsports. Most of the year it was sheer torture to put on nylons and fancy clothes unless I knew there would be air-conditioning. Since the temperature only dropped a few degrees in the evening, there was little relief at night.

Our first Christmas in the tropics *felt* different. It was strange to dress in sleeveless cottons and to see Art with his shirt collar open. We have photos of the family in front of our dry scraggly Christmas tree—a tree we didn't keep long because it looked combustible. In one picture sweat is glistening on our faces. But we were all smiling.

Our home was a small one-level rectangular house that was pleasant and comfortable, although the wiring wasn't adequate. We could only use two window air-conditioners at the same time—turning on the third would blow out the fuses. But we managed, even after we bought another cooling unit for the kitchen. We just arranged for everyone to be in the same part of the house at the same time!

The roof leaked and the owner promised to have it repaired, but since he lived in Miami, our roof was not uppermost in his mind. When Art was suffering with the flu, it rained unusually long and hard and water began to drizzle from our bedroom ceiling. Art got on the telephone—which had taken four months to acquire—and loudly and angrily told the landlord that he was sick in bed.

"Rain is dripping on my feet!" he shouted. I then heard some sort of threat having to do with the American government and lawyers and lawsuits and lots of money. Art's invectives must have been taken seriously because workmen soon arrived to repair the roof.

We installed our washing machine and dryer on the patio off the kitchen because there was no place inside for them. Since there was a laundry sink attached to that side of the house, we assumed the laundry area was supposed to be there. We didn't worry about rain since it didn't very often. The sun was relentless though, and eventually Art had to rig up a roof over the patio. Rust proved to be a problem because of the high humidity.

Art was doing some fix-it jobs one weekend and when he went to the outdoor sink to wash up, there was no soap. I was perplexed since I had recently put out a fresh bar of the industrial-strength variety. When the soap disappeared a second time, I asked Rita about it. Her answer made me shudder. "It's the rats," she said. "They eat that kind of soap."

It wasn't long before we discovered where the rats were nesting. A foul smell, faint at first, then stronger, settled over the laundry area. When I turned on the dryer, I knew where the noxious odor was coming from. I turned off the dryer, removed the clothes, and waited for my husband. Mine was not the sort of news that the breadwinner appreciates when he comes home from the office, but Art was as anxious as I to get rid of the awful smell.

"I'll have to turn the dryer over," he said. As he tipped the machine on its side he told me to hold on to the corner for balance so it wouldn't drop. It was me that nearly dropped when an ugly rat jumped out of the back of the dryer and raced between my spread feet! It looked as big as a pony.

"Hold on to the dryer!" Art commanded and he turned it about forty-five degrees. Another rat took flight—and then another! I don't know why they all ran in my direction; it was as if there was a lighted pathway between my feet. Terrified as I was of the rats, I also feared dropping the dryer on my toes. We turned the machine again and waited. No more fleeing rodents. But there was a dead one—caught in the impeller—that Art retrieved and disposed of.

The furniture we had shipped from Nebraska had arrived in a large wooden crate about the size of a walk-in closet. When it was empty, Art made a door in it and we had a handy storage shed—a place to put the lawn mower and to store the skis that we wouldn't need. When a cheeping sound first emanated from the direction of the storage shed, I thought it was a baby bird, but two days later the cheeps became squeaks. Art pulled the shed away from the wall and there was the nest. No mama, but several tiny baby rodents. With gloves Art scooped up the whole lot: shredded paper, bits of rags, pieces of soap and babies. He started to put them in a bag.

"No, no, we can't," I whimpered. "They're just babies."

"They're baby *rats*," my husband emphatically pointed out. "And they'll grow up to be big rats and they'll reproduce. Do you want them to multiply in our yard?" No, I didn't.

We had a little mouse living under our refrigerator. She went in and out the kitchen door at will. Somehow, I didn't mind having her in my kitchen—she was small. I was much more concerned about the sizable iguanas that wandered in and stubbornly hid under the sofa. And the cockroaches that hid everywhere. But when I saw *two* mice skitter beneath the refrigerator, I decided that a honeymoon couple may result in several mice too many. I set the traps.

We had never had a bidet before; now we had two. In addition to the use for which they were intended, we found them handy for washing the children's habitually dirty feet. Mine too, as a matter of fact, since I wore sandals every day. After the dust and trash in the streets, I so enjoyed dipping my feet into the cold water of the bidet when I came home from shopping. I don't know how common bidets were in Maracaibo. They were evidently not familiar to everyone. A little girl who came to play with Kathy mistook our bidet for the toilet—twice.

My feet grew a whole size by the time we left Venezuela. (No longer would I have difficulty buying shoes in Fulda.) The sandals I wore weren't rubber-soled or thick and sturdy like those I have today. They were the cutesy thonged variety—fashionable strappy shoes in colors to match my dresses. And they were very flat. My feet became flat also. Part of the blame for my spreading feet had to be placed on the hard terrazzo floors. I never saw carpeting in Maracaibo. Some homes, ours included, had an area rug in the living room, but all other floors were bare. I was on my feet all day and almost every evening. Social affairs were usually cocktail parties or stand-up buffet suppers; seldom did we attend a sit-down dinner.

Foreign Service Requisite: sturdy feet.

Among the several indigenous tribes in Venezuela were the Guajiros, *indios* that numbered about 25,000 people in the 1960's. Their name came from their origins, the Guajira Peninsula, which lies between Colombia and Venezuela.

The *indios* who lived in the Maracaibo area watched the moon landing on television along with the rest of the world in July 1969. After American astronauts walked on the moon, the Guajiros decided to do a special dance, the "*Chicha Maya*," in honor of that historic walk. They invited American Consulate families and other members of the North American community as their guests. We watched the dancers "celebrating man and woman" as they vied for each other's attention in their movements and steps. The women wore traditional brightly colored, flowing robes with huge wide sleeves. As they circled we saw their bare feet thumping rhythmically on the dusty earth. Male dancers dressed as they did on the street, in loincloths or short wrapped skirts topped by western-style shirts.

Señora Gonzalez, leader of the dancers, explained, "The Guajiros feel that the landing on the moon demonstrates the brotherhood of man." There was indeed a feeling of brotherhood that day and being part of it was one of our family's unique experiences.

Art and I rediscovered the fun and gratification of amateur theater work and we spent many of our evenings at play rehearsals, theater group meetings and performances. The Maracaibo Players also played together, kids included, on many a weekend. Whenever I think about sheer fun, I remember Maracaibo. I don't know about blondes, but theater people definitely have more fun.

Art was in *The Odd Couple,* along with Hal and Fred who *were* the odd couple personified. He also had a part in *Twelve Angry Men.* When Betty directed *Sunday in New York* I had the Jane Fonda role and Art played my brother. We had a small audience for the final dress rehearsal so we carried on as if it were a performance.

One scene in the play takes place in a Japanese restaurant where the characters are drinking sake, rice wine. Our sake was usually 7-UP, but that night someone had substituted straight gin. During a pause in the conversation I took a big swallow—and choked! Jolted by the strong unexpected taste, I coughed and sputtered and couldn't continue my lines. When the others discovered the gin, they began to laugh—and laugh—and there followed some very inventive ad-libbing.

Fred and Betty, who had lived in Maracaibo longer than most of us, were not only our elders, but also the leaders of the group. He was the rooster and she was our mother hen. They kept us going, advising and coddling us. They were experienced theater people from whom we learned a great deal. They invited us to family picnics at their home, partly because they had a swimming pool and partly because they were wonderful hospitable people. Fred was the brewmaster for a local brewery so he was in charge of refreshments for picnics and cast parties, at least the liquid part of the refreshments.

Our friends, those in the Maracaibo Players and others, were international. Unlike in Frankfurt, most were not in the diplomatic corps; they were business people, teachers, and bankers. Many expatriates were associated with or suppliers for the oil companies. We became acquainted with many local people, Maracuchos, through the Junior Chamber of Commerce and through friends of friends. Maracaibo was a socially active community, perhaps better described as a party town. It seemed that everybody invited everybody to every event. Since this was almost every night, we met a lot of people.

Venezuelan food was considerably different from European cuisine. We especially liked the marinated, grilled and shredded beef that always came with black beans and rice. *Queso blanco,* a local white cheese accompanied almost every meal. *Plátanos,* plantains, were ubiquitous—baked, fried, boiled or made into habit-forming salted chips.

Tequeños were my favorite: long strips of pastry wrapped around finger-sized pieces of white cheese and deep-fried. I tried to make them, but I never mastered the wrapping. My cheese always oozed out and melted into the hot oil. I also loved hot fresh *arepas,* flat round corncakes that were fried and slathered with butter. They were heavy as shot puts but they were delicious.

Pastry turnovers, *empanadas,* filled with meat and/or vegetables, are common throughout Latin America. Venezuela had its own varieties, but we weren't fond of the ones Maracuchos made at Christmas-time. They were stuffed with an unusual mixture that included olives—pits and all.

Supermarket beef was not aged and it was tough. We had a difficult time getting used to the wild gamey taste. Only one cut of beef could be roasted and that was the tenderloin. Loin it was—tender it was not. I experimented with marinating the beef and I used a good deal of tenderizer, lemon juice and Worcestershire Sauce.

Mi Vaquita, "My Little Calf," was a famous restaurant in Maracaibo that served mouth-watering tender T-bone steaks, which were perfectly aged and the biggest I had ever seen (until I went to Texas many years later.) The management offered a second steak free of charge to anyone who finished the first. I didn't think anyone could eat such a huge piece of meat until our old school friends, Bill and Mary, came for a visit from California. Bill ate the entire steak—with ease—and ordered another.

Our kids loved to eat at El Rincón, "The Corner," one of two restaurants that had a playground and a large screen that showed cartoons continuously. Alex's favorite was the deep-fried shrimp and I thought the fried chicken was the best anywhere. Art and I were usually oddities at El Rincón. There were seldom any other parents there—unless they were also American. Maids accompanied the local children.

Contraband goods, primarily food and cigarettes, came over the border from Colombia. Salesmen came around the neighborhoods with wheels of European cheese that weighed several kilos—too much for the average family. But the seller would wait while we telephoned around to find two or three friends who would share. One time we bought an enormous Dutch salami. It was a treat since that kind of sausage was not available in the stores.

I could never get used to the vile intrusive roaches that seemed to be everywhere. And I couldn't get used to the poverty—one of the worst of life's roaches.

In the beginning I gave coins to every ragged child I saw, against the advice of expatriates who had been in the country longer than we. Finally, I had to agree with them; a coin here, a *bolívar* there, didn't do much for the long term. After I became involved in charity work, however, I realized that this was the best way to help.

The first time I saw a little boy crawling out of a garbage dumpster at the supermarket, I felt—it's difficult to describe how I felt—shocked first, then outraged, sad, and mostly, helpless. There were hundreds of abandoned children in Maracaibo and thousands throughout the country. Whether the child at the dumpster, who was only four or five, was abandoned or a hungry member of a jobless family, I would never know. The unemployment rate was high and the standard of living was lower than low.

Señora de Leoni, wife of the Venezuelan president during our first year in the country, sponsored several mass weddings. Hundreds of couples were simultaneously and legally married with the full rites of the Catholic Church. A lot of children became legitimate through those services, and they were less likely to be abandoned by couples who were married.

Most Venezuelans were Catholic and they were churchgoers. Our maid came to me one day in tears because she didn't have enough money for the white dress her daughter needed for her confirmation. I was appalled that the twelve-year-old child couldn't be confirmed without the proper attire! Rita's husband was unemployed because of a back injury, making her wages the only income for the family of seven. I frequently sent food home for them and occasional small gifts for the children. But my conscience wouldn't allow me to buy a "church uniform" for a family that was so needy. Finally I told Rita that I would make the dress on my sewing machine if she could supply the fabric. In the end, however, the child borrowed a dress and veil from a friend and that resolved the situation.

The North American Association, comprised of Americans and Canadians, promoted charitable activities in Venezuela. The group's major fund-raiser was a Fourth of July raffle. Valuable prizes were donated for the event—automobiles, airline tickets and major appliances. The drawing was held during a ball in Caracas and in Maracaibo we had a black-tie dinner-dance to celebrate the raffle *and* American Independence Day.

Committees geared up in the late spring and almost everyone we knew sold tickets or worked in some other capacity for the big raffle. Women set up tables outside supermarkets and remained there for half-day stretches selling tickets. It became tiresome toward the end and we had to put other activities on hold, but it was a worthwhile project, which benefited many, many children. Our state of Zulia alone raised more than $200,000 each year.

After experiencing firsthand the community spirit in Maracaibo I decided to organize a benefit for leukemia research. My sister's first child died of leukemia when he was five and the dreadful disease took its toll on the entire family. I discussed the idea with friends and got an enthusiastically positive response. We formed a committee and decided to put on a Casino Night with poker, blackjack, bingo and a made-for-the-occasion Wheel of Fortune. The proceeds would be donated to St. Jude Children's Research Hospital founded by Danny Thomas in Memphis, Tennessee.

One of our committee members checked with the local authorities to preclude our violating any laws or regulations. The only taboo was gambling with actual currency so we printed up "play" money, which we called Benefit Bucks. Winners exchanged Bucks for prizes, all of which were donated.

Volunteers spent weeks knocking on doors of shops, restaurants and business offices, asking for donations. I was continually amazed at the generosity of the community, especially since we were an unknown entity. Westinghouse donated a television set, an attractive lure, as the door prize. We received all sorts of small appliances, radios, household items, giftware, liquor, food baskets, haircuts and manicures, restaurant dinners, jewelry and other things I have forgotten. The Hotel del Lago donated the space, served snacks and provided a cash bar.

Casino Night was a huge success. The gamblers were at it until the wee morning hours and everyone had fun. More than fifty volunteers worked and played and enjoyed the event along with our patrons. We were gratified by the large attendance and no one minded that it was crowded. The result was a check for over $2000 that I sent to St. Jude's.

I was so elated by our accomplishment that I immediately began planning for a benefit the following year. We would use a larger room, sell more tickets and make more money—it could become a tradition. Instead, the second Casino Night was almost a disaster.

The night before the second benefit I received an ominous phone call from a Venezuelan businessman we knew. He told me that the local authorities did not want us to repeat Casino Night. "There's a new regulation," he reported. My heart plummeted to my toes. We hadn't inquired about regulations that year. The Junior Chamber of Commerce had sponsored a casino party earlier in the year—so why pick on us? Our friend said that a local official (equivalent to a city councilman) wanted to meet with me at City Hall the next morning—an invitation I couldn't refuse.

I arrived at the meeting feeling nervous and agitated. After the usual civilities the official announced pompously, "The city has decided it cannot condone gambling." I blurted out a string of excuses, reasons and promises and with no shame at all, I begged.

"We can't cancel now! We've sold hundreds of tickets! The event has been publicized for weeks!" I was thankful the conversation was in English; I couldn't have begged in Spanish. Finally, with syrup in my throat I reminded the official,

"This year, half of the proceeds from our benefit are going to your local cancer society, the Liga Anticancerosa en Maracaibo. We've promised—how can we disappoint them?"

After a moment's hesitation the man told me, "Have a nice bingo evening and leave out the other games." I had a niggling suspicion that he had intended to make that statement from the outset. I was out of arguments; it was time to leave. His good-byes were akin to a verbal pat on the head.

As I drove home, I suddenly stopped in front of a beauty salon. I went in, had my hair done and my nails manicured. I must have been possessed—I've always hated manicures and I don't like to sit still while someone is fiddling over me. But I didn't want to talk to anyone. I needed time to mull over the situation.

Meanwhile the word had spread—as it has a way of doing—and people wanted to know what was going on. When I got home, I called several members of the committee and told them about the meeting. "But we're going through with it anyway—all of it!" I had made the decision while I was sitting under the hair dryer. My cohorts all agreed.

We made some contingency plans, nevertheless. We decided what to do if someone—the police?—came to shut us down; what to do if I was arrested; where to take the money at the end of the evening. We all agreed that Art should stay at home. He was an American government official and we didn't want *that* sort of problem. I had never before broken the law intentionally nor disobeyed an official. But that time, my sense of fairness was offended. Why did the government wait until the last day to warn us off? Truthfully—I didn't believe there would be any dire consequences. If the city imposed a fine, I just hoped we would make enough money to cover the fine and still make our donations.

The show went on. Unfortunately the rumors went on also. Many people didn't show up—some because they thought we had canceled, and others, because they were concerned about "trouble." Fewer people in a larger room put a damper on the ambiance. During the evening we spotted a reporter from a local newspaper and we told him that photographs were not permitted, but his presence made us nervous. The evening ended in a somber mood. Our profits were slightly less than the previous year and we were disappointed. But there were no incidents.

I deposited the money early Monday morning while Ian, our treasurer, rushed to complete the bookkeeping. As soon as he finalized the accounts I wrote two checks. I mailed one to St. Jude's and I delivered the other to the Liga Anticancerosa. Then I quickly closed our bank account. Done. Over. Finished.

Not quite. A picture appeared a few days later in the newspaper—a picture of several game tables with smiling gamblers holding cards. The caption read "Casino Night." Several uneventful days passed by and I began to draw easier breaths. Until Charlie, the manager of the Hotel del Lago, called.

"How about coming to lunch tomorrow?" he asked—and I knew something was up. He said that several officials had paid him a visit asking questions about Casino Night. "They're threatening to arrest the organizers."

Charlie was the original schmoozer. According to him, he told his visitors that if they arrested anybody they would have to include the guests who came to gamble. "We had some high-ranking government people here for the benefit, as well as an army general and several colonels." He declined to give out the names of the notables, of course. Some of what he said was twaddle and some was true, but you had to know Charlie. He also expounded on the attributes and generosity of the women who had given their time and efforts to benefit a Venezuelan organization. That's when he invited the city government people—all men—to have lunch with those same charming women. He told them: "You'll soon agree that no harm was done."

Charlie told me to invite several committee members to the lunch. "Bring the best-looking women and tell them to wear something pretty and sexy." Keep in mind that it was 1970, Charlie was Cuban, and this was Latin America.

In a little private dining room at the hotel Charlie introduced everyone and we shook hands and exchanged pleasantries and I tried hard not to hyperventilate. In the end there were no arrests—but my friends and I got a good scolding. We had "embarrassed the city government" by going ahead with our gambling games after they had asked us not to. I conceded that my decision was improper. What could I do? We promised to be "good girls" and never do it again!

Afterward Charlie had a good laugh. He was proud of himself for saving the day—and saving my hide. I gratefully congratulated him on his diplomacy.

Charlie was married to a genuine American southern belle called Buggie. They were friendly fun people who involved themselves in the community. In addition to his diplomatic talents, Charlie could sing. He often entertained us and Buggie would join in with castanets or a tambourine or her own voice. Invitations to their parties were sought and coveted. Unfortunately for their friends, the couple was transferred out of Maracaibo rather quickly after someone was shot in Charlie's office. The whys and wherefores were never clear.

I signed up as a substitute teacher and my first assignment was perfect: junior high English for three weeks—which stretched into nine. My training was in secondary education so I appreciated the opportunity for experience and I loved the kids. Another opportunity was not quite so pleasurable. Sara, principal of another school, talked me into teaching first grade for two weeks. Those were the longest two weeks of my life!

Teaching English as a foreign language was a new challenge. When several of my friends reported that there was a plethora of potential students and not enough teachers, I tried it—and I liked it. In fact, I liked it so well I continued it for many years. This was a vocation that traveled with the Foreign Service.

The combination of theater work, our children's activities, a Spanish conversation group, the Toastmistress organization, volunteering, social events and obligations plus teaching kept my calendar filled—and my soul fulfilled. Art seldom suffered from a dull moment, either. He joined the Junior Chamber of Commerce, which held frequent meetings and activities, and he played a little golf.

Though far from being an expert golfer, he played a tiny bit better than one of his Venezuelan partners. One morning they were joking back and forth and Art teased his friend. "Armando," he said, "You're a worse golfer than I am—why do you keep playing?"

"Because, Arturo," replied Armando with a grin, "Golfing keeps me humble."

A short time after our arrival in Maracaibo, I wrote to my parents: "Art and the other vice consul are driving into Colombia tomorrow…to check on reports of possible guerrilla activity. It scares me, but Art thinks it will be interesting." It proved to be an informative trip—and not a dangerous one. But such trips always made me jittery.

Art's job required other traveling for other reasons. During the months preceding Venezuelan national elections he visited several parts of the state, talked to the citizens and gathered information. Reporting was a major part of Foreign Service work and the consulate sent his reports on to Washington.

I went along on one of Art's more entertaining business trips. We flew to Judibana, a Creole oil camp on the opposite side of Lake Maracaibo. (Creole was the name of the petroleum companies owned by Standard Oil.) Somehow "oil camp" prompts images of army barracks or bunkhouses at round-up time. Judibana, in fact, was quite different. It was a small town with pretty homes and lovely gardens, a guesthouse, club, swimming pool and restaurants.

An American family had asked Art to witness a wedding in his capacity as consular officer. While there he set up office hours in the guest quarters and provided other consular services, saving several Americans a lengthy trip to Maracaibo. For the first time we toured a refinery and began to learn about the oil business.

When the work was finished, our new friends wined, dined and entertained us. We had luscious food—I remember the huge lobsters—and posh accommodations. A delightful three-day working vacation.

Art did some jail time in Maracaibo—jail visiting. One weekend he went to the aid of an American businessman who had been arrested for no apparent reason except revenge. It seems that the American had fired his Venezuelan lawyer and in order to punish his former client, the lawyer arranged for the man's arrest—late Friday afternoon on a holiday weekend.

When Art attempted to get the American released from jail, it was impossible. The lawyer had known that no one was let out of jail until the required appearance before a judge. And on a Friday afternoon before a holiday no self-respecting Venezuelan judge was available. The lawyer had his revenge: the American had to remain in the city jail for several days—relying on his family to carry in his meals. But Consul Hughes was able to do one thing for his countryman. After a bit of negotiating Art succeeded in having him moved into one of the jailers' rooms. The poor man was locked up still, but the atmosphere was less harrowing than sharing a cell with criminals.

Another call from the city lock-up sent Art to bail out a belligerent American traveler whom I'll call Mr. Z. He was in Caracas on business and had flown to Maracaibo for a brief visit. Foolishly Mr. Z had left his passport in his hotel room in Caracas. When a customs agent at the Maracaibo airport asked Mr. Z for his passport, the American replied that he didn't have it. The official took hold of the visitor's arm to prevent him from moving on and Mr. Z took offense. He angrily shoved the official and then threw him a hefty punch—and he was immediately hauled off to jail!

Mr. Z defended his unruly behavior by claiming that he didn't understand who the man at the airport was. It was true that the officials at Grano del Oro tended to look like scruffy individuals rather than tidy examples of officialdom. Nevertheless, the customs agent was following orders—for a good reason. Hijackers had diverted several aircraft to Cuba during the previous year so officials were carefully checking passports and identity papers at all airports.

During a visit to Paris several years later our friend Bill, a former neighbor in Bethesda, introduced us to an acquaintance of his and Art thought he looked familiar. When Bill mentioned we had been in Venezuela, the man began to spin out a story about his ill treatment in Maracaibo. Suddenly Art recognized him. "I was the consul who got you out of jail!" he interrupted. It was Mr. Z. He immediately changed the tone of his narrative—giving it a more positive slant.

Violent crime was unusual in Maracaibo. Muggings and armed robbery were not common felonies and murder was usually a result of inter-family fighting and domestic squabbles. Burglary and theft, on the other hand, occurred frequently. We knew many people whose homes were broken into during the night. Opening your eyes and seeing a stranger in your bedroom gives a frightening twist to the phrase "rude awakening." The audacity of the perpetrators was quite amazing.

Our friend Carol awoke with a start when someone opened the drawer of her night table—right beside her. She had put a good deal of cash in the drawer that day after selling raffle tickets. Her screams sent the thief running—with the money. His partner fled also with items he had taken from a suitcase that was lying open in the living room. Carol's husband Ron had just returned from the States and hadn't yet unpacked his bags.

When the police arrived, they insisted on taking the suitcase with its remaining contents to headquarters as evidence. "Procedure," said one of the officers. When Ron went to the police station the next day to reclaim his bag, he discovered that what the thieves hadn't stolen, someone else had. His camera and two new copies of *Playboy* magazine were missing!

Javier and Deena, who lived in our area of town, awoke to a strange noise. They peeked out of their bedroom, which was off a corridor from the dining room, and saw two strangers bagging up the sterling silver. Panic set in when they discovered that one of the thieves was wielding a machete! Since the dining room was situated in the middle of the house, they couldn't reach their children's rooms or the exits without coming face to face with the machete man. Flight was impossible. They had no choice but to wait until the intruders went out the front door with the loot. And out they went—prematurely it seemed.

The thieves had heard a ruckus in the street. Neighbors they had robbed earlier had called the police who arrived just as the perpetrators were hurriedly loading the stolen goodies into a get-away vehicle. It turned out that the neighborhood watchman was part of the machete gang.

Our friends got back all of their possessions after the initial investigation. That was probably because Javier came from Colombia and knew how to grease palms.

Gail was in bed when three thugs with guns got into the apartment. Her husband Ian was not at home. Terrified as she was, Gail wasn't about to get up because she was naked! As the robbers moved about looking for loot, she heard one of them whisper to the others in Spanish, "Don't wake the children!"

Our property was surrounded on two sides by a tall stone wall and on the other sides by a six-foot high chain link fence topped with barbed wire. Most homes in Maracaibo were similarly protected and those who could afford it also had alarm systems. Although fencing discouraged theft, it didn't completely deter it, as many of our friends were finding out. After two of Art's shirts were stolen from the patio clothesline, we decided not to leave clothes outside again.

One hot afternoon our maid Rita left the door open to her room, which had an outside entrance, and she went around to sweep the grass on the other side of the house. (The maids thought lawn rakes were strange implements and they preferred brooms.) When she returned to take a shower she discovered that someone had been there—her room had obviously been searched. She had only one thing of value, a pair of gold earrings, and they were missing.

Some time later rumors circulated through the neighborhood that a gang led by "Carlos" was responsible for recent thefts. Art and I had seen a group of rowdy and cocky teenagers several times, ambling through the streets looking around. The next time Art saw a familiar young man near our house, he called him over to the gate. (In his weekend work-clothes, my husband was often mistaken for the gardener or handy man.) The youth swaggered over, curious.

"Do you know Carlos?" Art asked him in Spanish. "Tell Carlos I have a little present for him."

Art slowly revealed the *regalito*, the present, he had behind his back: a .22 rifle, which he gave an arrogant pat. The teenager moved hurriedly down the street. The rifle wasn't loaded nor would it be, but the threat—perhaps—forestalled any more theft from our home.

The Colombian maids had a network and they all knew each other, it seemed. They visited back and forth and swapped stories, especially on Thursdays when they had the afternoon off. Rita would return on Fridays with all manner of gossip and tall tales. I listened politely but wondered—where do they *get* this stuff?

"The water is going to be shut off for several days." That was a popular story. "The Colombian maids are going to be rounded up and deported!" That one made us nervous. "The grocery stores are going to be closed and all the workers will strike." Another improbable prediction.

Occasionally though, there was a tiny thread of fact woven into a rumor. One day when the water did stop, I was grateful to discover that Rita had stored water in several pitchers and containers and filled the bathtubs.

The most disturbing rumors circulated just before the Venezuelan elections. There was concern that the elections would be called off, resulting in mass demonstrations—and demonstrations often turned into riots. Our consulate people increased security precautions during that unsteady period. Art varied his route to and from the office and he cautioned me to do likewise. Everyone was extra vigilant. The sale of alcohol was prohibited from Friday midnight through Sunday, voting day. Subsequently there were few social events that weekend. But the gossips were wrong—elections proceeded as planned. Much to everyone's relief, the process was peaceful and orderly.

President-elect Rafael Caldera came to Maracaibo shortly before his inauguration. He was the second Venezuelan president we had the opportunity to shake hands with. I'll never become too old or too jaded to appreciate meeting heads of state.

After the 1968 presidential election in the United States many of us in Maracaibo were reminded—with amusement—of a premature newspaper headline published three decades earlier. A Chicago paper had printed: "DEWEY DEFEATS TRUMAN." This time a Maracaibo paper ran the banner: "HUMPHREY WINS."

Art and I had watched bullfighting in Barcelona a few years earlier. I burst into tears at the end of the first fight and refused to look when the unfortunate dead animal was dragged through the dirt and out of the ring. But I loved the ceremonious opening parade: the pomp, the music, the costumes, the horses and the enthusiasm of the crowd. The bullfight itself was intriguing—once I had accustomed myself to the inevitable ending. I admired the talent and grace of the toreadors whose movements hinted of the ballet.

The annual festival of Chiquinquerá was a fun time we looked forward to in Maracaibo. Although the festival had religious origins, it was also a celebration of family and community. Bullfighting was the main event and one year we watched the famous bullfighter El Cordobés perform in the ring. His real name was Manuel Benitez and he came from Córdoba in Spain. In his "suit of lights" he had an elegance which, combined with his lithe svelte body and handsome face, was admired by fans all over the world.

Unfortunately, his performance that day was mediocre—the slow lazy bull was an uncooperative opponent. In bullfighting parlance: "He had a bad bull." A local newspaper quoted El Cordobés the following day: "I will not return to Maracaibo!" He was irked because the judge didn't award him an ear. When a bullfighter performs well in the ring, the judge may reward him with an ear from the fallen bull. An extraordinary performance may rate both ears! The floppy appendage is sliced off the dead animal on the spot and presented to the toreador who parades around the arena proudly waving his prize.

We had a bad bull, also. During one of the bullfights a particularly frenzied bull entered the ring jumping and leaping. He ran in circles totally ignoring the red cape. Suddenly, somehow, the feisty bull leaped over the guardrail—and the wooden fence—onto the narrow pathway in front of the first row of spectators. It was a stunning feat! We were sitting just above in the third row—too awestruck to be afraid. Fortunately for all of us, the now-frightened animal ran in a lateral direction and was soon brought down.

Several years later we took our teenagers to a bullfight while we were vacationing in Spain. They hated it! Alex was horrified, Kathy covered her face, and they both complained indignantly about cruelty. They were baffled that their parents were enjoying such an awful display. It was not the educational and cultural experience we had hoped for.

Laura, the consul's wife, phoned one morning and we were chatting about the festival and the bullfights that were coming up the following weekend. The phone call turned into a bizarre episode.

"If you're not going on Saturday," Laura said, "May we borrow your *bota*?" A *bota* is a leather pouch used for carrying and drinking wine or water. In Venezuela, Spain and other countries it was traditional to take the (full) wineskin to the bullfights.

I started to reply when a male voice interrupted. "Hi, how are you doing?"

I was stunned—it was Art! He was at the consulate—Laura and I were at home.

I quickly said, "Art, Laura was just asking to borrow our *bota*."

My husband's reply was unnerving. "I wouldn't loan it to them even if we weren't using it!" I felt as if I had just stepped into a movie. It was clear Art didn't know the boss's wife was on the line.

Laura quietly said, "I'll talk to you later, Pat." And she hung up. I sputtered and stammered and tried to explain to Art that the phone lines must have been crossed because all three of us were connected. We hung up abruptly, no longer trusting the telephone.

By the time Art came home for lunch—earlier than usual—I was beside myself. How were we going to fix this? Art meant what he said, but he certainly didn't intend to say what he meant—to Laura. He was annoyed because John and their sons had borrowed his golf clubs the previous weekend and had returned them all grassy and mud-encrusted.

On Sunday after several failed attempts by both of us to speak to Laura, Art took her aside, alone, and explained. He apologized for his harsh words and told her the reason for them. Laura, a warm gentle person, accepted his apology graciously, if not enthusiastically. After a time of cooling off and perhaps wariness on her part, our relationship returned to normal. Art agonized over whether or not to confess all to his boss and be done with it. He never did and I don't think Laura told her husband what had happened. John's attitude toward us didn't change—nor did his well-known sense of humor diminish. He didn't borrow the golf clubs again, however.

Some years ago when the trash collectors in New York City were on strike, Art showed me a newspaper photograph. "Does this bring back any memories?" he asked.

The picture showed mounds of garbage, in bags and out of bags, piled and strewn along the streets. According to the accompanying story, there was a dangerous increase in the population of rats as well as other nasty vermin.

We both recalled a similar strike in Maracaibo. The stench, intensified by the high temperatures, was sick-making. Our three weeks' worth of garbage was sealed into every bag, box, and container we could find. And there was no garbage disposal in our sink to lessen the volume. Flies and cockroaches seemed to multiply at the speed of sound and rodents were ubiquitous. At first, the wild dogs fought over the garbage but it soon became too putrid even for them.

Strikes in Venezuela were seldom quiet and peaceful. Several Maracuchos died and many were injured in the rioting during those three weeks. And there would be other riots.

In the days before security became a major concern at Foreign Service posts, I wasn't aware of what to do and what not to do if caught in a threatening predicament. I behaved very stupidly when it happened. (Today, officers and family members are given briefings on this subject.)

I was hurrying to get to a play rehearsal and I drove directly into the middle of a riot. I could have turned and taken another street; I could have pulled over and investigated; or I could have made a U-turn and returned home—but I didn't. Nor did I even suspect I was heading into a dangerous situation. Today, I would know better. I saw the black smoke from several blocks away and I wondered briefly where the fire was. Mostly, I was preoccupied—thinking about my lines in the play.

Suddenly angry young men and boys were surrounding my car—they were shouting, chanting, cursing and waving their fists. To my right I could see a burning truck tire in the street. I slowed to a crawl, desperately searching for a way through the mob. As more people surged around me, I felt as if the car were being carried aloft in some kind of tumultuous procession. My throat tightened as my hands gripped the steering wheel. I managed to make a left-hand turn—only because that was the direction the crowd was moving. I found myself on a slightly elevated concrete expanse in front of a small strip-mall, directly across the street from the consulate. The building also housed the USIS library, Casa Americana, where we were to have the rehearsal.

Acrid smoke was coming from another burning tire but I couldn't tell where it was. I suddenly saw flames shoot skyward. Now I was terrified! A black station wagon belonging to the U.S. government was on fire in front of the consulate. The billboard was also ablaze. The freestanding structure, about seven feet high with glass-fronted cases, held photographs of astronauts and information about the American space program. Fire quickly consumed the display.

My husband, bound for play practice also, had left home in a different vehicle. I knew he must have arrived before me but I didn't see his jeep. But then, my line of vision was partially obstructed by moving agitated bodies. I thought Art might have gone inside the building. Would the rioters force their way inside?

I couldn't understand any of the shouting and yelling. Normally my Spanish comprehension was adequate but that night it was nonexistent—until I heard the word "Americana" and again "Americana" like an echo. I saw fingers pointing at me and the mob around my car seemed to thicken.

Someone tapped on my window (I had already locked the car doors) and a young man called to me in accented English, "Are you American? You shouldn't be here," he hollered. What an understatement! When he tried to explain in Spanish, I understood only the words "against Americans," but it was more than enough.

At that moment a truck careened into the parking area not far from my car, scattering the riled-up crowd in all directions. Out of the back of the truck jumped scores of armed national guardsmen. Several of the *Guardia National* approached and surrounded me—perhaps they had recognized my diplomatic license plates.

I had a sudden burst of bravery—or stupidity—and rolled down the window. I heard bits of English and rapid Spanish accompanied by a lot of gesticulating. Without fully realizing what I was doing, I let my car, which I had kept running, coast down the small incline. Four guardsmen, like escorts, walked me into the street—one alongside each fender. We reached the next block where the crowds were heavy but less agitated and many people appeared to be spectators rather than participants.

Another block further, fewer people, less pandemonium. At the intersection I was able to make a left turn. I paused, waved to my rescuers and headed home. As I left the business district the noise decreased, but I could still smell the smoke. The suburbs were quiet and our street was empty. But instead of going home, I drove to the consul's house, speeding all the way.

As my brain resumed rational thinking I worried: where was Art? Did Bart, the new consul, know about the rioting? I thought I should "report" to someone. I rushed into their home just as the phone rang—it was my husband. He gave Bart a report and then I got on the phone. At that moment I started to shake.

While I was talking to Art, Bart's wife Calista handed me a glass of cold golden brown liquid. "Drink this," she ordered. I drank. My stomach slowly warmed and the trembling diminished. She had given me a medicinal shot of straight Scotch whiskey.

Art told me what he was doing while I was caught in the middle of the melee. "I was watching you," he said. As soon as he smelled burning rubber, he suspected there was a demonstration. He circled around, parked his vehicle in the next block, and walked to a corner pub. He ordered a drink and, along with the other patrons, observed the crowd through the window. And he listened.

"I saw you drive into the mob and park. I also watched the guardsmen escort you down the street—I knew you were all right." While I was worrying about his safety and whereabouts, my husband was drinking a beer and calmly observing my predicament!

Before calling his boss, Art had gone to check on the consulate. The demonstrators had scattered by then and he didn't see anyone in front of the building. Broken glass crunched under his feet. When he opened the outer door with his key, the night guard suddenly appeared.

"They were going to kill me, they were going to kill me," the terrified watchman wailed in Spanish. He had a gun but he had stayed hidden.

Although the demonstration had started at the university for some innocuous reason, high school students soon became involved. Other grievances were added to the initial complaint and eventually anti-American ideas fueled the already hot tempers. The major issue was American involvement in Vietnam.

A year later more rioting took place. American soldiers had crossed into Cambodia, and Venezuelan students railed against our country. That time, Art and I managed to stay clear.

Rita didn't show up for work one Monday and after several days, a message came that she was ill. We were concerned about her and after asking for directions, we made our way through the *barrio* to her home. She and her family lived in a tiny ramshackle hut that was spotlessly clean inside. We took enough food for several meals. The following week I decided to hire another domestic temporarily. But when Rita came back—unannounced—she was miffed to find another maid in our kitchen and she left for good. We were sorry because our family was fond of her.

Our new maid, Carmen, was round, robust and had an enormous appetite. She was as slow as a pregnant snail but eventually she got the work done. Including cooking the most delicious deep-fried *empanadas* I had ever eaten. She made them with a cornmeal pastry.

Carmen's reluctance to discipline our son was a problem in the beginning. Alex was seven and he quickly learned that he could take advantage of her when his parents were not home. I mentioned this to some friends and they reminded me that in Venezuela "the male rules." Boys are seldom punished or disciplined. Art and I had frequently observed this cultural tendency—much to our displeasure. After a lot of discussion and stern admonitions Alex and Carmen eventually came to terms with each other.

Carmen would only iron clothes early in the day. "There's electricity in my body after I iron," she explained. Many of the maids believed that if they took a shower or used water after ironing, they would be electrocuted. Carmen liked to take a shower and put on a clean uniform before dinner, so she had to do the ironing in the morning.

A shattering crash woke me one night—I sat up in bed as if I were spring-loaded. Panicky I shook Art, whispering, "What was that? What was that noise?" The only identifiable sound by then was the air-conditioner in the window.

My husband mumbled sleepily into his pillow, "Maybe a picture frame fell off the dresser."

I knew it was more than that, but I was too scared to get out of bed and investigate. I shook Art again and he turned on the lamp that was on his side of the bed. In the light we could see a big hole in the window where several of the glass louvers had broken. On the floor underneath was a fist-sized hunk of concrete and scattered shards of glass. Art put slippers on and went into the other rooms. From the darkness he peered out the windows but he saw no one in the streets or in our yard and there was no sound outside.

Art brought my sandals and the broom and I gingerly got out of bed. While I swept he shook out the throw rugs that were beside the bed. We still saw glimmers of glass on the floor and knew this job needed a vacuum cleaner. Not wanting to wake up the children, we decided to wait until morning. We arranged two heavy chairs in front of our door to keep out little feet that might wander in and step on something sharp.

We finally, uneasily, went back to bed and turned off the light. As I lay down I felt something cold next to my cheek—there was a jagged piece of broken window on my pillow!

We never knew precisely what happened. The missile that came through our window was part of the concrete curbing that was broken up on our corner. It was "probably" lobbed randomly over our fence. The perpetrator "probably" didn't know who we were. Art tried to convince me that if people were out to get us they would have pursued their objective. He "probably" was right because there were no other such incidents.

As I approached the age of thirty—with no sensible way to avoid it—I discovered I was still as naive as a maiden fresh off the farm. I knew there were people who had extra-marital affairs. A few people—occasionally—somewhere—but no one I knew. Until now. Maracaibo was a small-town city where everyone knew everyone else's comings and goings, literally. Rumors abounded and they were usually true.

I had heard about Venezuelan men who had mistresses. Many brought the "other woman" to social events while the pregnant wife stayed home. I was totally appalled when I observed the errant couples with my own eyes. But hadn't I heard that Latin men are passionate and arrogant? So…it was cultural.

But soon Americans began to figure into my adult sex education. Some merely flirted openly; others gave in completely to their whims and desires. One of my married friends told me repeatedly that she would like to have an affair with so-and-so. Another confided that she was going to meet a man (whom I knew!) for an afternoon tryst.

During rehearsals for a play, the leading actor and actress became attracted to each other and rumors were rampant that they were having an affair. The rumors must have been true; they left town, divorced their spouses and got married. We later heard the marriage didn't work out.

Another friend confronted her husband about his alleged affair. He denied sexual consummation but admitted he had strayed. They worked through the problem and their marriage survived (and still does). The other woman, over-wrought by her unrequited yearnings, soon left the country with her husband.

Gradually I was becoming worldly-wise. Nothing more, I thought, could shock me on the subject of extra-marital dalliances. Until I was propositioned. My friend Mary Ann, unflappable and thoroughly outrageous, came over one day and announced, "Dimitri saw you in the play and he's interested in you. When can you meet him?" Dimitri was European, young and single. I knew him only slightly but I knew he knew I was married. Mary Ann, who had been asked to set up a liaison, added with a sly smile, "He wants to have an affair."

I thought the whole idea was brash and presumptuous and I declined—of course! I didn't regret the boost to my ego, however; the man was attractive and charismatic. I have called him Dimitri, by the way, because I can't remember his real name. I do remember feeling very uncomfortable the next time I saw him.

When my parents came to visit we traveled to other parts of the country. At Merida in the Andes Mountains we rode the cable cars and admired the snow. We drove up to Eagle Pass, so high that Alex suffered from altitude sickness. We boated down the river Limon and gaped at the "stick villages" where people lived in huts raised on stilts over the water.

During the trip we stopped at a roadside fruit market and Mother and Daddy said they were impressed with my bargaining skills. Actually, I wasn't very good at it—I gave up too easily and too soon—but my parents didn't have any means for comparison.

We stowed the pineapple I bought in the trunk of the car to eat later and I put the huge bunch of bananas next to me in the front seat so we could eat them along the way. Venezuelan bananas were short plump and very sweet.

It wasn't long before we discovered the ants—hundreds of them, scurrying busily all over the front seat and into the back. The fruit had harbored a whole city of little black creatures. It was not an easy task reclaiming our car from the ants. We got out, shook ourselves vigorously and swatted at our clothes. We repeatedly brushed down the car seats and flipped out the floor mats. Finally we went on our way again. That evening I found more ants—playing inside my purse!

We visited an isolated area in the lower Andes where the calendar seemed to be far behind. The Motolonis who lived there were an indigenous tribe of war-riors that were still extremely primitive. Before the 1950's, we were told, they killed any stranger who appeared in their territory. Now they were taking slow hesitant steps toward the twentieth century.

As we approached the Catholic mission that ministered to the *indios*, we heard the whooping and laughing of children who were playing in and around a small swimming pool. Some of the older kids wore threadbare swimsuits; others, especially the little ones, wore nothing at all. We were impressed by how well behaved they were, the older children looking after the younger.

The mission was small and the accouterment sparse—there were few financial resources. The overworked but dedicated nuns ran a gift shop where they sold baskets and other items woven by the women. Hand-made spears of all sizes were also for sale. Though they were a novelty to visitors, the spears were vital weapons for the Motoloni males who used them for hunting and for protection.

When I recently asked my mother what she remembered about our visit to the mission, she recalled the teenager and her small baby. "The father had abandoned them and the young mother was worried that she might be separated from her child." Many of the men were not yet ready to accept the outside world. "The nuns let the girl and her baby stay at the mission where she worked and helped with the other children."

In the early summer of 1970 we packed up once again and sent our HHE on to Washington, DC. Art would be working at the State Department. We moved to the Hotel del Lago to spend our last weeks in a *casita* surrounded by the palm trees I loved.

I was in the little kitchen on a Saturday morning readying the ingredients for a hearty family breakfast of bacon and eggs. As I struck a match to light the stove—BOOM! An enormous blinding fireball exploded from the range, knocking the oven door from its hinges. The hot red-orange orb rose—then dissolved in the air—leaving smoke and heat. I found myself screaming with my hands over my face.

I hadn't been directly in front of the stove. Luckily I had turned to the side as I lit the match because I was talking to my husband, who was in the other room. That propitious conversation prevented me from being badly injured. I was so terrified during those first moments that I didn't know if I was hurt or not.

Art flew into the kitchen, took a quick look and pulled me into the bathroom. He put the plug in the sink, turned on the cold tap and plunged my hands in. "Keep your hands in the water," he told me. He raced to the kitchen and got a tray of ice cubes and dumped them into the bathroom sink. He sat me down and with my hands still in the basin, he repeatedly swished icy water over my angry red forearms. He wet a wash cloth in the cold water and held it to my chin and cheeks. He brought more ice and did it all again.

After a little while I stood up—and made the mistake of looking in the mirror. My hair! That terrible odor that was stuck in my nostrils was burning hair. I touched some singed curls—they broke and fell into the sink in tiny pieces. I have never thought of myself as a vain woman. But at that moment the pain from my first and second-degree burns was far overshadowed by the pain of losing some of my hair. And we were hosting a party that evening to say good-bye to our friends!

That afternoon the hairdresser cut away burnt hair from around my face and trimmed the rest to even it up. She put in curlers but I couldn't tolerate the heat of the hair dryer and I went home. I had to wear a wig to the party. (Wigs were popular in the 60's and many of us kept one handy to wear after swimming.)

I spent a miserable evening at our party holding an ice-cold glass against my cheek or my chin or my arm. The burns weren't serious—similar to a bad sunburn—but my skin was already blistering.

In regard to the stove, we discovered that the oven knob had been turned, switching on the gas. There was no odor so we didn't know that gas had accumulated, causing it to explode when I lit the match. But I was fortunate. My burns healed quickly and my hair grew back—though not so quickly.

We went back to Washington, bought a home in the Maryland suburbs and settled in to a different lifestyle—again. And we missed our Maracaibo friends.

7

THE PERILS OF PACKING

Government service is truly a moving experience. Pack and move, pack and travel, unpack, pack again, move again. Each time it seems as though we pack away our very lives, at least temporarily, in all those boxes. In the meantime, we exist—in limbo. Real living only reoccurs once we are unpacked and "at home," whether that home be ours (and the mortgage company's) or a loan from the government. Moving is not a simple process. We don't just pack and leave with a good-bye nod of the head—it's far more complicated. Never mind the far-fetched theory that moving becomes easier with practice.

The procedures are different each time we move. We leave familiar communities and travel to countries that are new to us. The packing companies are never the same and the modes of transport differ. The children are at different ages than during the last transfer. The clothing we pack varies according to the climate and also the social customs at our new post. Will we need overcoats and galoshes or lightweight clothes for the tropics? Tux and tails, gowns and gloves? What we pack also depends on what will be provided by the government and on the rank of the officer. Will we take our own china and sterling flatware? Our silver candlesticks? Will we need our lawnmower and pruning shears?

We have more possessions each time we pack up; inevitably, we collect and accumulate "things." We buy artwork in Denmark, woodcarvings and crystal in Germany, olive wood and pottery in Israel. Friends give us farewell remembrances such as pictures, paperweights, jewelry and books. Our children have the usual collections: model airplanes, stuffed animals and dolls, comic books, matchbook cars and scores of books of all kinds.

The first preparation for a move is to *sort*: save and stow? or toss and trash? This entails a great deal of decision-making, but doing it every few years keeps us from becoming pack rats. When our relatives complain about having too much "stuff" in their basements or attics, I have good advice: "You need to move!"

When we leave Washington, important pre-pack preparations include physical exams and dental check-ups for everyone in the family. One of us may also need to see the allergist or the gynecologist, the orthodontist or the optometrist. Depending on our destination, we may need inoculations against such dread diseases as yellow fever, hepatitis, meningitis, or rabies.

Our colleagues Frances and George proceeded through the usual two-day physical examination process in the department's Medical Division. They were preparing to leave for their assignment in Venezuela. The following morning George complained that his left arm was painful.

"It's the cholera shot," he said to his wife.

"Cholera? I didn't get a cholera shot," she replied.

When they returned to MED they reported the discrepancy to the nurse who had inoculated George.

"Caracas?" She checked both of their files and then exclaimed to George, "I thought you said you were going to Karachi!"

Before, between, and after the medical appointments, we shop. We stock up on clothes and shoes for the next year since we don't know specifically what we'll find at the new post. If there won't be a PX, BX, or commissary, we buy a large quantity of toiletries—our preferred brands of shampoo and toothpaste, for instance. If there is no Embassy Health Unit at our destination, we need to take an ample supply of over-the-counter medications and first aid treatments. I am not implying that we can't or don't use toiletries and medications available in foreign countries, but we have learned to be prepared.

Food is always high on our shopping list. (Any list, actually—we're a food-oriented family.) Although we haven't felt deprived at any of our posts, there are always a few family favorites that we miss when they aren't available. Chocolate chips and peanut butter immediately spring to mind, as well as Earl Grey tea. We take a supply with us.

Before we left Washington for Yemen, we ordered "consumables:" cases of fruits, vegetables, pickles, mayonnaise and ketchup, flour, cereals and other commodities, as well as detergents and cleaning products. For some posts, where many basic foodstuffs are not available, or are prohibitively expensive, the government pays the shipping costs for a pre-specified amount of consumables. This was a new challenge: determining what to order, how much to order, and the best source for that order. We shipped 2000 pounds of supplies with our household effects and we made two subsequent orders from post during the next two years.

Not surprisingly, I made mistakes. I ordered too many cans of peaches and pears because a Yemeni in Washington had told me there was not much fresh fruit available. We discovered the situation had changed a great deal since he had last visited his homeland. I included a whole case of Worcestershire sauce in our second order. I had panicked when the cook mistakenly used a whole cup of it instead of one tablespoon to make a salad dressing. I didn't order enough canned juice because we had been informed that orange juice was available locally. It was—but it tasted like dead orange soda. Initially, I didn't send any non-fat powdered milk, but I ordered several cases after we discovered that all the local milk was the reconstituted full-fat variety. On the positive side, I was glad I shipped American laundry detergent because the products available in Sanaa were heavily perfumed.

During the final weeks before our departure, I bought almost anything that was on special at the supermarket—items that we were not ordering by the case. I bought too much shampoo and not enough deodorant and hand cream. I bought corn chips and nuts that turned stale by the time we opened them; marshmallows that hardened into rocks; pretzels that had broken into tiny pieces during shipment. Some things were not so special after all.

We have to prepare our home before we leave Washington on assignment. Large repair work and small fix-up jobs have to be done, walls painted perhaps, and windows washed. We need to decide which curtains and rugs to leave and which to store. Then…we call the realtor and prepare ourselves for the renting process.

Art and I have read and listened to the advice of realtors for years: the do's and don'ts of showing your house; how to achieve the best "curb appeal;" tricks to make the rooms look larger. The experts say the home is most welcoming when an apple pie is baking in the oven, sending out a heart-warming, mouth-watering aroma. When the pie baker has other priorities, however, scented candles make a nice substitute.

One time a prospective renter arrived several hours earlier than his appointment. Contrary to all advice, I was in the kitchen crushing garlic and slicing onions! But those must have been homey familiar aromas for our visitor, a foreign diplomat, because he wanted to rent the house immediately with all the furniture.

As the departure date looms into sharper focus, we send out change of address notices to our credit card companies, magazines, bank, insurance providers, family and friends. We order plenty of checkbooks and deposit slips. And sometimes at this point in our preparations, we have to get a bank loan to pay for the preparations! Keep in mind that we may be in language training (or area studies, or spouses' orientation, or the ambassadorial seminar) while we are simultaneously making the above arrangements—in addition to trying to sell our car.

Finally, whether we are in Washington or abroad, we face the pack-out deadline. I get the vapors when I think about the verb *separate*. We have to separate our belongings into several categories: household effects, often called sea freight because that's how they usually travel; airfreight (extra clothing and odds and ends to tide us over until the HHE arrive); and suitcases, which will accompany us. When we're at home we separate furniture and other items for storage. When we're leaving a post we isolate our possessions from those that belong to the government and will remain in the house. And if we have a student going off to college, we have to arrange for an additional shipment. Some people break out in hives at this point.

Foreign Service Requisite: stamina.

Airfreight, it should be noted, seldom arrives in a timely fashion. One wonders if "air" means that our things travel by carrier pigeon. And no matter how we "separate," something always gets mixed up. In spite of the sticky tags and signs we attach to things, mistakes happen. Alex and Kathy's books and most of my cookbooks went into storage instead of reaching Copenhagen with the HHE. We didn't see them again for nine years.

People who are relatively stationary in their living arrangements often ask me, "How do you like moving so often?" Well...that depends on when I am asked. My answer tends to reflect my present circumstances: I have just moved; I am preparing to move; or I am settled in. I'll leave the various answers to your imagination.

The first time we packed out I was a novice and I assumed that all moving company employees were experts. I didn't pay an iota of attention to the nice young man who packed the portable typewriter on top of the stemmed Pilsner glasses. I also didn't notice the box of talcum powder he put unwrapped on top of the typewriter. During the trip across the Atlantic powder sifted around and through and inside the typewriter—in spite of its zippered case.

When we were leaving Fulda, I couldn't find the butter after the packers left. I thought I had left it on top of the refrigerator—out of reach. A few months later we opened our boxes in Lincoln and we found the butter. In a box, still in its covered dish and only slightly misshapen.

I began to suspect that I ought to take a more active role where packers were concerned. I tried. But preparing to leave Lincoln the second time, I overlooked an open can of olive oil on the top kitchen shelf. Unfortunately one of the packers retrieved it. By the time our shipment reached us, oil had leaked slowly throughout the carton and had combined disgustingly with the strawberry jam that had oozed from its broken jar. The canned goods that were in the same box were not only slippery but most of the labels had slipped off!

As we accumulate more possessions over the years, the moving companies send more people to pack us up. No matter how observant we try to be, the strangest things can happen. Packers have put our wastebaskets full of trash into boxes. Friends told us their ashtrays were neatly wrapped up—with cigarette butts in them.

Sometimes it is impossible to keep watch. Barbara, a realtor we met, had a baby to take care of while the movers were swarming through her home and it was impossible to put off bottle time. After the little one devoured half of the milk, Barbara got up and walked into another room patting the baby's back. When the expected burp was accomplished, Barbara returned to her chair to finish feeding the baby. Alas, the baby bottle had disappeared! Several minutes passed while a packer searched the filled boxes for the milk—to the accompaniment of a wailing baby.

One of the packers must have tired of his work in Bonn—or else he had a dumb-out. Instead of wrapping and boxing the various small items in our daughter's nightstand, he simply removed the entire drawer and put it in the bottom of a carton. Unfortunately, the furniture belonged to the owners of the rented house, not to us. When we discovered the drawer later in Washington, we had to mail it back.

No matter how the *experts* pack our clothes—folded or laid straight in long boxes or hung in special wardrobes—they always arrive in a crumpled mass and each piece has to be pressed before it is wearable. My shoes were frequently squashed and misshapen from heavy items that were piled on top of them in the cartons. Leather handbags were thrown in, unwrapped, among the shoes and boots. One summer the bags stuck together because of the heat and pieces of black patent melded onto beige and gray. But I have learned a few things. Now I keep my shoes protected in their original boxes and I wrap my purses inside pillowcases.

By pointing out fragile and delicate items to the packers, we try to encourage better wrapping and handling. Items that need an extra measure of protection, not from theft but from abuse, can be well padded inside handbags. I also put small picture frames, fragile crystal, and especially my delicate Danish paper mobiles, inside my purses. Inevitably there are occasions when I don't have enough time to do all that hiding, tucking, and protecting. The only alternative then, is to follow a well-known procedure: I cross my fingers!

In the midst of a pack-out one Foreign Service woman put a large ham in a borrowed roasting pan with the intention of baking it for supper. But the ham disappeared from the stovetop! By the time she discovered the missing meat, the lift vans were loaded and locked and the truck was moving off down the street. When they met up with their HHE some months later, they found the ham still in the pan waiting to be roasted. It was no surprise that everything in the crate had a rancid smell.

A Foreign Service couple with an antique table told a sad tale that unfortunately is not unique. They notified the moving company in advance that they required a separate crate for their table and special handling to avoid nicks and scrapes. On the day of the pack-out, the movers brought the wood and other supplies and made a crate on the premises. A good beginning, it seemed. But the end was disastrous. The movers enclosed the valuable piece of furniture in the crate—and nailed the lid into the tabletop!

Only once did we have the pleasure of driving to our new post. No plane tickets, no airports, no taxis, no agonizing over what to tote. With our car loaded—over-loaded perhaps—we drove from Copenhagen to The Hague. For the first time I didn't have to part with my houseplants—no traumatic farewells to the greenery. We put the begonias, the philodendron, the hibiscus, and twenty-some African violets in layers in the back seat. (We left the large ferns for Toini.)

"Coals to Newcastle!" my friends scoffed. Some of these same friends transported their pets from country to country incurring great expense and frequent trauma to children and pets alike. Plants were *my* pets. I had grown and nurtured the violets from baby leaves and I loved taking them with me.

When the King family was leaving Maracaibo, their departure was considerably delayed because of Barney, a big bouncy hairy dog that was one of the family. At the airport Barney was not at all happy about being locked up in his made-to-order cage. And although the dog fit into the cage, the cage didn't fit into the opening of the baggage compartment. After being pushed, shoved and jostled with no success, the cage broke open and Barney was out of there! There was pure chaos on the tarmac as the huge dog ran, loped and leaped trying to evade several wary pursuers.

The Kings with their five children traditionally separated when they traveled. John and the boys were to leave Maracaibo first with the dog. But by the time someone caught up with the excited animal, their plane was ready for takeoff. Barney and the damaged cage were not. John and the boys departed, leaving Laura and my husband in charge of the pet.

Art arranged for the repair of the cage and after a good bit of coaxing and soothing, Laura reinstalled the dog. One problem solved. We then found out that the plane booked for Laura and the girls had no space in the pressurized compartments for Barney. But if they didn't take that plane, they might miss their ship to the States. After weighing the options Art recommended to Laura that they take off as planned. The airline people felt "reasonably" sure that Barney would be all right on the one-hour flight—in spite of the diminished oxygen supply.

The departure was traumatic but off they went. Art worried the rest of the day about the dog. Thankfully, word came the next morning that all the Kings, Barney included, arrived safely in Caracas, made their ship connections and were on their way home.

Heike and Helmut, friends from the German Embassy, took two dogs with them to Yemen. During a stopover, one of the cages was crushed and their South African ridgeback was loose among the luggage when the plane landed in Sanaa. The baggage handlers refused to unload—they were terrified of the "ferocious" animal. Helmut had to climb up the conveyor belt and carry the huge dog down backwards. The animal was more frightened than the employees.

As our friends were leaving the airport with their dogs and several pieces of luggage, a uniformed Yemeni approached them. He gave them an overly complicated story about their dog arriving without a cage and, therefore, they would need to have some additional papers signed and stamped. But, unfortunately, the department that dealt with those particular documents had just closed—alas! Now there would be "big trouble," the official complained. Heike was certain that the man had *baksheesh* (a bribe) on his mind.

Helmut had had enough. Instead of offering the expected bribe, he put the dog's lead firmly in the Yemeni's hand and said, "Fine. We'll pick her up tomorrow." The Yemeni suddenly had enough also. He nervously pushed the dog chain back at Helmut and scurried away. (Did I mention that the ridgeback weighed over one hundred pounds?)

Whenever we unpack, I immediately open the boxes marked "kitchen" since those items are the first we need. Second, I unpack the linens and search for the crocheted doilies and dresser scarves. Somewhere along the way I discovered that placing those bits of needlework and fabric on the dressers, chests of drawers, and end tables means we have arrived—we are home. No matter where that may be. Those simple linen items may look bereft for a short while, but as we unpack more boxes, the doilies are soon resting places for family photos, knickknacks, lamps, and eventually potted plants.

Waiting for our possessions to arrive is one of the "givens" of Foreign Service life—we spend a lot of time waiting. We can never be sure how long it will take, weeks at least, maybe months. While we wait, we wonder if our things will arrive safely? And will *everything* arrive?

When we were notified in Maracaibo that our HHE had arrived, we set a delivery date and moved out of the hotel. We were waiting enthusiastically on the doorstep of our new home when the truck arrived with our lift-vans—some of them! Yes, our ship came in, but it sailed away again with half of our possessions. Whoever was in charge of unloading had the brain capacity of a coconut. Unfortunately the crates that were again at sea contained the items we needed the most: stove and refrigerator and air conditioners. We considered moving back to the hotel, but decided to stick it out. We had been assured that the rest of our things would arrive when the ship docked again in Maracaibo—which turned out to be several weeks.

We borrowed two ice chests and two hot plates and we located our electric skillet. We had to shop for food and ice every day, but we managed to cook. We could also boil water, which was essential since the local water was not potable. With at least one of the hot plates in use most of the day, the kitchen felt like a sauna. It was January but we had left winter in the States. Several weeks later our ship came in—again—and this time with the remainder of our possessions.

In Bonn we waited anxiously for our shipment, which seemed to be lost. We endured several miserable weeks before the good news came that the lost was found. But relief turned to disappointment and disgust when we saw the condition of our furniture. The moving company had unloaded our lift vans and moved the contents onto a regular truck. They told us that the huge vehicle that had carried the crates from the ship was too large to manipulate the narrow streets of our suburb.

For some reason—although I doubt that *reason* played any major role—no one saw fit to wrap or pad the furniture. The pieces knocked about and rubbed and pushed against each other for several kilometers. By the time the truck came up the hill, most of our furniture was bashed, battered and bruised. The repair work and refinishing took many months.

Three years later, when we packed up to leave Bonn, a large van managed to get to our home. Our containers were loaded and locked on the spot and the van headed immediately to the port. The company told us, "Your effects will be in Washington before you get there." And the shipment did arrive at the port in Baltimore in only two weeks but it took more than three weeks to get it from Baltimore to our home—an hour's drive away!

We heard about a Foreign Service secretary who arrived at her new post and waited and waited for her shipment of HHE. It didn't arrive. Continuing to hope, she bought only the bare minimum of linens and kitchen items to tide her over. Her apartment was furnished and besides, there was not much available in the host country. Word came that her shipment was lost, but still she hoped.

Toward the end of her two-year assignment Washington notified her that they had, amazingly, located her effects in a warehouse. She eagerly anticipated seeing her own possessions when she arrived at her next post. But before her things could be shipped to her, the warehouse burned down—along with everything in it.

Theft occurs, worldwide, but fortunately our losses have been relatively few during all the traveling years. There were the two rugs that weren't put in the crates for storage in Washington. They were tagged and thrown on the back of the truck at the last minute. We should have known better—we never saw the rugs again.

In Bonn someone on the packing crew stole our three Hummel figurines along with several other items small enough to hide in a uniform pocket. One Hummel was a chimney sweep that I had bought in Frankfurt for two dollars. It always reminded me of Fulda. Twenty years later I had to pay thirty dollars to replace it. The second chimney sweep wasn't the same, however; it was just a figurine. The original had been a memory.

The majority of thefts take place not in a home but somewhere along the way. Many of our friends have lost invaluable possessions. We can always buy another rug or toaster and the insurance money will cover the missing TV and the Hummels. But a box of mementos and family photos or Grandma's china can never be replaced.

My Uncle Bud was an Air Force officer. He and Aunt Elva plus three children moved even more often than we did, and we frequently swapped stories about packing and moving frustrations. "Has a moving company ever sealed and locked your lift vans right in front of you?" When I answered in the affirmative, Elva continued: "You know, they only stay locked and closed until the truck gets around the next corner!"

My aunt has an infectious sense of humor that keeps a smile on her face most of the time. This tale, however, was not funny. When they came back from Bangkok, they discovered that one of their "locked" lift vans had been ransacked. Several things were stolen, including Elva's sewing machine. A footlocker was missing—one that contained papers, some old coins, but nothing of value. Monetary value, that is. Among the papers was a half-finished account of her experiences and life with Bud in the military. Another missing piece of paper was a letter to my aunt from Bess Streeter Aldrich, the author who wrote many wonderful poignant books about pioneer life in the Midwest. I read her stories over and over when I was growing up.

So we learn to be trusting and prudent at the same time. We have no choice but to put our possessions in the care of a moving company. We have no control over the truck, the ship or the airplane that carries our things. But we can exercise caution during the packing process. Keeping a keen eye—several eyes, if possible—on the packers helps to discourage petty pilfering. But the only way to avoid theft of your valuables is to hand-carry them. We divide between my handbag and Art's briefcase my few pieces of jewelry that have monetary or sentimental value. The rest, well...we can't carry everything.

Before the movers arrive, I frequently hide things that are not valuable per se, but which I could never replace. (Unfortunately, I often forget where I have hidden something and it is lost for months.) I tuck ring boxes and costume jewelry into the toes of our boots and in tea cans. I wrap small pieces of silver and crystal and put them in jacket pockets or handbags. I am sure the packers are aware of these hiding places but the hiding makes me feel better.

Pam and Joe, career Foreign Service people, watched carefully as the packers wrapped their sterling silver flatware and put it in the bottom of a china barrel and Pam diligently noted down the number of the barrel. Weeks later, when their lift vans arrived in Bonn, disorder and upheaval caused the usual distractions and neither of them remembered to look for the silver. At the end of the day, the movers gathered up all the packing paper and empty cartons and began loading the trash onto their truck.

Noticing that the china barrels were still in the yard, Joe said, "Let's check to make sure they're empty." The barrels were empty—except the last one. And in the bottom, they discovered their silver. Pam and Joe never knew whether the sterling had been accidentally "missed" by one of the movers or left intentionally to be stolen later.

When we arrived in Yemen, several colleagues complained of theft from their food shipments, which had been "inspected" by local customs officials. During the next year we frequently saw canned goods in the stores that had labels from Washington, DC super-market chains. I heard friends say, "I saw some of Norma's applesauce at the Hadda store." Or, "We just bought a box of John's taco shells."

I was surprised one day to see boxes of Girl Scout cookies—with a very high price tag—on the shelf in a Sanaa store. I found out that a shipment of cookies had gone missing through the mail a few months earlier. After that, the Girl Scouts no longer ordered cookies to sell—it was too risky.

We pack our own suitcases but once they are plopped on the conveyor belt at the airport we relinquish control of them. I've lost count of how many of our bags have been damaged: punctured, cracked, stained with grease or tar, squashed, bent—and a few totally destroyed.

Our children have had their own bag mishaps and traveling traumas. Alex's first trip home from college, for example. We were living in Denmark and we drove to Prague to spend Christmas with Nancy and Dan. Alex flew directly to Prague after he finished his semester exams. He had packed two suitcases; one arrived in Prague, one didn't. The missing bag was crammed full of clothing—underwear, in particular—and also Christmas presents from the family in Nebraska. The suitcase didn't show up until two weeks later, after we had returned to Copenhagen.

There had been no pilfering. All the gifts were accounted for—including a five-pound chub of summer sausage from Brother Dave. It wasn't spoiled; the smokehouse and the preservatives prevented that. But we threw it away after discovering several small cracks in the casing. Of course, the suitcase and its other contents smelled like salami for quite a long time.

Kathy's luggage didn't arrive when she landed in Copenhagen one May. The next day we bought underwear and socks to tide her over until her two bags showed up. She had just finished her junior year at boarding school and had packed all her personal belongings to take home for the summer. Luckily, she had mailed a box of casual clothes so she had a few things to wear. At the end of two weeks the airline still had not located the suitcases and they gave us fifty dollars to cover "necessities."

The luggage did not arrive—ever. The airline finally admitted defeat and asked for an inventory of the contents of the bags. They sent us a check and we attempted to replace Kathy's "things." Clothing was easy—she enjoyed shopping. But what about the mementos that she was bringing from school? The yearbook signed by her friends (some had graduated and scattered all over the globe) and the many photographs. There would be no substitute for the cassette tape of her musical performances at "Rock and Folk Night" when she was a freshman in Bethesda. We couldn't recover the diamond earrings that her first boyfriend gave her—they had belonged to his grandmother. We had neglected to remind her not to put valuables and irreplaceables in her luggage. We all learned from that misfortune.

Another bag story comes from Copenhagen. An FSO arrived at the embassy on TDY (temporary duty) but his luggage didn't. The airline felt certain his bags would turn up but they didn't. In less than a week his assignment was finished and he was on his way back home.

When he arrived at the airport in Washington the officer stopped to discuss his missing luggage with an airline agent. There behind the counter he spotted two familiar-looking suitcases—they were his! The luggage had waited for him while he went to Denmark and back.

During the years that our children traveled with us, keeping track of all our bags was a challenge. A home-leave trip required at least six suitcases and, early on, a diaper bag. Depending on the season, we also lugged coats, hats, scarves, mittens and maybe umbrellas. When we were on transfer, we needed seven or eight bags. I looked forward to when our children would be old enough and strong enough to take charge of their own bags and jackets. But by then, more "things" were required for each person and my load didn't get any lighter. Add four carry-on bags, a briefcase, and a large purse and it's enough to discombobulate a mathematician! And we were a family of four.

Francesca said she left Moscow with sixteen pieces of luggage. She and her USIS husband had four children, including a set of twins. My brain has difficulty processing the quantity of luggage Marilyn and her husband, Alex, had to pack and look after. Alex worked for USAID for many years and they traveled with at least five of their seven children from post to post.

Marilyn had a special bag that she always filled and carried along with her, a vertical-shaped bag that the airlines used to give away to passengers. She looked like she was toting a bowling ball but it was the family survival kit. Inside was the all-important peanut butter, plus crackers, squirt cheese, a jar or two of Old English cheese, a can of deviled ham with a pop-top lid, stuffed green olives, a jar of Tang and of course, chocolate chip cookies or maybe Oreos. The bag also contained napkins, paper cups, and at least one knife, fork and spoon. And right on top Marilyn put a wet washcloth sealed in a small plastic bag.

Marilyn, Alex and their five youngest children were on their way to Kenya in 1971 when they were stranded in an airport. The airline informed them that their departure would be delayed by several hours and an agent handed around chits for hot dogs and Cokes. Hot dogs? In the airport cafeteria? Not an appealing thought for this family. Within minutes the kids were sitting on the floor cross-legged, surrounding their mother who was cheerfully doling out supper from her bag. So much better than hot dogs!

I promised myself that when our children left us to seek their own fortunes, I would never again carry anything on a trip except a small handbag. Promises, promises. There is still the jewelry, a last-minute gift or two, my toothbrush, hairbrush and cosmetics, and a snack (in case the airplane is stuck on the runway for a couple of hours.) And now I carry "spare pairs," underwear and pantyhose, in the event that our luggage is lost or delayed. All this requires another bag—and somebody has to carry it.

To tell the truth, I have become so used to being encumbered that even when we travel by car, I sit with "things" on my lap: my handbag, sunglasses, snack, a notebook. I'm afraid they'll get lost.

Of all our packing and moving frustrations—loss and breakage and theft—the worst damage to our possessions happened in the Washington area in storage facilities.

When we went to Maracaibo in 1968, we left many of our things behind. Due to the tropical climate, we didn't need overcoats, boots, winter clothes, or blankets. And because few homes there had basements or adequate storage space, we decided to store many of our books, along with albums, scrapbooks and mementos.

Nearly three years later, after buying our first home and settling in, we took delivery of our storage. It reeked! We could smell the mildew as the first damp box entered the house. Photographs stuck together, covers fell off albums, and many books had to be thrown away. The leather buttons on Art's elegant Harris Tweed sport coat were slippery with mold. Our leather boots were no longer wearable.

"At least," Art and I told each other, "We can be grateful that our new furniture was with us in Maracaibo and not in storage." I still remember those words. Our furniture subsequently went into storage many times as future posts provided furnished housing.

Washington was wet with rain in November 1994, when our storage was delivered. As the movers were carrying in the dining room furniture, I spotted something dark on the buffet. I fetched some old towels and quickly began to dry off the rain—and the towel turned black! Immediately, I knew.

"Art," I groaned, "We have mildew—again."

Dampness caused by a leaky pipe in the warehouse had permeated our dining room and bedroom furniture and our lovely cherry wood desk. Some of the drawers wouldn't open, others wouldn't close. Our mattresses and box springs were still damp and green with mildew. Cartons of blankets and wool sweaters smelled like wet dogs; small leather pieces and wood items like cutting boards and spice racks were sprouting fuzz.

We had plane reservations for the next day; we were going to Wisconsin to spend Thanksgiving with Alex, Mary, and our grandsons. We set the thermostat on low heat hoping to dry out the dampness while we were away. Off we went, leaving mold and mildew behind, for a short home-leave. We returned to discover that our furnace wasn't working. The weather was cold and rainy and it was equally cold and wet inside the house.

We waited two days for the furnace repairman. I shivered and shook as I spent hours on the telephone talking to the storage company, the State Department and the people who agreed to come and get rid of our mildew. Meanwhile, the washer and dryer were running twelve hours a day as I bleached and soaked and attempted to remove the nasty odor from our bed linens and tablecloths and the baby blankets I was saving for posterity.

We purchased new mattresses and worked at salvaging what we could. We made numerous trips to the dry cleaners. We sprinkled baking soda between the cushions of the overstuffed chairs and sofas. We repeatedly sprayed the air with Lysol.

But mold spores are like roaches. They multiply rapidly and have to be dealt with immediately and mercilessly. A commercial company that specializes in water damage arrived—not immediately, but eventually—and went to work. They treated the furniture with chemicals and ran an ozone machine to clean the air in the house.

Art and I scrubbed numerous items with a Clorox and detergent solution. Nevertheless, we had to throw away many of our wood and leather things, as well as plastics that had stuck together as if they were glued. And again many of our books were ruined. It was a sad sight.

My sinuses hurt, my nose ran and my head pounded for weeks. Art's health was affected also, but he could escape to the office.

At last, the nasty smell faded and I began to feel better. It was early spring by the time everything was clean and put away. I welcomed spring like never before—glorious sunshine, open windows, and the sweet fresh fragrance of hyacinths.

In case my pages of peril are misleading, I should reaffirm that the positive aspects of our traveling life have far outweighed the negative. While moving has seemed like mayhem at times, I have always been eager to pack up again when a tempting opportunity arose.

8

THE RHINE AND THE ROCK

"Everything is relative," my husband frequently reminds me. Our feelings, opinions and reactions are relative as we compare the job, the foreign country and each new home to those of previous posts. We are impressed differently—relative to our earlier experiences.

From the Caribbean to the Mid-Atlantic and then to the Rhine River we changed climates, clothing, and customs. Daily Maracaibo sunshine became a faded memory as we adjusted to overcast muggy summers, foggy fall mornings and cold wet winters in Bonn. But in Europe again in 1973, our weekends in Bavaria, ski trips to Austria, and sightseeing in Paris, Copenhagen and Amsterdam were more than adequate tradeoffs for what we had left behind. Relative, indeed.

But between Venezuela and Germany, we spent three years in Washington, DC as first-time homeowners, gardeners, suburbanites and busy parents. Art worked shifts for almost a year, first at the State Department Operations Center and then at the National Military Command Center in the Pentagon. He enjoyed the job but I found the hours difficult when it came to family scheduling.

I met a Foreign Service wife who also worked shifts—at home. She slept when her husband slept and when he went off to work at the Ops Center she did her housework—no matter whether it was daytime or the middle of the night. Since they didn't have children, she was able to match her own schedule to his. I thought it sounded uniquely romantic. My balloon burst a few years later, however, when I learned that they divorced.

The second year Art was a staff aide to William B. Macomber, the fifth-ranking man at the State Department in his capacity as Under Secretary for Management. Art found the work challenging and the boss demanding. Ambassador Macomber didn't have children waiting for him at home. At the end of the workday, which seldom came before seven o'clock, he often put his feet up on his desk and called his staff in to discuss serious matters—as well as the not so serious. After an hour or so of nattering plus the average half-hour commute Art usually arrived home for dinner around nine or so.

My husband was involved in drafting the Policy on Wives or the "1972 directive" as it is commonly called—the policy that was intended to "liberate" the wives. The Department of State recognized, finally, that Foreign Service spouses were private individuals, not government employees, and the service—including ambassadors at post—had no right to levy any duties upon them. No more "report cards" for wives!

I thought the directive was a good start in recognizing the dilemma of spouses, especially those overseas. Some women, however, were displeased and others downright angry about the new policy because of what it *didn't* do. You see, the traditional duties of diplomacy didn't change. The uncompensated and, now, unrecognized wives would continue to perform those necessary duties—at least some of them would. The disenchanted still maintain that when the directive was issued in January 1972, that was "the day they fired the wives."

Suddenly—it *seemed* sudden—we were packing up again. Before leaving for our assignment in Bonn, Germany, we turned our lovingly decorated Hughes-customized home over to renters—a new and unappealing experience for us. At our new post we wouldn't have color choices or decorating options, we would again live in government-provided housing. But we had one choice: to live in an apartment in the suburb of Bad Godesberg or in a house further out. We chose the house because we wanted to be in a German neighborhood rather than in the Project. It remained to be seen whether or not we had made the right decision.

The Project in Plittersdorf (a suburb of Bonn-Bad Godesberg) was similar to HiCog in Frankfurt—but here it was a "little America." The apartments were roomy and pleasant and the grounds were nicely landscaped; it was more spread out and certainly more attractive than HiCog. And all of the American community activities were held there. A theater, church, commissary and PX were centrally located along with a swimming pool, bowling alley and a club with a large restaurant and family snack bar. What more could military and other government personnel want?

This Foreign Service couple wanted to experience living in Germany, not the States. We wanted our children to play with German children and to learn the language. We wanted to have German neighbors—and we wanted to live in a house.

And so we did—a cozy three bedroom split-level house with an exquisite view of the mountains. The lower level opened on to a terrace with a little bubbling fountain. Spread out below was a large expanse of green grass—and an orchard! Well, almost. There were six apple trees and two cherry trees. When I first discovered the fruit trees, I thought of the movie *Sound of Music* with the song: "I must have done something good…" I could almost smell the apple pies and cherry tarts baking in my oven. By the third harvest, however, I began to wonder if I was being punished for some earlier sins. A lot of work comes with an orchard.

Choosing the house instead of an apartment in the Project was doubtless the right decision; the location of the house, perhaps, was not. Alex, at eleven, and seven-year-old Kathy met few German children and they seldom played with those few. The local school schedules were different from those at the American (Department of Defense) School that our kids attended. And they were soon involved in extracurricular activities—Scouts, sports, music and ballet lessons—that kept them in the Project after school. When they went out to play on Saturday mornings, the German children were in classes.

Our neighborhood was international, however. Brazilians lived next door to us, several American families were nearby and we became close friends with the Canadian family down the street. Their son was the same age as Alex and the boys spent a lot of time together bicycling and playing street hockey. Rob had four older siblings and for Alex he exemplified a new sense of freedom. As our son said years later, "I would have followed Rob anywhere."

But we didn't meet any German neighbors for a long time and I was disappointed. Much later I found out that it was customary for the *newcomers* to pay a call to introduce themselves. We were to learn many new things about German culture.

We abruptly realized that we needed two cars, since I was to spend a great deal of time as live-in chauffeur. The Project was a twenty-minute drive from our village of Mehlem if the traffic was light. For the morning car-pool run, however, we had to allow forty-five minutes. This was a major life-style change—in the States the children had taken the school bus. And when they were in school, I was driving myself to the homes of my English students and to my own German classes. I also joined a bowling league, took a few piano lessons and volunteered at the school.

I remember our three years in Bonn primarily as family time. Our children were old enough to learn about history, to absorb a new culture and to appreciate their surroundings. We traveled, toured and went sightseeing together; we also talked, played games and established new family traditions.

Surrounded as we were by the sights and smells of German food, Art and I couldn't help but pass along our love of the cuisine to our children. Though they were already familiar with sausages and schnitzel, there were more taste-treats to come. While most American kids were begging for lunch at McDonald's or Pizza Hut, Alex and Kathy wanted to eat *Bratwurst* and *Brötchen* at a sidewalk stand.

Perhaps Bonn was the harbinger for the oft repeated "So much food; so little time," a lament that has been our family motto since long before it was used on a TV commercial. When we plan a family gathering, we talk on the telephone about what we will be eating. When we're together, we talk at the breakfast table about what we're having for lunch; at lunch we discuss the dinner menu.

Early on we located the neighborhood butcher who also sold cheese, and the baker who was almost next door to the butcher. Both were within walking distance and walk and shop we did almost every Saturday morning. We carried home the ingredients for our hearty and habitual weekend lunch of *Aufschnitt*: cold cuts, cheeses, and three kinds of bread. We bought extra; the leftovers went into bag lunches during the week. Be assured—those were authentic cold cuts—an endless variety of fresh sandwich meats made from ham and other cuts of pork, veal and beef. Not a bit of turkey—and definitely not low fat. We hadn't been threatened yet with bad cholesterol.

All of us, except Kathy, liked *Fleishsalat*, meat salad. Small pieces of cold meat vaguely resembling bologna were combined with celery root, onions, herbs and other ingredients in a light creamy mayonnaise sauce. Occasionally, Art would splurge and bring home *Krabbensalat* with tiny shrimps, another specialty.

We also liked soft cold meats, the spreadable varieties of liverwurst, *Teewurst* and *Mettwurst*. We tried them all in one shop and another where the butchers were always eager to hand over small samples. Alex's favorite was *Leberkäse* or *Fleischkäse*, a loaf made of finely ground meat, baked, then chilled, and thickly sliced for a sandwich. (It was also good fried.) Kathy developed a passion for cheese, all varieties except those that smelled "bad." All of us, except Alex, liked *Butterkäse*—a mild, thinly sliced German cheese. At least once a week we ate sausages, fried or cooked on the grill. *Bratwurst, Knockwurst, Bockwurst* or *Weisswurst*—we liked them all.

Art became an ardent fan of herring, creamed or marinated in Germany, swimming in sherry and dill in Denmark, and later in The Hague, he ate a number of whole new herring. Kathy confessed some years later that she thought herring was a bird and she wouldn't touch it. She was even less inclined to eat it after she found out it was fish!

As our first Christmas approached we asked our children what they would like for dinner on Christmas Eve. I had planned turkey and all that goes with it for the 25th, so perhaps we could have a lighter meal on the 24th before we opened our gifts. After a short discussion, Alex and Kathy agreed on a German meal—cold cuts.

"That way we won't have any pans or skillets to wash and we can get right to the presents!" That was how Alex explained his choice and his sister was in full agreement. So was I—no cooking for mama on Christmas Eve.

By the next year, however, we had discovered Nuremberger *Röstbratwurstel,* a little-finger-sized sausage that is a specialty from southern Germany. We had one small frying pan to wash that Christmas Eve. In succeeding years our traditional holiday supper gradually expanded and we added a "few" items. Still today when the ingredients are available—and depending on where we are and how many of us are gathered together—we have many more dishes and pans to wash. We start with smoked salmon, peppered mackerel and herring. We have several cooked sausages and more varieties of cold meats and cheeses, at least four kinds of bread and we've added relishes. (We finish with Danish rice pudding and cherry sauce—the only dish we have added that is not German.)

Bonn was our first embassy experience; Art had worked in consulates at our two previous posts. The embassy was large with offices representing not only the Departments of State and Defense, but also other agencies such as USIS, FCS, FAS, Customs, CIA, IRS and FBI. Art was one of thirteen officers in the Political Section and his job was unique to the Bonn embassy. He and his immediate superior represented the United States in the Bonn Group. The subject of their work was Berlin, however, not Bonn.

After the Cold War began, three of the victorious allies of World War Two (the US, Britain and France) established the Bonn Group to coordinate the governing and administration of their sections of occupied Berlin and to deal with Russia, the other occupying power. In some instances, when appropriate, the West Germans participated in meetings involving policies and plans for the future of all Berlin.

Berlin issues were fascinating and frustrating. When the Russian bear roared, there were urgent meetings in Bonn. When they stomped over the line, we stomped back in their direction.

Bonn is old. It grew from a Roman military camp to a city of several hundred thousand people. Even though it was the German capital for over half a century it was still "a little town in Germany"—a sobriquet popularized by the novelist John LeCarré. The fine old university is highly respected in academia. The Redoubt houses a wonderful concert stage called the Beethoven Halle. Beethoven himself was born in Bonn and his birthplace became a proud museum. The Godesburg, remains of the town fortress, dates from 1210 and the beautiful stately Minster is more than 750 years old.

The department stores rivaled those of any large city and the restaurants offered culinary creations that represented all of Europe. The old and the new could be seen along the many pedestrian walkways and the sidewalk cafes invited you to while away the day merely "people-watching." Bonn was as quiet and mellow as a small town.

A Christmas market, *Christkindl Markt,* celebrated the holiday season in most German towns and cities. In Bonn the market was magical: beautifully decorated stands and tents offered all manner of Christmas wares from trees and greens to carved nutcrackers and foodstuffs. There were a few indoor shops along the aisles where you could stop and warm up, but most of it was outside. The popular way to keep warm was to sip some hot spiced red wine while you shopped. The fragrance of the wine combined with that of warm burnt-sugar-coated almonds reminded you: "It's Christmas!"

Our favorite tree ornaments are German—tiny carved figures of nutcrackers, angels and musicians, brightly painted and delicate. Although many countries mass-produce them today, the loveliest are still found in Germany at the *Christkindl* markets.

Surrounding Bonn were extensive suburbs, small towns and villages that grew together and became Greater Bonn in the late 1960's. Bad Godesberg abutted Bonn on the south, along the Rhine, and next door was Mehlem, where we lived. Once a separate village, Mehlem still maintained much of its "out in the country" charm: friendliness and freshness, small shops, outdoor markets, tiny narrow streets, family vegetable gardens, cows and chickens.

From the moment of our arrival I looked forward to having our own vegetable garden. The following spring we dug in, literally; we spaded and weeded and we planted. While we weren't totally successful, we were pleased with our first efforts. Our onions died but we had fresh carrots, kohlrabi, beets and plenty of string beans.

Several rose bushes were already established and Art worked hard at making them prosper. It was exasperating at first, finding out which German products we needed for fertilizer, plant food and bug spray. And new German words to learn.

Art complained one weekend, "There are so many aphids on the roses they have to stand in line waiting for a place to feed!"

"Would you like to grow some strawberries?" our British friend, Val, wanted to know. She needed to thin out her plants in the fall and she brought me a box full. I spent an entire morning merrily transplanting the fifty-some small plants into our garden, which Art had reshaped and expanded in anticipation of our new fruit crop.

When the landlord informed us early the following spring that he was sending over some gardeners to do a yard cleanup, we were grateful and more than a little relieved. The property was large and required a great deal of work mowing, cleaning, weeding, and spraying—not to mention harvesting. We were finding it difficult to keep up.

I returned one day from running errands. My parents were visiting and I heard my mother calling me. She didn't say "Come quickly," but her tone implied speed. I found her on the upper balcony, pointing down to the yard. There were two men below, partially obscured by the trees and I couldn't see what they were doing.

"Isn't that your strawberry bed?" my mother asked with incredulity spreading over her face.

I sprinted for the stairs, ran through the lower level and out the back door. I didn't slow up until I came to the mid-section of the yard where I found the gardeners wielding their spades.

Yes, it was my strawberry bed—but there were no strawberry plants to be seen. The whole plot had been spaded and turned under! To say I was upset would be making a molehill out of a mountain. I was disappointed, frustrated, perplexed, and extremely angry! I started to shout but couldn't dredge up the German words I needed for the situation. The gardeners remained calm, not understanding my agitation but suspecting that I wanted information. Strawberries? They only saw weeds. What were they doing? Preparing the ground for spring. Evidently our landlord had used the term "gardeners" rather loosely.

Later that day I gently tiptoed through the garden with a small hand rake, attempting to salvage any bit of a strawberry plant that had a root attached. I rescued four or five and I gently replanted, watered and nursed them along all spring. But they never did produce any fruit.

Few embassy people in Bonn had full-time domestic servants because it was too expensive, but weekly help was affordable. After I began teaching English lessons four mornings a week, I hired a *Putzfrau*, a cleaning lady, for two half days a month.

Irene, pronounced "ir-ray-nah," was a young German woman with a soft voice and shy pretty smile. She always had shiny pink cheeks, a bright healthy look that was typical of Germans. (Probably because they spent more time outdoors than the average American did.) In a few hours she accomplished more than I could all day—if I were ever at home all day. She whisked quickly but thoroughly through the basic cleaning, then spent the remainder of the time doing what she liked best—ironing. Because she was so pleasant and likable, I found it difficult to correct her or suggest she do something "my way." She had full rein at our house.

Nevertheless, I finally bucked up my courage one day and told her: "Irene, please don't iron the underwear—it really isn't necessary."

Social evenings in Bonn tended to be small sit-down dinners rather than large buffets as in Maracaibo. The atmosphere was more formal because most Germans were inclined to be formal and reserved, at least until a friendship was well established.

We were enormously impressed by our British colleagues' style of entertaining. The first evening we went to a British home was not only a cultural experience, but also a learning one for Art and me. After the coffee and dessert our hostess, Val, stood up and said, "Ladies, shall we leave the gentlemen to their port and cigars?"

Art, eager to be courteous, reacted too quickly and started to leave the table with Val before he had digested her first word, "ladies." When he realized he had made a mistake, he returned red-faced to his place where he rejoined the men—for the port but not the cigars.

While the gentlemen discussed tedious business, we women went upstairs to a large boudoir and guest bathroom. We took turns "powdering our noses" and our hostess offered up various colognes, hand creams and hair spray. I found the tradition pleasantly understated and refined.

One evening after dinner at the home of another British couple, I lamented that I wasn't an experienced hostess like our English colleagues. Val, Veronica, and Mrs. C entertained so graciously and with apparent ease that I felt like a novice.

"This evening, for instance," I told Art on the way home, "Mrs. C intermingled her guests, moved them around and kept conversations flowing. She always makes everyone feel comfortable and special."

Art's reply was surprising. "She certainly does," he said with a sarcastic edge to his voice. "But may I remind you that these diplomatic gatherings have more than a social purpose? We're also supposed to discuss a little business and gather information."

He explained what had happened that evening. Before dinner he had managed to speak with a German he knew from the Foreign Ministry. After a bit of maneuvering Art got the official alone in a secluded corner of the terrace and they began to discuss an extremely sensitive issue. Art thought he might finally get the answer to an important question. Just at that inopportune moment, our charming hostess spied the two men and interrupted.

"Now gentlemen," Mrs. C chirped, "I want you both to come inside; you'll love meeting Mrs. Heilemann who has just arrived." A diplomatic breakthrough foiled? Perhaps. Art didn't have another chance to speak alone with the German. We still refer to that incident as "Mrs. C's musical chairs."

Foreign Service people were expected to entertain in their homes in whatever style suited them—and the customs of the host country—and the government provided representation funds for this purpose. The money allotted to the Political Section was shared among all the officers. Although Art was now a mid-level officer, his superiors who had more responsibility obviously got more of the funds.

We did our share of entertaining, but with few embellishments—no uniformed waiters or caterers at our parties. We liked having small dinners but a few cocktail buffets were inevitable. Depending on the cost of the food I was serving, the availability of funds and the type of occasion, only infrequently was I able to hire someone to help. I cooked and we laid out a buffet or served family-style, which suited our style just fine.

There were two popular English-speaking German women who worked parties, together or alone. They were eager, experienced and they could do everything: cook, mix drinks, and clean up afterwards. There was such a demand for their services among the diplomatic community that they were engaged weeks in advance. On only two occasions was I able to hire one of them, Helga. And on those evenings—I entertained with great aplomb.

Unfortunately, some of our other parties were not so successful. I hired a woman, sight unseen (never again!) to help with a large dinner because I understood she could help with the cooking. I asked her to do the final preparations for the meal while Art and I entertained our guests before dinner. When I went into the kitchen at the appointed time to dish up the food—it wasn't ready. The woman didn't know how to cook the rice and she had been embarrassed to tell me. It was another long half-hour before we had dinner.

Prior to our Christmas Open House buffet I very carefully planned the menu so there would be enough money to hire an experienced bartender. He was to help Art serve drinks, pass hors d'oeuvres, and help me keep the buffet table stocked. And perhaps my husband and I would be able to enjoy our own party.

The bartender proved to be helpful and efficient. Our guests obviously enjoyed themselves but the food ran out before the evening did! After replenishing the trays and dishes the waiter told me, "*Alles weg.*" All gone—finished.

But I had prepared more than enough, hadn't I? Had I badly misjudged numbers and appetites?

After the last guests left, I paid the bartender and sent him on his way. He had washed a few glasses, but, typically, he didn't "do" clean up. Wearily I carried a load of dirty dishes to the kitchen—and was astonished to find a platter of food on top of the refrigerator! With trepidation I looked inside the refrigerator and found more party food. The bartender hadn't been so efficient after all. I learned a lesson that evening: checking supplies would henceforth and always be *my* responsibility.

The worst nightmare for a hostess is running out of food. Whether it is a buffet dinner or cocktail party, the sight of a denuded table or the sound of the words "There isn't any more" can be devastating. It happened to me several times—I simply did not plan and prepare enough food. When you invite another couple for steaks on the grill, you only need four rib eyes plus four large baking potatoes. (Except in the Middle East, as I was later to learn.) Those are about the only proportions you can rely on. As the guests increase to more than four people, the only thing you can predict is the *unpredictability* of appetites and numbers. If you buy extra steaks, several guests will drop out at the last minute or admit to being vegetarians. If you don't prepare "extra," someone is bound to call and ask if they can bring their out-of-town guests.

I continue to struggle with that most exasperating part of menu and party planning—deciding *how much* food. The decision can be especially challenging in countries where the invitees are not inclined to RSVP. Being a frugal person, I believe it is shameful to waste food—but not having enough is mortifying.

On another occasion in Bonn we almost ran out of food, but it had nothing to do with planning. Visitors had arrived at the embassy and my husband invited them, along with other embassy colleagues, to have drinks and snacks at our house after work. I didn't have much notice—but this was the way it was sometimes in the Foreign Service. Although Art assured me, "Don't worry, it doesn't need to be fancy," he specified *substantial* food. He expected the group would be hungry after a long hard day of meetings.

I spent the afternoon making finger food, dips, and a shrimp dish. I planned to stop by the commissary and buy salami and cheese, the substantial food, after I picked up Kathy from her ballet lesson.

But I didn't make it to the commissary—I had an automobile accident on the way and had to leave our battered car at a nearby service station. I managed to get home just in time to set out the prepared food and drink fixings before the guests arrived. While they attacked the buffet table, I went to the phone, called my friend Jane who lived nearby, and pleaded, "Help!"

Within twenty minutes Jane arrived with cheese and cold cuts from her refrigerator. She went right to work slicing, spreading and serving. She was a practiced Foreign Service wife—exactly what I needed. The food was just barely enough. But, as Jane said, "You didn't invite them for dinner, you know!"

When finally the guests were gone, Art asked me why I was so nervous and why my face was flushed. I had to tell him about the wrecked car—even though it was his birthday.

In regard to entertaining, we were still learning. And the most important thing I learned during those years was that entertaining properly was an ongoing experiment. The process continues.

There was never a lack of activities in Bonn—for any of us. I volunteered to be a part-time Girl Scout leader during the American bicentennial year of 1976 and many of our troop activities followed a pioneer theme. I invited the girls to our house one day and taught them to make bread. They had fun kneading the dough and punching it down, but their patience wore thin while we waited for it to rise.

Our "little America" in the Project provided a sports program with games for every season and for all ages. Kathy and Alex tried them all. Even Art participated in Little League softball—as an umpire. He also played "big" league basketball and took up tennis. And one year he sang with a madrigal group.

Frequently on Saturdays the American kids swapped and sold their comic books and magazines. There was a wide swath of sidewalk in front of the commissary and PX—plenty of room to set up shop. Our kids were always in pursuit of new reading material and it was a fun way to acquire some spending money.

They also earned a few Deutsch Marks collecting newspapers for recycling. They went around the neighborhood asking for old papers, loaded them into Alex's old red wagon and hauled them to our garage. When the newspapers threatened to overflow the allotted space, the kids crammed them into our car and I drove the entrepreneurs and their wares a few blocks down the street. The papers were sold by weight and it was a good business for a while. Unfortunately the price bottomed out and that was the end of that venture.

Sperrmüll Tag was the day the trash collectors hauled away all the things that were too big for the regular weekly pick-ups: old refrigerators, battered furniture, rubber tires, mattresses and worn out rugs. Garages, basements and attics relinquished their collections of rubbish and the cast-offs were hefted out to the curb a day or two before the pick-up.

After dark on the evening before the trash men came, the bargain hunt/flea market atmosphere took over. People of all nationalities cruised the streets looking for treasures they could rescue from the doom of the landfill. Some of us even picked up a useful item or two during daylight hours. Yes, I too succumbed to the thrill of the chase. The handsome clay flowerpots I recovered, for example, were whole and undamaged—and I needed them.

Coming home on the bus, Alex (then twelve years old) spotted an interesting-looking television set he could tinker with, plus several towering piles of newspapers. He convinced me to go with him to fetch home his discoveries in the car. On the way back we happened to drive by a gold-colored antique chair that called out to me, but the trunk was full. We headed straight for the recycle man, dumped the newspapers and Alex pocketed a few coins. We went back to fetch the chair, which was sitting crookedly against the curb because one leg was a little bit broken. But never mind, it looked really comfortable and we took it home.

When I proudly showed my husband the chair, he was not impressed. "It isn't an antique—it's just worn out." He further insulted my prize by declaring, "And it's not just a little bit broken, it's useless!" But maybe he could fix it and then I could re-cover it…

And maybe not. When the next *Sperrmüll Tag* came up on the calendar, my Charlie Brown chair went out to the curb in front of our house.

Frau Dohse was one of my English students and I wonder if I didn't learn more from her than she did from me. She taught me about German culture and food, and she showed me, again, the kind and generous nature of the German people. She had a lovely face with smooth soft skin and a pure smile. Gray-haired, petite, and in her sixties, she looked like everyone's favorite grandmother.

I asked Frau Dohse one day about the asparagus. "Why is white asparagus so popular?" There were eagerly-awaited asparagus festivals every spring in Germany. One could order an entire restaurant meal that consisted of almost nothing but the white spears. I told her that I had cooked some at home but we found it tough and bitter.

"You must first peel it," was her answer. The next time I arrived for our English lesson, she had a huge bunch of freshly washed white asparagus and a peeler all ready for our food lesson. She showed me how to peel it, explained how to cook it and sent it home with me. We loved it!

Another time Frau Dohse instructed me in the old-fashioned preparation of beef heart. I'm not sure why I wanted to learn except that it sounded so thoroughly German. I bought the heart and I cooked it according to her directions—but none of us liked it very much. We did, however, profit from her lesson on *Sauerbraten*, sweet and sour braised beef. "It all depends on the vinegar," Frau Dohse emphasized.

Art will frequently ask, "Do you remember Dieter Schultz?" (or Erik Jensen or Moshe Ramon or…) If I answer no, my husband reminds me, "But he came to our house for dinner in Bonn." (or The Hague or Maracaibo or…) I admit that I have difficulty remembering someone whom I have met only once or twice—ten or fifteen years ago.

"I remember faces but I'm not good with names" is a commonly heard statement. At our first post, Frankfurt, I became aware that I didn't have a penchant for remembering names nor did Art. But I discovered that it was easier to recall a name that I had seen in writing

In Bonn Art and I came up with a painless solution for remembering people—at least a few of them. It usually worked, as long as too much time didn't pass after the initial meeting. I have since learned that our method is called "word association" by the experts. It wasn't a miraculous cure for name-loss, but it proved to be an excellent aid.

On our way home from a social event we always talked about the people we had met—so we decided to write about them also. Before going to bed we would jot down at least two things about each person, a physical description and then perhaps something we remembered from a conversation. Since Art and I usually sat next to and conversed with different people, we helped each other match up the spouses.

In Europe it was common to supply a guest list to the attendees before the event, unless it was an enormous affair. We saved all the lists—with our descriptions and comments scribbled here and there—and we referred to them whenever our memories needed a prod. Our late-night penciled remarks read something like this:

Mr. and Mrs. Alte—German:

> Ernst: mustache, fluent English, For. Min. Per.
> Ingrid: blond, has 5 dogs, long purple dress

Mr. and Mrs. LeBlanc—French:

> André: glasses, white socks, polka-dot tie, spoke only French, Cons. Off.
> Mimi: lisp, torn black nylons, talked about sex, laughed loudly—a lot

Although we couldn't see the Rhine River below us because of dense foliage, our house was located only a few blocks uphill from the famous waterway. Our upper terrace offered first-class viewing each New Year's Eve when spectacular fireworks burst and arced skyward in glorious color all along the Rhine.

Across the river and spread out before our picture window was the splendor of the *Zieben Geberge*, the seven mountains. The nearest and tallest was the *Drachenfels*, Dragon Rock, where Siegfried slew the legendary dragon. Perched on top were ruins of an old castle. A cog train took tourists up the side of the mountain to enjoy the exquisite scenery and to eat in the new restaurant.

During my parents' visit we crossed the Rhine and took the railway up to the top. At the visitor's area there were high-powered binoculars that one could use after dropping in a coin. My mother had a surprise when she turned the dial and focused the glasses on our house across the river. There was Alex walking through our living room! Thereafter, she and daddy wondered if someone was watching *them* as they played scrabble and gin rummy at our table by the window.

Recently I asked our daughter what she remembered most about Bonn and she immediately replied, "Our view." We all thought of it as distinctly *our* view. Kathy was a John Denver fan and after we left Germany the sounds of "Rocky Mountain High" always reminded her of *our* mountains.

Our taste buds experienced a new sensation the day we went up the Drachenfels. The seductive aroma of fresh popcorn is always hard to ignore, so we bought two boxes from the snack bar to eat while we were admiring the view.

My reaction to the first bite is hard to forget—I thought the popcorn was spoiled. It was crisp and fresh but tasted peculiar. By the time all five of us tried it, we realized that it had sugar on it rather than salt. It didn't taste *bad*—it was just such a shock.

Years later we were again surprised by sugared popcorn at a circus in Tel Aviv. To avoid startling your mouth unduly, I recommend inquiring about the seasoning before buying popcorn in a foreign country.

Aside from the popcorn Art and I adjusted enthusiastically to the cultural changes we experienced. Although we had lived in Fulda and Frankfurt, we discovered many customs in the Bonn area that we weren't familiar with. We considered the differences challenging and in most cases fun, but our adolescent pre-pubescent son found some of the cultural adjustments difficult to accept.

The lessons that Alex and his Canadian friend Rob learned while riding the city bus were particularly frustrating. Our son was astounded the first time an elderly German woman quite forcefully removed him from his seat—because she wanted it. Another bus ride brought him a whack on the knee from an old man's cane. When Alex complained to us, we reminded him that he should always offer his seat to an older person.

"But the bus was practically empty," he grumbled, "Why did they need *my* seat?" Hmmmm. Culture, tradition, habit. Or ancient rite of passage? What could we say?

Whenever the boys attempted to open a window on the bus, they were firmly discouraged from doing so by angry shouts from the other passengers. Art had an answer for that: "Germans don't like drafts." Having spent some time in smoky German *Gasthaüser* (inns and pubs) we were well acquainted with the natives' aversion to drafts, which were considered unhealthy. Better to breathe stale smoky air than to get the *grippe* from fresh air coming through a window. Only when one was outside—in it—was fresh air healthful.

Kathy and Alex found another cultural practice unnerving. Germans had a propensity to stare—openly—with no hesitation or qualms whatsoever. Particularly when we were newcomers to Mehlem, the villagers would walk by our house, stop, and gaze with interest through our big windows. If the kids were playing in the front yard, curious eyes watched them intently.

Ingrid, an American friend originally from Germany, told me that an old custom dictated that people keep their front drapes open. "If you close them the neighbors get suspicious—you must have something to hide." Ingrid said that's why so many people use lace or sheer curtains; one can "sort of" see through them.

The comparison and contrast of spatial relationships is often a topic in cross-cultural discussions. We Americans like space around us—breathing room between our bodies and the ones standing next to us. Likewise our British cousins, who particularly prefer "organized" space—they queue up at the mere indication of a wait. Germans, however, are more likely to crowd and push against each other and they're reluctant to stand in any form of line. Perhaps it has as much to do with patience as it does with space. Other nationalities, including Israelis, have similar tendencies—to them a crowd means pushing, shoving, and lots of noise.

I'm five feet tall—some people would call it five feet short—and I have a need for space that borders on claustrophobia. Being surrounded by people taller than I and unable to see "out" is decidedly unpleasant no matter where I am. An incident in Bonn amplified my spatial mania way past the unpleasant to the edge of fright. The occasion itself was a happy one, the anniversary of the constitution of the Federal Republic of Germany. There were celebrations all over the country and, always relishing a good *Fest*, we went to join the fun.

The four of us went into the city and jammed ourselves into the moving tightening throng of people in the square outside the old *Rathaus*, the Town Hall that dates from 1737. A band was playing loud jolly music. Black, red, and yellow banners festooned the area and huge balloons hung everywhere. Restaurants and pubs around the triangular plaza had put out extra chairs and hired additional waiters. People ate, drank and toasted the country; they sang and swayed and sang some more. German *Gemütlichkeit* was in the air. By the time the ceremonies began there wasn't a centimeter of empty space. The speechifying went on too long, but when finally it was over, the crowd began to move and shift; we all needed some breathing room.

In an instant—as if a switch had been thrown—everyone wanted a souvenir balloon! These were not ordinary birthday party balloons—they were enormous heavy orbs. And suddenly the number-one goal of everyone under the age of eighty was to acquire a balloon. People began to leap in the air and grasp at the rubber, trying to hang on to its slippery skin. Bodies that jumped up didn't necessarily come back down in the same space they had vacated—the surge of the crowd didn't allow them to. Consequently the leapers became heavy missiles thudding down upon whomever couldn't move out of the way because there *was* no out of the way. And those who had the dubious luck of catching a balloon had to make space for the prize in order to keep it.

I was twice knocked to the ground. Elbows pummeled my head; hands and arms blocked my vision; whole bodies obstructed my breathing apparatus—and my sanity became unstuck! I began to shriek and scream maniacally—frightening my children and astounding the crowd around us.

Fortunately, we were near a café. The waves of people parted; Art wrapped his arms around me and I found myself sitting in a chair hyperventilating. The Germans sitting nearby were solicitous and helpful; they kept the revelers away and soothed the children. My children! They had also been bashed around and now their mother was acting weird. Once I was able to breathe normally—and I had *space*—my hysterics subsided. But I was so embarrassed by my behavior that I began to cry and I dissolved into a puddle of frustration. Later at home I studiously avoided the sight of the balloon that the kids took home with us!

One evening a policeman came to our door along with an older-than-middle-aged gentleman with a grave look on his face. They introduced themselves, we shook hands and invited them inside.

"Do you have a young son?" the officer asked. It was the sort of question that causes parents to go wobbly in the knees. Alex was at home so we at least knew he was safe. There wasn't time for any speculation because the next question came quickly. "Does your son have a slingshot?"

We knew the answer was "yes." At the policeman's request, we called our twelve-year-old up from his room and he brought the slingshot. (He later told us it was called a "wrist rocket" because it had "ultimate power.") Then we all filed out onto our terrace. A serious discussion ensued, in German, accompanied by arm waving and finger pointing in a leftwards direction.

The older man lived a short way downhill from us. He had recently put new double-glazed high-tech glass in his living room window—and a rock had hit the window! Alex admitted that he had practiced slinging rocks (and a few marbles) from the terrace; he wanted to see how high and how far each would go. All he could see below were trees, but one stone evidently flew through the branches and landed with force against the neighbor's window.

"Did you hear any glass breaking?" I asked Alex. But the neighbor interrupted to say that the window wasn't shattered, only pocked. Nevertheless, it would have to be replaced "at great expanse."

The policeman, the neighbor, Art and Alex trooped downhill to inspect the wounded window and Art agreed that the slingshot "probably" was the culprit. He offered his apologies and Alex did the same. Our son was terrified (his word) by the entire situation, which was punishment enough, we thought. The policeman and especially the victim were relieved to hear that we had proper insurance.

The neighbor, now cordial and pleased that the window would be paid for, told Art, "My wife and I would like you and your family to have coffee with us soon." The invitation never came, however, and we were disappointed.

Along with the job came some boring evenings that we would rather have spent at home with our children. There were dinner parties during which the conversations were conducted solely in German and French and before we finished dessert my brain began to fail me. We went to cocktail parties with hundreds of strangers and ninety percent of them talked about the weather. But more often the perks of the job resulted in our good fortune and we spent many stimulating evenings with remarkable people.

One such person was Eleanor Lansing Dulles. Art was the embassy control officer for Ms. Dulles' visit, thus giving us the pleasure of escorting her to Ambassador Hillenbrand's residence for a dinner in her honor. Since his wife was temporarily away from post, the ambassador asked me to be the hostess.

Ms. Dulles was almost eighty and, in spite of poor eyesight and partial deafness, she exhibited an energy and enthusiasm that impressed all of us. And there was nothing frail about her memory. She told numerous stories about her earlier years with the Department of State where she was an acknowledged expert on post-war Germany. She had earned the title "Mother of Berlin" for her work in revitalizing the city's culture and economy.

Being the sister of two famous men (John Foster, a former Secretary of State, and Allen, a former director of the CIA) did not deter her from gaining a respected and admired reputation for her own government work. But it was difficult to be a woman at State in the 40's and 50's, she told us. "I just had to work ten times harder."

Art was one of the control officers for another visitor, Secretary of State Henry Kissinger. Art particularly remembers the 1976 visit that took place in Grafenau, a small town in the Bavarian forest. The high-level conference pertained to the situation in South Africa.

"The tension." That was my husband's answer when I asked him what he recalled about the Kissinger visits. "There was always a lot of tension in the air." The Secretary was a perfectionist and he had a quick temper. He didn't like to be bothered with details, but he didn't like to be left out of any decision-making either.

When one of his aides or an embassy officer asked, "What shall we do about..." or "What do you want to..." Kissinger would burst out: "Don't bother me with that!" But just as the officer was leaving the room, he would hear a soft rumble from the Secretary. "Maybe I should take a look at that."

The care and feeding of top officials is another of the duties of a Foreign Service officer. A tremendous amount of planning and long hours of work precede an official visit and nearly all embassy personnel have some part in it. Art would be involved in many more such visits over the years.

Winter meant ski-time for our family and we went to Berwang—twice. This small village in the Austrian Tyrol exists only for sports: skiing and snowboarding in the winter, walking and climbing in the summer. As we drove toward Berwang the first time, I was watching the map and I knew we were nearly there. What a disappointment; we saw only beige and brown fields on all sides. There wasn't even enough snow for a snowball fight! Then, as if we had crossed some magical border, we came around a curve and everything before us was a brilliant white—a sparkling snowy wonderland!

Half-timbered inns decorated with painted flowers stood at the foot of the mountains. As we drove up the narrow main street we saw small shops that sold skis, sweaters and souvenirs. As soon as we got out of the car we heard the Austrian greeting "Gruss Gott" from every passer-by. The tantalizing smell of wood smoke welcomed us and the crunch of crisp snow underfoot made it all real.

We signed up for ski lessons. The first day Art and I were in the same class but I was soon demoted to a slower group. The children learned quickly and by week's end they hated to stop skiing even for the lunch break. I relished my lunch and hated to return to the cold after a yummy meal. The food was typical Tyrolian fare—heavy, delicious and plentiful—although Alex never seemed to get filled up.

At the first meal in our *pension* we found large envelopes with linen napkins inside. We wrote our names on the envelopes and found them again at our table the next morning. We discovered in the evening that we still had the same napkins, now sporting a drop or two of gravy or egg yolk. No matter, our innkeepers were frugal people and our personalized wrappers cut laundry costs. By mid-week our napkins began to resemble stained baby bibs. But we wouldn't complain, even after the spaghetti dinner. One patron, however, wanted a change. At the end of the meal, he intentionally spilled sauce on his *serviette* and requested a clean replacement.

The family didn't ski together the third year. Kathy went on a school-sponsored trip and Art and I joined friends for a ski week in Obergurgel, Austria. Friends Dixie and Dave offered to keep Alex that week—their son Doug were in the same class as Alex. The useful American custom of looking after one another's children was frequently practiced among us in Bonn.

Art and I returned home from our ski holiday late at night. As we began unloading our bags from the car, Art noticed a profusion of footprints in the snow around the front of the house. "Someone's been here," he said. The kids were still with their friends as we had arranged.

"Maybe Alex needed to come home and pick up some more clothes or something," I replied. "He had his key."

"Looks like he had a party." Art was suspicious, but I just laughed.

We lugged the suitcases into the house and Art took his skis to the storeroom. When I turned on the living room light I "felt" something was not right, but I didn't know what it was. Art came into the room, hesitated only a few seconds and declared, "The furniture—the chair and couch have been moved."

We were tired and without further pondering the placement of the furniture, we partially unpacked and fell into bed. Like Scarlet O'Hara, I would think about it tomorrow.

Art was right. Alex, Doug and Rob had had a party while we were gone—a party of thirteen-year-olds—without any adult supervision. Uh-oh. When the boys' story unraveled, we found out they had sent written invitations to their friends, including several girls. They gave directions regarding which bus to take and arranged to meet the girls at the bus stop near our house. Dave and Dixie didn't suspect anything when Alex and Doug fibbed about a party at Rob's.

The deception was well planned but the party was disappointing, as Alex later admitted. The girls soon left—they were uncomfortable when they realized there were no parents at home.

We grounded the boys and subjected them to a lecture about the dangers of unchaperoned adolescent entertainment. Long afterwards, when we parents had cooled down, Art and I chuckled with Dave, Dixie, Estelle and Pete about how organized the boys had been in their role as hosts. Pete mused, "Too bad they don't spend as much time and effort on their studies."

The American Women's Group brought American women together to provide friendship, fellowship, and a foundation for sponsoring social and charitable activities. In Bonn, as in many large cities abroad, the AWG also invited women of the host country to become members. In the fall and again in spring the Welcoming Committee arranged a coffee or tea to introduce and welcome new women. Traditionally the event took place at the home of the Deputy Chief of Mission whose wife was kind enough to offer her spacious house plus the aid of her housekeeper or maid. It was common practice—which we would experience first-hand a few years later—for the DCM residence to be used for large social and cultural gatherings. No one else, except the ambassador, had the space.

Naomi Cash, wife of the DCM, made a comment that reflected the changes taking place in the Foreign Service—changes that were affecting spouses. After one of the welcoming events that I had chaired, I went into the kitchen where the staff was washing up the cups and glasses. I picked up a tea-towel and said, "I'll help dry."

"No, you won't!" said Mrs. Cash emphatically. "I wouldn't want anyone to come in here and get the impression that I *required* you to help clean up."

I argued with her good-naturedly—I wanted to help—but she was adamant. She referred to the Policy on Wives and with a sly smile on her face she took the towel out of my hand.

Mrs. Cash was an old-style dedicated Foreign Service wife who was accustomed to doing unpaid work for the government. She was definitely not one of the dragon ladies, those infamous wives who puffed themselves up to their husbands' status, gave a mighty roar and told the other women what they should do, how, and where. The legend of the dragon ladies is not a myth—the creatures did exist. Their numbers have dwindled but there are still a handful continuing to breathe fire here and there. Today, however, the other wives don't have to pay attention to them.

Unfortunately, one of the negative effects of the 1972 directive was a new reluctance to work together, to gather the talents of the distaff members of the embassy and to use them for the good of the community. Because "someone" might get the wrong impression. No longer did some wives feel comfortable asking other spouses for help. Because a request might be misinterpreted. Consequently, our *esprit de corps* diminished.

We were happy in Bonn. Although Kathy had pined away for the U.S. at first—mostly because among her peers it was the "in" thing to do—she soon forgot to complain. When Art suggested extending our tour from three to four years, the rest of us enthusiastically agreed—and so did the State Department.

An unexpected phone call changed our plans—again. Arthur Hartman, Assistant Secretary for European Affairs, asked my husband to return to Washington to be his special assistant. Mr. Hartman's request showed confidence in Art's work and the offer was difficult to refuse. There would be no fourth year in Bonn.

That was the fastest move we ever made and the easiest—on the nerves. We had only two weeks to pack up, so there was no time for cogitating and dithering—we just did it.

It was August 1976 and Art's parents were on their way to visit us. Art met them at the train station in Bad Godesberg and waited until he parked in front of our house before telling them the news. The packers had already begun so he was compelled to prepare them for the mess inside.

When Art's dad Wendell came in the front door, he looked around at all the boxes stacked in the hallway and said to me with a grin, "Tsk, tsk. You've been here three years and you still haven't unpacked!"

Helen always adjusted quickly and easily to life's little quirks and upheavals and in those unavoidable circumstances she didn't flinch. We had planned for them to have several quiet days relaxing, enjoying the view and spending time with their grandchildren before our sightseeing trip. Instead, they pitched in and helped us through the chaos.

When the moving van left, we packed our suitcases and off we went to see the sights. As we meandered through the small Swiss town of Suhr, where Helen's father was born, Art approached a friendly-looking couple on the street and asked them for directions to the Town Hall. They were curious about us and impressed with our German. To our surprise they invited all six of us to their home for tea and *Kuchen*. They were a kind hospitable family and we enjoyed a lively conversation with them.

After visiting the courthouse in search of records bearing the Zehnder name, Helen's family, we split up to roam in different directions. Alex and his grandfather wandered through an opening in the side of a hill and discovered a cave. It wasn't just any cave—it was a cheese cave.

Alex ran to find the rest of us and by the time we got there Wendell had made friends with the workmen who were turning and rotating wheels of cheese. One man was using a forklift to shelve the enormous discs. Another worker was operating a machine that had brushes to wash the waxed cheeses. They treated us to a special tour of the aging and storage cave, a dark damp place that smelled moldy, but nevertheless was fascinating.

The owner took us into his adjacent shop and gave us hefty samples of all his cheeses. There was Swiss, of course, and Tilsiter and a soft aged cheese with a powerful sharp smell. They tasted especially good since we were at the *source*. We purchased several pounds and stowed them in our portable cooler with the water and soft drinks.

Alex found cheese about as appealing as eating live bait. (Even today he only allows mild cheddar and mozzarella to pass his lips.) During our trip he had preferred to sit in the back of our borrowed van, so we appointed him "keeper of the cooler." Soon, however, he begged to resign. Whenever someone asked for a drink or snack he was obliged to lift the lid of the cooler—and a strong aroma assaulted his nostrils. The pungent cheese became more so every hour. Alex moved to the front of the van.

All too soon we were back in Bonn. We washed our clothes, gathered our belongings and re-packed our suitcases. Art's parents returned to Nebraska and we four flew to Washington for yet another phase of Foreign Service life.

As we said *auf Wiedersehen* to Bonn, I wondered when we would return to Germany. The third time definitely had been a charm—would there be a fourth?

9

LAUGHING IN A FOREIGN LANGUAGE

"*Keine Stärke, bitte.*" It was a simple German phrase and Art was certain the words were correct. So why did the laundry starch his shirts? He had said, "No starch, please."

My husband had studied German in college and although he wasn't fluent he had a solid vocabulary and a good grasp of the grammar. After arriving in Fulda with the army his German improved with daily practice so when the post laundry facility starched his shirts yet again, it was time to complain.

Confronting the German employee, Art produced the laundry ticket on which was clearly written "*Keine Stärke.*"

"Ach! You mean '*Gar keine Stärke,*'" the man replied emphatically. "No starch AT ALL!" One little word—*gar*.

There is more to a language than vocabulary and grammar. There are nuances and inflections and funny little untranslatable words that give a language its own peculiar and interesting character. That's why studying a foreign tongue in school doesn't necessarily prepare the student for an intelligible conversation with a native speaker. A simple word or a short phrase can change the connotation or the tone of a sentence to something the speaker does not intend. The result can be humorous, disastrous, confusing and even embarrassing.

The mistake Art made in a restaurant in Fulda is a good example. He asked the waitress in literal German "Do you have any milk?" Flushing from pink to scarlet, the young woman shook her head and scurried away.

Our German friends around the table were grinning and looking at each other in amusement. Ottmar was sitting next to us and when his own laughter was under control, he explained why the waitress was embarrassed. Art had asked her if she was lactating.

An American woman, who spoke almost no German, went into a beauty shop in Bonn to have her hair done. Using simple words and sign language she explained to the hairdresser what she wanted.

"*Zitrone?*" asked the young German. My friend was puzzled at first until she remembered that *Zitrone* meant lemon. Ah, she thought, lemon juice is good for the hair. She smiled and nodded her assent.

With a suspenseful mystery book to read she paid no attention to what the beautician was doing until her hair was dry and ready to be combed. But when she looked in the mirror she didn't recognize the stranger who was looking back at her—with blond hair! Earlier she had been a brunette. It seems the *Fräulein* had mistaken her for another woman who periodically had her hair colored "yellow."

Hiking in the hills of southern Germany, Kathy and Jeff came upon a huge sign that looked important but which neither of them could translate. It began: "*Lebens Gefahr.*" The words weren't familiar so Jeff wrote them down and they continued on their walk.

That evening they asked their hosts what the sign said. They were shocked to find out that *Lebens Gefahr* meant mortal danger! The sign had also instructed them: "Do not proceed—it is forbidden to cross the glacial field!"

One can only imagine the confusion encountered by foreigners traveling in our broad country. Even for Americans the language can create minor confusion from one part of the nation to another.

Our children, aged eight and four, still had Spanish in their ears when we were assigned back to Washington after Venezuela. They went with us one evening to visit a distant relative in the Maryland suburbs. Our hostess offered Art and me a cold drink and then asked Alex and Kathy, "Would you like a soda?"

They reacted as if they had been invited to drink hemlock and both said "No, thank you" rather quickly. A short while later Alex whispered in my ear that he had spotted a bottle of 7-UP on the bar. "Can we have some pop?" he pleaded.

I suddenly realized that our kids thought they had been offered a glass of club soda. They had learned "pop" in Nebraska, but they didn't know it was a shortened form of "soda pop," an outdated term. Art and I now stick with "soft drink" which seems to have a broad following.

Back in Washington again a few years later, an older Alex went into a supermarket and bought some candy and a package of gum. The checker took his money, gave him a receipt and turned to the next customer.

Alex said, "Excuse me, may I have a sack, please?"

"A what?"

"A sack," repeated Alex.

"Oh—you want a *bag*!" and the woman handed over a small paper sack—uh bag.

I studied Spanish in high school and continued to pursue it at the university. When I finished I was rather proud of my command of the grammar, but unfortunately my comprehension of spoken Spanish was mediocre. Somehow the words encountered an obstacle course as they traveled from my ears to my brain. Still I could converse adequately with a passable accent—although I was never able to convince my poky tongue to trill the R's.

When we traveled to Spain on vacation from Fulda, it was my turn to communicate. Art didn't speak Spanish at that time. Reading menus, ordering food, asking directions—no problem, I was ready for the challenge.

Spain is one of those countries where the language has different pronunciations within its own borders. Spanish speakers in Andalucia in the south and Catalonia in the northeast have a soft "th" sound, which one doesn't hear in the center of the country. During our first hours in Barcelona I thought there were a surprising number of citizens with lisps! The sound was new to me—my instructors in school had been from Madrid and Havana where that pronunciation isn't heard.

When I asked the innkeeper in Barcelona what time lunch was served, he replied, "*Doath.*" I didn't know if he said twelve (*doce*) or two (*dos.*) Eager to avoid a mistake I risked embarrassment by asking for a show of fingers. Fortunately two o'clock was lunchtime or he wouldn't have had enough fingers.

In Venezuela there are also differences. We lived in the north where the Maracuchos pronounced their Spanish more cleanly and distinctly than in other parts of the country. In Caracas for instance, words were slurred and many endings were omitted altogether.

Even in small European countries we found surprising variations in pronunciation. The Dutch language we heard in a northern province sounded quite different from that in the south of the Netherlands. And foreigners who could understand Danish in Copenhagen found it impossible to comprehend on other Danish islands.

Our country is no exception, although the differences are relatively minor. We who hail from the Midwestern prairies like to think we don't have an accent. No Southern drawl or Texas twang, no Bronx brassiness. We don't diphthongize our vowels like Wisconsinites and we don't move our consonants around the way

New Englanders do. They like to add "r" to a final vowel. Jackie Kennedy, for example, referred to the White House dishes as "chiner." Conversely, Bean-Towners still talk about the Boston Tea "Pahty." Our friend Michael from New York calls my husband "Aht."

English speakers in other countries have asked us, "Where do you come from? We can't place your accent." That's because we from the Plains States speak plainly.

In college I enjoyed my Spanish classes immensely and, hoping I would excel at another language, I decided to study German. I needed only one semester to realize I was not gifted in foreign language learning. Spanish was easy and German was difficult—those were the hard facts. That disappointing bit of self-analysis proved to be correct, not only then but also for my future foreign language endeavors.

In the early days of Foreign Service training Art was required (and I was permitted) to take the Modern Language Aptitude Test. We scored within a few points of each other—on the lower end of the aptitude scale. During the early 1990's controversy regarding the "em-latt," as it is familiarly called, prompted some ongoing research projects. But to date there is still a great deal of support for the MLAT's effectiveness. Proponents say this test has proven to be the best available predictor of language learning success.

Our test scores predicted that we would probably not be successful at Chinese, Japanese, Arabic or any other "hard" language. In practical terms that meant the Foreign Service would have been ill advised to assign Art to a two-year hard language program—an expensive investment.

A student's motivation may outshine his aptitude, however, and in such cases hard work and long hours of study may yield a command of the studied language that is superior to what was predicted by the MLAT. It happens. The effectiveness of the instructors, class size and home situation also have some influence on the students' success rate. But I believe foreign language learning is a talent like music, dancing and painting. Some of us have it, some of us don't.

While we were studying at the Foreign Service Institute, a professor of linguistics entertained us now and then with a good story. One was about an American who was serving in Nicaragua and dating a young local woman. One evening when he arrived to pick her up to go dancing, he met her grandmother. The young woman wasn't quite ready so the *abuela* began to chat with the American.

"I am so glad that you are taking my granddaughter out—she really loves to screw and she has been practicing!"

The man's mouth fell open and he didn't know what to say. Then he realized that what the grandmother meant was "twist." It was the 1960's and the twist was the latest thing in modern dance.

Spanish, even with its variations in pronunciation and accent, nevertheless still sounds like Spanish from country to country. But there are individual words that may have different meanings or connotations. The word *palo*, for instance, means a stick and also a hit or a blow. But by adding a diminutive ending, the word becomes *palito* which is slang for "a little drink"—at least to the Maracuchos.

An American friend who spoke excellent Spanish traveled from Maracaibo to another South American city on business. After the meetings he invited his local colleague to go for a *palito*. The Latino was surprised at the invitation—Americans were not usually so open about their dalliances.

When the pair ended up in the hotel cocktail lounge the local man realized with amusement that the American had invited him for a drink. A *palito* in his country was a casual and quick sexual encounter.

There were two butchers frequented by the expatriates in Maracaibo, a Frenchman and a German, and only one of them spoke English. An American whom I'll call Annie spoke no Spanish when she arrived but she was resourceful and not the least bit timid. When she went meat shopping for the first time, she wasn't certain of the butcher's nationality, because he had greeted her with "*Buenos días.*"

She looked over the choices in the display case and thought about what to say. Like many other Americans in a foreign country, she assumed that a loud voice was necessary in order for the man to understand her words. In a forceful robust tone she said "oink oink!" several times and pointed to the pork chops. Then she held up four fingers. The butcher was at first dumbfounded but then he smiled and pulled four chops from the case.

Emboldened by her success Annie then gestured to a large piece of meat and inquired "Moo? Moooo?" The meat man nodded. When she held up two fingers and loudly said "kilos," he again nodded his head. Aha, this is working, she thought to herself.

Annie was silent for a few minutes while the butcher was wrapping the meat. Suddenly he began to laugh and, evidently tired of the game, he announced in English, "We also have some very nice 'cluck-cluck' and a fine fat 'quack-quack.'"

We watched television infrequently in Venezuela, but I remember how funny it was to watch Bill Cosby "speaking" Spanish on the program "I Spy." A few other popular shows from home were relayed and dubbed including "The Tom Jones Show."

When Gill discovered that her Colombian maid was an avid Tom Jones fan, she commented that the singer, like herself, was from Wales. Sara, who spoke only Spanish, evidently tracked this information through her gray matter while she watched the program. Afterward she made an astute observation. "I thought you said he was Welsh like you."

"He is, yes," Gill responded.

"But *he* speaks perfect Spanish!" Sara pointed out.

Since the insult was clearly unintended, Gill restrained herself from informing the maid that Tom Jones could only *sing* in Spanish. She also decided to let Sara keep her illusions about the many Hollywood stars whose movies were shown locally. As Gill said to me with a chuckle, "Command of the Spanish language was no doubt a prerequisite for the actors' MGM and Paramount contracts!"

On Saturday mornings Alex and Kathy watched cartoons, which they had looked forward to all week. In Spanish, as in English, the antics of familiar characters were entertaining and there is no doubt that TV helped to improve our children's comprehension of the local language. Immediately before the cartoons the station aired an exhilarating rendition of the Venezuelan national anthem. Alex understood that the music was Venezuela's version of "The Star Spangled Banner" but I didn't think either child paid much attention to the words.

During a visit to Caracas I took Kathy with me to the hotel hairdresser where she sat quietly reading a book while my hair was combed and teased—in the usual 1970 manner. Suddenly an immature but self-assured voice began to belt out the Venezuelan anthem—in perfectly accented Spanish. My daughter was singing along with the television: "*Gloria, bravo pueblo…*"

I turned around and watched Kathy cheerfully singing every word, but still looking at the book she had in her lap. She was oblivious to the women who were staring in amazement at the four-year-old American child.

In addition to our memory banks from which we make continuous withdrawals, I believe we also have separate vaults that house our subconscious memories. Unbeknownst to us, certain stimuli can cause a vault to open and release its contents. What comes out of our mouths as a result of that transaction may surprise us. Especially if one of the vaults is a safety deposit box for a foreign language.

Hidden away in one of my mother's vaults was the Bohemian dialect. She grew up in a small town in Nebraska where most of the people, including her parents and grandparents, spoke Czech and/or Bohemian. She didn't study the language with a teacher and a book—she learned it as a kitchen tongue. After she married and moved to another town, however, she seldom heard Czech. She was in her sixties when she visited then-Czechoslovakia for the first time. The familiar homey sound of the language, which she heard on the streets and in the stores and restaurants, renewed warm thoughts of her childhood.

Mother and family friend Maxine were shopping one day in Prague. They went into a little store to purchase the renowned hollow eggs that were hand-painted by local crafts people. When Mother said something unintelligible, Maxine was non-plussed.

"*What* did you say?" Maxine whispered, poking her with an elbow.

The clerk, who had clearly understood my mother's request for two dozen eggs, began to wrap them up. As she watched the saleswoman, my mother suddenly realized that she had spoken her family's language, which she thought she had lost, for the first time in many years.

My dad used to say, "The brain takes pictures and files them and they come back to us at the appropriate times." Or sometimes inappropriate times.

One of *my* vaults opened a few weeks after our arrival in Copenhagen. Kathy and I boarded a bus and I tried to ask the driver how to get to the other end of the city. I began with English but the man shook his head. I then used my meager supply of Danish but he didn't understand me. Finally a combination of German and Danish yielded a modicum of success.

After we took our seats Kathy whispered to me, "Why did you think the bus driver would speak Spanish?"

"Spanish?" I didn't understand. "What are you talking about?" My daughter informed me that I had spoken several sentences in Spanish, and I didn't know it.

From snippets of Danish conversation I became aware of the name Jose' Annersen, including references to Jose' Annersen Boulevard. I was curious and finally I asked someone, "Who is he?"

"You know—Hans Christian Andersen's fairy tales." That reply confused me even more until my American friend explained. "The Danes refer to Hans Christian by his initials H.C. You're hearing the Danish pronunciation 'Ho Say.' It's not a Spanish name, believe me."

I felt less foolish a few weeks later when a new arrival asked me, "Who is Jose' Annersen and why is there a street named after him?"

The Danes do not pronounce the d in Andersen—nor in Madsen, Sandersen, etc.—which had added to my confusion. Where I grew up there were many families of Danish descent so the names in Denmark looked familiar but they didn't sound the same. Andersen was Annersen, Jensen was Yensen, Jorgensen was Yurensen and Berg sounded something like Be-yero.

Of all the countries we have called home, Denmark was where I had the most difficulty remembering names—perhaps because they were too familiar. There were also a lot of repeats. A cocktail party guest list would include several Rasmussens, Olesens, Sorensens and of course numerous Jensens. In Germany I had no trouble remembering Lipschitz and Muhlhausen and I could always recall Zielhuis and van Heemskerk in Holland. But in Denmark I confused Erik with Henrik and Jens Hansen with Lars Larsen—or was it Hans Hansen?

"A foreigner can only speak Danish with a hot potato in his mouth." At least that was the rumor that circulated in Copenhagen. If you didn't want to risk the hot potato, you could try a large marble—moving it about with your tongue would help to produce some of the difficult Danish sounds.

Roed groed med floede paa. That was the test. Kathy said the long-timers at her school challenged new students to repeat the phrase with a proper Danish accent. Along with a staccato lilt it should sound something like: "rooth groot meth floothuh po." The phrase means "red porridge with cream," and once learned it is not forgotten.

When Art and I were traveling in Italy we met a friendly South African couple at the campgrounds in Florence. We liked them immediately and accepted their invitation to join them that evening for a glass of wine under the stars. John was an animated storyteller whose speech was peppered with four-letter expletives. His wife, too, used "damn" as if it were a common adjective. But when John referred to the Italians' "bloody hooting," she objected.

"John! Watch your language!" she scolded. Hooting was simply horn honking—but "bloody" was a nasty word not to be used in polite company.

That was 1964. Art and I were just beginning our education about the world outside the United States. As the years scrolled by we discovered all kinds of interesting and amusing meanings and connotations for words used by non-American English speakers.

During our first weeks in Bonn the children had only a few of their own books and games to keep them occupied when we weren't out exploring the area. We had a longer than usual wait for our household shipment, which had temporarily escaped its keepers, but once we discovered the post lending library, they spent hours and hours reading. Alex and Kathy, ages 11 and 7, delighted in the copious books written by Englishwoman Enid Blyton in the 1940's and 50's. It didn't occur to me at the time that they might be confused by some of the British terms.

Alex thought the young people in the stories spent an inordinate amount of time in bathtubs until he discovered that "having a bathe" meant swimming. Kathy, too, was confused by the bath situation. Why did the children wear bathing costumes? She also wondered why the characters "motored" to Italy; it seemed to her a long way to go on a motorcycle!

The "torch" bewildered them the most. Neither could understand why British children were allowed to go about at night carrying live fire. Alex eventually figured out the flashlight connection.

When an English friend announced, "I'll knock you up" I thought I had heard the ultimate in Brit wit, especially since he was speaking to both my husband and me. Art, having heard the expression before, gleefully explained to me that it had nothing to do with procreation—our friend simply intended to drop by and knock on our door. In American slang, the phrase means "to impregnate."

"Keep your pecker up!" was an entreaty intended to cheer me up when I was ill—and it did. I laughed at my British well-wisher and replied that I lacked the appropriate anatomy.

"Your chin—keep your chin up!" my friend chortled. I decided I liked the British interpretation of the expression much better than the crude American reference to a body part possessed only by men.

There are several British terms that I prefer to those used by Americans. When the former have a stomach cramp they blame it on "wind." It's a nicer cleaner word than gas, it seems to me. They watch the "telly" while we sit in front of the boob tube. That should tell us something.

Americans take vacations while the British go on holiday or "hols" as Alex remembers from the Blyton books. A holiday sounds much more enjoyable than simply vacating homes and offices, which is what our term means. Our British friends have gardens and we have yards. With or without vegetables and flowers a garden sounds lovely and the word evokes pleasure. A yard is merely a piece of enclosed ground.

"Did you ring your mother?" or "I'll ring for the maid." Telephones and bells quite rightly *ring* in the United Kingdom. In the U.S. we call, which is only one step away from shout. I do draw the line, however, at giving my friend "a tinkle."

In The Hague my Dutch teacher recommended that her students watch the news on television. "Excellent practice for the ears," she said, and television would help build our vocabularies.

A few days later my classmate asked her, "Why are the newscasters always talking about the Nazis?"

Amused as well as pleased by the question, our instructor wrote the Dutch word *natie* on the board and pronounced it "nazi." "This is what you heard," she explained, "It means nation."

Another country, another language…I wondered if my brain had enough compartments. But learning to read Dutch came easier for Art and me than Danish. Many words were cognates, related in origin and kin to English or German. A *park* was a park, for example, and a *man* was a man. *Boek* meant book and *hier* meant here. House and out were also cognates but they were diphthongized in Dutch. A Canadian would have had no problem with *huis* and *uit*.

Reading and comprehending Dutch, however, didn't automatically transfer that ability to speaking the language. Rule number one was: you can't speak Dutch with a dry throat. Saying good morning, for example, required extra saliva far back on the tongue. As written, *goede morgen* appeared easy, but it sounded much different than it looked. Grammar books said the Dutch "g" was pronounced with a rasp, but it sounded to me like the speaker was clearing his throat. Confusing, yes. Rule number two: imitate, don't analyze.

Our cook in The Hague came from West Flanders in Belgium. He spoke Dutch and French fluently and English passably. Lovable as Patrick was, he could be quite feather-brained on occasion. On my birthday, for example, I asked him to make fried chicken. I looked forward to eating crispy crunchy chicken and not having to prepare it myself or clean up afterward.

We sat down at the table and Patrick served the chicken—baked. I was disappointed but decided to overlook his mistake. Not long after, I asked him to bake the fish we were having for dinner, but instead he fried it. I suspected that Patrick wasn't paying attention to instructions and after several similar mistakes, he and I sat down for a serious discussion. What I discovered was an interpretation quirk. I looked up bake, roast and fry in a Dutch dictionary and found *bakken* for all of them. No wonder Patrick was confused.

When our brood was home from college for holidays and summers, Patrick, two years older than Alex, frequently joined them and their friends at parties and gatherings. (Their favorite hangout was a Mexican restaurant that had a Turkish chef.) As they got to know each other better Patrick felt it was his duty to teach them "dirty Dutch"—in case they would hear such words.

During those years my son generally ate his biggest meal of the day after midnight so when he and Patrick came home late one night, Alex headed straight for the refrigerator. As he pulled out a dish of leftovers Patrick offered to heat the food on the stove.

"No thanks, I'll just *nuke* it!" was Alex's response, referring to the microwave.

Patrick stared at Alex in amazement. The boss's son was showing off—using an extremely nasty Dutch word. "Where did you learn *that*?" he wanted to know.

After Alex explained about the microwave, Patrick told him with great amusement that "nuke" sounded like the Dutch slang word for copulation!

We were long gone from The Hague before I heard the "dirty Dutch" stories. I was aware, however, that our cook and our kids were learning languages from each other. Kathy was studying French and she frequently practiced with Patrick. She also teased him a great deal about his literal interpretations. "The table she is set" and "The dinner he is ready" were typical Patrick-isms. They reminded me of Mark Twain's parody on the German language in which he made fun of the gender of nouns.

Our daughter went to France one summer during her college years to study French. We worked out a budget of sorts and agreed on a sum of money that would satisfy her needs throughout her month's stay in Amboise. The money she took with her would have been sufficient if she hadn't had her socks and her underwear dry-cleaned!

Kathy was staying in the home of a French family and although she did small bits of washing in her room, midway through the month her jeans, skirts and blouses needed to be laundered. She spotted a sign that looked familiar—a form of the French word for "clean." After watching several people go in with armloads of clothing, she assumed this was the right place and she took in her own armful. Unfortunately, the establishment did dry-cleaning only and retrieving her clothing was costly. Following her panicky phone call, we wired extra money to her.

Jeff saw an interesting chicken dish on the menu in a Paris restaurant. He wanted to try it but because of his preference for the white breast meat, he asked the waitress if the chicken was *poulet blanc*?

With a withering look and a tone of exasperation the woman replied in French, "All chickens are white, aren't they!"

One evening after a dinner in Sanaa several of us were talking about the hazardous driving conditions in the mountains of Yemen and inevitably the conversation turned to automobile accidents. Manuel, who spoke English with a charming but thick French accent, narrated the harrowing story of a car crash involving his family. After explaining that he and their son were in the front seat of the vehicle when it crashed, Manuel then nodded to his wife and continued. "We looked behind for Yolande but she wasn't sitting. We got out of the automobile and then we found her. She was in ze tree!"

We exploded with laughter at what seemed an absurdity—until we saw the grieved look on Yolande's face. The laughter stopped abruptly. Yolande explained in French that her injuries required extensive surgery and she spent many months in and out of hospitals. The remembered pain was evident in her eyes.

One doesn't normally laugh at such a tragic story. The poor woman was thrown through the back window along with shredded glass and propelled forcefully into the branches of a tree. Where is the humor is *that?*

It wasn't the story that was comical. It was Manuel's manner of telling it: his accent, his very formal English, his climactic statement "She was in ze tree!" He stimulated our laugh reflexes and we couldn't avoid that first automatic response. Ah, the power of words…and accent and intonation.

Molly has the gift of tongues. Her command of Hebrew as well as Arabic was the envy of her colleagues when we were together at the embassy in Tel Aviv. She had previously been posted to Amman, Jordan, and was later assigned to Jerusalem where she needed both languages. She was the only Foreign Service Officer at that time to have achieved the high score of 4—in both Hebrew and Arabic—at the Foreign Service Institute.

When it was time for spring gardening, Molly went to a large well-known nursery in Tel Aviv and picked out scores of young plants. Having made her selections, she was ready to pay. Being familiar with the local customs, she confidently expected a discount due to her sizable purchase—and she said so.

"*Ma?*" ("What?") The clerk gave her an incredulous look. An impassioned discussion in Hebrew followed, with the Israeli becoming more negative and Molly becoming more insistent. She didn't merely ask for a discount—she demanded one!

The clerk frowned, shook his head and continued to ask, "*Ma?*"

A blinking red light in Molly's head suddenly lit up the Hebrew word she was using for discount. It was wrong! Her loud persistence came to an embarrassing halt. What she had demanded from the clerk was "pleasure." Molly didn't say whether or not her bill was discounted in the end, but she assured me that she never went back to that nursery.

Israelis cheerfully and frequently tell a joke that insults themselves and their countrymen. The anecdote illustrates how language and culture are inextricably intertwined.

Armed with a microphone a reporter is interviewing people in an international setting. He first approaches a man from Bangladesh and says, "Excuse me. What is your opinion of the meat shortage?"

With a quizzical look the Bangladeshi asks, "What is *meat*?"

The reporter turns to another person. "Excuse me. What is your opinion of the meat shortage?"

The interviewee happens to be a Soviet who replies, "What does *opinion* mean?"

Again the reporter asks the question and this time an American responds. "What is *shortage*?"

The journalist next approaches an Israeli and repeats, "Excuse me. What is your opinion of the meat shortage?"

Bluntly the Israeli asks, "What is *excuse me*?"

When an Israeli driver or pedestrian stopped someone on the street to ask a question, there was no preamble—no "Pardon me" or "Please, can you tell me...?" The Israeli was curt and brusque. "Where's Shalva Street?" or "This is Herzlia?" As the response was being given, the driver already had his car in gear and he was moving on. He may have nodded his head but he seldom said "Thank you."

Rude? Uncivil? Did the average Israeli lack basic manners or was this common behavior dictated by the culture?

Art and I enjoyed taking long walks through our neighborhood in the Tel Aviv suburbs and people often stopped to ask us directions. We noticed that when the question was asked in Hebrew, the tone was abrupt, even harsh. However, if the Israeli suspected we were foreigners and he spoke in English, the voice was more affable and accompanied by what Westerners call courtesy. We made a similar observation in Yemen. Although the Arabic language is rich with polite expressions and words of courtesy, these were noticeably lacking on the street and among strangers.

A person's tone of voice often has more significance to the listener than the actual words. Initially I thought the Yemenis argued and bickered a lot; at least, it sounded like argument to me. Arabic speakers told me, however, that the Yemenis were merely "discussing" something.

At the advanced age of twenty Kathy had a favorite toy—a hedgehog hand puppet that Uncle Dan and Aunt Nancy had given her for Christmas. It was a unique puppet, fuzzy, with realistic features including its cute little nose. During the holidays that year the whole family traveled to Egypt. Returning to the hotel after a day of sight seeing, Kathy discovered the hedgehog was missing. All of us had played with it, taking turns like children and entertaining each other. We couldn't leave Egypt without it.

My first attempt to find the puppet was a pathetic failure. How do you describe a make-believe hedgehog? And how do you explain what a hand puppet is—over the telephone? The housekeeper on the other end of the line was pointedly silent while I babbled. She finally told me in halting English to call someone else. I did. I called Art into service.

He went directly to the front desk, described the missing item and suggested that someone check the laundry room, and specifically, the sheets that had come off of Kathy's bed. The assistant manager of the hotel spoke excellent English but even so…a hedgehog hand puppet? But he followed up on Art's suggestion that perhaps "the toy" was lost in the bedding. It was. Soon Kathy was reunited with her—and our—favorite plaything. The hedgehog remains our number one challenge in the descriptive vocabulary category.

Insha'Allah is a constantly used phrase in the Arab world, but it can be confusing to foreigners. I was familiar with the words before we went to Yemen and I knew the translation was "God willing" but I didn't truly understand the meaning for a long time.

Lady Bird Johnson used to proclaim, "Lord willin' and the creek don't rise." That old-fashioned southern expression is accepted as a half-humorous/half-serious response to a question that requires a yes or no answer. But there was no doubt that Mrs. Johnson was saying "yes."

When I said to a Yemeni, "We would like to have you join us for lunch on Saturday," the answer was always *"Insha'Allah."* Was that a yes or a no? Or did the Arab mean "maybe—if God wills it." I could understand God having the final say-so, but did the Yemeni *want* to come to lunch or not? The advice from those more familiar with the language and the culture was, "Yes, you may assume the invitee will come."

I could easily fathom the cultural custom of deferring to the will of God; whether or not the creek rises may also be God's will. What I had to learn was that *insha'Allah* was not a matter of Arabic vocabulary and it had nothing to do with yes, no, or maybe. The expression was a result of a religious observance. I was able to understand *insha'Allah*—and to accept it as a response—only after I read the translation from the *Quran* (Koran): "Do not say of anything: 'I will do it tomorrow' without adding 'If God wills.'" Period.

For those of us who lack the speaking-in-tongues gene, learning a new language can be painfully slow and enormously time-consuming. The best proven method is to concentrate only on the language, forsaking all but the most necessary chores and obligations. Leave the dust-bunnies under the bed, let the faucet drip, lock up the Robert Ludlum mystery, forsake cookie baking and gardening and definitely don't go to work. The language class has to be your only office; outside the classroom an audio tape and lesson book must be your constant companions.

Sure. For the diplomat or military person or anyone whose paycheck ultimately depends on relative success in speaking the foreign tongue, the foregoing requisites can be adhered to. For the female spouse, however, there may be other, more challenging time constraints to deal with. The baby must be fed and tended to and the laundry won't wash itself. And paying for several months of child care on a young officer's salary is just not do-able.

If the kids are in school and mom can manage to attend language classes, there are still music lessons and dentist appointments and sports schedules and somebody has to drive. Grocery shopping is essential. Cooking and dishwashing are necessities that can't be avoided unless your ship comes in and brings you a full-time housekeeper.

I could let the weeds and aphids devour my flowers while I was studying and I could ignore the dust bunnies until they grew to be full sized rabbits. I could listen to my language tape while I washed pots and pans and wiped Kool-Aid off the kitchen floor. I could practice vocabulary words with the kids while we were to-ing and fro-ing in the car. I could pop frozen pot pies in the oven to bake while I folded laundry and dreamed of gourmet creations I would cook if each day had twenty-seven hours.

What I couldn't do was avoid ironing. Art needed shirts and taking them to a commercial laundry was an extravagance that wasn't in our budget. (Sure he could iron, but I preferred that chore to changing the oil in the car or cleaning the leaves out of the gutters.) I couldn't *not* take Alex to browse through the new skateboard store and I couldn't miss shopping with Kathy for a prom dress. At birthday times there were still the from-scratch cakes to make and decorate according to someone's specifications. I couldn't disappoint the birthday boy or girl (or husband) because I had sentences to memorize.

To say that I'm not bilingual would be stating the obvious. I'm not fluent in any of the foreign languages I have pursued—and there have been six. But I have gained immeasurably from studying each one: communication skills, a better understanding of the workings of my own language, windows into new cultures, necessary shopping aids and enormous personal satisfaction. I can't imagine living in a country without knowing something of its language.

I prefer to risk embarrassing blunders such as "I am so sorry you came this evening" (which I cheerfully told a dinner guest in German) rather than not study languages at all.

In an International Herald Tribune interview by Carol Krucoff, gifted linguist Charles Berlitz said, "Knowing just one language is like living in a huge, wonderful house and never leaving one room."

10

THE MERMAID AND THE MAGIC

There is something magical about Copenhagen. It's not only the beguiling petite mermaid who sits alone out in the harbor or the spirit of Hans Christian Andersen that dwells in the soul of the city. It's not just Tivoli, which combines the noisy laughter of an amusement park with the peaceful beauty of lush colorful landscaping and elegant theaters. It's more than the *stroget,* the walkway that draws strolling citizens as well as curious tourists along its pedestrian lanes adorned with shops, cafes and salons whose sights, smells and flavors envelope you snugly into the Danish atmosphere.

There is a magic that goes beyond the monarchy and its majestic palaces, the intriguing museums, the Royal Theater, the quaint canals and all the charm and freshness of the city. I can't explain it—but I felt it.

After our sojourn in Bonn we spent the next four years in Washington on the outer fringes of the diplomatic scene. It was good being home, closer to our family and in sync with our own culture. By 1980, however, we were eager for our next foreign posting and we itched to bring the suitcases down from the attic. Because that's the way it is with Foreign Service people.

Spring brought the welcome news of Art's assignment to the embassy in Denmark as Deputy Chief of Mission, the number two slot. This was the Big Time: career advancement for Art, more responsibility for both of us—and certainly a lot of fun. I remember thinking—more than once—now *I'll have to behave!* I'll be expected to do certain things because I'm the DCM's wife and I'll have to refrain from doing other things for the same reason.

Art and Kathy and I arrived in Copenhagen on a warm June morning—but our luggage didn't. Ambassador Warren Manshel and his wife, Anita, had invited us to a dinner they were hosting that evening in honor of Foreign Minister Kjeld

Olesen. We had packed appropriate clothing for the black tie affair but Art's tuxedo and my evening dress were in a suitcase that somehow had gone astray.

Toini, the house's long-time Finnish housekeeper, met us at the front door of our new home. When she heard of the luggage dilemma she responded calmly. "You don't worry, I fix." (And she would continue to be a fixer throughout our stay in Denmark.) We stripped off our traveling clothes, left them in bundles outside our bedroom doors and climbed baby-naked into our beds for a nap. Not only were we jet-lagged but our energy and enthusiasm, which had been working overtime, had suddenly peaked and plummeted.

We awoke to clean underwear, blouses and dress shirt freshly washed and ironed and suits that had been brushed and pressed. Art's suit would suffice for the evening but mine consisted of a jacket and pants—definitely not suitable for a formal dinner. Neither was the straw hat I had worn.

Not to worry. Chuck and Janet, the embassy couple who had met us at the airport, found a solution while we slept. They borrowed an entire outfit for me: silk dress, shoes, pantyhose, evening bag and a matching umbrella! They had surmised I was about the same size and height as Judy, another embassy spouse, and they were right. Her clothes fit me perfectly and I was quite presentable at the Ambassador's soiree. Our luggage, thankfully, was delivered later that night.

Walking home after the dinner—we lived only a few blocks from Rydhave, the ambassador's residence—Art and I could still see a faint illumination in the sky. Danes had told us that in summer the night never becomes completely dark. That information was followed by apologetic warnings about winter when daylight lasts only a few hours. I soon discovered that the Danish people were somewhat obsessed with their country's climate.

"You've just arrived? Ah…then you haven't experienced one of our Danish winters…" This foreboding comment was frequent and I almost expected it to be followed by "Just you wait!" The accompanying regretful facial expression always gave way to a shake of the head, a quick intake of breath—a reversed sigh it seemed to be—that only a Dane can do while saying "Ja!"

We lived in a charming two-story frame house with large elegant rooms that were perfect for entertaining, but it was also a cozy comfortable family home. In addition to the grand staircase in the front hall, there was another stairway that led from the bedrooms down to the kitchen. Fourteen-year-old Kathy loved to scoot down the back stairs while we were entertaining, fill her dinner plate in the kitchen, hang about and listen to the conversations coming from the dining room.

The large living room that we called our "sun room" jutted out toward the east—its three sides surrounded by huge full-length windows. French doors opened onto the terrace and stairs led down to a patio and lovely gardens. We had roses, dahlias, baby's breath, numerous flowers I couldn't name, plus a lilac bush. There was also a plot ready for our first experiment in potato growing.

From the elevated position of the sunroom we could look past the end of our property across a busy road and out into the Sound, the *Oeresund.* The view was even more spectacular from our bedroom. Beyond the trees we could see sailboats passing by and watch the colorful figures of wind-surfers skipping over the water. At night when there were no traffic sounds we often heard the hum of ships' engines.

The American government bought the stately white house on the old Strand-vej (Beach Road) after World War II and it has since been the DCM residence. Many of the Danes whom we came to know had visited our predecessors over the years and they delighted in telling us the history of the house. We heard that Nazi officers occupied the property during the war and kept prisoners chained in the basement. The most colorful storytellers warned us of the strange sounds we might hear from the far corners of the cellar—ghosts still haunted the place.

After hearing these tales I thoroughly but carefully investigated the unfinished parts of the basement. I found some old pots and pans, a huge plastic jack-o-lantern and bits and pieces of trash, but no sign of unhappy spirits. I hoped that if any still resided there beneath us, they would know that we weren't to blame for their incarceration.

While Art settled in to his new job as the ambassador's deputy with its inherently long full workdays, Kathy and I took advantage of the lull before our HHE arrived and the unpacking began. We became acquainted with the buses and trams and explored the city. We walked and gawked and played and talked. My daughter was wonderful company.

Our nest had shrunk by 25 percent. Alex graduated from high school before we left for Denmark and he decided to stay in the States and work until fall classes began at the University of Nebraska. I missed him dreadfully and thought it unfair for a mother to be separated from her son for six long months. We wouldn't see him again until the Christmas holidays.

Several times during our first weeks in Copenhagen Kathy remarked to me knowingly, "I see we're having a guest for dinner again." I was so accustomed to my family of four that I frequently set a place for Alex at the dinner table.

The World Conference of the United Nations Decade for Women convened in Copenhagen that July with representatives from 136 countries. Not only did 2300 official delegates descend upon the city but another 6000 women took part in the parallel conference, the Non-Governmental Organization Forum.

The ambassador gave a welcoming reception for the American delegation. The "hat lady," Bella Abzug—better known as the congresswoman from New York—wore a big floppy hat, plain but gorgeous in my eyes. Betty Friedan was a delegate as was Lynda Bird Johnson Robb. Ms. Robb was there, not as the daughter of a former President or wife of a future governor and senator, but as an active participant in the conference.

Kathy and I joined the masses of unofficial but eager attendees for several sessions of the Forum. We became totally caught up in the complex issues the women talked over, argued about, and fought for. We learned about female "circumcision" for the first time and we were horrified. The practice, now more commonly called genital mutilation, continues today in Africa and elsewhere, in spite of the fight against it.

The Arab/Israeli dilemma was one of the most volatile subjects under "discussion." Many of the Arab women equated Zionism with racism while a number of Jewish women railed against the terrorist tactics of the PLO (Palestine Liberation Organization). Initially we were appalled at the angry outbursts and verbal battles, but we couldn't help but be impressed by the dedication of the speakers. Unfortunately there was more talking and shouting than listening.

Jihan Sadat of Egypt was a panelist at one of the sessions. When she took her place, a large contingent of Arab women stood up and stormed out of the auditorium. In spite of the sporadic hissing and booing from a few members of the remaining audience, Mrs. Sadat courageously defended her husband Anwar Sadat and their country's decision to participate in the Camp David accords of 1978.

The conference was a formative experience for my daughter. She has always remembered the women talking, arguing, and shouting. "But they wouldn't listen to each other!" She pursued women's studies in college.

Among the delegates to the official conference—as well as within the Forum—there *were* areas of agreement. Women from all over the world denounced discrimination based on race as well as gender. They proposed several resolutions promoting the status, health and well being of women and they called on the UN to increase its budget for women's projects. That was 1980.

KISS was our next challenge. The Danish acronym stood for Copenhagen intensive language school. Kathy and I signed up for Danish classes hoping to learn the difficult pronunciation and at least the bare bones of grammar. Intensive it was: classes three mornings a week and many many hours of homework. Unfortunately, when we attempted to practice what we had learned Danes invariably spoke to us in English. We can still spout a few of the dialogues we memorized: "*Har du et ringbing?*" and "*Ja, det har jeg.*" These days, however, I don't have any opportunity to ask about someone's notebook in Danish.

While we worked hard in class we also worked up a hunger that could only be satisfied by stopping at a bakery after our lesson. We habitually bought a loaf of bread for lunch—a large loaf so we could eat half of it on the bus-ride home. Sometimes, we bought a bag of *wienerbrod* and then we had to skip lunch. The delicate sweet pastries were called "Vienna bread" because they were patterned after those created in the Austrian city long ago.

Wienerbrod should not be confused with American sweet rolls called "Danish;" they are not at all comparable. Authentic Danish pastry has no equal. (Except maybe in Vienna. Maybe.) These luscious buttery flaky rolls made in various shapes and sizes may be lightly studded with nuts and glazed by a hint of icing, or subtly accented with sweet/tart fruit, or filled with tasty custard, whipped cream or cheese. But it was the pastry that starred; the toppings and fillings were secondary.

A short walk from home we found lovely sandy beaches heavily populated with golden tanned bodies. Even on cold breezy days, if the sun was shining, the Danes were basking. On our first visit to the beach I was notably conspicuous in my one-piece swimsuit. Although the other females wore one piece, it covered only the bottom portion of their torsos—they wore nothing on the top. The Danes stared at us, clearly foreigners, so I *had* to buy a two-piece outfit. The next time Kathy and I went to the beach we removed our tops as soon as we got there and attempted to look native. No one paid us a bit of attention. We became quite comfortable among the strangers on the sand.

One weekend the three of us walked north along the beach to get acquainted with the area. We strolled and looked out at the water until—heads suddenly popped up from sand and blankets and turned in our direction. We realized with a jolt that all the swimmers and sunbathers on that stretch of beach were naked! Feeling like trespassers, we quickly backtracked. I found it curious that the majority of bathers at the nude beach were middle-aged and elderly, and there were more men nudists than women. On all the beaches there was an air of complete ease and comfort.

Tom, an oil company friend from Dallas, told us about his friend who went to Denmark to work for the A.P. Moeller company. The man drove all night from wherever he had come and hit the outskirts of Copenhagen just as the sun was peeking up. He parked his car and walked along a beach to stretch his legs and enjoy the sunrise. Tired from his long drive, he decided to lay down and rest on the soft sand.

When he awoke several hours later he thought he must have slipped through the pearly gates: on either side of him was the bronzed body of a woman—completely nude. It was a pleasant welcome to Denmark.

While we were between ambassadors in the spring, Art and I hosted a reception at Rydhave for a female Danish accordion band. The young musicians were set to tour the United States and we wanted to give them a friendly American send-off. It was a warm sparkling day and we offered drinks and hors d'oeuvres in the garden.

A few weeks later we found out that several of the accordion players had a spot of misfortune in a Midwestern town—they were arrested! The musicians were out walking, enjoying spring weather that was much warmer than in Denmark, when they came upon a park. Being typical Danes, they loved the sun—so off went their blouses and whatever was underneath, if anything, and they lay down in the grass to sun bathe. They were charged with indecent exposure. But the young ladies didn't remain in jail long. They convinced the authorities that they were innocently unfamiliar with local laws. They were Danish—doing what Danes do on a sunny day.

George Ballanchine came to Copenhagen with his New York City Ballet and charmed the Danes with his extraordinary choreography. Although Mr. B always said his company had no stars and no prima ballerinas (programs consistently listed the dancers in alphabetical order) Peter Martins definitely shone brightly at every performance. He was Danish and he dazzled his hometown audiences. (He would later become Artistic Director of the company.)

Following City Ballet's opening night at Tivoli, Ambassador and Mrs. Manshel hosted a party in honor of the company at a discotheque called "Daddy's Dance Hall." Danish food was abundant and American-style hamburgers were cooked to order by the local Burger King. Several hundred happy invitees ate, drank and merrily danced until early morning. The absence of Ballanchine and Martins was disappointing but it didn't deter anyone from having a splendid time. The City Ballet dancers were fun to talk to and Art and I enjoyed their disco-dancing almost as much as their ballet performance earlier in the evening.

Denmark was synonymous with DANCE—at least it seemed so to me. Never before had we had the opportunity to see so many magnificent performances—nor to meet dancers and learn about their lives as well as their careers. The Royal Danish Ballet featured boyishly handsome, curly-haired Frank Andersen as a perfect Puck in *A Midsummer Night's Dream*. And Liz Jeppesen with her big beautiful eyes was delightful in *Coppelia*. I was partial to Niels Kehlet and Johnny Eliasen (perhaps because I met them both) who danced and played the buffoons in *Kermesse i Brugges*, a delightful Bournenville ballet.

But no other performance in Copenhagen—or elsewhere—has ever awed and enchanted me like that of ballerina Maja Plisetskaja from Moscow's Bolshoi Theater when she danced *The Dying Swan*. It was the most beautiful dance and the most emotion-evoking performance I have ever seen.

Artist Inge-Lise Koefoed was one of our first Danish friends. Her unglazed porcelain relief, aptly named "Vibrations," was Denmark's gift to the Kennedy Center for the Performing Arts in 1976. Blond, pretty and petite, Inge-Lise had a dancer's soft fluid movement in her walk. And when she talked about her work she moved her hands in graceful circular expressions as she interpreted her art forms.

After lunch together one day Inge-Lise gave me a tour of her studio. She explained her sources of inspiration by showing me the many scattered collections of what she called "nature's free offerings." As we looked at a seashell, then a bird's feather, she talked about the circles of life, the beauty of motion, and "the music we find in nature." These themes were apparent in her paintings, her sculptures and in the collages that she accented with rice paper. She used similar motifs in the designs she created for the exquisite porcelain lidded boxes for Royal Copenhagen Porcelain.

Inge-Lise invited us to a party she was hosting with Gabriella and Henrik, the director of the Royal Theater. The party was casual and crowded, everyone mingling and circulating, talking and laughing. In some cultures the guests, women especially, find a chair, settle in, and remain in the same spot all evening. Not the Danes—they're friendly gregarious people. The occasion resembled an American potluck supper; we each brought a bit of food and a bottle of wine to share.

Among the guests was writer Anders Bodelsen who told us about the filming of one of his novels, a mystery. The movie *Silent Partner* starred Donald Sutherland. Anders wasn't happy about the changes the producers had made in his story. I later saw the movie on television but I had some difficulty following the suspense—it was dubbed in Danish.

Niels Kehlet, a dancer who was well known for his high leaps and his peren-nial good cheer had been a classmate of Inge-Lise's. During the party we heard several people offer him congratulations and in answer to our question we learned that he had been dancing with the Royal Danish Ballet for 25 years. A few weeks later we attended the special performance at the Royal Theater in honor of Niels' diamond jubilee.

Inge-Lise also introduced us to a photographer named Jan van Steenwijk. After traveling for three months through 29 American states he returned to Copenhagen and published a book called *Always on the Road*. His splendid color-ful photos of streets, roads and highways leading to the beauty of America are accompanied by his thoughtful, almost poetic text.

In Copenhagen we had our first night watchman—he came with the job. Pre-viously I had thought security was something to worry about only in other parts of the world, in far-away scary places where dictators ruled or armed insurgents were the norm. By the 1980's, however, the State Department was focusing on personal safety at all of its posts.

The security man circled our house, making certain the doors and ground-floor windows were locked, and then he walked the parameters of the prop-erty—three times every night. I was taking a late evening stroll through our gar-den the first time I saw him. When I walked back to the house, I couldn't get in; he had locked the back door even though he knew I was outside. Though I appreciated the man's dedication to his work, I thought he was overdoing it somewhat. I had to ring the doorbell long and hard to awaken Art who was not pleased that I had "locked myself out." I learned to carry a house-key.

It took a little time for me to get used to the guard's nightly routine. With our bedroom windows open I could hear his boots crunching over the gravel in the front of the house. I was never a sound sleeper and during the night in my half-awake state, I sometimes anticipated the watchman's arrival and departure. I would check my bedside clock to see if he was on time.

One night my internal worry-bell pealed: wasn't the guard *too* predictable? If *I* knew his routine, wouldn't a potential intruder also be able to learn his schedule? The next morning I explained my concerns to Art, knowing that he had no idea when the watchman came and went. "Hmmm…" he said in diplomatese. "Per-haps his watch schedule is not in our best interests."

Shortly thereafter I noticed that the security visits were no longer routine, but random.

Along with the rank and the unique privileges of the DCM position came also the responsibilities we had anticipated, including entertaining. Not only bigger—but more. Representational dinners were frightening and intimidating at first, perhaps because they were more formal in Copenhagen than at our previous posts. And after four years in Washington I was out of practice. I was a Nervous Nellie before our first sit-down dinner for twenty-four but Toini talked and walked me through it and helped to allay the panic that threatened to immobilize me at "show time."

I learned a lot under Toini's tutelage. Until Denmark I had never had help with the major cooking so leaving the final meal preparation to someone else—in *my* kitchen—took some major mind-set adjustments. I soon discovered, however, that having Toini and her husband Erik at the wheel was almost as good as autopilot. Toini always encouraged me to have a "*lille* rest" and take a long bath before our evening events. I later realized she wanted me out of the kitchen so she could work without my fussing and nervous pacing.

Erik was a Dane who worked for the Customs Department by day and hired out as a waiter by night. As soon as Art and I set a date for any kind of party, dinner or reception at home, Erik arranged for the additional bartenders, waiters and kitchen help. At the end of the event, Erik made a list of the liquor, mixes, juice and soft drinks that had been consumed and advised me if we were running low on any supplies.

Toini and I planned the menus together, I did the shopping, and we shared the cooking. After the guests arrived, I seldom needed to return to the kitchen. She was responsible for finishing the main course and arranging the food on the serving platters—which she did beautifully—and instructing the waiters.

I usually made the desserts but there was one specialty that only Toini could prepare: Baked Alaska. It was the sparkling climax on many special occasions. Erik turned off the dining room lights just before he and the other waiters brought in the elegant desserts—flaming and expertly presented. The drama never failed to hush our guests and then to produce that now-familiar combination of breath intake and sigh from the Danish women.

After numerous dinners, lunches and cocktail receptions I began to feel like a pro and my former persona, Nervous Nellie, was replaced by that of "Perle Mesta of the North" (at least in my own eyes.) There was one party, however, which caused me to take a lot of deep breaths and I didn't have time for one of Toini's "*lille*" rests.

We hosted a farewell dinner for our friends and colleagues, Sonja and Walt. Their guest list included a Danish school friend of Sonja's, Ida Davidson—the very same Ida Davidson who owned a well-known restaurant in Copenhagen! That fact alone was enough to give me the vapors, but when I found out that Toini and Erik would be on vacation—which meant that I would be doing *all* the cooking—that's when the deep breathing exercises began.

I spent three days preparing the food, which included labor-intensive rolled stuffed round steaks with a Dijon cream sauce. I knew the meal would be good and attractive and properly served, but when the curtain went up, my self-confidence hid in the wings. Nervous Nellie returned. The arrival of Ms. Davidson, however, calmed most of my fears. She was a warm friendly woman and didn't appear to be the type who would roll her eyes or grimace upon tasting my food. The event played itself out smoothly and the evening was successful. Before she left the restaurateur complimented me on the meal and I felt as though I had taken a curtain call.

The Permanent Secretary for Greenlandic Affairs, Erik Hesselberg, was our guest of honor one evening. He had a keen sense of humor and I always enjoyed talking with him. The dinner plates had been removed and we were waiting for dessert when I was struck with a dreadful realization—one that caused me to bite my lip in mid-sentence. Mr. Hesselberg had diabetes. I don't remember what I had made for dessert that night but it was definitely something sweet—and definitely forbidden for this guest.

As if I had sent a telepathic message, Erik Rasmussen appeared at that exact moment and served the secretary an attractive colorful plate of mixed fruit. I had to concentrate hard to keep my face from showing relieved surprise. Mr. Hesselberg, smiling broadly, gave my hand a pat and said, "Thank you for remembering that I am diabetic." It was Toini and Erik who remembered—just in time.

Marion, the Canadian ambassador, was seated next to Art at another of our dinners. After dessert Art drew my attention across the table and by using a bit of unorthodox sign language, he implied that we were ready to leave the table. The more he motioned, the more vigorously I shook my head.

When Ambassador MacPherson noticed Art's befuddlement she gave him a nudge with her elbow. "There's another course coming, Art," she informed him, pointing out the cutlery that still lay horizontally and unused at the top of each place setting. Art was accustomed to having dessert as the meal finale and had forgotten that I had decided to finish with a cheese course that evening.

As the cheese and crackers came around, Marion chuckled and told Art: "Stick with me, kid, and you'll do all right!"

When we finished eating, Art always repeated the ritual Danish word "*Velbekommen*" to signal the diners to follow their host to the next phase of the evening—which was usually coffee in another room. As the guests left the dining room they passed by the hostess—who had positioned herself in a strategic spot—and each continued the tradition by saying "*Tak for mad.*" Thank you for the meal.

Another delightful old Danish custom was one Art and I have continued to observe because we find it so endearing. According to tradition a man must attract the attention of his wife or partner during a dinner party—even if they are seated far across the room from each other. As their eyes meet, he lifts his glass in a silent toast to her alone. The woman then responds by raising her glass to him. If the gentleman fails to remember his lady in this manner—alas—he is required to buy her a pair of gloves at the first opportunity. (Art had to buy me a pair of gloves—but only once.)

At certain functions it was customary to toast the Danish monarch. Still, I thought it was a bit odd when an American military attaché asked us to observe the ritual. Bill and Pat had invited friends to an elegant dinner party in celebration of their silver wedding anniversary.

As everyone stood up Bill lifted his glass and said solemnly, "To the queen…" Before the rest of us could respond he turned to his wife and continued "…to the queen of my heart."

Winter came with its long hours of darkness but the season wasn't "awful," as some Danes had gloomily predicted. By December our lights and lamps were on throughout the day; the mere four to five hours of daylight were often shadowy and hazy. But never had I loved candlelight so much as that first winter. Though we had often used candles on our dinner table at home, the Danes showed us how the glow brightened one's humor as well as one's house on a dark cold day. A home alight with candles was *hyggelig*—cozy, snug, comfortable and friendly.

Perhaps it was because of the darkness that the Christmas season was so special in Denmark. The Danes illuminated the holidays not only with candles, but with brightly colored decorations, exquisitely cut hanging mobiles, sparkling trimmed trees and red hearts everywhere. Bodies as well as spirits kept warm with hot mulled red wine called *glogg*.

The American Women's Group was alive and well and active in Copenhagen. Traditionally the club's Christmas party was held in the DCM's residence and I was delighted to continue the custom. The house was an ideal setting for such events; we had a piano and lots of space. Enough room, in fact, for two Christmas trees.

A committee furnished cookies and other treats and brought the *gløgg* ingredients, which Toini whipped together and heated in large pots on our stove. Imagine one hundred-plus women, carols ringing from the piano, happy voices, candles aglow and the aroma of spiced wine—intoxicating the senses! Still today when I smell mulled wine my heart longs for Christmas in Denmark.

Ronald Reagan's first inauguration turned into an excuse for Danish protesters to show their displeasure with the United States. Just as Art was leaving the embassy garage that January day in 1981, he spotted a group of fifty-some people swarming across the street and converging onto the sidewalk and steps of our building. Art radioed inside to the Marines; they were already alerted and had notified the police.

Many of the demonstrators had painted their faces to look like cadavers. They lay down in front of the embassy doors and simulated death—complete with "blood" dripping from their mouths. Some lay on top of their comrades to portray stacks of bodies. Others carried lit torches and the remainder held placards painted with the years during which—they purported—the United States was the aggressor/invader of innocent countries in South America.

Art parked his car down the street and then approached the lone policeman who was standing on the fringes of the crowd. "Do these demonstrators have a permit?" Art asked. The answer was "No."

"Then ask them to leave—they're blocking access to the embassy." The officer replied that it was not a good idea at that time—he would wait until his superior arrived. Art was not satisfied with that response but there was nothing he could do at the moment except wait. Until—he detected a concerted movement among the protesters and saw eyes looking up at the Stars and Stripes. Our flagpole was situated just outside the front doors of the embassy.

With his two-way radio my husband called Post I, the Marine Guard station inside the front lobby. "Send some Marines out here right away. They should stand next to the flagpole—at parade rest. But don't let 'em get the flag!" Immediately two Marines in riot gear (flack vests and helmets) rushed out the doors and took up position at the flagpole. The mob shied away.

Additional policemen soon arrived and ordered the demonstrators to leave. The response was slow, but when the officers began to pull some of the "bodies" to their feet the crowd gradually moved away.

Art later told me about the advisory that circulated among security and intelligence people: watch out for protesters with baby carriages. That meant they carried a supply of beer—not babies—and the demonstration would be long.

The climax to that day was the superb news that our colleagues had been released from their imprisonment in the American Embassy in Tehran.

"The life of a diplomat is full of intrigue and fine dinners." As far back as the year 1140, traveling emissaries appreciated good food. The quote comes from *The Devil's Novice*, a Brother Cadfael mystery by Ellis Peters. Though the intrigue is questionable I heartily concur with the fine dinners. More than eight centuries later Art and I were humming with satisfaction over the good food we encountered along with our diplomatic duties.

Ambassador Manshel enjoyed his fine dinners, also. At a farewell lunch given by the Ministry of Foreign Affairs, the ambassador spoke of his fondness for the Danish people and their country.

"And I'll be taking a part of Denmark home with me," he remarked as he patted both hands over his midsection. "About fifteen pounds worth!"

My favorite meals consisted of *smorrebrod*, perhaps because they delighted the eye as well as the palette. In fact, the overall appearance of the Danish table was eminently important. The flowers and candles, fresh linens and bright dinnerware—all were color-coordinated and designed to show off the food.

The word *smorrebrod* means buttered bread, but less literally it connotes openfaced sandwiches. Each began with the bread, good solid bread (not the pre-sliced fluffy American variety), and can be white or any variety of rye, thickly spread to the very edges with butter. On this standard base the toppings were exquisitely created, assembled and meticulously garnished. Mind you, the garnish was more than a frill of parsley or a sprinkle of paprika—it was an integral enhancer of the sandwich.

The fish *smorrebrod* usually came first or on a different tray from the other varieties. The herring (smoked, marinated or creamed) were accompanied by an icy-cold draught of akvavit—which means "water of life"—and washed down with beer. Sometimes there were also smoked salmon and smoked trout, but always there were shrimp *smorrebrod*. Tiny pink curls—most probably from Greenland—mounded high over the bread, sprinkled with feathery fresh dill and topped with a lemon twist.

Alex's friends at home had never heard of a shrimp sandwich and were a bit leery of his description—especially his claim that the best were to be found at the airport. Alex always ate a shrimp *smorrebrod* while waiting for his departure call.

I can still picture the colorful inviting array of *smorrebrod* artfully laid out on huge platters—they begged to be admired before consumed. Thinly cut roast beef was topped with crunchy fried onions or freshly grated horseradish. The pork loin was best with pieces of pickled beet or sweet and sour shredded red cabbage. Triangles of cheese sported thin rounds of colorful radish or cucumber. Overlapping slices of hard-cooked egg were often topped with Danish caviar.

A spoonful of remoulade was sometimes centered over a cold cut and creamy Italian salad skirted the edge of a roll of ham. Thin pieces of salami had a decoration of onion rings and slivers of tomato. Sliced breast of duck or chicken came with various dollops of salads or sauces. And these were only a few of the possibilities. Ida Davidson's restaurant offered more than 200 choices of *smorrebrod*.

Denmark consists of one peninsula and hundreds of islands between the North and the Baltic Seas so it's not surprising that seafood had a habitual place on the family menus of the five million inhabitants. Salmon, red snapper, plaice, cod and other varieties were poached, baked, fried or sautéed in butter. The Danish standard bearer, however, was a cured rather than a cooked salmon.

Gravad laks began with a large filet of fresh salmon generously covered with salt, pepper, sugar and fresh dill and then left to marinate for several days. When it was ready, the fish was sliced extra thinly and served with a special honey-mustard and lots of bread. (To be fair to Denmark's neighbors I have to add that the other Scandinavian countries make their own versions of *gravad laks*.)

Meatballs called *frikadeller* were unique and best without any sauce to enjoy the delicate flavors. Made from ground pork and veal, the balls could be large and than sliced for *smorrebrod* but usually they were bite-sized and eaten as an appetizer. Though some recipes used milk or cream Toini said true *frikadeller* were made with *Dansk vand*, the local fizzy mineral water nicknamed "Danish water."

Danish ducks were the best I'd ever eaten. Toini roasted them to a crispy brown finish and made a tasty sauce (in Europe gravy is called sauce) to which she added red wine and orange zest. I still remember her rotating the ducks one by one over the burner of our gas stove to scorch off the pinfeathers—and occasionally scorching a finger or two.

Now and then we purchased delicious smoked ducks that came with a fiery red sauce. *Sprengt and* was duck cured in brine before cooking and Danes ate it with a potent horseradish sauce. Very few of Denmark's gastronomic delights were spicy but when the food was hot, it was *very* hot.

When Ambassador Manshel left Denmark to return to private life in New York, Art became *chargé d'affaires*. He remained in charge of the embassy until the new ambassador arrived seven months later. Through obligations and invitations—all in the name of work—we saw a great deal of Denmark and met a great number of Danes. Sometimes the work was so enjoyable we almost felt guilty for accepting Art's paycheck. Almost.

In May we joined the annual excursion hosted by the Danish Foreign Ministry for heads of missions and their spouses. We visited the northwestern part of the country touring an area along the North Sea and inland around the Limfjord. From church to castle, from open-air museum to modern factory we looked and listened and learned.

We arrived mid-morning at Hjerl Hede, the "Old Village" made of reconstructed buildings representing moorland life in earlier centuries. Coffee, tea and luscious *wienerbrod* were waiting for us. Our hosts urged us to eat something—lest we become hungry before the next sumptuous meal. They made certain that no tummies at any time went unstuffed.

Before the aforementioned second breakfast we drank a tot of bitter-tasting Gammel Dansk. Made from orange rowanberries, the dark liqueur was called "Old Danish"—and it certainly tasted old. The Danes said, "Start the day with a Gammel Dansk and you'll feel well and strong all day." They also admitted that "maybe" the taste has to grow on you. I thought "maybe" by the time you're old, you can't taste it any more!

The Foreign Ministry people treated us more like royalty than diplomats throughout our two-day trip, which was crowned by an evening dinner-dance hosted by Foreign Minister Kjeld Olesen and his wife Hanne. (The following year—alas—we weren't invited; the new ambassador took our place.)

Denmark's Queen Margrethe was the first monarch we met, our first true royal. I could be very sophisticated about my reactions and describe the meeting as an everyday occurrence but I won't because it wasn't. (I could also say it was one of the perks of the job; it was but I won't.) The events surrounding the royal handshake were what made it special and memorable.

We traveled to the peninsula of Jutland for the annual July Fourth Rebild Festival, which brings together thousands of Americans and Danes from both countries and elsewhere. The city of Aalborg fills with visitors for several days of merry-making and patriotic celebrations organized by the Dansk Americansk Klub and the Rebild National Park Society headed at that time by Erik Emborg.

The first event was pure fun. The King Christian IV's Guild, boasting such famous members as Queen Margrethe, Ronald Reagan, Danny Kaye and Victor Borge, invited us to participate in a solemn secret induction ceremony. We soon learned that the only solemnity was in the origins of the Guild: it began as a clandestine social club during Nazi occupation and possibly harbored a few members of the resistance. After World War II membership grew to several thousand people from all over the globe.

Nick, the chief bencher, officiated with his clever mix of serious history and present-day humor. But I can't write any more about that because it was secret.

During the pre-membership rites one of the historical lessons of the Guild included a glass of mead. The fermented honey liqueur was a common beverage when Christian IV reigned in the first half of the seventeenth century. Fortified by our eye-opening drink of mead, we initiates had to weave our way snake-like through the city center—left hand on the right shoulder of the person in front and all the while singing "Auld Lang Syne" accompanied and led by a snare drum. Then back to the Guild house where the serious rites—that I can't explain because they were secret—were concluded and the fun part continued.

The long-time members treated the inductees to a morning snack of Danish *rode polser,* long skinny red sausages similar to hot dogs but so much better. Along with the *polser* came belts of akvavit, called *snaps.* When our mouths weren't full, we sang the goofy *snaps* song—again and again. "I like the *snaps* and the *snaps* likes me, thrilling as only a *snaps* can be…"

At the conclusion of the ceremonies each proud new Guild member received a "gold" key to the door of the old stone house that dates back to the era of King Christian IV. Whenever we return to Aalborg we can gain immediate entry to the meeting place of *our* Guild. I can't write any more about that, of course—except to say I keep my key in a most secret place.

This was our first visit to Aalborg and although we had a full program of activities we decided to make time for the livestock exhibit. Our family had always loved county and state fairs at home and here was an opportunity to see another facet of Danish life. Mr. Werner, however, couldn't fathom adding animal viewing to our schedule.

Jorgen Werner, a Dane who was the embassy protocol officer, accompanied us throughout most of the Rebild festivities. He interpreted for us when necessary and stood ready to remind us "who's who" in case we forgot a name or a face. He was thoroughly professional and embassy officers relied on him to know who the Danish players were in political as well as social situations. Jorgen was also a classic stuffed shirt—but one whom we became fond of.

When we actually went *into* the barns and *inside* the chicken coops and pigpens, Mr. Werner was aghast! I tried to placate him with the information that we had extra shoes in the car, but he continued to dither. We petted a few fuzzy lambs and spent some time watching the piglets nurse until our keeper said we really must drive on to Rebild. I think he was afraid the family of the acting ambassador would be seen up to our ankles in farm doo-doo.

The Fourth of July festival was named for the Rebild National Forest, a gorgeous wonder of nature with lush green hills and acres of tall trees. Somehow a natural bowl settled itself amongst the hills and rocks and became a perfect venue for the annual celebration. Tents perched on the rim—one was the dining hall and another served at the disposal of the royal family.

That was where we met Queen Margrethe. She was pretty; she was regal; she was glamorous—all that I had imagined a queen to be. She wore a chic spring coat in a pale pastel color. The matching brimmed hat tilted at an unusual angle over the left side of her head giving her a jaunty look.

The queen had invited the day's special guests and notables to a reception and since Art was the official representative of the American government, that included us. It was a heady experience. We shook hands with the Queen, her husband Prince Hendrik, and their two young sons. The royal family mingled among the guests making casual conversation but I was so bedazzled I couldn't speak—I just gaped.

Our children, following their own agenda, arrived at the queen's reception a bit later than Art and I. Alex remembers rehearsing over and over in his mind exactly what he was going to say to the monarch. He wanted his sister to "go first" but she was gripped by sudden shyness and she refused. Alex found moral support at hand, though, and asked Mr. Werner to introduce him to the queen. Our son was instantly overwhelmed by his own efforts to be polite *and* correct and his planned speech was reduced to, "Pleased to meet you, Your Majesty."

For both teenagers the Rebild experience was awesome. They were enormously impressed with their dad's clout as chargé and they enjoyed the attention that came their way because of his position. And dining with a Hollywood celebrity wrapped up the package with a pretty ribbon.

The celebrity, singer and actor Pat Boone, was an apt choice to be the American guest speaker for the festival. The theme was "Family" and he and his wife Shirley have four daughters. Boone's reputation as a wholesome family man and non-smoking teetotaler still followed him 25 years after he became a recording star in the mid-50's. Art and I met the Boones during the Guild initiation where they were having as much fun as we were. Shirley turned down the glass of mead but Pat quaffed it *and* the akvavit along with the rest of us.

When we gathered for lunch under the "big top"—hundreds of us—the singing began. There were innumerable toasts, and a rousing holiday spirit pervaded the tent and the hills around us. By the time the meal ended everyone knew the *snaps* song, every verse…"Please go to hell with your juice and tea—*snaps* is the drink for me!"

Mr. Boone cheerfully accommodated the autograph seekers, hand-shakers and groupies who surrounded him. At one end of the long lunch table was a bosomy coifed California woman who shouted across to the Boones: "My sister lives only three blocks from you and she says you're wonderful neighbors!" An elderly couple recalled to Pat that they had heard him sing "in person—back in 1960-something." Americans as well as Danes greeted him with, "Do you remember…" and "Oh, please sign this for us…"

Art and I were enormously impressed by the Boones who were genuine good sports. They participated in every activity of the festival with enthusiasm, humor and apparent pleasure. And although Mr. Boone didn't sing our kids' kind of music, they appreciated his stature as a popular and respected celebrity—and they thought he was cool. Alex took special note of the singer's white bucks and matching belt, California-style.

Everyone trekked over to the sun-sparkled stage for the afternoon's program of music and speeches. Thousands of already warmed-up patriotic voices sang the Danish and American national anthems. When it was Art's turn at the podium, he gave his opening remarks in Danish and read the Independence Day greetings from President Reagan in English. After he began speaking a group of young Danes silently stood up from their places on the hillside—exhibiting their T-shirts which read in Danish, one letter each, USA OUT OF EL SALVADOR. Although a few were more vocal against the United States, it was a quick and quiet protest. The festivities went on.

That evening back in Aalborg we all wanted to look spiffy for the formal banquet and dance. Mrs. M, the young wife of Boone's manager, took a liking to our daughter and asked if she could "do" Kathy's make-up and hair before the dinner. Art and I had typical parental reactions: I agreed and he frowned.

Kathy, who at the time envisioned a career in the entertainment world, thought she had *arrived* due to the attention she was getting. Mr. M advised her to find a good photographer and put together a portfolio of portraits. He told her, "If you ever want a career in Hollywood…" and he turned and diplomatically handed his business card to Art.

Mrs. M applied Kathy's make-up with a light hand and gave her advice on mascara, eyeliners and color. The results were subtle and I thought our daughter looked lovely with just the right hint of sophistication. When Art grumbled about the "rouge," I reminded him, "She's fifteen already!"

To which Art replied, "She's *barely* fifteen!"

I had sputtered the same riposte a few months earlier. In the spring Kathy irrevocably decided she would finish her last two years of high school in the States rather than Denmark. As parents we didn't want her to go away to boarding school, but we wanted to do what was best for her education.

I made an appointment with our Danish doctor for Kathy's physical exam, as required by her new school. When the forms were completed Dr. Berg leaned back in his big chair, folded his hands and looked at me—then at Kathy—then at me again.

"And what are we doing about birth control?" he asked bluntly. Kathy blushed and I blanched. Neither of us was prepared for such a question.

"I don't think we need to do *anything* right now," I replied defensively. "Kathy is barely fifteen!"

There were several "tsk-tsks" and then Dr. Berg told us he had two daughters and he gave them the Pill as soon as they were sixteen. He emphatically advised, "It's never too soon to be prepared." In 1981 the Danes were much more liberal in this area than were Americans.

When the Alvin Ailey American Dance Theater came to Copenhagen, Art and I hosted an opening night buffet-reception for the group at Rydhave, the ambassador's residence. The home was spacious and it seemed sensible to make use of the staff there, especially the cook who had been idle since Ambassador Manshel had left.

During the party Kathy approached Mr. Ailey nervously and, thrusting a program at him, blurted out, "My daddy is giving this party—and may I have your autograph?" She had only meant to identify herself but she was so awestruck her words came all atumble.

The king of choreography completely charmed her with his reply. "You could have my autograph—even if your daddy weren't giving the party."

When the time came for Kathy to leave for boarding school, we found the Alvin Ailey troupe at the airport—waiting for the same plane. They thanked us again for the party and promised to look after our daughter during the flight. I was a millimeter away from tears, but the good-byes were somewhat easier knowing that our teenage daughter would undoubtedly relish every minute of the trip—and she would have a good story to tell her friends.

As one left the nest, another returned. Alex didn't go back to the university that fall, he stayed in Denmark with us, working at the embassy and making friends. I was happy to continue setting three places at the dinner table.

In the Foreign Service as in many other careers and jobs, you can't choose your boss. You can't vote for the most genial supervisor or sign up to follow the smartest ambassador throughout your career. You can't even be assured you will work for the same chief throughout an assignment. Mostly, you do your best for whomever you work—even if you get a bad taste.

Art knew almost from the beginning that he would like working for Arthur Hartman a few years earlier. The boss called from his home one early morning and after giving my husband some instructions, Hartman remarked that he was looking out his window. The sprinkling system had mistakenly activated during the night and left a lake of water over his yard.

"I'm sitting here watching the birds on my grass." Art thought right then—any senior officer who took time out to watch the birds would be a good man to work for!

Art was fortunate with his Forrest Gump box of chocolates. He worked for some soft-centers, some semi-sweets, several tough chewy caramels who were hard to swallow—but he only worked for one nut.

An American President has the right to replace ambassadors and is not legally bound to appoint career people. Ambassador Manshel, chosen by Jimmy Carter, was not a Foreign Service Officer, but he was well-versed in foreign affairs. He proved to be an intelligent serious Chief of Mission who was respected by the Danes and by his staff at the embassy.

The same could not be said about Reagan's choice, the nut. Art received some covert information—warnings actually—about the new man before he arrived. We hoped Art's sources had exaggerated but the reports were unfortunately true. The new ambassador wasn't a sturdy hard-to-crack nut like a pistachio or Brazil nut. He was more like a chestnut—he had various layers and he needed a good roasting.

When Ambassador John Langeloth Loeb, Jr. landed in Copenhagen, he made a reasonably intelligent arrival statement. His subsequent remarks and comments and conversations, however, showed signs of a serious disconnect in his circuit board.

At a dinner party one evening honoring the visit of former President Jimmy Carter, Loeb made a rambling speech extolling the attributes of the Loeb family business. Forty-five dreary minutes later he concluded by saying, "I'm so glad to be here in Sweden!"

Carter was heard remarking quietly to his tablemates: "He won't keep this post long."

The Danish newspapers initially described Loeb as "charming" and "elegant" but subsequent journalistic reports left flattery behind. One paper quoted a "high" official in the Foreign Ministry: "He [Loeb] is the lowest Denmark has ever been offered by the USA." And he had only been there for ten months.

The earliest discovery about Loeb—and the biggest disappointment—was that he was not a serious ambassador. He knew little, nor cared, about foreign relations. Instead, sexual relations were uppermost in his mind—and other parts of his body. A parade of young attractive women sashayed in and out of Rydhave spending more time upstairs than downstairs. The housekeeper complained she couldn't get her usual work done when there was a female guest because she spent so much of her time "changing sheets."

Alex recognized one of the ambassador's houseguests and reported gleefully, "She's the Gong lady!" While my mind was struggling with his suspect adjective, Alex told me about an American television program called the "Gong Show." The ambassador's friend was allegedly the hostess, an early version of Vanna White.

Admittedly, the man shouldn't be criticized for wanting female companion-ship. He was single (twice married and twice divorced from the same woman) and Denmark was a liberal country. Danes didn't care who did what with whom as long as the sleepover was not adulterous.

But when the ambassador asked embassy employees, the CIA station chief for one, to procure "dates" for him, he not only stepped out of bounds, he sank into the muck. Apparently, Loeb believed that officers in the intelligence field were knowledgeable about—as well as accustomed to—sordidness. Art, as well as offic-ers Wes and Mike, reminded him repeatedly: "It's not appropriate for the Ameri-can ambassador to pick up women off the street."

Loeb made the unwise decision one day to show several visitors around the residence. He particularly enjoyed pointing out the framed pictures of himself with famous people. When the group went upstairs someone happened to open the door to the master bedroom. There—mounted on a tripod—was a video camera aimed at the bed! The story spread like a brush fire, eliciting innocent indignation and loud protests from the ambassador. "The camera just happened to *be* there, it wasn't being *used* in the bedroom." He didn't understand that the kindling had been smoldering for months.

Morale at the embassy began to slip and slide downhill. The Foreign Service Nationals (Danes and third country employees who were locally hired) were embarrassed by the ambassador. The American staff members were ashamed of him. Art, Matt, Wes, Roger, Jim, Mike and others worked overtime to hold the embassy up and to keep Loeb out of trouble—or at least to minimize the fallout when they couldn't accomplish the latter. The Defense Attachés as well as the officers in ODC (Office of Defense Cooperation) also had to practice damage control—frequently.

For a short time the fickle public eye turned an envious green and focused on THE parties. In June Ambassador Loeb hosted two spectacular affairs on consecutive evenings. The guest lists were better reading than a Blue Book with such titles as Queen, Duke, Countess, Baron, Viscount, Earl, Lord and Lady, Ambassador and Aga Khan plus Danes who were highly placed in the government, in business and in cultural endeavors. Invitees came from far-off California and Texas and from New York and Washington, DC. Others popped over from Italy, Ireland, and England. Among the untitled guests were a Danish sculptress, an American oil man, a film producer, a banker and entertainer Art Linkletter.

Party Number One took place at Solyst, a grand old country-style mansion that housed the historic Royal Copenhagen Shooting Association. The dinner was intended to fete a couple from California who were "dear friends" of the ambassador—and even dearer friends of President Reagan about whom the guests were frequently reminded. A medical emergency unfortunately prevented the dear couple from attending, so the rest of us were asked—repeatedly—to toast the dear absentees.

Party Number Two, a black-tie dinner-dance at Rydhave, was in honor of Queen Margrethe and Prince Hendrik. Her Majesty was elegant in a long gown of colorful plaid silk taffeta. Before dinner she circled the garden with Ambassador Loeb who introduced her to some of his other guests, and she stopped often to chat with people she knew. She was neither exuberant nor excessively formal but cordial in a way that put others at ease.

Ambassador Loeb's parents, New York financiers Mr. and Mrs. John L. Loeb, Sr. were among the guests. One of the rumors that had preceded as well as followed our wealthy ambassador was one regarding his mother. It was whispered aloud that President Reagan had initially offered the diplomatic appointment to her. In New York City Mrs. Loeb was looked upon as an unofficial ambassadress to the UN community and was well known as a fund-raiser. She reportedly had told Reagan: "Give the ambassadorship to Johnny."

Art and I spent some time with the senior Loebs, wanting them to feel welcome. Mrs. Loeb graciously complimented Art on how well he, as DCM, ran the embassy. I thought at the time there was something besides praise behind her words. I was also convinced that the Loebs were a matriarchal family.

Art confirmed both after he talked with her in private. "This is Johnny's last chance to accomplish something," Mrs. Loeb told Art candidly. "He hasn't done so as yet."

The garden at Rydhave was lovely that evening. Flowers were everywhere. The weather was pleasantly warm and because it was summer in Denmark, the sun was shining until after ten o'clock. When it was time for dinner, Ambassador Loeb escorted Queen Margrethe along a plush red carpet and into the huge marquee that had been erected for the occasion. Red, white and blue decorated the inside where linen-covered round tables held candles and flowers in the same color scheme.

Standing at the entrance to the marquee were two Marines in dress uniform. They added a certain panache to the grandeur, I thought, but Art had objected to their presence.

"The Marine guards should not be used as decoration," he had argued. "That's not part of their job." But the ambassador had his way.

Seated near me at the dinner table was a California woman who didn't appear to be enjoying herself. Her name was not a familiar one but she made it clear she was attached to a famous personage at another table. "Ms. Grumpy" expressed her pique early on by complaining loudly about the wine. She unceremoniously grabbed the waiter's sleeve and told him to keep her supplied with gin.

By the end of the first course Ms. Grumpy, well on the path to inebriation, was talking more to herself than to anyone else. She steadily graduated from sounding peevish to being downright acrimonious. When the waiter came to remove the dinner plates, she remarked caustically to no one in particular, "You can bet we'll have strawberries next! I don't know why people can't think up some other kind of dessert this time of year. Always strawberries…"

Within a few minutes the fresh strawberries and whipped cream materialized as if she had ordered them. Two guests across the table nudged each other, grinned and proclaimed almost in unison: "Doesn't the dessert look luscious!" Ms. Grumpy muttered to herself, stood up rather unsteadily and tottered off.

My good friend Candace had a dinner partner who preferred vodka to the wine. The waiter brought it in a large water glass, probably hoping it would last throughout the meal since the wait-staff had a great number of guests to serve. The man was delighted to learn that Candace and Wes were from his home state of Ohio and a merry conversation ensued. As the vodka disappeared from the glass and was re-supplied, Mr. Ohio began to show signs of intoxication—his face became flaccid and his lips failed to form intelligible words.

A woman sitting on the other side of Candace became increasingly aware of Mr. Ohio's appearance. Having no idea that he was swilling vodka, she whispered to Candace, "Poor man. He must have had a stroke."

After a short musical program by members of the Mormon Tabernacle Choir, guests strolled in the garden while the staff moved tables and rearranged chairs to make space for the dance floor. Most of the women strolled into the house in search of the powder room.

Candace and I were dismayed when we saw the long line waiting to use the ladies' room—and Queen Margrethe in the middle of the queue! Although other women had stepped aside and urged her to move ahead, she had declined. "I'll wait in line like everyone else," she said.

We felt like negligent hostesses. "The queen should be taken upstairs," Candace and I agreed in whispers and she scooted off to find Livia, the housekeeper. But the answer was an emphatic "*No.*" Livia had stern orders from the ambassador that no one was to be allowed upstairs "under any circumstances." The Queen continued to wait.

My turn to give Livia a try. I found her near the stairs and pleaded with her: "If I escort the queen upstairs, I'll take all the responsibility." Again the housekeeper refused and I didn't want to put her job in jeopardy. When I left Livia, she was standing guard at the staircase—to keep out infiltrators.

In spite of the insufficient facilities the evening progressed smoothly and it was a great party! The band was versatile and the dancing was lively. More than once Queen Margrethe gathered up a group of guests and organized the Danish equivalent of a quadrille. She and a few other Danes demonstrated the steps to anyone who wanted to learn. When Art and I headed home just after midnight Her Majesty was still dancing.

When Kathy came home from boarding school for spring break, it was apparent how much she had matured. She had also acquired a fierce independence and was rankled by the tiniest bit of parental advice. If we suggested she carry an umbrella when she went out, she accused us of "treating her like a child." She had just turned 16. Alex's growing up process was more gradual, or at least it seemed that way because he was with us until he was 18. He didn't appreciate parental interference either, but he didn't say much—he just ignored us.

One afternoon Kathy and I were cooking together in the kitchen when she suddenly reached into some unseen pocket of frustration and produced an emotional discourse about her young life.

"I'm very grateful for all the advantages that I've had because of daddy's job in the Foreign Service," she began. "Traveling, meeting interesting people, learning new things...but...." Her voice became heated and she finished with: "But I will never do this to *my* children!" I felt totally deflated—as if the air had been painfully punched from my body.

Foreign Service Requisites: thick skin and strong stomach.

But I got through it and Kathy got over it. By the time she was in college she was extolling the virtues of Foreign Service life. Alex, too, had his share of wear and tear from our moving life, but today he says the "good stuff" outweighs the negative. Both of them agree: "The hardest part of moving was leaving behind our home—and friends."

For teenagers another of the downsides of living overseas was the lack of job opportunities—particularly during the school year. Embassies hired college students during the summer months but depending on the post, jobs were limited and so was the money. So Alex and Kathy learned to work parties and they were good at it. They helped in the kitchen, they passed appetizers, and they helped clean up. Most of the time they thought it was fun—and they appreciated the pocket money.

Their favorite gig was at Lois and Matt's. Our embassy friends held an annual Open House Brunch on New Year's and our kids worked alongside the hosts' daughters, aided by a professional or two. Lois poached whole salmons, perfectly, and laid out a luscious buffet. At those parties the young people spent a bit more time cleaning up than usual—by that time they had managed to sip a little champagne out in the kitchen.

One summer we exchanged houses with a Foreign Service family posted in London. Toini was taking her vacation while we were away so I asked Erik's cousin Irene to come in and clean the bedrooms before the guests arrived.

When we returned from England Alex went into his room and came back out shouting. "Where are my beer cans?" For years he had been collecting cans and bottles from all over the world and he had displayed them in a fancy pyramid. His friend Chris had brought him a can all the way from St. Kitts.

I immediately thought of Irene. "She probably put them away someplace since the little girl was to sleep in your room." I felt sure we would find the collection in a closet or cupboard. We didn't, so I phoned Irene. I was astounded by her answer.

"I threw them away!" She thought they were trash. Alex still hasn't forgiven her.

Visiting the Tuborg Brewery was enlightening as well as fun—especially for our son who hadn't toured a brewery until then. Remembering the ads for an American beer that claimed its goodness came from "pure Rocky Mountain spring water," Alex asked the tour guide, "What kind of water do you use?"

We were surprised when the Tuborg man replied, "City water, of course." At night when usage was down, they filled their huge water tanks from the public supply. He explained that whichever water they wanted—spring water, mountain water, regular, carbonated—"We can make it!"

Tuborg also made concentrated beer that they exported in tank trucks. Water was added to the product after it arrived at its destination. After that revelation I wasn't too surprised to learn that the Danes were just as clever at making cheese—any kind of cheese. They developed their own feta (a sheep's milk cheese) which they proudly made out of cow's milk.

The Copenhagen Theater Circle drew us into its orbit. CTC was an amateur English-speaking group with a multinational membership: Canadians, British, Americans, a New Zealander and an Irish woman, and Lone, a Danish artist. There were other Danes, including Cyril Glynn, a dapper mature gentleman, who was the only professional member of CTC. He had been the stage manager at the Royal Theater for many years.

One of our productions was a one-act play set in a smoke-filled cocktail lounge. A group of smokers puffed frantically on stage attempting to create the right atmosphere just before the curtain opened. Although we generated a lot of smoke, it dissipated too quickly. Art was the stage manager and he asked Cyril for his help. The pro came up with a smoky solution—as well as answers to other problems—all trade secrets, of course.

Terry, a Canadian, was an excellent actor and director. He always said that his chief theatrical goal was to play the part of Lady Bracknell in *The Importance of Being Ernest*. Perhaps he has accomplished that by now. Theater people *do* have fun!

The young men who are chosen for the Marine Guard program are special; only the best are selected to serve at our embassies and consulates abroad. Some are in their teens and others barely twenty, only a few are older. With their military-style cropped hair many still look like boys. But when it comes to their duties they're men—well trained and prepared.

What a wonderful surprise to discover that Brian, a newly arrived Marine, came from my hometown of Grand Island, Nebraska. We had grown up in the same neighborhood but had never met. During his previous posting in Reykjavik Brian met Anita, a pretty blond Icelandic woman who followed him to Copenhagen where they would be married when he finished his tour of duty. Regulations forbid Marine Guards to be married while on assignment.

The date was set, the minister was booked, and the church was reserved—but the reception? Brian and Anita discovered it would be costly to rent a place. It was Art who had the idea: "Let's invite them to have their reception at our house."

Toini and I made canapés; two embassy women made a gorgeous traditional wedding cake; Brian arranged for champagne, beer and soft drinks; and Anita ordered flower arrangements for the table. The families arrived—Brian's from Nebraska and Anita's parents from Iceland.

It was a fairy tale day. As the bride and groom came out of the church into the September sunshine, they walked beneath the crossed swords of the Marines while the music of bagpipes celebrated their marriage. A silver Rolls Royce with uniformed driver elegantly transported the royal pair to our home—and took them away again after the reception. The bagpiper in full kilt preceded the slowly moving limo out of our driveway, piping his special music until they disappeared down the street.

When the 150 guests were gone, I looked around at the flowers and I began to sniffle. Was it over already? I thought of my niece, Laura, who always cried at bedtime on Christmas or her birthday—or anyone else's birthday—because she didn't want the day to end. I wasn't ready to unwind yet, so Art and I joined some friends at "Joe's," a pub near the embassy where they made great hamburgers.

"Joe's" was full of people when we arrived including David, one of the embassy drivers, and the piper. When the bagpipes began to play, everyone hushed. David, Scottish through and through, came to me and said, "The piper's goin' to play for you." Then he explained that the song was called a *pibroch*, which the piper would create as a thank you to me. "He's doin' ya a great honor," David told me proudly.

The *pibroch* was hauntingly beautiful and I was touched beyond words. When the song was finished the kilted piper bowed to me and said, "Thank you for the day."

A tray appeared with two small glasses of a dark liqueur. "Now ya must link arms and take the drink together," David instructed. We did—and the ceremony was concluded. Aye—the day had a storybook ending.

As our stay in Copenhagen approached two and a half years, Art was already reviewing possibilities for our next assignment. He was like most FSO's—as soon as they are unpacked and settled they start looking over the fence. But in this case it looked as though Art's superiors in Washington might prefer he stay on in Denmark another year to help forestall the train wrecks that continued to be engineered by John Loeb.

Articles in the Danish press regarding the ambassador had become less and less favorable. One paper quoted a politician who said he was bewildered by Loeb's "nearly comic behavior." Perhaps the kindest thing printed about him was the observation of an anonymous woman: "He's very sweet but not very smart." And the word spread. An American newspaper published a story about "amateur diplomats" in which the writer referred to Loeb as "another appointee with problems."

We left Copenhagen the end of May for our long-planned vacation and to attend Kathy's graduation from The Mercersburg Academy. We were enjoying the change of pace and scene when Washington notified us that the scenery in Copenhagen would change definitively with Loeb's early departure. Another piece of good news followed: Art was being assigned to the Netherlands, as DCM.

The unenviable task of informing Loeb that his assignment was curtailed fell to the Vice President. In less diplomatic terms—George H.W. Bush telephoned the ambassador and fired him! Loeb was crushed and so distressed he didn't leave the residence for several days. His continued anguish was evident in spite of the make-up he applied in an attempt to hide the signs of his mewling. The pancake and powder were still obvious when he returned to the office—so too were his red eyes.

When we returned to Copenhagen after our home leave Art found the atmosphere in the front office chilly and gloomy. The ambassador ignored Art's greeting—no "welcome back" handshake materialized. It soon became apparent that the man blamed Art for his ambassadorial demise.

Meanwhile, a friendship had developed between the Werners and us. As a Dane working at the American Embassy, Jorgen suffered as much as the rest of us through Ambassador Loeb's foibles. Perhaps the frustration was a bonding agent. When Jorgen and Ester invited us to dinner Art enjoyed the conversation about wines, vintners and vintages. The Dane was a connoisseur and my husband admired his cellar. When Jorgen gave Art a bottle of a special red wine he said, "Save this for an occasion you want to celebrate!" With a glint in his eye and camouflage around his words he discreetly hinted at the impending departure of John Loeb.

When it became certain we would leave Denmark before the ambassador (who stayed until October—two years after his arrival), Art decided to save the wine gift for another special occasion.

We celebrated Mid-Summer's Night with our good friends Michael and Ema at a restaurant where we ate outside in the long summer light. The Scandinavian countries observed Mid-Summer when it was day all night—perhaps because of the long winters when it seemed like night all day. To Americans the date simply marks the end of spring and the beginning of summer. We were keenly aware on that evening of endings and beginnings. Our time in Denmark would soon come to an end.

The Vice President and Mrs. Barbara Bush arrived shortly before our departure. They followed a relentlessly whirling schedule and whisked out of Denmark the next day. The brevity of the visit as well as the agenda were characteristic of official high-level visits. A "country team" briefing for the Vice President was first on the agenda. The ambassador, DCM, and all heads of sections/agencies met in the (secure) conference room at the embassy. And because Mrs. Bush was included, the DCM allowed me to sit in also.

The ambassador again showed his worth. The staff had given him written "talking points" (the mission's purpose, accomplishments, goals) but Loeb decided to wing it. It was obvious he wanted to impress Bush with his capable command of the meeting. Ignoring his notes the ambassador babbled and rambled on, mercilessly impressing the Vice President with his stupidity. When Bush interrupted to ask a question, he received an incoherent answer from Loeb. Then another. The Vice President looked bewildered at first and then frustrated.

As I scanned the faces of the officers, I half expected their eyes to roll collectively in a silent cry of, "We give up!" I was surprised to see that it was Barbara's eyes that rolled! She tried, but she couldn't quite hide the look of amusement on her face.

After the briefing Mr. and Mrs. Bush met the embassy staff and their families in the embassy auditorium. The Vice President graciously thanked everyone for their service and then he and Mrs. Bush moved among the crowd, talking and shaking hands. Bush had been our ambassador to China some years before and the two of them had a special affinity with Foreign Service people and an understanding of how appreciative *we* are when *we* feel appreciated.

The family game of "Royal Rivalry" began that day. Alex, in spite of the crutches he needed to support an injured knee, managed to hobble to a strategic position in the auditorium to have his picture taken with the Vice President. Kathy was on a trip out of the country and when she returned, her brother used every opportunity to remind her that he had shaken hands with Vice President Bush—and she hadn't. Alex was ahead—two royals to one.

After their lunch at Amalienborg Palace the Vice President attended to his duties and Mrs. Bush went sightseeing—from a boat. It was a splendid way to enjoy the surroundings of the city and to get a closer look at the Little Mermaid. I had taken the boat tour numerous times but never before with such illustrious companions as on that day with Barbara Bush and Lisbeth Schlouter, the wife of the Prime Minister.

The Bushes were staying at the ambassador's residence so it was from Rydhave that the motorcade departed that evening for Elsinore. Prime Minister Poul Schlouter was hosting a banquet in honor of the Bushes at Kronborg Castle, the famous setting for Shakespeare's "Hamlet." Our printed schedules said the ride north along the coast would last 45 minutes. I thought there must be a mistake; Elsinore was a bit farther than that.

Since it was my first time to ride in a motorcade, Art gave me detailed instructions: we arrive early; we get into our designated vehicle; and we wait. "The motorcade waits for no one except the principals," he warned me. "In this case—the Bushes."

Art and I rode in Car H along with the nurse, Ms. Sommers. (A doctor and a nurse always traveled with the Vice President.) Promptly at 7:15 p.m. twelve vehicles left Rydhave, not counting the escort of motorcycle policemen with sirens singing. It was exciting and I had to keep reminding myself to stay calm and act as if this sort of thing were the norm.

Within a few minutes I understood why the trip to the castle would take only 45 minutes—speed! We traveled fast and the drivers maintained the same distance between vehicles the entire trip. There was no slowing, no hesitation. Posted at the intersections and crossroads were additional patrolmen who had stopped all other traffic. My excitement turned to fright and the butterflies in my stomach began to feel like bats!

Car H was in ninth position, which meant there were cars ahead and cars behind us. One mistake by one driver or one blown tire and we'd be road kill—all of us! In the name of security, of course.

But we arrived safely and as soon as we entered the famed castle I forgot entirely about the high-velocity ride. Enormous brass chandeliers hung from the high ceiling and lit the Knight's Hall with candles. There was no electricity. I wouldn't have been surprised to see Hamlet or William Shakespeare appear smiling from the shadows.

Two hundred guests sipped and smiled and strolled before dinner. The women were begowned and bejeweled and the men looked elegant in black tie. We ate a sumptuous meal of salmon and roast beef but for once the food lacked importance. I was totally enthralled by the charm of the castle and the overwhelming sense of privilege to be dining there.

At precisely 10:55 the motorcade left the castle and we sped back to Rydhave. The Bushes were standing on the porch of the residence when Art and I got out of the car and we walked over to tell them goodnight. Mr. Bush asked, "Art, have you seen the ambassador?" The question surprised us—Loeb was supposed to have returned in the same car as the Vice President.

I suggested the ambassador may have returned in another vehicle and had already gone inside. "No. He's not in the house and we haven't seen him," Barbara said.

Art quickly established that all vehicles in the motorcade had left the castle—and no one had seen Loeb. It appeared that the Bushes wanted to wait for their host so we four stayed on the porch making amiable small talk. After some speculation and conjecture about the whereabouts of the missing ambassador, the Vice President inquired about our transportation home.

"We're walking," Art told them. "We live just around the corner."

"You two better head on home then," Barbara said with a sly smile, "Or you'll be blamed for *this*, too!"

The following morning Art found out that Loeb had "missed" the departure of the motorcade from Kronborg. Roger, an embassy officer, and his wife JoAnn were leaving the castle when they discovered the ambassador had no transportation. They drove him home. Some people surmised that Loeb intentionally didn't get into the limo at the appointed time. Continuing to show he was in command and to exert his self-importance, he expected the motorcade to wait for him. It didn't.

Fourteen years later the Loeb saga continued. Art was reminiscing with a longtime friend when they both recalled the vice presidential visit to Denmark in 1983. Peter had been on Bush's staff and remembered the arrival of Air Force Two at Kastrup Airport. He said that as soon as the Bushes got off the plane Ambassador Loeb—with a grave face—pulled the Vice President aside and spoke earnestly to him.

A minute later Bush concluded the conversation with: "Take it like a man, John."

We packed up—again—and said our farewells. That part of Foreign Service life never became easier. I would miss our home on the Strandvej—still today it's my favorite of our homes away from home. I would miss magical Copenhagen and I would especially miss our friends. We had a special bond with our American colleagues and hopefully we would see them in Washington or elsewhere. But our Danish friends…would we meet them again? Good-byes are tough.

Matt and Lois, the Community Liaison Officer, organized an embassy farewell for us. The Americans and the FSNs came with hugs and handshakes—except for Ambassador Loeb who had ceased speaking to Art. Matt, who would take over the duties of DCM until the new man arrived, gave a clever and funny speech that made us proud and also made me cry.

But this time I wouldn't sob all the way to the airport—we weren't flying. We loaded our blue Audi with suitcases and bags in the trunk, scores of houseplants on the back seat and on the window ledge, and heavy round discs from Art's weight bench in front under my feet. On the floor behind the drivers' seat was Jorgen Werner's gift of red wine—carefully padded and encased in cardboard. That special bottle was destined to travel thousands of miles with us.

Kathy was traveling in Europe and Alex elected to stay in Copenhagen to work for two more weeks. Thus it was that on July 17, 1983 only Art and I said good-bye to Toini and we left the big white house on the Strandvej…and drove all the way to The Hague.

11

HOME IS WHERE?

HOME LEAVE

The vacation that wasn't...The home leave that should have been left...The R & R from hell...These are the blunt descriptions and oral epithets that many Foreign Service people affix to one or the other of their trips home. So I wasn't surprised that nearly all the women who have written books about diplomatic life tell tales of harrowing home leaves and R & R trips that were completely devoid of "rest and recuperation."

It's not that the trips are useless or unnecessary and they're not always viewed negatively from hindsight. Some can be quite pleasant. Home leave—the phrase itself—sounds warmly alluring. Surely the visit must be relaxing and cozy and most of all—homey. We all look forward to that long-awaited trip "back home" to see family and friends, back to the familiar and the comfortable. Yes, but from a wife's point of view....

Home leave also means medical and dental appointments. An overdue mammogram because that equipment isn't available at their present post. A visit to the orthodontist to have their son's braces checked. A trip to the dentist to replace a crown that was poorly done at the previous post. An urgent appointment with the doctor because the little one has tonsillitis with a raging fever. After she returns from the pharmacy, she discovers her husband has the flu.

Home leave means shop, shop, shop. Several hours spent at Giant, Shopko or K-Mart stocking up on contact lens supplies, toiletries and cosmetics that either aren't available or are prohibitively expensive in their present country of residence. A stop at the specialty music store to get a small gadget to repair the gizmo on their daughter's guitar. Another futile search for reasonably priced American-made gifts to take back to post. An attempt to locate a craft store that carries the chartreuse embroidery thread a friend asked her to buy.

A dreary day in and out of formalwear shops as her husband tries on tuxedos. His old one has been pressed so frequently and improperly that it's shiny. A visit to the mall—maybe several malls—to buy clothes. She has gained weight and his trench coat has worn out. A search for slim-fit jeans for their son since Sears has discontinued their mail order business. A concentrated hunt for three different watch batteries. A quick turn through a linen store to find fingertip guest towels. Theirs are in storage and there aren't any in the residence. She checks several florists looking for large squares of oasis for flower arrangements—another item not available at post. And everyone in the family needs new shoes.

A half-day spree at a grocery store filling her cart with chocolate chips and dried apricots, rye flour and corn meal, long-life cream, and peanut butter in non-breakable jars. She tries to avoid the treats and snacks that she knows the kids will crave as soon as they return to post because she also knows these goodies would be too difficult to pack and too expensive to mail.

When she has finished the shopping—or it has finished her—she scrounges around the back room of a supermarket locating empty boxes. She buys several rolls of strapping tape. She and her husband frantically ransack the relatives' basements and garages for Styrofoam popcorn and other useful packing materials. Together they wrap and pad the precious purchases and box them up. At the post office they suffer the indignant stares and mutterings of the people in line behind them when it is discovered they have fourteen boxes to mail.

Home leave especially means visiting. They've been away for two years and they want to spend time with their families. Blessed are the couples whose parents and siblings reside in the same part of the country! For others—his are in southern California and hers are in North Dakota. There is the elderly favorite aunt who is not well and begs them to visit her in upstate New York. The college roommate just had a baby and she lives 400 miles west of their official home leave address. The class reunion is in Nebraska and the family reunion is in Minnesota. And he wants to visit their Foreign Service friends who have just retired in Colorado.

Home leave *should* include recreation. Her sister wants her to watch her nephew perform in a wrestling match. His niece's piano recital is a must. The children want to see all the latest movies because they *never* get to see good movies at post. Her parents want them to go to so-and-so's cocktail party because everyone is "just dying" to see them both. Another relative wants them to see the farm he just purchased—it's thirty miles out and they have to walk the last mile because there is no road. She didn't pack any boots.

Her husband wants to go to the concert at the university—it's the same evening her cousin has planned a dinner party in their honor. If they spend time with any friends, they'll need to get in touch with them all or someone's feelings will be hurt. She buys the latest bestseller but never opens the book until she's on a plane—returning to post.

Home leave is the *only* time for necessities. Her husband has appointments at the State Department in Washington for the obligatory consultations. She meets with their real estate agent regarding the renters who have just painted their bedrooms horrendous colors. He reads Consumer Reports and then price-shops for a new air conditioner. They have to renew their driver's licenses. She takes his suits and her fragile silks to a dry cleaners because there are no such facilities where they live.

Both of them—ideally—accompany their soon-to-be-a-senior student on visits to prospective colleges. The eldest needs help moving from the dorm into an apartment—followed by shopping for kitchen supplies. If they're between assignments, they spend all available "spare" time studying up on their next post—the country's history and government, its customs and climate. And so goes home leave.

There are always necessities, chores and errands that must be attended to during home leave. And there are the unexpected and unpleasant pop-ups that we can't avoid. But home leave also has positive aspects: the good times we spend with our families. Alex and Kathy always got extra-special treatment from their grandparents, who indulged and pampered them. My tummy gets a familiar warm feeling when I think of the fried chicken my mother always made because she knew it was my favorite. Art didn't like fried chicken, but no matter—his mother made lemon meringue and chocolate pies just for him.

There were delightful weekends at "The Cabin" with Brother Dave, Jan and their five children. When Art and Dave's sister Ardith joined us with husband Dick and children, there were eleven cousins of various ages all in one place. It was crowded, noisy, hectic and blissful!

Today most of the "children" have their own kids and it's increasingly difficult to coordinate everyone at the same time. Still, most of us manage to gather for a Sunday in summer and we fit easily around Dave and Jan's patio and deck—lounging comfortably while hamburgers cook on the grill. Nancy and Dan, who were married in Frankfurt, are still in the Foreign Service and try to arrange their home leave so we can all be together for a family wedding or other special reunion.

One of our earliest home leave get-aways in Nebraska was a July camping trip with my sister Carol and her family. Delm had borrowed a camper, a large vehicle that more or less housed us all—four adults and five small children. Carol, pregnant at the time, made up a duty roster for cooking and cleaning up. Each of us did our respective chores with the opposite spouse—to forestall familial bickering. She wanted our short time together to be idyllic.

It was probably fortuitous that we had only planned to camp for an extended weekend. We parked by a lake and the kids played in the sand, water and dirt for long hours, thus necessitating lots of bathing. The weather was hot and we consumed gallons of liquids, juice and Kool-Aid and beer and iced tea, thus the commode was repeatedly flushing. The tank ran out of water before we ran out of weekend! And miles to go to the next fill-up.

The State Department grants home leave at the end of each of our overseas assignments—like a reward for the successful completion of our duties. Actually the trip home is mandated by law to keep us in touch with the country we are representing and, perhaps, to remind us of the flag and apple pie. Home leave may also be taken midway through a tour of four years or during a hardship posting.

Foreign Service assignments range from 18 months to four years depending on the post, the specific job, and/or the rank of the officer. Junior officers remain the shorter length of time, as do officers at hardship posts (countries where living conditions are extremely difficult and/or the stability of the host government is precarious). The ambassador and deputy chief of mission may stay longer at a post than other officers.

I have found the (average) three-year posting to be just right even though several months on either end are spent unpacking, preparing and packing up. Opinions vary among my friends as to a preference for staying in the same place for four years. A lot depends on the desirability of the post and the host city, and also on local education opportunities for children. I can't tender an opinion on the four-year posting since the only place we have ever lived for that long was Washington.

Rest and recuperation—or "R & R" in Foreign Service lingo—is a government-sponsored break during an assignment. It differs from home leave in two ways. One: transportation is paid for the officer and family only to a pre-designated (read "civilized") city depending on where the officer is posted. Or the R & R destination can be the nearest American port city. In other words, away from post, but not always all the way home. Two: only officers at hardship posts or particularly difficult areas are entitled to R & R.

We managed to do some recuperating during our R & R's but rest was illusive. To me R & R meant "race and run," others have used the phrase "rant and rave." Just like home leave. But I'm forced to confess that some fortunate families have thoroughly enjoyed their R & R's and their home leaves and have actually rested. One or two, maybe.

One of the best things about home leave—second only to family togetherness—is enjoying the foods that we have missed while at post. Though we have never been deprived of anything essential, our family loves to eat and sometimes we have lacked *variety*, the spice of mealtime as well as life.

I confess that some foods we yearn for when we don't have them are things that we don't eat very often when they *are* available. If I don't have cottage cheese or red bell peppers, fresh turkey or scallops I miss them dreadfully. But when they are at hand at my suburban supermarket a mile away, I don't buy them very often.

When we were in Israel and Yemen we longed for pork, especially sausages. In Sanaa I ordered British sausages through an importer but we were sadly disappointed—in all ten kilos of them! They turned out to be bangers and didn't bear the tiniest resemblance to what we were hankering for. I should have known better.

Some of those same sausages turned up at a potluck after-tennis lunch. As we were serving ourselves from the grill, I commented to Katy, one of our friends from England, "Aren't those sausages awful?"

"I think they're quite good," she chided me. "After all, we grew up on bangers!" I felt as though I had insulted the Union Jack.

In Maracaibo we missed frozen orange juice and we longed for it again in Sanaa where we couldn't even buy oranges for making fresh juice. Canned juice may be marginally nutritious but it lacks something—flavor. Potato chips were missing in several countries but I could manage to forget about them—for a while. Corn, fresh or frozen, wasn't available in Europe until the last few years, except as animal feed. When summer came, I longed for fresh corn-on-the-cob, wherever we were.

American fast food is incomparable; the varieties are endless and so are the calories. And the prices are right even if the nutrition isn't. But it's fast and it's typically American—even the tacos and the pizza. When we're posted at home we eat fast food infrequently, but when we're away I long for a Burger King Whopper or a genuine roast beef sandwich from Roy Rogers, some finger-lickin'-good Kentucky Fried Chicken, and especially those huge crunchy icy-cold Blizzards from the Dairy Queen.

Home fills the stomach as well as the heart. When we arrive in Nebraska Kathy goes straight for the Runzas: unique hot pockets of sautéed cabbage and ground beef enveloped in bread dough—the cheese is optional. They're always fresh, perfectly seasoned—and to die for—if you haven't had one for two years. Our daughter thinks Runzas are a gift from the Food Fairy!

Alex would rather have a steak, the Number One food where we come from—grain-fed, properly aged Nebraska beef. At Driesbachs in Grand Island or at Misty's in Lincoln we always knew we were home when we bit into tender succulent steaks. And cooked over a home grill, accompanied by corn on the cob and shared by the family, they're even better.

We eventually have to put an end to the shopping and the mailing—maybe we haven't finished but enough is enough. We have completed all the urgent tasks on our list. We've made all the visits we had time and breath for, including endless phone calls. We are medically and dentally renewed. We have eaten all the Whoppers, fried onion rings, Runzas and fajitas we craved. Home leave has come to its inevitable end. Maybe I'll have just enough time for a haircut before we gather up the luggage and the kids and race for the airport. Our suitcases are heavier and our carry-on bags are fatter than when we started out.

There is only one thing we didn't do enough of on home leave—rest—but we'll have to do that on the airplane. (Too bad about the bestseller.)

HOMECOMING

Art and I still refer to Nebraska as home. We grew up in that state and most of our family is there. We return as often as possible and we identify with Nebraska—it's Big Red country! But we also refer to our current post as home. When the vacation is over we are eager to return to Bonn or Copenhagen or Tel Aviv (wherever we have laid out the dresser scarves and crocheted doilies) and put our heads on those familiar inviting shapes—our own pillows.

If home is where we hang our hats—it is also where we park our empty suitcases. "Coming home" to Foreign Service families means returning for a Washington assignment. We get our belongings out of storage, we completely unpack, and we put the suitcases in the attic. We lifers, long-term career people, usually buy a house in the area early on and Washington becomes home—especially to our children. Granted, the "feeling" of home may come sooner or later—depending on the individual speed of assimilation.

Our first homecoming was in 1970. After living in Germany and Venezuela we returned for our first Washington assignment and bought our first home in the Maryland suburbs. Our neighbors came over to introduce themselves. Someone brought iced tea and cake when the moving van arrived, another brought sandwiches for our lunch. We were guests for dinner and again for breakfast. The older children walked with Alex to the school bus stop and the younger girls invited Kathy to play the next day. We settled into our then and future home comfortably—and with eagerness.

Growing up in the Midwest Art and I knew all our neighbors and their families. Our mothers traded home-baked goods back and forth, especially during holidays. They helped out when someone was sick and gladly loaned an egg or a cup of sugar. I didn't know if the same neighborliness existed elsewhere and in larger cities. In Bethesda, Maryland, it did.

Neither of our children thinks of Nebraska as home. Even though Alex was born in Lincoln and studied at the University of Nebraska, he and Kathy called Bethesda their home until they married. A few years ago I asked them, "What do you tell someone who asks where you are from?" Their answers were alike.

"It depends on who is asking and why." If the situation calls for a short easy reply they say "Washington, DC" because that eliminates an explanation about the location of Bethesda. If a longer conversation is anticipated they expound on the Foreign Service and the countries where they have lived.

Alex has frequently answered, "Everywhere."

"Culture shock" is a topic we increasingly discuss, advise upon and warn about in Foreign Service circles. It affects us all, negatively or positively, at one time or another. Indeed the adjustments each family member must make adapting to a new culture can be stressful and painful, easy and rewarding, merely frustrating, or totally impossible. For our family the adaptations have been satisfying and worthwhile—eventually.

In recent years we have recognized another challenge to the nomadic life. Experts in cross-cultural problems and solutions have dubbed it *reverse* culture shock. In simple terms, it's like doing a double take upon returning to one's own country. It's how we react and what we feel when we come back to the States after an absence of several years. We are faced with a totally different life style and dissimilar responsibilities that can make reentry as difficult and challenging as an entirely new culture abroad.

At first we notice what has changed since we left. We may think home *feels* different somehow. In reality it is we who have changed. We have been altered by what we have done, those whom we have met and everything we have experienced abroad. The longer we have been away and the longer we have served with the Foreign Service, the truer this becomes. That familiar refrain, "everything is relative," sings to me again.

Social life in Washington is different from that at post. We spouses don't have the same built-in opportunities to meet women from other countries. We don't have any of the support systems that we have learned to rely on overseas: no welcoming women's group, no packet of local information, no embassy people stopping by to say hello. Sponsor programs at post and "Hail and Farewell" events—especially traditional with the military—get each family up and running in the first week. Friends are quickly made and relied on overseas. Not so at home.

For friendship we tend to gravitate toward colleagues in the Foreign Service. Those with whom we socialized three years ago, however, will likely have been reassigned during our absence. But with the constant changeover in the service, friends from our previous posts will turn up—just when we're ready to leave again. We may return to friendships in our neighborhood if we return to the same house—and if the neighbors are still there.

On the positive side there are few command performances at home. Nobody is required to entertain in Washington. Spouses don't feel compelled to attend every country's National Day reception—we may not even be invited. Perhaps it's a matter of opinion whether or not this is a positive part of the home assignment.

The non-career spouse faces the boxes and cartons, calls the utility companies, waits for the repairmen, and cleans up after the painters while the officer goes to work and meets his colleagues. In this aspect, there is little difference in being home or abroad. When we have children, we meet people through the school, parents of our children's friends. We may become involved in volunteer work or we may take a job outside the home—once we have settled in. But somehow making friends and "belonging" takes longer when we're at home. We feel as if we are on the fringes.

In Washington I don't share in my husband's duties and participate in his work as I do at post. Particularly after being a DCM spouse and then an ambassador's wife abroad, I found the changes in responsibility and self-image plus the lack of stimulation disconcerting and strangely disappointing—at least initially. Those of us who years ago chose to be at home with our children and simultaneously make our husbands' career our own, poignantly experience reverse culture shock on re-entry.

In her book *Pay, Pack and Follow* Englishwoman Jane Ewart-Biggs talks about those feelings resulting from reverse culture shock. She says the Foreign Service couple at home no longer works "in tandem."

Today's diplomatic spouse who has a personally rewarding and perhaps lucrative career is happy to return to it after her absence—assuming she can pick up where she left off. Some careers travel and some survive a hiatus, but others stagnate. This is one of the biggest spousal problems that the Foreign Service faces today. More and more, spouses want to continue their own careers.

There are other lifestyle changes that require patience, hard work and adjustment. The changes are not unpleasant—they just take some getting used to. As homeowners in the Washington area we are solely responsible for cleaning up after our renters, a process that may involve minor or major work before we can move back in. Once settled we become immersed, like most of our fellow citizens, in the regular maintenance and repair of our abode, including the yard work, most of which is taken care of for us when we live in government housing abroad. (One of the compensations for our fully occupied social life abroad representing our government.)

Many of our colleagues tell ghastly tales of the damage done to their homes by renters, damage that their agents weren't aware of or ignored. Broken windows, holes in walls, carpets ruined by pets, and total deterioration. There are also stories of realty or mortgage companies going bankrupt and using the rent money for their own purposes. One couple had to fly home from Europe after they received a foreclosure notice from their mortgage company. Their agent had pocketed the rent money.

Coming home every few years to the supervision of our own home and the continuing pursuit of roots is what we trade for the responsibilities we have at post. Instead of delving into a foreign culture, learning a new language, planning dinner parties and receptions, organizing bazaars, visiting orphanages and collecting clothing for a hospital, I clean, iron, paint cupboards, wash windows and pull weeds. My husband the diplomat, instead of heading a mission, dealing with crises, delivering a *demarche*, cutting ribbons at opening ceremonies, touring archeology sites, speaking to business groups and flying to oil camps, spends his weekends at home doing chores. He repairs leaky faucets, plasters a ceiling, installs shelves, mows the grass and shovels snow.

In Washington there is no Irene to iron, no Rita to clean, no Toini to arrange the flowers, no Desmond to serve the drinks, no Patrick or Robert to prepare luscious meals, no Abdul Hameed to take care of our clothing. There is no one but Art and I to clean up the dirty dishes after dinner. But there is privacy, which we cherish, and there is pride in our well painted, polished and self-decorated home. There is enormous satisfaction in having MY kitchen to myself and cooking and baking to my heart's content. I LIKE being mistress of my own house.

When we come home after several years abroad, curious friends ask me, "Don't you miss having servants?"

"Only after dinner," is my honest reply. I don't miss the bickering that is inherent in a household where two or three people work together day after day. I don't miss having to remind someone not to wash black socks with white shirts or training a cook to use less butter and garlic. It's a relief not to panic when a waiter doesn't show up for a dinner party or when a staff member is ill. I definitely don't miss hiring and firing and negotiating salaries.

After we returned from Yemen I didn't miss being fully covered and clothed at all times. At home I can walk around my house naked if I am in the mood for a Benjamin Franklin style "air bath." In the summer I can wear shorts and a white T-shirt—without a bra. I can wear my nightgown to breakfast. But occasionally I wish Desmond or Abdul Hameed or Toini were around to help with the dishes after dinner.

The re-entry adjustments I refer to are meant to be editorial musings rather than complaints. The truth is I love being home in Washington, which is filled with opportunities and possibilities. The city is beautiful: the Reflecting Pool, the White House, The Kennedy Center for the Performing Arts, the parks and gardens. History abounds: the Capital, Arlington National Cemetery, the monuments and memorials. The area has a wealth of museums and galleries and offers culture and entertainment for every taste. Food tastes are catered to as well; our own Bethesda was dubbed the restaurant center of the metropolitan area a few years ago.

Washington, however, is expensive on a government salary. During our two home assignments in the 1970's we had to budget every nickel. When our washing machine wore out we needed to replace it quickly. To get the best price we had to pay by check—credit cards weren't universally accepted then. And to save delivery and installation charges Art and Alex loaded the new washer into our station wagon, brought it home and hooked it up themselves. After paying for the machine our bank balance sank to less than fifty dollars—and payday wouldn't come for another ten days. I prayed that the clothes dryer would hang on.

Our family entertainment centered on the National Zoo, museums and parks, and free events such as the Cherry Blossom parade in the spring and the Fourth of July concert and fireworks. Our kids remember waiting in line for over two hours on a frosty winter weekend to see the Tutankhamen exhibit from Egypt. Some years later they saw the entire King Tut collection in Cairo and were reminded how privileged they were and how culturally rich their lives had been.

Richard Nixon's and Jimmy Carter's inaugurations took place in front of our eyes—actually quite far in front of us—but we were there with Alex and Kathy for those historical events. We allowed them to skip school one day to go with us to the White House grounds to watch the welcoming ceremonies for Marshall Tito of then Yugoslavia. They returned to class the next day boasting to their friends that they had seen President Nixon. We were a lot closer for the inauguration of Bill Clinton. Due to Art's job we sat in reserved seats for the ceremony, a privilege we were able to share with (by then grown up) Kathy and her fiancé Jeff.

We were posted abroad for nine years during the 1980's. We lived in three countries, studied three languages, and we changed cultures from the European to the Middle Eastern. Our children grew up—Alex married and Kathy moved to New York City to study. One summer toward the end of that decade, I realized anew while on home leave how "far away" we had been and what disparate lives we had led compared with those of our siblings. Only Art's sister Nancy has traveled similar roads.

While we were visiting relatives in Minnesota, Art's cousin invited him to see her new car. I dallied behind for a few minutes and as I approached the garage I heard a strange, almost atonal voice that I couldn't identify. I walked in just as Art opened another car door and there was the voice: "Your door is ajar, your door is ajar." I had read about talking cars, but I had never *seen* nor *heard* one until that moment. I was dumbstruck.

The following week in Nebraska I had two more surprises. At my mother's we were catching up on each other's news, chattering away, and I offered to refill our ice tea glasses.

"I like crushed ice in mine," my mother said. What? I'm supposed to crush the ice? I thought she was joking. She wasn't. Her talented new refrigerator offered a choice of ice cubes or crushed ice plus a spigot yielding icy cold water—all without opening the refrigerator door!

In Lincoln at Brother Dave's I was talking on the telephone in the dining room. Art and his brother were sitting nearby having a boisterous conversation that intermittently produced loud guffaws. Twice I had to cover the receiver. "Would you hold it down, please?" I implored. "I can't hear!"

After I hung up, Brother Dave looked at me with a sly smile and asked, "Why didn't you take the phone into the bedroom where it's quiet?" I was holding a cordless telephone.

Our children found it necessary to teach me some new-fangled facts of life—an exchange of roles that they relished. I commented to Kathy, for instance, that I frequently heard a clicking sound while I was using her telephone. "Mother," she groaned, "That's call-waiting!" I had never heard of it.

Alex found it necessary to explain what a music video was and what the TV show "Cheers" was all about. He also informed me in a professorial tone that a FAX was a facsimile. "A copy, mother!"

I was not a back-roads country girl, but I felt a bit backward when we returned home. We had lived in five foreign lands and had dealt with varying degrees of culture shock—we were world travelers, weren't we? Still I found myself in awe of the modernities of my own country.

I frequently forget to use our garbage disposer the first weeks after our return. None of our homes abroad had such a device, except for the new residence in Yemen. I overclean the fruits and vegetables until I get used to being in the U.S. where most produce is pre-washed and certainly doesn't need soaking solutions. I often recoil early in the morning when I dip my toothbrush in the running water from the tap—until I'm awake enough to remember that the water is safe.

My friend Ema told me she had a difficult time with grocery shopping after she returned from Denmark. "The supermarkets here are so big and there are too many choices!" She was completely overwhelmed by the numerous brands and varieties of coffee, for example. "At first it took me so long to make decisions that I could only buy a few things at a time. I would have to go back again the next day."

Another aspect of re-entry gave us a gentle jolt in 1994. We returned from Yemen, reclaimed our house, checked in at the State Department, then flew to the Midwest for a short visit. We drove back east two weeks later in our new car, which we had picked up in Wisconsin. Since the county Motor Vehicle Administration is located a half-hour north of our home we thought it wise to stop there, register the car and renew our driver's licenses at the same time.

To our surprise and considerable dismay, neither goal was possible—we didn't have the required proof that we were residents of the county. Art had his State Department photo identification and we both had passports plus current

Nebraska driver's licenses, all of which proved *who* we were but not where we lived. We explained our situation and told the clerk that our Bethesda address was in the MVA files three years back. But no—we had no tangible proof of our current residency. We would have to come back with more information, (which we did after receiving our first home utilities bills).

During the drive home Art commented, "Looking at the humorous side…for the past three years in Yemen everyone knew who we were and where we lived. Remember how many times we wished we were anonymous?"

Re-entry also meant a return to those pesky parking meters. Art and I each found twenty-dollar tickets on our windshields—not because we exceeded the time limits, but because we forgot to put in our money! There were no parking meters in Sanaa.

Many years ago I became afflicted with the Stow and Save Syndrome. (My friend Francesca calls it the "siege mentality.") This is a malady frequently suffered by people (mostly women) who have lived in countries that are not well endowed with consumer goods. Again the peanut butter and chocolate chips example. I saved them if I didn't know when or if they would be available again. My mother mailed chocolate chips to us in Maracaibo but I wouldn't use them for months. By the time I opened the package they were gooey from the heat. Eventually I learned to stow them in the freezer. In Sanaa I ate sparingly of our last jar of peanut butter—I wanted it to last until our departure. By the time I was halfway through the jar it was stale. In Tel Aviv I stored away our favorite cereals thinking they would taste the best when we missed them the most. But in the Mediterranean humidity—they became soggy *before* the milk!

I bought things I didn't need because I *might* need them later and by then they *might* not be in stock. In Sanaa the availability of imported canned goods was particularly unpredictable. I didn't hoard, though, I only bought two or three—and then I saved them.

The Stock-Up Syndrome is an adjunct to the Stow and Save ailment. It occurs—and reoccurs—when we return from a post where saving was a must. This affliction is every bit as serious as its sister syndrome. The symptoms can be especially worrisome to family members who haven't suffered the precursors. Our children who fortunately don't remember any deprivations from their early years (due to their mother's astute shopping, stowing and saving) are astounded by the size of my larder. Kathy has joked, "Is there a medication for this disorder?"

Alex opened our fully stocked freezer and inquired, "Mother, there are only two of you—who else are you cooking for?"

Within a few weeks of our homecoming my pantry houses all the usual items plus such things as sesame oil, artichoke bottoms, tahini, dried cherries, bamboo shoots, Lapsong Souchong tea, hearts of palm and several kinds of baking chocolate. I have needed each of those items in the past, so I must have them on hand—in case I need them again. And we always have the required selection of pastas: spaghetti, penne regate, rigatoni, farfalle, lasagna, orecchiette, fusilli, ziti, fettuccine and orzo.

I keep back-up jars and bottles of everything I have in the refrigerator: ketchup, salsa, pickles, capers, Worcestershire sauce, mayonnaise, green olives, Kikkoman's soy sauce, horse-radish, several kinds of mustard and several varieties of vinegar, plus a wide selection of jams and jellies. If we have unexpected guests, I want to be prepared.

As the Stock-up Syndrome completely envelops me I buy anything that is on special—especially if it's half-price—and then I purchase several of each. Many months pass before I realize that most commodities, whether they be fresh, frozen or non-perishable are "on sale" often. Perhaps I don't need to have ten pounds of chicken breasts or nine cans of tomatoes or eight boxes of cereal or four packages of herbal tea on hand.

Food is not the only thing I save at post and stockpile at home. Gift-wrap, ribbon, pretty bags and boxes were not available in some countries so many Foreign Service women recycled them. A large piece of wrapping paper could be cut, trimmed and used again. Gift bags, bows and decorations would pass from one friend to another until they began to show signs of strain. At home I still find myself reusing these things.

Useful items like paper clips, rubber bands and string were wildly expensive in some parts of the world so I collected them for re-use. Sturdy plastic storage bags and twist ties were often not replaceable so I never threw them away. Envelopes of varying sizes were also rare. Sometimes I put mailing labels over the previous addressees, attached fresh stamps and reused envelopes. I recycled Christmas and birthday cards by cutting off the greetings and using the pictures as post cards.

I remember a friend in Maracaibo who was "short," as they say in the military—not in stature but in time. She and her husband were soon due to return to the States. She had only one pair of nylons left and because they were expensive locally, she refused to buy new ones until she got home. The couple was feted at several farewell parties and frequently I heard one of her friends inform her in a hushed voice, "Oh, Jane, did you know you have a run in your stocking?"

With an artful look of surprise, she replied (repeatedly) "Oh my, I wonder how that happened!"

Remembering that story I always made sure I had plenty of pantyhose on hand. In fact, during one R & R trip I stocked up and I still have several pair—as yet unopened.

Foreign Service life meant change and a change of venue meant a new home. The change may not have come exactly when we wanted it and it may not have been the change we anticipated. But change came. After two, three or four years we packed up and flew off to another assignment, another country—another home.

12

DUTCH TREATS

We arrived in our new country of residence without having studied the language—a first for us. It was fortunate that the DCM residence in The Hague was situated on Sophialaan, an easy-to-pronounce avenue. We were able to read some of the highway and street signs because of similarities to German and English, but we hadn't a clue about most of the pronunciation. We had acquired a Dutch language book and attempted to learn words and phrases we thought we would need upon our arrival, such as please, thank you, and especially, "Where is the bathroom?" We were relieved to discover that one gets by quite well with English in Den Haag. Nevertheless, we would soon be taking Dutch lessons.

Arriving at our new post by automobile with our luggage safe in the trunk was another first experience (and one never to be repeated.) From Copenhagen we headed south and took the ferry from Rodby Havn to Puttgarten. We continued south then west and by the time we reached the Netherlands my "pets,"—the African violets that covered the rear seat and back window ledge—were limp and wilting. And so were we. That day in July 1983 turned out to be the hottest day of the summer. I would like to say that I shone or glistened but in fact I was sweaty just like Art. Our car was not air-conditioned.

The violets survived and after their trauma of being transported nearly 500 miles they perked up and began to thrive. Their adjustment period was shorter than mine. I had to weave through the now-familiar latticework of culture shock: the daily challenge of strangeness; the excitement of a new adventure; the longing for my previous home and the friends I knew so well; the surge of exhausting energy as we unpacked boxes and put our pictures on the walls. Then began the gradual re-stitching of ourselves into yet another unique pattern.

By the time the dresser scarves were in place, our clothes were pressed and hung up, and the dishes were put away in the kitchen, I felt almost at home. The embassy people welcomed us with good cheer and, as is usual at an overseas post, acquaintances and colleagues soon became friends. Since we all experience the absence of extended family and, for some, children away at school, we bond quickly and firmly. While we need our possessions to make a house a home, we also need friendships to feel at home in a community.

When the couple across the street welcomed us to the neighborhood, we discovered we had already met—in Copenhagen. Erik with his wife Ebba had come to The Hague two years earlier as Denmark's ambassador. We passed many pleasant evenings together "putting our feet up" and taking a break from the usual diplomatic round of social events. The occasional case of Tuborg beer found its way across the street to us, as well as Ebba's advice and shopping tips.

The conversation turned one evening to butlers and waiters and the training of staff. Erik, an enviable storyteller, recalled a dinner party he and Ebba had attended at the invitation of the Danish Queen. After serving himself from the silver tray proffered by the waiter, Erik fumbled and dropped the serving fork onto the floor. The server immediately but quietly said, "I am so sorry, sir, I should have been more careful."

"But it was I who had dropped the damned fork!" declared an admiring Erik.

"What do they *do?*" was my urgent question to the wife of the previous DCM. I was inheriting three servants and I didn't know what to do with them! I was frantic to know about their duties and how I would supervise *three* people.

We had a cook—a full-time trained cook—we had never had one before! What would he do for eight hours a day when we weren't entertaining? I suspected that Art and I would be invited out frequently—how could we possibly keep a cook busy? The woman explained that our cook, Patrick, would make breakfast, prepare the mid-day meal for us and the staff, cook dinner of course, and when he wasn't preparing for guests he would use the time to make meat stocks, soups and sauces. Mmm…all right. I could also have him bake lots of cookies, breads, cakes and pies to put in the freezer. That would keep him busy.

But this cook didn't *do* cookies or pastries; he didn't know how to bake. Hired the previous year, he came to the DCM residence straight from culinary school with traditional training in food basics. His repertoire was limited but his specialties, including fish dishes and sauces, were excellent. He knew about wines and cheeses and he laid out a beautiful fruit plate—but he couldn't bake cookies! Ebba told me this was typical. Their German cook refused to bake—he was a *chef.*

When Kathy arrived that summer after touring by train around Europe, she explained to Patrick that chocolate chip cookies were—and should continue to be—a staple in our house and she taught him how to make them.

Patrick, in his early twenties, had an adolescent grin, an infectious laugh, and an impish sense of humor. It was impossible not to like him. His manners were impeccable. He served family meals with an unrushed correctness and his own special flair. His voice was gentle and he was never obtrusive. He was a willing worker, eager to please us in every way—and he was also addle-brained, forgetful and messy!

He cleaned up the kitchen one Thursday night after dinner and then left for a long weekend at his home in Belgium. Art and I went away also and when we returned Sunday evening, I turned on the oven to heat some bread. After a few minutes the smell of cooking meat pervaded the kitchen. I discovered two pork chops that Patrick had forgotten in the oven several days before. That was only the first of many surprises our cook would leave in the oven for us.

Desmond was the butler, a properly trained, perfectly mannered British butler. He was in his mid-fifties with a full crop of salt-and-pepper hair, but he looked years younger. Art's sister Nancy was in awe of the entire concept of a butler. She and Dan came to visit us just after we moved in and she asked me incredulously, "What does a butler *do*?" I wasn't yet sure.

But I learned during the first week that Desmond's duties quite naturally stemmed from the proper definition of a butler: the head male servant of the household. Checking the etymology I found out that "butler" derives from the word bottle. So our butler had charge not only of the silver, but also the wines and liquors. And more.

Desmond did what one expected a butler to do: he polished the silver and he shined shoes; he polished the banisters and he shined mirrors; he served drinks in the parlor and he served toast in the sick room. He hired party help, wired the Christmas tree lights, and fired up the grill. He laid the wood, lit the fireplace, hung the pictures and harangued the repairmen. He answered the door and the telephone and he answered our summons. He repaired, fixed and tinkered, and he dusted, vacuumed and swept. When the maid was away, he washed the linens, ironed the shirts, made beds and cleaned bathrooms. He did whatever needed doing because he was a pro—and he never complained.

Except once—obliquely. Night after night Desmond had fastidiously cleaned up after the workers who were, too slowly, remodeling our kitchen. Patrick had been on vacation during the worst of the mess and was due to return. That afternoon Desmond announced he was going to leave early. "Patrick can clean up in the morning," he said in exasperation, "After all, the kitchen is *his* responsibility."

Pretty dark-haired Irene (our third employee with that name) was the "upstairs maid" and since there were two floors upstairs she had five bedrooms and four bathrooms to look after. There was a sixth bedroom that Patrick used, but he was obligated to keep it clean himself. In addition to the upstairs Irene did the laundry and ironing, served at dinners and receptions and she made beautiful flower arrangements for the tables. Occasionally she brought her portable sewing machine and helped me with the mending. She was multitalented—like Toini.

Originally from Portugal, Irene spoke no English but she had learned Dutch. Since I didn't speak any Dutch in the beginning we managed to communicate in Spanish. She was shy and sweet and a pleasure to work with.

I learned to avoid the kitchen whenever something other than food was heating up. Desmond and Patrick had frequent noisy rows—the butler was too bossy and the cook was too touchy, especially before parties. Sometimes harsh words bounced around the kitchen and Irene had to plug her ears. The spats usually petered out and voices were softer and calmer the following day. With several people working cheek by jowl day after week after month, each with distinct personalities and individual quirks, there are bound to be conflicts now and then.

With all this efficient household help it would seem I didn't have a thing to do in my new home. Not so. Before our HHE arrived I spent several hours each day cleaning out the kitchen cupboards, the storerooms, and the linen closet. Our predecessors, many of them it seemed, had a penchant for saving the government's chipped glassware, cracked china and battered pots and pans. Some had left behind worn-out items of their own such as plates whose color and pattern had faded, pitchers and mugs with no handles, rusty cake pans and cookie sheets, mismatched pieces of tinny flatware and lonely lids to long-gone casserole dishes. There were also small appliances that hadn't coupled with electricity for many a year. In every corner sucked in by cobwebs and old dust were bits and pieces of some other DCM's kitchen remains.

Although Desmond had kept the butler's pantry clean and organized, I pulled out glasses, plates and cups that couldn't be used because of nicks and cracks. It was search and destroy all over again. These exercises that began in Copenhagen would be repeated at our subsequent posts. I have often speculated on the reasons people left unusable dishes and kitchenware in the cupboards. Maybe they didn't know the broken items were there? They couldn't take time to remove them? Perhaps they didn't care? I cared. When we moved into a residence the place became our home, perhaps temporarily, but our home nonetheless. I wanted to know what was in my home and that included every cabinet and cubbyhole. And I expected every item therein to be useful and workable.

My husband the FSO was responsible for everything in the house that was provided by the government, from the furniture to the drapes to the sterling silver down to the smallest sauté pan and potato peeler. When we arrived at post and again before we departed, regulations required Art to sign a document attesting to the existence (and the condition) of every item on the inventory.

The inventory was important not only from a legal standpoint but also in order to replace supplies that were broken or worn out. The Pertinent People in Washington could peruse the inventory and put the proverbial tick mark by "DCR (the deputy chief's residence): The Hague," for instance, when the numbers matched the need and the allotment.

Inventory complications arose, however, when "someone" (a servant? an embassy employee? a spouse?) ran a finger down a stack of plates and came up with a count of 73. The number on the last inventory was 75 so although two plates were broken during the year, 73 was still an adequate number of plates, right? Not necessarily so. You had to inspect every dish, top and bottom. I found seven plates with old ugly cracks and nine that were badly chipped. That meant 16 dishes were not fit to set before guests at our dinner table. The gold rim on six other plates was faded and worn—some miscreant had put them in the dishwasher, which is against the rules. I set those aside to be used only if necessary.

According to my count "DCR: The Hague" didn't have 73 dinner plates, it had 57. When Washington received our request for eighteen new plates, the Pertinent People probably looked at our inventory list and their eyebrows darted upward. They wondered what was going on at *that* post! There was more eyebrow action when they saw our order for two dozen glasses.

L. Paul Bremer III, known as "Jerry," and his wife Frances arrived a week after we did. He was the newly appointed and duly anointed ambassador, but I agree that *The Ambassador's Wife is an Ambassador, Too.* That is the title of an article written by Peggy Durdim for the New York Times Magazine in 1964. Her premise continues to be valid decades later. The majority of wives who accompany their ambassador husbands to post are exemplary envoys.

Francie was smart as well as intelligent, charming and also disarming. She had done her homework and could converse knowledgeably about the art, literature and politics of the Netherlands as well as that of the United States. She not only knew *what* to talk about but *how*, yet her conversational style was low-key. She introduced herself simply as "Francie." She was a people person.

With the arrival of a new ambassador and a new DCM the embassy staff was challenged by changes in dynamics and methods in addition to personalities, but everyone responded eagerly and with vigor. Morale in the workplace improved swiftly and noticeably week after week. After the unpleasantness associated with John Loeb in Copenhagen Art and I felt an immediate lift in our spirits in regard to the jobs ahead.

When Alex and Kathy joined us in The Hague they shared the fun of exploring and examining every corner of our hundred-year-old house. Alex noted the location of the fire extinguishers and planned the family's escape route in case of fire or a security threat, something we had neglected to do. He was quick to inform us that fleeing from the master bedroom (our designated safe haven) by way of the balcony would be neither speedy nor, for me, physically feasible. We took his suggestions seriously, spoke with our security officers and they immediately made changes in the emergency exit plans.

With our son and daughter with us once again, we decided to invite the Bremers and their two children for a casual family dinner. We still remember it as "the evening of Patrick's infamous chocolate eclairs."

After discussing various options we decided on the main course and then our cook asked us, "What would you like for dessert?"

"Let's have chocolate eclairs," Art replied quickly with a wink in my direction. Years before I had asked him the same question while planning for a special occasion. He had answered "chocolate eclairs" knowing full well that I didn't know how to make them. This challenge was repeated many times until I began to adopt the name chocolate éclair for whatever dessert I made. Now Art thought that finally he would get his chocolate eclairs since we had a cook. We didn't know yet that Patrick couldn't bake *anything*—let alone chocolate eclairs.

Before the dinner he spent all afternoon making dough and baking it—one batch after another—after another. I was aware that at least one tray of pastries had burned when an unmistakable smell wafted through the house. I intentionally avoided the kitchen and stayed out of his way—something I had learned from Toini. This was our first dinner party and I didn't want to make the cook nervous. But when I heard some heated exchanges coming from that direction, I asked Desmond if there was a problem.

"Patrick doesn't know how to use the oven!" explained the butler with annoyance. "He thinks the pastries are baking too slowly so he turns up the temperature and they burn. Then he makes another batch and they turn out soggy!"

Small but beautifully decorated chocolate eclairs appeared that evening for our dessert. The pastry wasn't quite right—mine was scorched on the bottom—but the filling was tasty and we ate them. I appreciated Patrick's efforts, especially after Kathy confided later that dozens of eclairs had ended up in the trash can during the course of the day. We never again asked Patrick for such a sacrifice.

We were attached to the Heart Association—our home was, that is. The Dutch organization had its offices on the other side of the building. The large structure abutted the front sidewalk; there was no approach, no front lawn, and no porch. Cars parked fender to bumper in front and all along the divided avenue. With offices next door and traffic flowing directly beneath our bedroom windows we feared noise and disruption. At the end of the workday, however, the cars disappeared and the street was surprisingly quiet. We could look out and enjoy the huge handsome trees that lined the median all along Sophialaan. And we never heard a heartbeat through the common walls.

Living plunk in the middle of the city was another new experience; at previous posts we had been located in the suburbs. The front of the house with nary a blossom or blade of grass was deceiving: within the high fences that surrounded us on two sides, we had a huge green yard with a beautiful array of shrubbery. There were flowering bushes and colorful bulbs in the spring, an enormous splendid copper beech and a walnut tree that produced nuts. We felt cozy within our space and isolated from the hubbub of the streets. There was a greenhouse in the back of the garden where sweet peas thrived along with radishes and lettuce, spinach and cucumbers.

Out the front door we were only a short stroll away from the post office, two bakeries, a stationery store that did photo developing, a dry cleaners, several fresh flower stands—and oodles of restaurants. I needed my car only to drive to the supermarket and to social functions. I accomplished all my other tasks and errands on foot. What a pleasure that was.

An ambassador becomes accredited to a foreign government only when he or she presents the required credentials to that government's head of state. Although an American appointee is sworn in at the State Department in Washington, DC, where he assumes the title of ambassador, he isn't official in the assigned country until he tenders a letter of credence from our head of state and a letter recalling the previous ambassador.

In America the head of state and the head of government are embodied in one person, the President. In many countries, however, a Prime Minister leads the government and the head of state may be a president or, as in the Netherlands, a monarch. It was Queen Beatrix to whom Jerry Bremer presented his credentials at her palace on Lange Voorhuit, two buildings away from the American Embassy. (Though Amsterdam is the capital of the Netherlands, the seat of government is in The Hague.)

Elegantly old-fashioned horse-drawn carriages are a continuing tradition in Holland and the Dutch government offered this mode of transportation to foreign envoys to deliver them to the queen. But alas—American security precautions prevented the Bremers from riding in the carriages. Automobiles instead drove Jerry and Francie to the palace along with the four embassy officers whom the ambassador had chosen to accompany him. The palace guard was there to meet them along with flag bearers and a band, all in full regalia as was the Dutch protocol official who directed the ceremonial activities.

We observers who had come to bear witness—actually to take photographs and ogle—were kept at a safe distance behind security barriers by a multitude of overzealous police officers.

Francie was lovely in a cream-colored suit set off by a bright teal blouse and a broad-brimmed hat. The men outshone her, however—a fact she was well aware of and, I suspect, amused by. Jerry, Art, Mike (political chief) and Frank (USIS) were resplendent in their required and rented morning suits: coats with tails, appropriately diplomatic striped pants, top hats and gloves. (According to the rules the top hats were not for wearing, only for carrying.) Paul (Defense Attaché) was equally elegant in his naval dress uniform and he looked distinctly comfortable in his familiar attire. The other four wore silly grins atop their morning suits as if they felt rather foolish in such alien clothing.

After the band played both national anthems the six Americans entered the palace. They came out again a short half-hour later sporting genuine smiles and looking more relaxed. Jerry was now official.

Walking home after the morning's impressive events, I heard the clop-clop of approaching horses and turned just in time to see a carriage round the corner in the direction of the queen's palace. I smiled to myself. Another ambassador was about to be launched.

Later in the month, the third Tuesday in September, to be exact, I saw another carriage. I had gone out on foot to do some shopping when I became aware that crowds were gathering on corners and along the street. Heads were bobbing, necks were stretching and, as the Dutch conversations around me became more animated I stopped to look and listen. I heard the clacking of hooves and there, coming down the street—was a stunning golden coach drawn by eight horses.

It was *Prinsjesdag*, the day Queen Beatrix rides from the palace in the royal family's carriage to the Binnenhof for the opening of parliament. There she delivers the "Speech From the Throne," the monarch's annual address to the nation. It is a regal stately affair, but the atmosphere in the streets that day reminded me of fairy tales.

The street in front of our house underwent an important change not long after our arrival. Reinforced concrete posts several feet high were inserted at the curb outside our door, prohibiting vehicles from parking in front of the building. At that time, 1983, the American government was upgrading all security precautions at its embassies and consulates around the world. New stone boxes sporting flowers and greenery soon lined the sidewalk in front of the chancery. They were heavy and strong and meant to be in the way of any wayward or sinister vehicle that might attempt an attack on our facilities.

Hydraulic barriers came next. Now, in order for a vehicle to pass through the gates and enter the embassy grounds, the driver waited for the guard to signal that the barrier could be lowered. That was done only after a trained eye had inspected the vehicle: inside the body, under the hood, inside the trunk and, by way of special mirrors, underneath the carriage.

Changes are sometimes difficult to adjust to. Shortly after the barriers were installed, a vehicle found itself hung up and unable to enter or exit the embassy grounds. The guard had raised the steel bar prematurely—while the car was above it. There was a mighty crunch.

Ambassador Bremer was escorted at all times by a bodyguard or two. A trained driver was at the wheel of the specially armored and reinforced vehicle in which he rode. He and Francie were not able to sneak off for a private dinner in a quiet little restaurant or go for a walk through the neighborhood by themselves—they always had a chaperone.

Kathy remembers when security was especially tight and her father insisted on sitting with his back to the wall whenever we were in a restaurant or other public place—a learned habit that he still has. He explained to her in great detail one afternoon what to watch for and what to do in case of a terrorist attack. "And then," she recalls, "After he had me all worried and nervous, he told me he was going upstairs to take a nap!"

We came to the conclusion, soon after arriving in The Hague, that a goodly number of people had dogs. We saw the evidence, which was also recorded by our olfactory senses, all along the sidewalks. One day a few blocks from home I spotted small figures repeatedly painted on the cement throughout the neighborhood. It was difficult to tell what animal the picture represented—I initially thought it was a rodent. But after I had traversed and sidestepped around a patchwork of pet surprises, I realized the picture was supposed to be a dog.

A few weeks later during one of our walks through the city we discovered more animal pictures but with two Dutch words written underneath: "*Niets Poepen.*" A plea to pet owners: the sidewalk was not the place to relieve nature.

In Holland the decline in the number of children has been matched by the increase in the number of pets—and houseplants.

We had a pet—for a short time. We inherited Jerry the Cat from our predecessors who promised to send for him when they were settled in the States. Art and I reluctantly agreed to keep the animal after Desmond said he would arrange for transportation when the time came. Jerry was an outdoor cat, they said, and "would be no trouble."

One early morning at 0-dark-thirty the Outdoor Cat signaled his presence in our bedroom by leaping up and landing on my chest like a fur shot put. It was not a pleasant awakening and my hysterical screams sent Jerry bounding out the terrace door and up into a tree where he hid and cried most of the day. He obviously missed his former family and we who were not accustomed to pets of any sort were not appropriate substitutes.

Cat stew came to mind another day when I discovered Jerry on the kitchen counter circling a fresh dish of butter. Outdoor Cat indeed! After several more months of cat tricks it became apparent that the former owners had deserted their pet. With the help of Peter, who cooked for our Danish friends across the street, Desmond found a new home for Indoor-Outdoor Jerry.

Among the restaurants within walking distance from our home was one that specialized in pancakes. Dutch pancakes were a treat for foreigners—including us—although our Dutch friend Gijsbert, whom we met later in Yemen, said he thought pancakes were "nothing special" for the local people "except perhaps at children's birthday parties."

If you are conjuring up an image of fluffy American-style flapjacks you're on the wrong taste track. Think of French crepes and you'll be closer to *pannekoeken* in flavor and texture. The Dutch version was flat and round, covering a humongous plate about fourteen inches in diameter. You could order your pancake with bacon or ham or cheese enveloped in the batter or you might prefer yours as dessert topped with apples or strawberries and crowned with whipped cream. The Dutch were likely to cover theirs with *stroop*, a thick dark-colored syrup.

Food in The Hague was international in variety. There were restaurants featuring Italian, Chinese, French, and Swiss cuisine, and little cafes that offered delicious Middle Eastern *shwarmas*. But most prolific was Indonesian food. The *rijsttafel*, rice table, originated in the former Dutch East Indies and became extremely popular in the Netherlands. The meal consisted of several small dishes of meat, chicken, and vegetables prepared in a variety of ways and a sampling of each went on top of the rice. Peanut sauce was predominant but there were other sauces and condiments, some of which were fiery hot. Guests who came to visit us had usually heard of the famous *rijsttafel* and were eager to sample it. Those who liked a kick with their food were quite happy with the heat. Others were impressed by the unique flavor of the peanut/meat combination.

The goat, however, drew mixed reviews. Some restaurants included goat on the menu but depending on the method of preparation and the accompanying sauce one couldn't distinguish it from any other meat.

Sharon, our former neighbor from Bethesda, was repelled at the very mention of goat meat and announced she had no intention of trying it however it was camouflaged. There were eight of us at the table that evening and we ordered a variety of dishes—enough for twice our number! Afterwards as we discussed the pros and cons of the food, Clark told his wife she had eaten goat—and she had liked it! Sharon is still not convinced.

The Dutch oven made its way to the United States many years ago and most American families have one of these large heavy lidded pots. Actually the name probably came by way of German immigrants who were called Pennsylvania Dutch. Today combining several ingredients and cooking them slowly to marry the flavors can be accomplished on top of the stove or in the oven—with a Dutch oven. Hearty food frequently was an *eentopf*—or one-dish meal. We especially liked *braune bohnen*: tasty brown beans with vegetables and sometimes a tiny bit of meat for flavoring. Another typical *eentopf* was made of split peas.

History records an additional meaning for "Dutch oven." According to *A Dictionary of Slang and Unconventional English* the term also signifies "the olfactory state of the bedclothes after one has broken wind."

Herrings were perhaps the most historically typical Dutch food. As in Germany and Denmark they were prepared in numerous ways, marinated or in cream sauce, whole or chopped, with or without onions. But raw unadorned herrings were a Dutch specialty. So special in fact that *Vlaggetjes Dag*, Flag Day, was almost a holiday. On that date at the end of May the newly painted and polished ships of the herring fleet, all colorfully decorated and hung with flags, went out from Scheveningen and from Vlaandingen to open the fishing season. The queen received a gift of the first herrings and then from June to September the green or *groene haring* were fresh and at their best at herring stands all over the country. The Dutch and many a brave foreigner could be seen in front of the kiosks, heads back, holding new herring by the tails and sliding them into eager mouths, chewing slowly, then tossing the tails away. On occasion, a tail also disappeared into an open mouth.

The Dutch were also fond of smoked eel, a not-so-famous delicacy. Eel was not particularly popular among Americans, perhaps because it was just plain unfamiliar. Always willing to try new things, I politely accepted an eel sandwich offered by my Dutch hosts, Joudie and David, but early into the second bite I traded it for ham. I just couldn't get around the tough spine down the middle of the eel. It was impossible to chew and I didn't know what to do with it!

The Dutch made some of the best cheeses in the world and they exported well over half of what they produced. Gouda and Edam are well known in the United States, but harder to find are delicious Maasdam, Leerdam, Leiden, and aged Old Amsterdam. And one had to *live* in the Netherlands to enjoy the wonderful farmers' cheeses because most were not exported. These tasty cheeses, each a little different, were found in the countryside and at small town markets.

When the Dutch people marked the 40th anniversary of their country's liberation by Allied Forces at the end of World War II, Art and I witnessed a unique corner of history. From September 1984 through May the following year there were memorial services, parades, solemn ceremonies and jubilant celebrations. There were emotional remembrances and happy reunions as thousands of veterans returned to the Netherlands from the U.S., Canada, England and other parts of Europe. Brigadier-General James M. Gavin, commander of the American 82nd Airborne during the war, was one of the returnees who took part in the Market-Garden commemorations.

Queen Beatrix frequently headed the roster of royals who attended the unveiling of freshly hewn memorial stones and the dedication of shiny new brass plaques. But those were times when shaking hands with royalty and rubbing shoulders with dignitaries were overshadowed by the enormity of the occasion. The queen's father, Prince Bernard, presided over several events and he talked openly with us about his personal gratitude for the sacrifices of so many soldiers. At one of the celebrations we met Princess Margriet. Dressed in an elegantly simple suit and small matching hat, she looked very much like her sister, the queen, and she was equally as friendly and at ease with strangers.

But the real celebrities during the anniversary were the veterans. Some were elderly and frail; others were no more than sixty and already planning to return again in ten years for a 50th reunion. I saw several chins quiver when the men talked of their buddies who didn't live through the liberation. I saw winks and nods and heard lots of laughter as they reminded each other of funny stories and personal jokes. All of them spoke proudly of their war service.

Vera Lynn, the queen of song during WWII, reigned again in Oosterbeek when she sang to a grateful and admiring audience during one of the celebrations. "We'll meet again, don't know where, don't know when…" That unforgettable song from the war era summoned up smiles, tears, and tumultuous applause.

The christening of the "Liberty" took place at Keukenhof in that magical kingdom of flowers. Liberty was the cultivar name reserved for a new orange tulip approved by the Royal General Bulbgrowers Association. A member of America's 503rd Division, Combat Engineers had the honor of christening the tall stately tulip for the grateful Dutch citizens who appreciated "…the great personal sacrifice brought by the people of the United States of America in carrying out the liberation of the Netherlands."

And at home that year the American people at last dedicated a symbolic resting-place in Arlington National Cemetery for the unknown soldiers who died in Vietnam.

In The Hague we were again captivated by amateur theater. The Anglo-American Theater Group was large, cohesive and full of talented people who put on several productions each year including a well-known British staple, the pantomime. For the uninitiated the term pantomime is misleading. A "panto" is not mime, but a musical comedy usually based on a familiar children's story or a fairy tale that has been rewritten to appeal to a modern audience of both children and adults. Wanting to participate I was willing to portray any character that was needed. One year I was a clown and Yona, the expert, taught us how to paint our faces with lots of gooey colorful makeup. I agreed to be one of a gaggle of adolescent boys in the next panto. I had a whopping three lines to say and it was such fun!

Art played Uncle Ben in *Death of a Salesman*, a marvelous production that showcased the abilities of Roberta, a multitalented American woman who had been a professional actress. She later produced a play based on the letters written by John Adams to his wife Abigail while he served as our first ambassador to France. Art narrated the play and the Adams were portrayed by two other gifted thespians, Gail and Ruth, both educators at the American International School.

Our days were busy, most evenings were occupied and we never had the time to be bored. When Art left the office and put behind him (briefly) issues such as INF (Intermediate-range Nuclear Forces,) security threats, sanctions against Libya, and preparations for official visitors, he played tennis and softball, only taking time out to heal a broken ankle. We attended official functions and cultural events not only in The Hague, but also in Amsterdam and Rotterdam. We hosted houseguests on a regular basis: family, friends and official visitors from Washington, DC. And we entertained a host of Dutch officials and parliamentarians, foreign diplomats, colleagues and friends.

We had the unique privilege of entertaining members of the Harlem Opera Ensemble from New York City. When they came to The Hague to perform "Showboat," one of our favorite American musicals, we invited them to our home for Sunday brunch. What a lively group of people! They were pleased to be invited for a home-cooked meal and to spend a relaxing afternoon with other Americans. We ate from trays on our laps and as I looked around the group, I was totally in awe of the musical talent represented there in our own living room.

Each year at the end of May we drove to the province of Limberg where we commemorated American Memorial Day. Over 8300 of our service people from World War II are buried in the American cemetery at Margraten. After the services The Netherlands American Institute of Limberg hosted a dinner in Maastricht. The organization was established to further friendship between the two countries, and through NAIL Art and I made many friends in the southern part of the Netherlands.

General Josef Luns was with us at another NAIL dinner in Maastricht, this one in celebration of Thanksgiving. I suppose we ate turkey, but what I remember is laughing throughout the meal. That grand gentleman, a true extrovert then in his seventies, was formerly Secretary General of NATO. I could imagine him winning over various warring factions and solving unpleasant international disagreements with humor and laughter. I was completely enamored by his charm, wit and endless anecdotes.

Barbara Bush came to The Hague. The Vice President accompanied her, of course, but his wife was definitely the more memorable person. Mrs. Bush's reputation for down-to-earth friendliness preceded her—and followed her—wherever she went. The Bushes paid a visit to the embassy, shook hands, thanked the employees for their service and left everyone mightily impressed—as they had in Copenhagen.

Prime Minister Rudd Lubbers hosted a dinner in honor of the Bushes in the Treveszaal, a banquet room at the Binnenhof, seat of the Dutch parliament. Located in the center of the city, the Binnenhof, which means inner court, is a complex of historical government buildings, parts of which date to medieval times. The hall where we dined was not medieval; it was beautifully lit and elegantly appointed, crisp white linens and fresh flowers decorating the tables.

As the waiters were clearing away the plates and we awaited dessert, I left my table and with some urgency went in search of the powder room. I unfortunately am one of those people who can't hold their drink—in the physical sense, not the behavioral. We had left home hours earlier in order to be in place at the Binnenhof before the dignitaries arrived. We sipped a cold drink while we mingled, diplomat style, during the reception and enjoyed the wine as well as water that accompanied the long many-layered meal. And the chances were favorable that a toast would be proffered as soon as the dessert was served—which meant swallowing more liquid.

As I left the restroom feeling much relieved, it occurred to me that Mrs. Bush might also like to be relieved. Instead of returning to my place I approached the head table and tapped her on the shoulder. "Excuse me, Mrs. Bush," I whispered, "I have located the ladies' room and I'd be glad to take you if you would like."

She turned to me with that toasty warm smile of hers and replied, "That is so kind of you; however, I have just been given *the signal* and you know what that means—we'll be going soon. I'll just have to wait. Thank you!"

A scant minute later, the Vice President stood up, followed by his wife and the Prime Minister and they said good night. The rest of us stayed and ate dessert. There were no more toasts. It dawned on me as I sat there that Mrs. Bush would not have been allowed to leave the banquet room without a security escort. Perhaps she has accustomed herself to "waiting" as she must have to do frequently.

Prior to the George H. W. Bush visit Art and other embassy staff were conferring with the Vice President's advance team and a Dutch protocol representative.

Queen Beatrix had invited Mr. and Mrs. Bush to a private lunch with her and Prince Claus. All of the day's details had to be gone over thoroughly: departure and arrival times, security precautions, travel routes, pathway and entrance to the palace and other minutiae.

Art asked the Bush people how many cars would make up the motorcade and the answer was "fourteen."

The Dutchman gasped.

"Fourteen?" My husband was incredulous. "Fourteen vehicles for a two-on-two lunch?"

The advance team at first looked sheepish and then one by one became defensive. "So many people…so many cars…needed…necessary…useful…."

Art burst through the defensive line then and insisted on particulars: "Who is to be in each car—and why?"

"Our security people." Security. Uh-huh, right. "The doctor and nurse." Medical. Uh-huh, okay. But who else? Aids, assistants, advisors…

After some extreme excuses and silly suggestions the negotiations led to elimination and a total of six vehicles was agreed upon. The queen's protocol man once again began to breathe smoothly.

The truth is, on the day the Bushes ate lunch with Queen Beatrix and Prince Claus, the motorcade that carried them to the palace consisted of more than six cars—but only one or two more.

It is difficult to say what I liked most about Holland. The cheese? The beer? The friendly Dutch people? The pancakes? The miniature replicas of the city at Madurodam? If I had to make a decision—if I were heavily pressed to name my favorite feature of the country—I would have to say the flowers, which were unquestionably gorgeous. There was an enormous variety in a plethora of colors. Fresh cut flowers and houseplants were inexpensive and one never had to drive or walk far to find a flower stall; they were everywhere.

Spring bulb flowers were magnificent! You can believe all the tourist literature and all the sales pitches—tulip time in Holland is as spectacular as it sounds. At Keukenhof park, your soul as well as your eyes were blessed with an unsurpassed beauty as you strolled the gardens and inhaled the fresh air with its aroma of clean dark earth and the spring-time fragrances of freesias, hyacinths, tulips and so many others. While the outdoors offered its naturally sequential parade of bulb flowers, the greenhouses welcomed you inside where the plants were replaced almost daily to give flower lovers a constant garden display. Every daffodil, each bud and blossom, every iris, each blade and stem of green were planned to contribute to the entire scene.

Growing up in Nebraska I was familiar with auctions, particularly livestock auctions where manure odors were country pleasant and the sight and sounds of the cattle and the pigs made me wish I were a real farm girl. I was particularly fascinated by the voice of the auctioneer. The speed and rhythm and sudden undulations he used as he communicated with the buyers and sellers were awesome. My best friend Diane's daddy was a cattle feeder and he knew all about being an auctioneer. When he demonstrated for us, rapidly manipulating his tongue and tone as he called out livestock prices, I thought it must be like using a foreign language.

The early morning auction at Alsmeer was somewhat different. Alsmeer is the site of the Netherlands' flower auction that was unlike any sale I had ever experienced. First and foremost, the aromas. Our tour guide led us through the huge chilly warehouse where employees were sorting and counting scores of varieties of cut flowers and preparing them for shipping. The almost-at-peak blossoms gave off the most heavenly fragrances one can imagine.

The auction itself took place in a coliseum-shaped room where hundreds of buyers perched in a circular arrangement and watched a lighted board above their heads. The auctioneer rapidly relayed information about the varieties of flowers, their prices and availability. To a lay person his voice was as mystifying as that of the livestock auctioneer. By electronic means, the buyers silently and quickly made their selections and those purchases were soon en route to markets in Europe or trucked to nearby Schiphol Airport and flown abroad.

Did you know that tulips and daffodils don't like each other? If they are put together in a vase they will whisper withering insults to each other and the bouquet will wilt prematurely. Or something like that.

A Dutch military officer and his wife invited us to dinner one evening and I wanted to take a gift as is customary. I arrived home from another social event rather late in the afternoon and to save time, I asked Irene to go to a nearby kiosk and purchase a bouquet. She came back with a lovely bundle of yellow and white flowers that Art and I gave to our hostess, Karin, when we arrived.

Inspecting the flowers the woman announced in a supercilious tone, "You should never group tulips and daffodils together; didn't you know that?"

There they were, those fighting flowers—together! I had been in such a hurry, I hadn't noticed. But I was flabbergasted that our hostess had the audacity to point out the flaws in her gift. On the way home I silently hoped the flowers murdered each other by morning and left sad petals all over Karin's floor.

Foreign Service Requisite: thick skin.

With over fourteen million inhabitants, the Netherlands was a densely populated country with dense traffic to match, especially in the major western cities where nearly half the population lived. It was no wonder there was a lot of cycling, not only to avoid traffic hassles and parking problems, but also for pleasure outings in the countryside. In fact, bicycles numbered between ten and eleven million. We had three bicycles in our garage and Art enjoyed a turn or two with his on the occasional weekend. Kathy rode her bike back and forth to her summer job at the embassy—until she was knocked flat by a bus in a traffic circle. She was only bruised, but after that, she agreed that bike riding in our neighborhood was a risky venture. Too many cars and trucks and trams and buses.

Alex and Kathy were in college during the three years we were in The Hague. The summers and holidays they spent with us were full of fun, friends and freedom. Culture shock was short-lived and shyness was long past. There were lots of young people to hang about with, not only Americans and Dutch, but also other nationalities and they all made friends quickly. When someone had a visitor from out of town, the group liked to head for Amsterdam to see the sights and visit the Heineken brewery.

Our location was advantageous—the kids could walk to all the local hangouts. Most of their friends lived in the suburbs and drove to our place where they left their cars and joined the walk. The streets were safe, they stayed in a group, and we didn't have cause for concern. Morning "bed-check" was often necessary when a mother called to inquire if her son were with us, usually because she needed her car. I would creep quietly into the guest bedrooms and check the pillows to see who might have spent the night in one of our twin beds. Parents knew we were glad to have their kids stay in our home, particularly as a deterrent to drinking and driving.

When Page and Merk were married, it was THE social event of the year for the young people and their elders as well. Planning a wedding in a foreign country could be a nightmare but Mike and Mary, the parents of the bride, executed this one in style. Mike was our Air Force attaché and as plans for the nuptials were progressing, the European fashion magazine *Elegance* decided to feature photos of the wedding. "American diplomat's daughter is married in the Netherlands…" It was a lovely touch and added to the excitement.

Perhaps the appeal for *Elegance* was the combining of American and Dutch customs, including transportation in Dutch carriages. The bridesmaids and groomsmen, at any rate, rode in traditional buggies but Kathy said the bride and groom had a "Cinderella carriage." Pretty as it was, the carriage was small and old-fashioned and Page had some difficulty stuffing her full skirted and hooped gown through its door.

Another Dutch tradition was the birthday celebration. Though birthdays are important almost everywhere, it seemed that they commanded a lot more attention in Holland. I was a bit curious at first when I noticed that every bathroom I visited had a calendar hanging on the wall or behind the door. But I soon I found out that those weren't just ordinary calendars, they were *birthday* calendars. The Dutch kept the calendars where they could see them every day—in the bathroom. That way no one forgot a relative's or a friend's birthday.

One fine May day I went zipping down the stairs in a bright pink dress ready to leave for the AEWG spring lunch. There came Desmond rushing up the stairs to meet me. "Go to your room and lock the door!" he ordered and back down he went.

The tone of his voice shocked me more than his words. I managed to squeak out "Why?" just as he rounded the banister at the bottom of the staircase.

"There's a security alert," he called over his shoulder, "Just go!" and he disappeared through the back hall.

I went to my room. I locked the door. And I immediately headed for the huge windows overlooking the street. I was too curious—and perhaps too foolish—to be frightened. Sirens were whining and brakes were squealing as I reached the windows. I saw policemen piling hastily out of their vehicles. I heard the racket of two-way radios and the insistent live voices shouting in Dutch. The windows were closed—I had latched them before I left the room only minutes before. I wanted to pull them open, but I thought it probably wasn't prudent. I moved into the dressing room adjacent to our bedroom and pressed my face to the windowpane. Our front door was directly below and I watched as several police officers disappeared beneath me into the house.

The hubbub in front of the house diminished after a short while and all I could hear were sirens clamoring on the other side of the block. I unlocked the bedroom door and cautiously peeked my head out. I could hear muffled voices—lots of them—coming from downstairs. I tiptoed to the top of the staircase and listened but I couldn't understand a word. I started down the stairs hesitantly and Desmond spotted me as I reached the landing.

"What's going on?" I demanded predictably.

Just as sternly as before, Desmond told me, "Go back upstairs—Mr. Blackburn's orders! I'll explain later." Blackburn was the RSO.

I could see policemen traversing the hall below, but I did as I was told and again I went upstairs. When at last I was allowed out of my room, the officers had left except for two who were guarding the front entrance.

Desmond told me what had happened. The buzzer rang insistently from the driveway gate and when Desmond asked who was there, an accented voice shouted in English, "We're coming in there and we're going to kill all of you!" Another voice spoke from the background but the words were unclear.

Right beside this intercom was the panic button and Desmond pushed it immediately. He then communicated with our security officers at the embassy. The police arrived swiftly and surrounded the neighborhood, which they thoroughly checked after searching our property. They didn't find the perpetrators.

When I arrived at the luncheon an hour or so late, Francie was relieved to see me. "I saw the police cars in front of your house," she told me. Another woman had to detour because a row of police cars had blocked off a major street on our block. Only then did I fully realize the potential threat of the situation and I felt a profound gratitude for the quick response of Desmond, the police and our own embassy security people.

Another incident of panic buttons and quick responses occurred at the embassy. Yona had spent the late afternoon at a child's birthday party and she arrived at the embassy after dark to meet her husband. Since it was after business hours, the doors were locked. Yona plodded up to the door in her floppy long-toed shoes. She waved her fat orange-gloved fingers and waggled her curly cherry red wig. She pressed her round squishy red nose against the glass and rang the bell.

The Marine on duty looked out and saw what he feared was a deranged person dressed in a clown suit—he pushed the alarm! Promptly two local guards grasped Yona by the arms and patted her down while she struggled to explain in Dutch that she was legitimate. When the guards released her she produced her ID card and told them her husband's name and phone extension. He was only slightly embarrassed by the misunderstanding but his wife, after the initial shock of being manhandled, thought the whole thing was a hoot! Yona was a professional clown. She performed at parties, taught clown classes and when she was in costume she tried never to be out of character!

The call came on Christmas Eve. Art's friend Arnie at the State Department informed us of our next assignment: Tel Aviv, Israel. Art had hoped for Israel and we were both delighted at the prospect of changing continents, cultures and climates.

The following months were a flurry of pre-packing activities, arrangements, and farewells. Whenever we had a free evening we poured through books about Israel, its short yet lengthy history, its people and politics. The Hebrew language would have to wait.

Art added another layer of bubble paper and cardboard around Jorgen's gift of red wine, which we were still saving for that "special" occasion. We couldn't carry it because our hand luggage was packed with fragile Delft plates for the family. We entrusted the wine to the packers—and once again crossed our fingers.

More good-byes. Another move.

We thanked our staff—we would miss them very much. Irene cried and I tried not to. Patrick hugged me. And Desmond said, "If you ever need me, wherever you are, just call me."

13

SAFEGUARDS AND SAFEKEEPING

Alex climbed into the driver's seat of the ambassador's glossy black Cadillac, looked around appreciatively and decided to "go cruisin'." He had discovered the keys to the vehicle in our kitchen and he knew that the ambassador was nowhere around. He also knew that his parents, who were hosting a reception, would be occupied for at least another hour.

He started the car, moved slowly and quietly up the incline of our driveway, out onto the street and away he went—no longer slowly nor quietly. He picked up Benita, fetched another friend, Ali, and the three of them took a spin through the streets of Copenhagen.

Unbeknownst to Alex, as soon as the Cadillac was in motion an alarm sounded in the embassy. The Marine on duty knew immediately that the car was moving, but he didn't know who was at the wheel because David, the ambassador's driver, was right there in the embassy!

Alex, twenty years old, was enjoying his command of the sleek automobile, but he wisely knew he'd better not enjoy it for very long. He drove Benita and Ali to their homes and hustled back to his own, where he parked the car in its previous spot. Slipping into the kitchen to return the car keys, he discovered his dad—hanging up the phone. The ensuing tongue-lashing was as thorough as it could be with guests in the next room.

Art was furious, the Marines were relieved, and David the driver was amused. His attitude was "boys will be boys" and so will young men!

Implements, mechanisms and apparatus for enhancing personal safety in vehicles, homes and in the workplace are essential at diplomatic posts. Ambassadors' vehicles are outfitted with alarms, sirens, locks and other safety devices including bulletproof windows and partial or full armor. The residences of ambassadors and

DCMs are equipped with "panic buttons," ideally one in the bedroom and at least one in the living room/dining room area. These silent alarms are placed in inconspicuous spots, but are easily accessible in case of trouble.

Had there been a panic button in the ambassador's residence in Sanaa, it would have been firmly pushed the night we were fired upon. Somehow the architects—or the engineers—or the security planners—forgot to install the device on the ground floor of the house. It didn't matter in this case; the Marine guard heard the blast the same time we did.

We had been in Yemen for only three weeks when it happened. Art and I were eating dinner in our over-sized dining room when we heard the unmistakable sound…"whoooosh"…followed by a thunderous explosion that we felt as well as heard.

We bolted from the table. Art reached for the telephone at the back of the room and dialed the Marine at the embassy next door. The answer to Art's expected query was, "We don't know yet."

The Marine asked, "What part of the house are you in?" When my husband answered that we were in the dining room, the Marine's directive was: "Shut the drapes and stay away from the windows!"

A camera at that moment could have preserved the looks of exacerbation and chagrin on our faces as we stared at each other realizing that we could *not* close the drapes. They were narrow side panels, not meant to be closed.

We ran upstairs to our private quarters, our designated "safe haven." My first knot of fear gave way to frustration as we waited for further information. There were no more explosions and no evidence that we were under attack. The local guards had surrounded the house and searched the area and the entire Marine contingence had been recalled to duty.

A bazooka, the RSO informed us later, had been fired from the wadi below us. The misguided missile had overshot its target, the American Embassy—next door!—and torpedoed through the roof of a building across the street. The Russian Military Assistance Mission had rented several apartments there but the Russians had recently gone back to Moscow. Fortunately, the apartment that was blown up was vacant and no one in the building was injured.

Armed Marines are posted at the entrances to American embassies and consulates. They have access to numerous bells and buttons and switches for responding to security emergencies. Maybe there are too many of those gadgets.

I was home alone one night in Sanaa when I heard a telephone ring. I went down the hall to answer it, but the sound seemed to change direction. I did likewise. When I finally picked up a phone, there was no one there. Curious, I called the Marine at Post 1 who was in charge of the switchboard after business hours.

"Do you know who was calling us?" I asked him.

"No one," the Marine told me. "I haven't put a call through to your residence all evening."

A few weeks later I stayed home with the flu while Art and Kathy (who was visiting) went out to a holiday party. The telephone rang and—again—the sound seemed to come from a strange direction. When the ringing stopped abruptly, I heard some one talking, faintly, but talking nonetheless. I darted from sitting room to bedroom to another bedroom, into a bathroom and back to the sitting room. Who was speaking—and where? I suspected the sound was coming from the ceiling but The Voice went silent before I could be sure.

I was unable to sleep. As soon as Art and Kathy came in the door, I blurted out my report of the disembodied voice. Art very politely and as kindly as possible told me I had an excessively active imagination. Or maybe it was the fever—or my stuffy head.

The next morning at breakfast I was adamant: "I *did* hear a voice!"

"You have nothing to be afraid of, Pat." Art was obviously cajoling me. He explained that there was no way anyone could be above the sitting room or the bedrooms because there was no empty space. He had looked at the house blueprints and had gone up on the roof to double-check. He said there was nothing above the ceilings except heating and air-conditioning ducts. I was not convinced. There could certainly be space enough for espionage equipment!

Kathy was with me a few nights later when Art went out for the evening. The phantom phone rang again. I rushed toward the sound—into the hallway leading to the bedrooms—and I knew then, absolutely, that none of our telephones was ringing. We both heard The Voice speak as soon as the ringing stopped. It sounded like code: short replies, quick sentences, curt. We could only distinguish occasional words but we were certain The Voice was speaking English.

The sequence was repeated a little while later: phone ringing, The Voice speaking, then silence. But this time we figured out where the ghostly sounds were coming from. On the sitting room wall near the ceiling there was a small round metal grill. That was IT.

Art believed me this time—I had a witness. He met the next morning with the security officer, the facilities management officer, and the Marine Gunny. And the mystery unfolded.

At Post 1 where the Marine Guard sat in front of the security monitors and the telephone, there was a toggle switch that activated a microphone. In case of an emergency the Marine could broadcast a warning through the intercom to our residence. One of the new Marines was toggling the switch unawares, as he reached to answer the telephone. The Voice was not a spy, but a friendly Marine.

The principal duty of the U.S. Marine Guard detachments abroad is to guard and secure what is inside the building—not including the personnel. This fact was divulged to us during an early session of the seminar for new ambassadors. Surprise registered on many faces when the class coordinator emphasized: "The Marines are not there to protect *you*."

One of the new appointees remarked with a grin, "Maybe we all should re-think this job."

The Marine on watch and/or his superior must assess the danger and the level of emergency in any situation and employ some or all of those aforementioned switches, buttons and levers. He can put the Marine detachment on alert or order an immediate recall. And he can call for a lock-down, prohibiting anyone from going in or out of the building.

Inside the embassy there is electronic equipment to be protected and there is paper, reams and reams of paper in the form of cables, facsimiles, letters, messages and records of all kinds. Some pieces of paper are ordinary, some are marked "Eyes Only," and a few are Top Secret. If the equipment and the paper cannot be protected from impending danger such as a terrorist attack or a natural disaster, the Marines can resort to the shredder and the incinerator.

Outside, however, local guards on contract to the embassy are responsible for guarding the building and the surrounding property. When the bazooka smacked into the apartments after barely missing the embassy and our residence, it was the Yemeni guard force who swarmed over our garden, checked for intruders, and searched for the placement of the launcher.

In Tel Aviv it was the Israelis who set up a twenty-four hour guard post out-side our temporary quarters after we arrived. I wasn't privy to the whys and wherefores, only that we were subject to a threat. And when the ambassador was out of the country and Art was chargé d'affaires, the Israeli guard force watched over us. And our home.

Prior to 1970 there were only a few United States embassies and consulates around the world where extreme precautions were needed and anti-terrorist prep-arations were routine. That changed. American diplomats, representatives of their government and its policies overseas, became targets of violent groups. Ira-nian extremists held American Embassy employees hostage for 444 days. Meanwhile the Palestine Liberation Organization broadened its geographic horizons and stepped up its menacing activities. The Red Brigade and the Bader-Meinhof gangs rose up and spread long fingers of fear throughout Europe. Countries that previously were considered safe and comfortable for diplomats now were plagued by the threat of terrorism.

The increasing threat level was apparent when we returned to Europe in 1980 after a four-year posting in Washington. We became more and more security-conscious as the decade progressed.

Our ambassador in Denmark was particularly concerned for his personal safety. He arranged to have an old police car parked in his driveway near the front entrance. It truly was an *old* police car; it barely made the distance from the vehicle graveyard to the residence, but Ambassador Loeb felt safer having it nearby. It would certainly deter any possible attack, he thought.

And it might have—except that the potential perpetrators would have known that there were no police officers accompanying the old car. Loeb couldn't resist telling every acquaintance and stranger about his clever plan to thwart danger. He explained at great length about the "fake" police car and the impression he expected it to convey.

The ambassador frequently announced with eloquence, "The best thing I can do for myself is stay alive."

Nancy and Dan were posted to Bonn in the mid-1980's. Had they not alerted us we would have been shocked at the changes that had taken place in the suburb of Plittersdorf since our assignment there ten years before. No longer could we enter the community, where most of the embassy people lived, and drive down memory lane. As visitors we didn't have access to the athletic field, the schools our children had attended, the American Club, all of the once-familiar places. Not without a special pass—and only after Dan had registered us as their guests.

When we were in The Hague, our college-aged son and daughter and their friends were advised to vary their gathering places so as not to be predictable. They were also told not to hang about in large groups. This was the antithesis of the usual parental advice of "stay together" and the assumption that there was safety in numbers. Art told Alex and Kathy—again—why and how to be alert and they listened with unruffled acceptance.

What was happening in our once-peaceful world?

In Beirut suicide bombers blasted the American Embassy and the Marine Corps barracks and later the embassy annex, killing and maiming hundreds of Americans. A car bomb destroyed the Frankfurt PX, injuring thirty-five people.

All in the 1980's. Meanwhile the Libyan henchmen of Muammar al Qaddafi threatened, terrorized and kidnapped. And in 1988 Libyan intelligence agents were responsible for planting a bomb on an airplane that killed 259 people.

We were living in The Hague when an unusually high state of alert began in the Netherlands—and other places—in January 1986. Lebanon's Islamic Jihad threatened to strike at "the most vulnerable points of American imperialism." At the same time Abu Nidal's group of Palestinian terrorists was reportedly planning attacks on Americans, Israelis and Jews elsewhere. The Dutch Ministry of Justice stationed more than 200 National Police officers at Schipol Airport. Additional guards surrounded our embassy and our consulates general in Amsterdam and Rotterdam, while heavily equipped observation vehicles kept watch. Ambassador Bremer arranged for an old beat-up dumpster to be filled with sand and placed outside the embassy—smack in front of the concrete flower boxes. Another layer of protection. Thousands of US troops were in the Netherlands for REFORGER, a long-planned periodic training exercise. The entrance to their campground was sandbagged and heavily guarded.

"Did you pack this bag yourself? Has the luggage been in your possession since you packed it?" These questions, asked by security personnel, are familiar to anyone who has traveled by airplane in the last decade.

After claiming their suitcases at Ben Gurion Airport, Alex and his fiancee' Mary had to unlock and open them at the request of a security official. Our son had passed his twenty-third birthday and was no longer eligible to carry a diplomatic passport—the possession of which may or may not have precluded the bag inspection. He and Mary had come to Israel to spend the holidays with us and their bags were loaded with Christmas presents.

The official pointed to a small gift-wrapped package and asked, "What is that?" Alex told him it was a compact disc. The man indicated another beribboned box and repeated his question. Alex's unfortunate answer was, "I don't know. Someone gave it to me to bring to my parents."

This was not the reply that a security person likes to hear and Alex realized it as he spoke. He quickly clarified that the gifts were from family members. He also explained that his father was the "number 2" at the American Embassy. In spite of this belated piece of information, the officer pulled several odd-shaped packages from the suitcase and told Alex to open them. A practiced hand felt the contours of the guest soaps and suspicious eyes inspected the socket wrenches. Finally with a last cursory look at the luggage, the officer said, "You can go." Alex's advice: don't gift-wrap the presents.

John, a friend of Kathy's who came to spend the same holiday with us in Tel Aviv, was detained and interrogated extensively. In the jargon of security people, John "fit the profile" (as Alex probably did also). Young man in his twenties, dressed in jeans, a couple of days' stubble on his chin, supposedly a student. But in John's case, there was an additional element that gave him a Potential Problem profile.

After John had booked his plane to Israel our family decided to travel to Egypt for several days. We invited John to join us and sent him a round-trip ticket from Tel Aviv to Cairo where we would meet him. The security officers were highly suspicious of his itinerary: land in Israel, stay 24 hours, fly to Egypt, stay four days, return to Israel. It was the short layover in Tel Aviv that sent up the red flags.

John explained…and explained. Finally one of the agents agreed to call the embassy. DCM Hughes could not be reached, of course; we had already left for Egypt. But the fact that John's alleged host, DCM Hughes, actually existed—as confirmed by the phone call—persuaded the security people that John was telling the truth. When he arrived in Cairo, he gave us a dramatic account of his lengthy grilling, told with a healthy grin on his face.

Kathy arrived at Ben Gurion Airport the following summer and she too failed a round of security tests. The security officer asked her why she had come to Israel and she replied that she was visiting her parents.

"Where do your parents live?" The agent wanted to know our street address, but she couldn't tell him. "I don't know, they have moved." She didn't admit that she had no idea of the previous address either.

"How long have they been in Israel?"

"One year," Kathy replied nervously.

"So your parents have lived here one year and you don't know their address?" The man was becoming peevish. Why was it that security people made you feel guilty when you hadn't done anything wrong?

"I never use their street address, I always write to them at the American Embassy."

"Ah—so what is the address of your embassy?"

The situation was worsening. "I don't know," she said. "I use the APO address." She then attempted to explain American Post Office. Finally, she dug into her handbag and produced her little address book, "Here it is, my parents' mailing address. And here is their phone number." Whether the officer was satisfied or not, that was the end of the questions.

I was troubled about the envelope all the way to St. Louis. My mind kept replaying the security questions at Ben Gurion Airport: "Did anyone give you anything—a letter or a package—to carry on the plane?"

"No." Actually the answer should have been "yes." But that was later, wasn't it? I couldn't refuse. Did I do the right thing? Maybe I made a mistake.

I was traveling alone to my mother's seventieth birthday celebration in Nebraska. While I was checking my bags, the ticket agent said the manager wanted to speak to me. I was expecting a familiar face—the manager of the airline was a friend of ours. Instead, I was introduced to the airline's airport manager, who informed me I would be flying first class to Lincoln. And by the way...

"We would like to ask a favor of you. Would you be kind enough to deliver some important papers to our office in St. Louis?"

I didn't hesitate a second. "I'd be happy to." Making a delivery was a small fee to pay in exchange for traveling comfortably in the first class cabin. And I had to change planes in St. Louis anyway.

After I boarded the plane the manager brought me a large manila envelope, which he opened and showed me the papers inside. He said they were routine but he wanted them to reach St. Louis as quickly as possible. And he repeated, "We really appreciate your help."

It wasn't until after take-off that I began to second guess myself. I opened the packet, looked again at the papers which were mostly lists and columns of numbers. There was nothing else in the envelope, certainly no lumps or bulges. But what if that man was *not* employed by the airline?

It was a jolt to hear my name over the public address system after I deplaned in New York. Good grief—I'd been caught! But at what? I answered the page with my heart beating like a jackhammer. I was greatly relieved to find a friendly smiling airline agent who said, "We would like to invite you to relax in our first class lounge until your departure for St. Louis." I did, after I took a lot of deep breaths.

Again, upon landing in St. Louis I heard my name broadcast. In a few minutes a distinguished gentleman introduced himself, thanked me profusely and relieved me of the manila envelope. He took my carry-on bag and my arm and said warmly, "May I escort you to our first class lounge?"

It was a comfortable and pleasant trip from Tel Aviv to Lincoln. But I would have enjoyed it more had I not felt unnecessarily guilty!

When Art joined the Foreign Service in 1965, anyone could walk through the front doors of the Department of State, stroll the corridors, climb the stairs or use the elevators. There were off-limit areas on the upper floors, but those were locked and clearly marked. Spouses as well as officers could attend to their banking needs, lunch in the cafeteria, make trip arrangements in the travel office or check the location of their HHE with the transportation people. They could return their stools kits to the Medical Unit or get their typhoid and yellow fever shots. Messengers came and went and deliveries were common.

That era is long past. Today, no one gets by the reception desk without proper identification. Employees have ID cards that must be worn and evident at all times. Visitors must be vetted and accompanied. Handbags, briefcases and packages are x-rayed. Security guards are posted throughout the lobby. With diplomatic passports spouses may obtain visitors' badges and after declaring their destinations may go there unaccompanied. But without that special black passport, the situation is quite different.

During our assignment in Washington in the early 90's my diplomatic passport expired and I wasn't to get a replacement until we were again posted abroad. I wasn't unduly concerned because I had a tourist passport. But when I went to the Department to see my husband, I learned I couldn't go upstairs until he—or someone from his office—came to escort me. I felt like a reform school alumna.

When the news of our assignment to Yemen came, the new diplomatic passport didn't—until two days before we left. Pre-departure preparations became a headache. I had consultations with the desk officer and administration people regarding our residence in Sanaa. I needed to discuss sources for supplies and I had inventory questions. There were briefings about regulations and financial record keeping. I couldn't get to those offices without an escort—I wasn't allowed in the corridors by myself.

Even *with* a diplomatic passport I wasn't allowed to go unescorted to Art's offices abroad when he was DCM and later ambassador. The executive offices were separated from most other sections by doors with cipher locks or elevators with secret codes. Spouses weren't allowed to know any of those cryptic numbers.

In our residences, nevertheless, I was entrusted with thousands of dollars of inventory. I counted the crystal, accounted for the silver and cared for the china. I watched over the furnishings and all the government property that was assigned to us. But I couldn't walk into Art's office—alone. I might overhear something of a sensitive nature that Art hadn't already told me. Or I might spy a secret cable a day or two before someone in Washington leaked it to the press.

Finally, however, the keys to the castle came my way. The RSO in Sanaa phoned to say he wanted to talk to me. After a short briefing Mike informed me that I now had "secret access." I was stunned—the government trusted me! I could now punch the numbers in the royal lift and I could push the magic ciphers on the door lock—all by myself. I was so excited to get to the elevator that I completely forgot the code that Mike had mouthed to me—I had to run back and read his lips again.

The State Department cable that announced my new security status relayed this information also: "...clearance is active for the length of the ambassador's appointment." We were to leave Yemen in two months! After nearly thirty years as a Foreign Service spouse the tired old adage "better late than never" took on a new emphasis.

Foreign Service Requisite: a sense of humor—and never mind the irony.

Security warnings during WWII admonished our military personnel: "Loose Lips Sink Ships." That litany can well be recalled today. As diplomatic discussions, negotiations, bargaining and walks in the woods help to stave off wars, our diplomats know that one loose mouth and peace goes south. Because one never knows who is listening and where.

I hadn't expected to hear voices in our walls in Sanaa, but I wouldn't have been surprised to find out there were ears. At the beginning of our Foreign Service life we learned the blunt truth about listening devices. Our leaders in the A-100 course in 1965 told us about what may be hidden in the walls of any of our future domiciles and/or offices anywhere in the world.

Frankly, I didn't believe that our homes in Western Europe had ears, although I did contemplate the possibility now and then. But since Art never discussed classified information with me, it didn't matter. If he wanted to inform me about a subject that was "sensitive" he would tell me out in the open air while we were walking. In Europe or elsewhere.

I was more skittish about saying something that "our" people would take amiss, rather than the other side. We all know that our government doesn't bug its own faithful servants but...somehow I always thought I should whisper when calling the ambassador a jerk or proclaiming that his wife looked like a side of beef in a tutu. When I wanted to criticize the U.S. government or, more specifically the Foreign Service, I always lowered my voice. In my own home abroad I would never say out loud that the President or the Secretary of State were puzzles with a few pieces missing. Who knew where those comments might end up?

In Tel Aviv I was particularly cautious. Certainly Israel was our friend and our ally but to Israelis, trust was secondary to the security of their country. (Jonathan Pollard, to whit. He was an American that spied for Israel.) I assumed our home was bugged but the fact didn't offend me. I assumed also that someone was listening to us in Sanaa. Whether it was the Yemenis or someone else I didn't even attempt a conjecture—it wasn't important to me. I didn't have loose lips.

There was no doubt about listening devices in Prague. We visited Dan and Nancy when they were posted to that beautiful but glum city in the early 1980's. Whenever we began a conversation with serious overtones about the Czechs, the East Bloc, the Cold War, or any subject relating to the Soviets or to our own government, Nancy would wave her hands about and shoot her eyes in the direction of the ceiling. She felt compelled to remind us of the microphones.

The Czechoslovak secret service knew the whereabouts of the American diplomats twenty-four hours a day. That was expected. When we all went to the opera, the *all* included Dan and Nancy's chaperones for the evening. After some time in Prague the diplomats learned to spot their followers even though the latter rotated duties and subjects.

Now and then when Dan felt like having a bit of fun he made a game of trying to lose the Czech agents. He enjoyed a number of wins, but he didn't mind if he lost. In the process he became acquainted with the little streets and back alleys of Prague along with some useful defensive driving techniques.

Heike and Helmut, German friends whom we met in Sanaa, told me this story. Their friend, who worked for a German foundation, received a gold cigarette lighter from Yuri, the Russian third secretary. Although his title was third secretary—of which there was a multitude—everyone suspected he was KGB, the Soviet secret service. That's why a colleague from the American embassy convinced the German that together they should "check out" the golden gift.

In Heike's words: "Yes, the lighter contained a little something."

Aware of that information a group of friends got together one evening and placed the lighter—with its listening device inside—on a table in front of them. "We all had a good talk with Yuri!" Heike finished her story by adding with a grin, "Yuri never spoke to us again."

While posted in Washington we became friends with a couple from the Egyptian Embassy. Rania and her husband had been assigned to Moscow in the early 90's and the system was "relaxing a bit" as she put it. She had succeeded in becoming almost friends with her maid. One afternoon the domestic announced, "I'll be leaving early; we have our meeting tonight." The "meeting" was the servants' required tattling session to the secret service regarding their employers.

Rania told us that the diplomats in Moscow referred to the listening devices as "Boris." Whenever a woman was unhappy with her (state-appointed) domestic she would say loudly, "Boris, I wish the maid would do a better job cleaning the kitchen!" Eureka! The kitchen would be spotless the next day.

One evening Art and I were sitting at the dinner table discussing a recent foreign affairs glitch, something about the start and stop peace process in the Middle East. We had just returned to Washington from our final overseas posting. I began a loud opinionated tirade and then abruptly clamped my hands to my mouth. Art looked at me quizzically and I responded by rolling my eyes and aiming my thumb toward the wall. With a start, I realized that an old habit had surfaced and I laughed.

Art, who at first feared I was having a medical emergency, didn't think the moment was nearly as funny as I did. He said, "You're still suffering from war wounds."

Warnings about listening devices in our walls and telephones plus other spying techniques were on the agenda of the State Department's security seminars in the 1980's and 1990's. The greatest emphasis, however, was on personal safety. A diplomat's resume' of expertise now included survival skills.

Terrorists may use arson to instill fear, cause pandemonium and to kill people, the fire safety experts informed us. They told us what to do—and what not to do—in case of a fire. Crawl along the floor and, if possible, get a wet cloth to hold over your mouth and nose. If the metal doorknob feels warm or if smoke is coming under the door, don't open the door. If you are in a hotel and you decide it is safe to leave your room, "Take your room key with you!" If you find smoke at the end of the hall or in the stairwell, you may need to get back into your room.

We were staying in a hotel in Bethesda after we returned from Tel Aviv. Art left the room early one morning and I went to sleep again—a deep sleep. Abruptly a piercing red light woke me and then an alarm irrupted into the silence. When the alarm stopped, a droning voice took its place. I struggled to keep my eyes open—until I heard the word *fire*.

I rolled out of bed onto the floor. I felt the doorknob—it was cool. I sniffed the air—there was no smell of smoke. I opened the door a crack—no flames or fumes. I hurried down the stairs, concerned that I didn't see any one else. When I exited the building, hotel personnel directed me across the street to where other guests had clustered. I seemed to be rather late in arriving. I didn't remember getting dressed, but I must have.

A short while later as we watched the firemen climb into their trucks, the hotel manager announced, as if reporting on the weather, that a small blaze in the basement had been successfully put out. "You may return to your rooms." At that moment I discovered my room key tucked in the pocket of my jacket. Lessons learned.

The security seminar also provided experts on firearms who showed us weapons and various types of explosives, some of them fully assembled and others taken apart. We learned about timers, fuses, and simple Molotov cocktails, and about plastique and how it could be camouflaged. One lecturer advised us what to do if our aircraft were hijacked and how to "lose" our diplomatic passports if necessary. He emphasized the importance of possessing a blue tourist passport. (Diplomatic passports are black.)

We watched an unnerving film on defensive driving and although there was no accompanying classroom practice, those lessons were not difficult to absorb. The main point was to avoid situations where defensive driving became necessary. The "rules" have been repeated many times by security officers at post: don't repeatedly drive the same route; don't leave your home and your office at the same hour every day. In other words, don't be predictable.

The experts coached: "Be alert to your surroundings." Not just the car in front and the traffic signals, be aware of the people and vehicles around you. Watch for the unusual. "Avoid congested traffic areas." During times of crisis and when there is an alert, we have learned instinctively to stay away from bottlenecks and choke points. I continue to follow another piece of advice: always keep your gas tank at least half full.

Constant awareness of our surroundings at home as well as the workplace was high on the list of survival skills to practice. During the classes and later at post, security personnel repeatedly reminded us to beware of an unexplained package or bundle on the sidewalk or in an isolated corner of a hallway. Suspicious vehicles parked in the block or nosy-looking strangers should be reported.

"If you are taken hostage...." That possibility is not one any of us wanted to contemplate, yet one of the seminar sessions forced us to look head-on at that very subject. We watched a filmed dramatization of a man being taken hostage and his subsequent solitary confinement. It was chilling. The lecturer stressed the importance of keeping your mind and body as active as possible. If you are not able to stand erect, continue to exercise the muscles in whatever parts of the body you can move. Use your brain by doing mathematical problems or recreate in your mind a chronology of happy events in your life. Important advice that one hopes never to have to use.

The increase in terrorism since the 1970's has made security seminars a prerequisite for American Foreign Service personnel going overseas. Many other countries also provide and often require training and briefings on personal safety for their diplomats as well as business people. We are taught, in the words of former Canadian Ambassador Sidney Freifeld "...how to make [ourselves] less predictable and less alluring as targets for gunmen and kidnappers."

When our daughter moved from Washington, DC to New York City to begin her graduate studies, we were living in Tel Aviv. It was 1987 and the (first) *intifada* had begun. Palestinian youths were throwing deadly rocks and Israel soldiers were shooting at them. The situation escalated to explosives, car bombs, destruction and killings.

Our friends in the States asked, "Aren't you afraid to live in Israel?" Our friends in Israel—of various nationalities—inquired, "Aren't you afraid to have your daughter live in New York?"

Again that old refrain: everything is relative. Afraid? No, I wasn't. Statistically, there was a greater chance of one of us being killed in a traffic accident than by a mugger in New York or a combatant in Israel. Kathy had spent three years living and studying in the heart of Washington and she was street smart. I wasn't worried about New York.

Prior to her move Art and I went to DC on home leave and this is what happened in three days.

Day One: Kathy and I sat down to lunch in a small café in Georgetown, an area near the Potomac River in west Washington. Sirens began to squeal and within seconds police officers swarmed through the street in front of the restaurant and we watched from the windows as they surrounded the block. No one was allowed to leave the café. Fast moving men in blue, guns at the ready, burst into the shop across the street, where we had browsed only minutes before. We ordered lunch and soon forgot about what was happening outside

The evening of Day two: We had dinner reservations at a well-known Georgetown restaurant—the very one from which the supposedly valuable Soviet defector, Yurchenko, disappeared in 1985. (He slipped his CIA escort, went into the men's room and didn't come out. He later resurfaced back in Moscow.) While we waited for our table we stood at the bar and had a cold drink.

Three policemen came into the restaurant and moved quietly in our direction. As I stared, the officers handcuffed and arrested the man who was standing beside me! He struggled, but only briefly.

The evening of Day Three: Kathy and I met Bernadette, a friend from Copenhagen days, at a pub on Pennsylvania Avenue a few blocks from the White House. The husbands declined to join us and it became "ladies' night out."

It was a lovely fresh summer night and we sat outside on the pub's front terrace. As the evening progressed the din from within became more and more raucous. We hadn't paid it much attention until the shouting, which included some nasty epithets, became interspersed with the sound of bottles and beer mugs shattering.

As we got up to leave, several young men bounded through the doorway and one of them flopped onto our bench. "I recommend you stay where you are for the moment," he announced, puffing for breath. "It's gotten really ugly in there and the fight is moving outside." He told us that students from rival schools had gotten into an argument, which had steadily escalated. Not wanting to traverse the space near the doorway, we reluctantly sat down again—just in time—as more lads came hurtling out of the pub battering each other as they came. Blood dripped from several heads and faces and at least two bodies fell heavily on the steps. Several young women, who presumably had lost their dates, came through the door hesitantly and then everyone sprinted for the street.

We quickly left our refuge and hurried in the direction of our hotel. As we rounded the first corner, police cars with insistent sirens were pulling up in front of the bar, a bit late we thought. We seem to have chosen the wrong locale for a quiet evening of conversation.

Security is and will continue to be an essential part of the daily lives of diplomats. I don't in any way resent the accompanying inconveniences but I most emphatically regret the state of society that makes them necessary. And in spite of all the precautions and safety measures, the bells and buttons, the guards and the gates, there are still mistakes. No system or organization run by human beings will be infallible.

There are small glitches. The embassy x-ray machine that broke down and wasn't repaired for weeks resulting in cursorily inspected bags and totes and purses. The guard who overate at the family celebration and later fell asleep at his post.

Colleagues told us about the flashlights that had no batteries for weeks. These were the very illuminators used to inspect the undercarriages of vehicles before the latter were permitted to enter embassy grounds. The local guards didn't bother to ask for new batteries. (And who was supervising the guards?)

Several foreign ambassadors in Yemen felt insulted because guards insisted on inspecting their vehicles before allowing them to park in front of the American ambassador's residence where they were invited to dinner. In one case an ambassador vehemently refused the inspections and so rudely intimidated the guard that the car was permitted to enter—unchecked. What His Excellency failed to recognize was that he personally was not under suspicion. But his vehicle with the possibility of something planted in it was a serious safety issue.

At one of our posts I discovered a stairwell door ajar. The stairs led up to the sanctum of the ambassador so, curious, up I climbed. Art was surprised to see me since I hadn't called for an escort. The following day the door was again unlatched. By the third day the unlocked door made me nervous.

I kept thinking about the Saudi Arabian ambassador who, earlier that year, had been held hostage after a "guest" burst into his office brandishing a weapon that the guards had failed to detect. Although a visitor to our embassy had to be cleared by the Marine and go through a metal detector, once inside, the visitor—if he had a sinister plan—could knock out his escort and hie up that unlocked stairwell.

I decided to risk being branded a busybody and I told the boss about the door. He in turn reported the situation to the security officer. The latter suspected that someone had failed to learn the numbers (that were frequently changed) for the cipher lock and left the door ajar for convenience. No evil deed was intended—probably. But the stairwell door was subsequently kept locked.

And then there was the mistake made by one of our canine colleagues. Perhaps *mistake* is not the proper word. Security dogs are enormously valuable and they are well trained in their sniffing duties. Their noses make few mistakes, but etiquette is perhaps not a top priority.

When Vice President and Mrs. Bush visited The Hague in 1984, they accepted the ambassador's invitation to stay at the residence. According to security procedures, any place that the Vice President would be had to be checked out before he arrived. That included Ambassador Bremer's home and most especially the guest rooms. In came the sniffer dog smelling his way through the house searching for explosives.

The dog seemed more excited than usual, his handler thought, but up they went into the flower-bedecked bedroom where the Bushes would sleep. The dog immediately defecated in the middle of the carpet! But there were no dangers to be detected—such as weapons or bombs—and there was just enough time to clean up the malodorous deposit on the rug before the guests arrived.

The larger mistakes, unintended and unsuspected, are paid for in lives. We've all seen the sad and gruesome evidence in recent years at the Khobar Towers in Dhahran, and at our embassies in Nairobi and Dar es Salaam. What more can our security people do? How much further can they go? The State Department's Bureau of Diplomatic Security (DS) has over 1600 dedicated employees who have an enormous and difficult task both at home and abroad.

Peter E. Bergin, then director of the bureau, said in State Magazine in 1999: "The terrorist threat to U.S. diplomatic facilities and personnel overseas is global, lethal, multidimensional and growing."

Proof of the increase in this threat over the last three decades can be seen in the Diplomatic Lobby of the Department of State in Washington, DC. Two memorial plaques honor foreign affairs people who died overseas in the line of duty. The West Plaque lists the names of 81 Americans who perished prior to 1967—all the way back to the early beginnings of our country. As of September 10, 2001, the names inscribed on the East Plaque Memorial number 115—since 1967.

During our thirty-three years of government service I read and heard numerous offensive remarks about the Foreign Service. Members of congress, journalists and ignorant lay-people—who have never left the comforts of home in the US—have made derogatory references to diplomats living in palatial mansions, champagne-sipping ambassadors, striped pants cookie-pushers, spoiled whining spouses, and a cushy Foreign Service life style complete with servants.

I haven't seen enough references to the *real* Foreign Service life, which is frequently life threatening. Diplomats are targets of bullets and bombs; they are assassinated and gunned down; they are attacked by violent mobs and political protesters; they are caught up in civil wars that they are powerless to prevent. They are hijacked, kidnapped, beaten, tortured and held hostage—all in service to their country. From the beginning of the war in Vietnam through Desert Shield, more American ambassadors than generals were killed in the line of duty. And Foreign Service family members share these risks and sacrifices.

One ambassador was killed during a peacekeeping mission in Bosnia. When his name was added to the Memorial Plaque, the Department of State press spokesman pointed out that the ambassador "was riding in an armored personnel carrier and wearing a flak jacket, not striped pants."

Lt. General Vernon Walters, former ambassador to Germany, had this to say on the occasion of the birthday of the United Nations: "I don't want the United

States to be the world's policeman, but I wouldn't want to live in a world where there *were* no policemen."

14

OLD TESTAMENT AND NEW TRIALS

"Attention, please. Mr. and Mrs. Arthur Hughes are requested to come to the front of the aircraft."

Art and I exchanged curious glances as we gathered up our carry-on bags and made our way up the aisle where the flight attendant asked us to be the first to deplane. We were puzzled—until we discovered Ambassador Thomas Pickering and his wife, Alice, waiting for us at the bottom of the steps. The ambassador's car was parked nearby on the tarmac.

Not since Maracaibo had we had such a warm and personal welcome—a prelude to our unforgettable three years in Israel. After the meeting and greeting we climbed into the armored vehicle and sped toward Tel Aviv. Despite the long flight Art went immediately to the embassy with the ambassador, a deed which further presaged our time at that dynamic and often frenzied post.

It was early August of 1986 and hot and dry. From the car window I saw only brown brown brown until, far off, there appeared a smidgen of green—an irrigated field or orchard, perhaps. Later on we learned about the drip irrigation system pioneered by the Israelis. Water was precious in that part of the world and not a drop could be wasted. Irrigation hoses had small openings at intervals along their length delivering water to plants and trees exactly where it was needed. One seldom saw a yard-variety sprinkler in Israel.

As we traveled throughout the country during the next months, we saw silvery green olive groves, white-dotted cotton fields, bright orchards and vineyards. We drove through agricultural plains, up small mountains, and along ancient rivers. We traversed dry deserts, walked along soft sandy beaches, tread volcanic soil and waded into the salty Dead Sea. Mounds of sand sculpted by the wind were frequently adjacent to gardens of green.

Jews came from all over the world to settle and develop the Jewish State. Hard working, strong, talented people drained the swamps and plowed and planted. They established kibbutzim and moshavim and they erected cities. Intellectuals, technicians, scientists, political activists, rabbis, artists, farmers and doctors built a homeland. Pioneer men and women—most of whom also became soldiers at one time or another—established the state of Israel, which became independent in 1948.

A Jew who is born in Israel is called a "Sabra." The word comes from a cactus of the same name that grows prolifically in the country. The Jewish Sabra is thought to be strong and sturdy and a bit prickly on the outside, but sweet on the inside. The cactus with its sharp quills and tough exterior also has a seasonal yellowish orange flower.

A great financial outlay for Israel since its statehood has been for wars and for its security. The land is bordered by the Mediterranean Sea on the west and on the other sides by Arab countries that have fought against the very idea of a Jewish State. Neighbors Lebanon, Jordan, Syria and Egypt have threatened and been threatened by Israel for much of the nation's history.

Nevertheless the Peace Process has continued—albeit with many interruptions—and those involved will persevere, probably for many years to come. Agreements have been made, promises have been broken, treaties have been signed and implementation has stalled—time and again. The pursuit of "a just and lasting peace" (a phrase that has pertinence, but that has been used so often it sounds stale) is what made living in Israel so fascinating for diplomats like us. Art's position as the number two officer at the American Embassy put him up front with issues that were of paramount importance to a large part of the world.

We made acquaintances and friends among both the Arabs and the Jews. We met hawks and we met doves but we met few birds that sat on the fence. Opinions were firm and seldom wavered.

Arabs living in the West Bank, territory now occupied by Israel, told us they were from Jaffe or Haifa even though they themselves had never been there. But the family had settled in those old cities many generations before. It was complicated—for a foreigner. Living in Israel, however, helped one at least begin to understand the depth of feelings that these two peoples, Jews and Arabs, had for a tiny piece of land that each claimed as its birthright.

We counted among our friends a family that lived in Gaza. Hatem, a medical doctor, ran a school for handicapped children and organized home study for children who were unable to attend school. Hatem and his wife Aida, a wonderful cook, and their four children forgave our inability to speak Arabic—they all spoke English—and they welcomed us into their home on many occasions. Likewise, they visited us in Tel Aviv and in Bethesda.

Security was a major issue in Israel and we took that concern seriously when we lived there, even though as Americans we didn't feel personally threatened. Soldiers carried their weapons on the street, whether on leave or going home for *Shabbat* (the Jewish Sabbath) with a duffel bag full of dirty laundry. Military service was mandatory at the age of eighteen except for religious students. Three years of duty were required of men and two years for women.

Where large numbers of people gathered in public places, there were soldiers as well as police nearby. Security officers searched handbags at the entrance to theaters and venues for large social events, especially those to be attended by Israeli notables. Frequently we passed through metal detectors. At the shopping mall we didn't enter until someone checked out whatever we were carrying—bags, parcels or umbrellas.

The embassy security office issued hand-held two-way radios to every family. Our instructions were to carry the radio whenever we would be "out of contact" for more than a short while. The radio would alert us to any sudden security emergency and we could use it to call for help. Art chose a call sign he knew no one else would be using: "Cornshucker," a remnant of his Nebraska roots.

Security briefings were mandatory and they were the first order of business for newcomers to the embassy. When a safety threat or crisis arose, the security office called a "town meeting" to explain the facts and answer questions. They kept us well informed and were quick with pertinent advice.

Ofer and Israel and Danny, Israelis who drove the armored vehicles for the ambassador and the DCM, carried weapons and they were trained in defensive driving. On Art's official car a thick layer of bulletproof glass had been added to the windows, making it impossible to roll them down. A few times when the air conditioner gave up, I was willing to trade safety for fresh air!

The security office thoroughly checked out and interviewed staff members before they came to work for us. Robert, our cook, said his interrogation was so thorough that "they asked me everything except what color socks I wore to bed."

In the late fall of 1987 an incident in Gaza, together with the unrest in West Bank refugee camps, heated to a flash point and Arabs vented their anger and hatred with violence. The Palestinian uprising, the first *intifada,* began. Thomas Friedman in a New York Times article loosely translated *intifada* as "shaking off." The Palestinians wanted to shake off the Israeli occupation. According to Friedman, "The name made so much sense that even the Israelis used it."

I was enormously grateful to have the two-way radio one summer afternoon when Kathy and her friend Carolyn and I were lazing around the swimming pool. A deafening explosion shook the ground, rattling the windows and propelling us out of our chairs. Wide-eyed and frightened, we rubbed our ears, unable to speak.

When my hearing returned and my brain reactivated I shouted, "Come on!" and we raced into the house and up the stairs. As I grabbed the radio, punched the buttons and yanked up the antenna, I thought aloud, "Sounded like it came from Zionism Square." The small strip mall was near our home. A bomb could very well have targeted diplomats, including the many Americans who lived in the area. There was also an Israeli military office a few blocks away.

The radio immediately reported an explosion—yes, Zionism Square—but no more information. "Continue to monitor your radios and stay away from there," the voice instructed. Sirens came squalling from all directions, police cars and fire trucks—many speeding past our corner.

It was only a short time later, although it seemed longer, when the radio came to life again. Security informed us there was no evidence of terrorism. A leaky gas container in the basement of a pizza restaurant had caused the explosion. The establishment was totally destroyed and there were several casualties among the employees.

"Be Alert." That was the number one advice we heard over and over following our arrival in Israel. I was alone when I was first "alerted." I came out of the shower, hurriedly plugged in the hair dryer and began to fluff my hair. Bud, the Science and Technology Officer, and his wife Sherry were hosting a reception to introduce us to his Israeli contacts. Just as I shut the dryer off, I heard some odd noises. I stood still, listening.

Knock—knock. The sound was coming from the ceiling almost above my head. I heard four more knocks, louder this time. We had just moved in and I had no idea what was above the bedroom or any other part of the house. I reluctantly picked up the phone and called Art. Maybe I was overreacting.

"I hear noises above the bedroom—knocking sounds," I fretted. "What's up there?" At that moment I saw the square outlined in the ceiling at the other end of the room—a trap door big enough for someone to crawl through! Now I was frightened. I told Art what I had spotted.

"Get out of the house and take your radio. We'll call the police."

I realized with a jolt that I was completely naked—which made me feel even more vulnerable. "I have to put some clothes on," I reported to Art in a panic.

"Don't hang up the phone then—keep the line open and throw something on fast." I did as I was told, then ran down the stairs and into the street.

Almost immediately I saw a police car driving in my direction—and then Fred, the RSO, arrived along with another police car. They surrounded the house with flashlights waving and radios chattering.

It didn't take long to determine that there was no intruder. Fred told me there wasn't any way a human body could get into the attic—a crawl space only—from the outside. "And I'm certain the trap door in the bedroom hasn't been used in a long time. The ceiling paint around the opening is clean and unmarred. But we'll come back tomorrow and check everything out in the daylight." Art arrived in time to hear Fred's report and to see that calmness had returned to his wife. We changed clothes quickly and arrived only a little late at the reception.

Security people along with the GSO inspected the attic the following day and found no signs that anyone had been up there in a long time. They saw several ceramic tiles that might have fallen over creating the noise. "Some rats probably knocked into them," someone commented nonchalantly.

The rat theory was not comforting but I was nevertheless relieved. I felt increasingly foolish, however, for causing such a fuss. "It's better to be safe," Fred reminded me. "Never hesitate to report anything you think is suspicious." And I didn't hesitate—the next time.

I pulled into the parking lot of a small shopping plaza one morning and took out my list of errands. As I reached over to lock the passenger door I glanced up and noticed a stranger on the sidewalk looking in my direction. He abruptly turned around and opened a newspaper. I went inside a gift shop and looked back toward my car. The man had refolded the paper and was writing on it as he walked closer to my car. Was he writing down my license plate number?

Quickly I purchased some candles while continuing to look out the shop's front window just past the cash register. Trying not to appear hurried—or harried—I strolled out to my car. I focused on unlocking the door and not looking up. Once inside the car I opened my purchase and used the bag as a camouflage while I searched for the stranger. He was there. He had again raised the newspaper but he looked over the top of it trying to appear nonchalant—like me. I took a scrap of paper and a pen out of my purse and jotted down his description.

Instead of finishing my shopping I headed home to call Fred. Before entering the main street I looked in my rear-view mirror. The suspect had lowered the paper and turned in my direction.

"What did he look like?" the RSO wanted to know after he heard my story.

"Middle-aged, tall and chunky. Dressed in dark green Bermuda shorts and a plaid short-sleeved shirt. I couldn't get a good look at his face because he had a baseball cap pulled down low over his forehead. A plain cap, black, no logo."

Fred called me forty-eight hours later. "A man following the description you gave me was spotted by Israeli security personnel lingering in the block where President Herzog lives." The president's personal home was across the street from the shopping square. "Thanks for the report and the good description," the RSO told me. That was the last information I heard. I suppose this was the proverbial case of "no need to know."

As Israel struggled with its daily crises and never-ending problems, both internal (politics) and external (its neighbors), our personal troubles were just beginning. We couldn't find a place to live. The USG had decided, wisely we thought, to give up the present awful DCM residence and buy or lease a more suitable property. The "buy" part was an on-again/off-again plan as budget constraints increased. The embassy itself needed to be replaced by a larger and more secure structure. Its present location was seriously vulnerable, surrounded by other buildings and wedged between the Mediterranean Sea and a main street.

By autumn housing possibilities were less than slim and we moved into our second temporary home, one large enough for the obligatory entertaining and also to accommodate our son and daughter and several other family members who were coming for Christmas.

Prior to the move Art and I went to a warehouse on the docks and sifted through our lift vans in search of "necessities." Our summer clothes were no longer adequate even though the coastal winters of Israel were mild. Into an embassy truck went all cartons marked clothes or shoes. We located Art's stereo and speakers plus a box of recipe books—necessities for each of us. And I just happened to find a box of Christmas decorations and some personal items. Those few boxes would have to suffice until our final move. Only a few months, we thought.

Art worked long hours and he was frequently on the road to and from Jerusalem, where the Israeli government was located except for the Defense Ministry. Sometimes he ate both lunch and dinner from a brown bag in the car. Many evenings I met him at the embassy and we went on to a social event.

"We need to start entertaining." I was still immersed in house hunting when Art made that inevitable announcement. "Check the calendar and write down some potential dates," he told me. Working around the invitations we already had, I found fourteen free dates during a six-week period and I gave the list to Art. By the end of the week he had made plans to invite guests for dinner or lunch on every one of the fourteen.

We needed a cook. Although I loved cooking and enjoyed setting a pretty table, I didn't want to spend my three years in Israel stretched between the kitchen and the grocery store. We had inherited two part-time maids but neither woman was going to be any help with entertaining. The woman whom I referred to (in private, of course) as the Old One wasn't really old, but hopelessly slow and lazy, and didn't know how to open a wine bottle. The other woman was efficient, but she didn't work evenings. I realized again how fortunate we had been in Copenhagen and The Hague where we had ready-made staffs that were trained and experienced—and we *liked* them. I longed for Toini and Erik, Patrick, Irene and especially Desmond.

Robert came to work for us in time to do the last of the 14 dinners and lunches and to cook us through the holidays with our eight houseguests. An American Jew, he had been living in Israel for ten years and he knew where to shop, what to buy and how. The *how* was important—Robert was fluent in Hebrew and accustomed to the customs. He was an excellent cook who thought food should be beautiful as well as tasty. He was imaginative, enthusiastic, and sometimes so overwhelmingly cheerful I wanted to put a bag over his head!

My mother's discomfiture was evident one evening when she was visiting us. When Robert brought the dinner to the table, his feet were bare and he wore a T-shirt that read: "Same Shit—Different Day." Robert was a laid-back person.

Now it was time to work on the other problem. I put out the word that I wanted to hire a butler. Subdued but typical responses were smirks and snickers. *A butler in Israel?* I held fast for a while but to no avail. Butlers were as rare as fairy godmothers.

One morning after making breakfast I decided to climb back into bed after Art left for work. This was unusual, but we had had several late nights in a row and I was weary. I told the Old One not to disturb me unless my husband called and said it was urgent.

I was awakened from a blessedly deep sleep by a rapping on the bedroom door and a voice calling, "Mrs. Hughes?" I kept my eyes tightly shut, hoping she would go away. She didn't. The door opened—so did my eyes—and there was the Old One standing over my bed. "Am I disturbing you?" she asked idiotically.

Disturbing me? As I stared at her she explained that I had a telephone call. I picked up the phone to discover that it was not my husband and it was not important. That was it! Butler or no, the Old One had to go. Before we moved into our third temporary house I hired Christie, a Philippine woman, to replace the other two.

In Israel we met—and Art had official access to—more politicians and government leaders than in most other countries where we had lived. Was it Art's astute diplomacy or our country's special relationship with Israel (and the three billion dollars the U.S. was giving to the country annually) that gained him easy entrance to the people he wanted to see? Perhaps all of the above.

Whether Art was chargé d'affaires or not, he met with Prime Minister Shamir and Foreign Minister Peres or vice versa. (The two switched roles during the period of the unity government.) He saw President Herzog and had a solid working relationship with Secretary of Defense Yitzak Rabin. He met with other cabinet officers such as Moshe Ahrens and Ariel Sharon, and with Teddy Kolleck, mayor of Jerusalem. Other embassy officers also had contacts among the local officials, who were forthright and eager for dialogue and discussions.

Israelis were open and outgoing people. One of my first observations was that they liked to argue. They called it *discussion* but it sounded like argument to me. They admitted with a hint of pride, "When three people get together, there will be a debate of four different opinions."

Many of the heroes of Israel's fight for independence became members of subsequent governments. We met them at dinners, at receptions, at benefits and even at sports events. Art played tennis now and then with Yitzak Rabin and sometimes his wife, Leah.

Whenever Mrs. Rabin saw me, her first words were "Where is Art?" or "How is Art?" if she knew he was away.

My husband was particularly fond of Ezer Weizman. When Art returned later to Israel in his capacity as a Deputy Assistant Secretary at the Defense Department, he was pleased that Weizman, who had become the Israeli president, remembered him. When Art walked into his office, President Weizman greeted him with, "What happened to your mustache?" Art had shaved it off, but only temporarily.

I found myself seated next to Abba Eban, statesman, writer, and former ambassador to the U.S., at a benefit dinner in Jerusalem. I was enormously impressed—at first. I tried to make interesting and intelligent conversation, but Mr. Eban's replies were short and disinterested and he avoided eye contact. Perhaps he was unhappy about where he was seated. There was no one on his other side.

When he took some small pieces of paper and a pen from his pocket and concentrated on his jottings, I gave up all efforts to converse, wondering if I should feel insulted—or inadequate as a dinner partner. I was somewhat appeased after the meal when Mr. Eban was introduced as the speaker for the evening. No wonder he was preoccupied and not inclined toward idle conversation—he was making notes for his presentation. The speech, delivered in his well-known British accented voice was as impressive as his reputation.

Leaders of the Israeli fine arts community were also accessible as well as interesting. Painter Josie Stern was gregarious and entertaining. At parties his friends begged him—and received little resistance—to "do drawings." He would hand someone a sheet of blank paper and instruct, "Close your eyes and make one stroke with the pen—a line, a curve, anything." I made a squiggly mark on my paper and within three minutes he turned it into a picture of an elaborately costumed dancer.

Artist Frank Meisler's shop in old Jaffa was full of wonderful eye-catching pieces he had sculpted in bronze, pewter, silver, and gold plating. He also created fountains and memorials and he designed synagogues. Judaica was the theme of many of his individual sculptures, but his work was not always of a serious nature. Meisler's sense of humor, which we had witnessed in person, was particularly evident in the pewter goat he designed with a tinkly bell around its neck—and shiny gold testicles.

Yael Dayan, author of several novels, was also an inspiring public speaker. We heard her commencement address at the American high school. The daughter of famed General Moshe Dayan, she was later elected to the Knesset, Israel's parliament.

Tamar Rose, a talented watercolorist, specialized in local landscapes. She and her husband, Bernie, invited us to experience our first *Seder* in their home. She and Art continued to play tennis together for many years whenever he returned to Israel.

Dignitaries, public figures and Hollywood stars came regularly to Israel, a popular place to visit. Former President Jimmy Carter with his wife Rosalynn and his mother, Miss Lillian, headed the list of American notables whom we met.

Edward Villella, formerly with the New York City Ballet, was one of the kings of dance. I was so excited to meet the dancer I had long admired, I was tongue-tied when we were introduced. But after lunch at Louise's (the Cultural Affairs Officer), Art and I bombarded him with questions about the Miami City Ballet he had founded. I soon discovered he was a regular guy and we had a regular conversation.

Armand Hammar, industrialist and businessman, gave a speech when he came to Israel. Before getting down to serious business, he humorously informed his audience: "I have nothing to do with the baking soda people!" Apparently his name was often confused with Arm and Hammer.

I took an immediate liking to Columba Bush and empathized with her concerns about being in the public eye. When they visited Israel her husband Jeb was Florida's Secretary of Commerce and he would later become its governor. But it was her father-in-law's position that put her and her family in the unwanted spotlight. George H.W. Bush was Vice President and had already begun his race for the Presidency. After the handshaking and acquaintance making at the ambassador's reception, Columba and I found a quiet corner and talked about publicity and the hoopla surrounding dignitaries. She was a sensitive down-to-earth young woman.

Zubin Mehta, director of the Israeli Philharmonic Orchestra, conducted a superb concert celebrating the fortieth year of the Jewish State. The site itself was impressive: the base of Masada, a mountain on whose plateau Romans besieged over 900 Jews in 73 AD. The *Jerusalem Post*, an English language newspaper, reported that the audience of nearly 4000 "was almost as star-studded as the clear desert sky that watched over the event."

One of those stars was Gregory Peck whose splendid baritone voice made him a perfect choice for Master of Ceremonies. Later at the reception Art and I talked with him about his work; he was currently filming a movie in Israel. I thought he was even more impressive with the gray in his hair and the lines in his face than when he was younger. He was friendly and humorous and he looked us in the eye while we talked. And I saw that the twinkle in *his* eye was still there—the one I remembered from the movie "Roman Holiday."

To aid an organization dedicated to helping autistic children, Leah Rabin, along with President and Mrs. Herzog, sponsored a benefit featuring *Othello*, the opera movie starring Placido Domingo. I was somewhat distracted during the movie by the presence of Mr. Domingo himself who sat directly in front of us, next to the producer Franco Zeferelli. In addition to having a big voice the singer also had a mighty handshake, which we found out when we met him after the movie.

Leonard Bernstein conducted a concert of his own music in Tel Aviv—a long way from *Westside Story* but vintage Bernstein. The audience was on its feet at the end applauding and cheering the famous composer. At the party afterward he swooped in, swinging his black cape—lined in bright shiny red—making a spectacular entrance that no one missed!

Although I don't consider movie stars royals, meeting them certainly makes life more interesting. And sometimes, embarrassing. At an elegant garden party I filled a small plate with canapés and without looking behind me I backed away from the buffet table. One of my three-inch heels met an obstruction.

"Ouch!" a voice winced. I was mortified to discover I had stepped on David Sole's foot! Handsome blond David Sole, star of TV's *Starsky and Hutch* and numerous movies. I stammered apologies—over and over—and he just laughed. He shook his foot a few times and forgave me.

Sylvester Stallone, in Israel to film the third *Rambo* movie, invited the embassy Marine contingent to lunch and a tour of the movie set. When he left the country he donated his weight-lifting equipment to the Marine House. The hotel manager said Stallone was finicky about linens. He bought himself a number of new pastel colored towels because he didn't like those provided by the hotel. I wonder what he did with his towels when he left.

Movie stars, royalty, notables—some impress us, some don't. It depends on our age, our background, our point of view. Martin Indyk, twice American ambassador to Israel, was inaugurating the first Jerusalem branch of McDonald's when, (according to Thomas Friedman's story), an Israeli teenager approached him.

"Are you the ambassador? Can I have your autograph?"

Slightly embarrassed, Mr. Indyk signed the boy's McDonald's hat.

"Wow!" the teenager said. "It must be great to be the ambassador for McDonald's and go all over the world and open restaurants."

"No, no," Mr. Indyk explained. "I'm the *American* ambassador." With that the boy lost all interest and walked away.

"Groupies" were numerous, at least in Tel Aviv where most of the foreign embassies were located. *Everyone,* it seemed, not only knew the previous American ambassador and his wife, but were socially intimate with them.

"We were very close friends of the Lewises," they would tell me, or "We knew them extremely well, *of course.*" No doubt Ambassador Lewis made many friends during his unusually long tenure at our embassy but many of his acquaintances, I surmise, became "dearer" after his departure.

Alice Pickering met a steady parade of these groupies. "The Lewises were our dear friends and they always…" (hosted the annual meeting of, gave a dinner for, honored us with a reception at…etc.) The litany always reached the same point:

"We're certain you and the Ambassador will want to carry on this tradition." It was a difficult position to be in at first, but Alice held her ground. Neither she nor her husband was interested in social maneuvering—they had a job to do.

I had a groupie of my own, at least temporarily. I was partnered with Pat, a Canadian friend, at a bridge afternoon. Concentrating on my hand after winning the bid, I mistakenly started to play out of turn. Smack! An Israeli woman slapped my hand! She glared at me and sniped, "It is not your turn!"

The game continued but I could no longer focus. Pat was nudging me under the table with her foot and rolling her eyes. We were both glad when that round was over and we changed tables.

After we finished playing bridge we were socializing over coffee. The hostess introduced me to someone, adding that my husband was the new DCM at the American Embassy. The hand-slapping witch, who was within earshot, stepped right up and began the drill: "Your predecessor was a *dear* friend of mine...I have known all the ambassadors and DCMs at your embassy for years...You must come for lunch...Let's get together." Yadda, yadda. I declined lunch when she called the next day. (And I never played bridge again.)

Katherine L. Hughes, author of *The Accidental Diplomat* (and our daughter), puts it candidly: "The ambassador's wife is treated according to her role, not according to her individual self. Even wives of the deputy chief of mission...experienced difficulties from their imposed role...."

I frequently had the same doubts as one of the wives that Kathy interviewed. "I think that's probably the hardest thing that I've had to deal with in the Foreign Service...you're not sure whether people like you for your own sake, for something they see inside you, or whether they are befriending you because your husband is who he is."

Several months and two house moves after arriving in Israel, culture shock began to pull me down. The gloominess began gradually but it hit sharply at times. I recognized that I was suffering from culture shock blues and I didn't like it—but I eventually got through it.

By the time I was climbing up out of the doldrums a visitor came to the embassy. The woman, trained in cross-cultural problems and other sticky issues for expatriates, led a series of small discussion groups. Typically, all the participants were female. We comfortably and frankly talked about the state of our psyches—how we felt when we first arrived in Israel and how we felt several months later.

The expert explained some facts about the "travelin' life" that many of us were not aware of. One premise was particularly relevant to me: the higher one's expectations are of the new posting, the harder the fall, so to speak. Bingo—there I was. I was so excited to come to Israel with its unique culture and ancient history that I expected my enthusiasm and eagerness to overcome all problems of adjustment. I was on a high plateau the first few months and then I began slipping and sliding.

Initially at a new post we are fully occupied with unpacking and settling in, meeting people, finding our way around the city, learning about the country and trying to see some of it. Many of us have children to look after, child-care to organize and schools to get acquainted with. We're in awe of new places and unusual experiences. In Israel there were archeology digs and biblical sites; the beauty of old and new Jerusalem; the stark realism of the holocaust memorial museum and the wonder of the Museum of The Book. The mix of Jewish, Moslem and Christian people who brought traditions from all over the globe provided a fascinating new world for us.

And within this new world were the usual and not-so-usual irritations of adjusting to a new home, different customs, language barriers, annoying manners—in addition to the basic issue of the Arab/Israeli conflict. During our cross cultural discussions the group agreed that none of the problems we encountered was serious or insurmountable. But there were so many of them! Small annoyances added to several successive irritations could lead to a very stressful day.

Traffic, for instance. The highways and major streets in and out of Tel Aviv were crowded and dangerous. Dangerous because Israelis drove like teenagers, fast and carelessly. They were also impatient. Horn honking, shouting, fist waving and fender bashing were the norm long before the phrase "road rage" was coined.

Courtesy was lacking in the public sector. Seldom did I hear the Hebrew word for "excuse me." Ordinary good manners that we were used to at home were scarce in stores, markets, post offices, dry cleaners and such places that provided services. Merchants seldom greeted their patrons with "hello" and even rarer said "thank you." A shopkeeper in the suburbs was likely to finish sipping his tea or reading the newspaper before he bothered to wait on you.

If you perversely persisted in being pleasant there was the occasional reward, especially after your face had become familiar in the neighborhood. After a long period of shopping at the same little grocery store, the curt and cranky clerk began to say "Shabbat shalom" to me on Friday afternoons. (The words were a traditional greeting preceding and during the Jewish Sabbath.) But that was the extent of our conversation.

When we answered our telephone and the caller found out he had reached a wrong number, (which happened often), the disgruntled person hung up the phone—with an ear-pounding bang! Excuse me? Sorry?

Electricity was annoyingly unreliable. I cooked dinner by candlelight one night when we had guests. Fortunately we had a gas stove because the power was out for almost three hours. When there was no electricity we also had no telephones. And when a heavy rain flooded the street around the embassy and water got into the cables, the embassy extension into our home didn't function. I tried reminding myself that for thirteen months in Fulda, Germany, I had no phone at all. It didn't help.

Tel Aviv had only a few American-style supermarkets in the 1980's but there was a large one along the highway where I sometimes shopped. Produce was fresh and plentiful, although it was not quick cleaned as we are accustomed to in America and parts of Europe. But it didn't matter since stuff tended to be splattered with foul/fowl droppings because birds were flying around inside the store!

One day after attending an archeology lecture, my compatriot Ellen and I stopped at the supermarket. After we had been elbowed repeatedly and jostled along the aisles of the store, she was fed up. "These Israelis! They won't allow a glass of milk on the same table with their meat but they don't care if birds shit all over their fruits and vegetables!"

Language was a constant source of frustration. Unless you had the opportunity to study Hebrew before arriving, it took several months to acquire enough vocabulary and grammar to shop and run household errands. Socially, however, we got along quite well without Hebrew; government people and politicians, as well as other diplomats, generally communicated in English. Though most of us *wanted* to learn the language, it was a slow process. I gave up on writing and reading and took an invaluable class called "Survival Hebrew." And I survived.

As Jane Ewert-Biggs says in her book: "…I began to realize that the major problems arising from our nomadic life were going to affect me rather than him." Her husband the Foreign Service officer was enjoying fascinating days learning about his new job, while she dealt with the frustrations of settling in.

Spatial proximity can be a big issue with Americans. Israelis like to be close to others—a polite way of saying "in your face." At a tennis match I attempted to buy some Cokes during the intermission. No matter how I tried to get to the counter, I was helplessly maneuvered further and further away. At one point I shouted in exasperation at the teenagers who surrounded me. "Please stop pushing!"

"Lady—this is Israel," one young man responded casually in English. "You *have* to push!"

I never got the soft drinks and I felt as though I had been mugged by the time I returned to my seat.

Catherine, who had visited Israel several times with her Foreign Service husband, told me she learned the ropes quickly. When they brought their young son with them for the first time, McDonald's fast food had just made its debut. The boy, longing for familiar food, wanted a hamburger for lunch. They went in—and found themselves surrounded by masses of people jostling and bumping together.

The boy was frustrated. "How do I order? I can't find the line—where's the line?"

"You wait," his mother directed. "Watch me and I'll show you how it is done in Israel!" And she proceeded to elbow her way to a hot hamburger.

In Israel it was "done" with the elbows as our friend demonstrated. Unlike the British the Israelis did not queue up; line forming was not a familiar concept. I was envious of people like Catherine who learned quickly to maneuver like the natives without being offended or offensive. I was a wimp.

Dealing with culture shock also meant becoming accustomed to the creatures that inhabited our new environment, especially the ubiquitous cockroaches. There were also stinging scorpions, fuzzy poisonous caterpillars, nasty rats and snakes.

I spotted three kittens toying with something in the street near our home. They were jumping about playfully then abruptly backing off. It was dusk and I couldn't make out the object of their game. Until I got closer—and I saw, for the first time, a scorpion nearly as large as the kitties. The creature was pink, almost translucent and had a deadly pointed tail. I feared for the kittens but I didn't hang around.

Fifteen months and three temporary houses after our arrival in Israel, we settled into a lovely home in the suburb by the sea, Herzlia Pituah. Two enormous palm trees stood guard in front of the house and when the lunar calendar was in our favor, the full crystal moon shone between the silhouettes of the palms. Tall poinsettia bushes, especially colorful in the fall, climbed up the wall outside the kitchen terrace. We also planted a banana tree that produced small, very sweet bananas.

We hadn't seen most of our personal possessions since we left The Hague almost a year and a half earlier. We merrily began unpacking and then hosted a thank you party for the GSO staff and the workmen who had given extra effort to get the house ready for us. In Israel, unlike the US, one bought or rented a house and that was it—the house. There were no light fixtures, no large appliances, no carpeting or drapes and often no closets in the bedrooms nor cabinets in the kitchen. A lot of work was needed to prepare a home for occupancy. (We would later discover that several of our hard-working Israeli employees whom we had so appreciated, had betrayed us.)

We flew to the States in December for Alex and Mary's wedding—a wonderful joyful event. Before our departure several Foreign Service friends asked the inevitable question: "Have you met the bride?" Happily, we could answer "Yes." Many parents who spend time abroad don't meet their children's chosen partner until the marriage.

Back in Tel Aviv we finished unpacking and had just begun to feel at home when our lovely abode turned into a disaster. The water pipes inside the walls began to burst—one by one. The hallway flooded, the kitchen floated, and workmen had to break holes in the walls and the floor to replace the piping—the builder had used garden hose! (He later spent some time in jail for fraud.) In the meantime we had repeated electrical problems resulting in expensive and extensive rewiring throughout the house. Months and months of messes.

Linda, whose family lived nearby, had similar water problems and we frequently commiserated and compared floods over Diet Cokes. But when one of their toilets exploded, she was way up the scale on disaster stories. The commode didn't actually come apart—a ferocious geyser issued forth from its depths spewing water over the bathroom and into the bedroom, soaking the carpet and some of the furniture.

Linda and I wondered if we were still under the influence of culture shock or just unlucky. We began to liken ourselves to Andy Capp's friend who went through life with the dark storm cloud over his head. But we lived through the floodwaters.

Foreign Service Requisite # 2: stamina (the psychological kind.)

I stepped over puddles and inched around workmen as I came and went to Hebrew lessons, American Embassy Women's Group, philanthropic organizations, archeology lectures and social events. I spent many satisfying hours working with the Outreach Committee of the AEWG. Our goal was to reach out to the community and contribute to its well being, not only financially but also with our time and dedication. AEWG organized two major fund-raising events a year, plus a few smaller projects, and most of the money was spent by and at the discretion of the Outreach Committee. We received numerous requests from institutions, hospitals and schools in need of funds. We adhered to two rules: we did not give cash donations and we did not contribute to a place without first visiting and learning as much about it as possible.

Only occasionally did we donate to an organization more than once. A prime example was the women's shelter in Herzlia. The women (some had small children with them) who sought refuge there usually arrived with nothing except the clothes they wore. As women we felt a special affinity for those beaten and beleaguered souls who had no place else to go to protect their bodies, their sanity and sometimes their lives.

An Israeli woman named Ruth Resnic saw a special need and she began the shelter, alone, in the 1970's. She begged and wheedled the government into providing a small house where women could stay temporarily. She enlisted volunteers and together they provided food and safety, solace and hope. Eventually Ruth convinced a few attorneys and social workers to donate their time and counsel. Later the shelter offered educational programs and helped the women find jobs.

Ruth has continued her work and travels all over the globe sharing her expertise and experience. There are now more than ten shelters as well as an emergency hot line in five languages manned by volunteers, including Arab women.

Spousal abuse occurs in every corner of the world including the United States—it is not an Israeli specialty. I had never before been involved with the victims, however, and in Herzlia I talked to many of them and heard their stories. Pregnancies aborted because of a man's boot to the belly. Broken bones after a fling down a flight of stairs. Vision impaired by repeated blows to the head. And these women could not get divorces without the husbands' agreement. Jewish courts rarely granted divorce over a husband's objection.

"Guess who's coming to dinner" was played out at our house more than once. The farewell dinner we planned for the political counselor, for example, was almost theatrical. On the morning of the event we set up three round tables to seat eighteen. Christie was ironing the tablecloths as I left to do the last of the grocery shopping. At mid-day just as I finished arranging the flowers Art called to say that two people had canceled.

Later Joe, our guest of honor, happened to see one of the invitees and said, "Looking forward to seeing you this evening."

"Oh, sorry, my wife and I won't be able to come." Something had come up. Scratch two more from the list.

Christie and I removed one table and rearranged the place settings to seat seven at each of the remaining tables. My husband phoned—two more dropouts. As we reset the tables yet again, I began to wonder if something mysterious was afoot.

But it was only politics. We found out there was a political crisis and leaders of both the government and the opposition parties were holding meetings. Certainly a priority over dinner with the Americans. In the end only eight of us had dinner together that night, next to a bare table that I hadn't had time to remove. What a disappointment for Joe—seven of us were Americans. But one Israeli came—he was parliamentarian Ehud Olmert, who later followed Teddy Kolleck as mayor of Jerusalem and then became the Deputy Prime Minister.

Diane had the opposite dinner party problem. Twelve guests showed up for dinner and they had only invited ten! She had to sneak out the back door and borrow two china plates from her neighbor.

We also played the "guesstimating" game: we guessed how many guests were coming and we estimated how much food to prepare for large buffets and receptions. Israelis were not quick to respond to invitations.

Entertaining was an unusual kind of challenge due to Jewish dietary laws and customs. Before going to Israel I knew enough not to serve pork or shellfish, but I hadn't understood that there were various levels of ritual observance. A minority of Israelis "kept kosher," meaning they strictly conformed to all religious dietary laws. Others did not eat meat together with dairy products but were unconcerned about the dishes and cookware. For the latter a cheeseburger or a roast beef sandwich laced with mayonnaise were forbidden. Many others didn't observe any rituals, but traditionally avoided pork and shellfish. Some Israelis followed no restrictions. We visited a kibbutz, for instance, that raised pigs and specialized in pork products.

When we invited people for dinner we asked, "Do you have any dietary restrictions?" If the response was "kosher," we ordered their meals from a kosher restaurant or a hotel. (In Israel all hotels, by law, keep a kosher kitchen.)

To be kosher, meat has to be prepared according to strict religious laws, from the slaughtering of the animal to the cleaning and cooking. These laws further require that silverware, cooking pots and utensils, actually everything in the kitchen, are separated for usage: one set for dairy foods and another for meat.

To insure that all our guests were comfortable at our dinner parties, we did not serve meat and dairy products at the same meal. This was difficult at first. I was accustomed to using a lot of cream: in the peppercorn sauce for the beef, to thicken the cream-of-leek soup or whipped and sweetened for the chocolate cake. Cheese also had to be eliminated if we served meat—no cauliflower *au gratin* or cheesecake.

For large receptions and cocktail buffets, we gave our guests a choice. We laid out the dairy products and meat on separate tables, mixed and garnished with lots of vegetables and fruits. If we ordered food from a kosher restaurant, we put it on yet another table and served it in the dishes provided by the restaurant. The latter issued a certificate declaring that the food and its preparation abided by kosher dietary laws and we displayed the certificate on the table. We were gratified by the appreciation expressed by our religiously observant guests.

Entertaining was a challenge also because we did so much of it. I spent long hours shopping and even with an efficient cook like Robert, who also did some of the meat purchasing, I usually helped with the cooking myself. Christie was a fast learner and hard worker but large parties were a tremendous amount of work for the three of us. We expected the hired bartenders to help clean up and wash glasses—if they didn't, we didn't hire them again. (Desmond, where *are* you?)

Before we had established a roster of good waiters and bartenders, Christie told me that her husband was "good at everything." So I hired him to help with a small dinner—a trial evening. When the man put ice cubes in the glasses of beer, it was immediately evident that he had had no experience at bar tending. After the guests left I found him sitting in the kitchen—gazing at his finger-nails—while Christie washed dishes. Maybe he could have learned to mix drinks, but I wasn't willing to teach him work ethics. We didn't add him to our roster.

An enormous crash interrupted our first sit-down dinner. We had just begun the first course of salmon mousse when a shelf in the kitchen gave way—sending china plates and platters smashing to the floor. Heads popped up and forty forks poised stiffly in the air until the last tiny shard of dinnerware bounced into silence. I made an inane joke about "more plates where those came from" and we all resumed eating and talking.

One autumn we had three receptions with over 100 guests each—during a ten-day period. They were working parties to welcome new embassy officers and their spouses and to introduce them to their Israeli counterparts and other diplomats. One of the new couples, whom we had known at a previous post, sent us an enormous bouquet of pretty flowers before the event and a thoughtful note of thanks afterwards. Seasoned Foreign Service people, John and Priscilla knew how much work a reception required of the unpaid spouse. No thank-you notes were received from the others whom we introduced.

Sometimes a week or two went by quietly with no guests and then wham—several events in a row. For example, the two large buffet receptions we gave on consecutive nights. I couldn't rerun the identical menu for the second function because some of the guests were invited to both. I felt like a yo-yo bouncing back and forth to grocery stores and produce markets for four days. Even with two refrigerators there wasn't enough space for all the supplies.

We weren't the only ones with a heavy entertaining schedule; the ambassador hosted many more events than we did. The defense attachés also had a tremendous number of guests, keeping the spouses as busy as the officers. Israel drew American visitors from the Department of Defense, the State Department, other departments, bureaus and agencies and especially from Congress, which kept the embassy fully occupied. During crises or peace talks or fact-finding trips (often combined with pleasure), a surfeit of official people (and some shopping spouses) shuttled in and out of Israel.

JoAnn's husband was the Political Counselor when we arrived—which meant heavy hostessing—and she also worked in the embassy's Community Liaison Office. During one particularly hectic period JoAnn declared with a grin: "What I need is a wife!"

I kept food receipts and made notes and Robert wrote down the ingredients he used. This was our third post as DCM so I had developed my own accounting system. After each function I tallied the food prices down to every onion, cup of sugar, can of tomatoes and tablespoon of Worcestershire sauce. We received reimbursement for all entertaining expenses including flowers, candles and hired help—except for me. I kept price lists for the items we used regularly—staples like flour, sugar, butter, eggs, rice, canned goods—and I broke down the cost by weight, by the piece or by cup. For alcoholic beverages I listed the cost of the bottle and also of a single drink. Unfortunately prices changed and I had to redo my lists at least twice a year. Had I owned a computer then (and had I known how to program it) my work would have gone much faster.

I have talked to spouses who said they couldn't be bothered with calculating the small stuff so they just estimated their expenses. A few women refused to spend any time with financial accounts at all and they claimed the maximum allowance for official functions at home. (Each post sets standard maximum amounts that officers may spend on lunches, dinners, receptions, etc., based on local prices.) I didn't want to estimate—and my accuracy (parsimony?) cost me a lot of hours.

"Two for the price of one" may be frowned upon today, but this reality is still lurking about. Those of us who enjoyed being a partner in government service and who believed in the importance of diplomacy were still giving our time and energy to the Foreign Service throughout the 1990's. However, with more women working outside the home, more entertaining was taking place outside the home—in restaurants. Many spouses just plain didn't want to do dinners. Homemade meals for official guests were on the decline.

Not only is restaurant entertaining less personal than at home, it costs a lot more. Catering is also expensive. Each department at an embassy or consulate (i.e. state, defense, agriculture, etc.) has a yearly entertainment budget and the total amount is divided among the officers in that department. If one officer hosts dinner in a restaurant he will use considerably more of the budget than another officer who entertains the same number of guests at home. This can be particularly significant at a small post. I was annoyed at two senior officers in Sanaa who had large parties catered in their homes once or twice a year. They thought—wrongly—that those events fulfilled their entertaining obligations. Large events can be useful, but they don't replace small dinners where conversation and discussion of issues are at the core of diplomacy. An officer seldom has a quality discussion with an important contact while the former is hosting a hundred people.

Large receptions and cocktail parties are beneficial, however—maybe even enjoyable—because they bring people together. But they seldom promote important dialogue. In his diary British Ambassador Biggs described receptions this way: "…a room full of people at close proximity shouting at each other."

To unmarried officers and to those officers (male or female) whose spouses decline to give lunches or dinners, I have this to say: can you make a pot of coffee or tea? Can you stop at a bakery after work and pick out a tasty cake or a local sweet? What about inviting two or three contacts for coffee and dessert after dinner? A lot of good dialogue can be accomplished in an hour and a half, spouse or no spouse. And you might even make a friend or two.

I didn't always have an apron on. After moving into our final home I got into my swimsuit as often as possible in the summers and got some exercise swimming. At least once a week I invited embassy spouses and children to share the swimming pool and sometimes my friends came over just to lounge in the sun and chat. Those were good times.

When Suzy and Sandra arrived one afternoon, Sandra commented, "That's the third time I have seen that man parked in the same spot." I immediately wanted to know *what* man.

We peeked around the fence that closed in one side of the pool and small garden and Sandra pointed out a car parked at the edge of the vacant lot next door. I realized that from inside the house, I wouldn't have noticed the vehicle. We agreed that if the man was still there when she and Suzy left, they would write down the license number and call me.

They did and I quickly phoned the RSO and reported. He was amused when he called me back. "The vehicle belongs to a security service that is employed by several people in your neighborhood. In between his rounds the guy likes to park there because of the big shade trees."

I was relieved and so was the RSO. "Let's not discourage him," he added.

Secretary of State George Shultz was a frequent visitor to the country—"shuttle diplomacy" was a continuing process while we were in Israel. Because of the enormous expenditure of time and energy by the embassy staff for a high level guest and his entourage, we decided after one visit to throw a "Wheels Up" party. As soon as the Secretary's plane lifted off from Ben Gurion Airport, embassy colleagues and spouses got together at our house for a potluck supper, some easy breathing, and a little fun. They were a tired group and no one hung around for long, but people knew the visit had been worthwhile and they felt appreciated.

An old-fashioned slumber party materialized during another of Shultz's visits. At the spouses' Friday wine and cheese gathering several of us remarked that our husbands would be spending the night in Jerusalem. A good time for popping popcorn and watching "Gone with the Wind," we thought. The movie evening turned into an all-nighter at my house, pajamas and all.

There were twelve of us, women from ages 28 to 48. We ate, talked, watched the movie, and we ate and talked some more. There were beds for eight plus sleeping bags and floor space for the others, but only two women actually went to bed; the others didn't want to miss out on anything. The impromptu slumber party was a great morale builder—and mostly it was fun.

"We're not religious," Amos emphasized when he and Yael invited us to a family meal on the Jewish Sabbath. We had been in Israel only a short time and they wanted us to feel comfortable. *Shabbat*, observed by Jews wherever they are, begins at sundown on Friday and ends as the sun sets on Saturday (when three stars are visible). As soon as we arrived Amos gave Art a skullcap, a *kippa*, (*yarmulka* in Yiddish) to wear. I was confused. I had thought that only the very religious men and boys wore the small round caps. I was to learn a lot about the differences and the intertwining of religious beliefs and Jewish customs.

At the dinner table Yael lit the *Shabbat* candles and Amos and their eldest son read passages from the Old Testament. Amos then blessed the wine—and we ate. They were not a *religious* family; they didn't keep kosher and they didn't go regularly to the synagogue. But they observed many ancient Jewish traditions.

Yom Kippur, the Day of Atonement, is the holiest of all days for Jews, who *observe* the holiday more than celebrate it. This is a time for prayer and atonement of sins and, for the orthodox, fasting. It is also the quietest day of the year in Israel. Except for emergencies no vehicles are allowed on the streets.

Purim is a fun holiday that celebrates the deliverance of ancient Persian Jews—with the help of Esther—from massacre by Haman. Children dress in costumes, take part in school plays and eat sweets made especially for the day.

Adults, too, often commemorate *Purim* with costume parties. Mirah, an Israeli journalist, traditionally hosted a huge fancy dress affair for her friends. An American colleague, a woman who weighed well over 250 pounds, appeared at one of Mirah's party stuffed into a fluffy ballet tutu and pink tights.

The best food in Israel came from the Middle Eastern/Arab cuisine: *hummus*, a dip made of ground chickpeas, sesame paste, olive oil and garlic; an eggplant dip; kabobs of ground lamb; pita and other flatbreads, to name only a few. We liked to eat in simple Yemeni Jewish restaurants that served grilled meats, flavorful stuffed vegetables and rice. First course or appetizer "salads" were Mediterranean: roasted peppers, eggplant and zucchini in olive oil, and lots of olives.

We had an old style Jewish dinner one Saturday afternoon in Jerusalem. Our hosts explained that the food was traditional *Shabbat* fare. In earlier times their families prepared the food before sundown on Friday and put it into a pot to simmer over a home fire or in the baker's oven all night to be ready for Saturday dinner. The religiously observant households were not allowed to work—which included cooking—during the Sabbath hours so the meal cooked itself.

As we ate the stewed concoction of meat, vegetables and heavy dumplings, the other guests reminisced about the *Shabbat* foods of their heritage. *Cholent* was the name they used for one-pot meals like the one we were eating. At the height of the nostalgic remembrances, Shimshon mused, "But this really isn't very good, is it?" Everyone laughed and nodded their heads in agreement. "So why do we do it? Because our parents and their parents did."

Not only did Jewish dietary laws influence cooking, but food traditions from various parts of the world have influenced Israeli cuisine. *Cholent,* potato pancakes, and *gefilte* fish were traditional Jewish foods from Europe that are eaten in Israel today.

Street food—fast food in Israel—included: rice-stuffed vine leaves; Moroccan "cigars," savory cylindrical fried pastries; *shuarma,* rotisserie-cooked pieces of seasoned lamb stuffed into pita bread; and *falafel,* deep-fried balls of mashed chickpeas. *Falafel* was almost considered the national dish of Israel, although it probably originated in Egypt.

Battered and bent armored vehicles and partially dismembered trucks lay scattered along the hilly highway to Jerusalem. These carefully preserved Israeli monuments were remains and reminders of 1948 and the war of independence. And on a rocky hillside in Jerusalem near Yad Vashem, the holocaust museum, stood another stark memorial: a rusty cattle car brought from Eastern Europe. A rectangular death box for the Jews who unwillingly rode the rails to prison and death camps.

Jerusalem is a hauntingly beautiful city that sits on the hills reflecting the sunlight. Since the 1950's, construction regulations have required that only "Jerusalem stone" can be used for new buildings in the city center. The beige and ecru-colored limestone gives the city a clean sparkling look.

Wandering through the narrow lanes and alleys within the walls of the Old City was always an adventure. Little shops displayed an array of ceramics, brass, olivewood figures and mother-of-pearl inlaid boxes, plus the inevitable souvenir T-shirts. A hot-selling T-shirt that amused tourists bore the logo: "America—Don't Worry—Israel is Behind You." Carpet merchants and antique dealers offered customers coffee, tea, and a chair to rest in while considering their purchases. These were serious shopkeepers, Arabs and Armenians, not the disinterested clerks I found in the Tel Aviv suburbs.

Bargaining is an art form and a talent I sadly don't have—another gene gone astray. (I am also lacking a chocolate gene.) Behind the old walls one was expected to haggle over the prices of almost everything. I wasn't good at it even though LaVerne, who had lived in Jerusalem, had given me ample instructions before we left for Israel.

"When you see something you want that is pricey, admire it profusely," she told me. "Leave the shop, return later and ask the price. Return again and suggest an alternative price." Depending on the item and the shopkeeper, you may have to return yet again for the serious haggling before settling on the best price.

"The merchant likes to know you are serious," advised LaVerne, who was an astute shopper.

The smells of the Old City still linger in the nostrils like the sights that have nestled in my memory. I could smell the combinations of spices and herbs long before I spotted the scores of large open bags. It was acceptable to handle the powders, leaves and seeds. You had to rub them through your fingers and sniff them to determine the quality.

Olives came in numerous varieties and the customer was expected to taste them before making a purchase. No native Arab or Jew would pay for olives, grapes or nuts without first sampling them. This was true, not only in the Old City, but also in outdoor markets throughout the country, including the huge Bedouin market we visited near Beer Sheva in the desert.

When the family was visiting we drove north and wandered around in the town of Netanya where we found a splendid market. Everyone had fun tasting the olives and selecting their favorites. We went home with several little plastic bags—each containing a different variety of olives. The following day I opened the refrigerator to put the olives in separate small dishes for us to snack on. I discovered that the maid had dumped all the olives into one big container—mixing up all the flavors!

American travelers and expatriates celebrate the Fourth of July wherever they can in the world. I think when we're abroad there is more of an emotional need to observe our country's national day than when we're at home. Maybe it's because we miss out on the hometown parades and band concerts, picnics with our families, and the patriotic celebrations televised from the mall in Washington, DC.

We seldom had fireworks at our foreign posts but we always had the "Star Spangled Banner," both the music and the flag it represents. The President sent his Independence Day message for the ambassador to read and—whoever the speechwriter was at the time—his words were always stirring.

Each post has an official celebration, usually a ho-hum reception to which the local ministers, mayors, and mavens—political and social—are invited along with ambassadors and representatives of other foreign missions. In large capital cities the guest list can number as many as a thousand. These receptions are necessary but not necessarily enjoyable. Weeks of work by the staff culminate in two hours of handshaking and tired feet. (Although Art says that on occasion an important contact has been made.)

Sometimes the spouses are invited, sometimes not, and the children are seldom allowed at the official party. In Tel Aviv Kathy and her college-age friends felt left out and—let's face it—put out because they were not included. The young women, especially, wanted to dress up and attend the festivities in the ambassador's garden and ogle the dignitaries. They decided instead to have a counter party at the DCM's residence, our home.

Kathy and Robert, the cook, made scrumptious snack food and friends supplied some of the soft drinks, beer and juice. Scott and Emily, whose parents were embassy friends, helped move the furniture, blow up balloons, decorate and set up the music. The party was successful and well attended—especially by people the hosts had never met! The food and drink ran out early in the evening but they partied on, celebrating *their* independence.

The *real* Fourth of July celebration was a community affair, usually a picnic organized by volunteers and/or the CLO. There were games for the children, hot dogs and hamburgers, and memorable camaraderie. The Apple Pie Contest was popular in Tel Aviv. Volunteer judges taste-tested the home-baked entries and gave a blue ribbon for the best pie. Afterwards, we sold slices of pie and added the proceeds to our charity funds.

Corn-on-the-cob headed the menu at those picnics. Israel grew the sweetest corn I had ever tasted—and I was nurtured on delicious Nebraska "roasting ears." One young son complained at being compelled to help clean it, but his father Adriaen, who was from Arkansas, put an end to the grumbling.

"Every young American boy has to learn to shuck corn!" he announced.

Two silver trays disappeared from our pantry. I looked and looked, thinking they had to be somewhere in the house, but they were nowhere. Art was out of town so I went to the embassy and talked—confessed—to Clarence, the ADMIN counselor. I was full of guilt because the silver was government property and I couldn't remember when I had last seen the trays. They were lovely pieces, but too heavy and cumbersome to use regularly.

Clarence wrote down the information and said he would look into it. "But don't lose any more sleep over this," he told me.

When Art returned I told him about the trays. He responded in much the same way as Clarence had, almost apathetic. What I didn't know was that there was already an investigation in process—Israeli employees of the embassy's General Services Office were suspected of theft. A long-planned joint operation by our security office and local law enforcement soon culminated in the arrest of several people.

When the police searched the homes of the suspects, they discovered large hoards of stolen goods—plundered from the embassy warehouses. I never found out if the silver trays were among the recovered loot. I suppose I didn't really want to know.

Because I *did know* personally all the perpetrators. They were in and out of our home weekly and I called them by their first names. I *liked* them. These were the people who did repairs in the homes of embassy personnel. They worked on electricity and plumbing and they moved furniture when we were having a large party. And when we were away, they had access to our homes in case of fire or other emergency.

One young man had invited Art and me to a *brit mila,* circumcision cere-mony, for his baby son. This same man, prior to the arrests, threatened the life of another employee to keep him from tattling. The numerous stolen items, and many were expensive, were almost insignificant compared to the trust these men violated. That hurt.

Though the crowd at the tennis match might poke you in the ribs, and the clerk in the dry cleaners might be surly, and the bank teller might show disinter-est, the Israeli people, nevertheless, have big hearts. We felt their warmth and saw the tenderness in our many friends. They invited us into their homes and shared their lives and their culture with us. Some Israelis may be prickly like the sabra cactus but their toughness has resulted in their endurance. And their sense of humor gives them strength.

Every Israeli had a story to tell. For many it was about the parent or grandpar-ent who died in a Nazi death camp. Or a relative who beat the odds and survived. There were many tales about subsequent wars, about death and survival. Some Israelis told humorous stories about gas masks and air raid shelters.

Yaron's father was wounded during the fighting in the Sinai. He watched many friends die and he swore he would never again set foot in any part of Egypt. Three bullets had pierced his heart and he eventually needed a transplant. Finally he was summoned to a Belgian hospital for the procedure. The irony of his renewed life was that he received a healthy German heart—implanted by an Egyptian surgeon. Yaron told this story with a big smile.

Another Israeli summed up his country's personality with a yarn about the dif-ficulties of living in Israel versus the pleasures of visiting the country. A man arrives at the Pearly Gates where an angel greets him. "Where do you want to go, up or down?"

"You mean I get to choose?"

"We can't decide what to do with you so we'll make you a special deal. We'll let you visit and then you can decide." And the angel sends the man down below where wild parties are going on. Sex orgies, dancing, great food, noisy celebrations and non-stop fun. Mmm, the man thinks, not bad.

"Okay, enough," announces the angel and zap! He transports the man upward.

In heaven the scene is pastoral and beautiful music is playing. The people, all dressed in white, are reading books and reciting poetry. The sky is blue and the temperature is perfect. Everyone appears to be contented.

Back at the Pearly Gates, the angel asks the man, "What do you think?

"Well, heaven is a nice place, but maybe a little boring. You know, forever is a long time—this is a hard decision." Then trying not to show his eagerness, the man says, "I'll take Hell!" And back down he goes.

But this time there are no beautiful girls, no music, no food or even water. It is hot and demons begin to torture him. "Help—please!" he calls out in anguish. "This can't be the right place. The first time I came, it was a party—totally different."

"But the first time you came as a tourist!" a booming Voice replies.

Kathy came for a last visit—due to the imminent and inevitable end of our assignment in Israel—and Art and I went with her to Ben Gurion to see her safely on her way back to New York. Halfway to the airport the radio crackled and a voice called for "Cornshucker."

Art responded and we all heard: "Keep your heads down—there may be live fire in your area!"

We looked at each other, stunned for a few seconds, before we recognized the Marine's voice and the humor in it. We laughed then, especially Kathy, who loved the goodbye salute from her friends at Marine Guard Post I.

We had kept our heads down for three years, we watched out for live fire, we curtailed some of our activities because of the *intifada*, and we strove to understand the problems and emotions that were causing it. We survived the crises, alerts and failed peace efforts and we worked hard. Whenever someone asks Art how he liked his time in Israel, he answers, "It was a *total* experience." For me it was the good, the bad, the ugly *and* the beautiful.

It was time to go home. We had been abroad for nine years and we were ready for a Washington assignment. Art retrieved Jorgen's gift of red wine from a dark corner in our bedroom closet. He checked the cork, rewrapped the bottle and added more cardboard to the package. Maybe there would be a special occasion in Washington.

15

THE OTHER ROACHES

The big bugs, euphemistically speaking, are those that have a serious impact on our lives. They are dirty and detestable and damaging like cockroaches—and all too often deadly. They occur in all parts of the world, some naturally and others with the help of humankind, some intentionally and others unwittingly. Among these are the tragedies and traumas that have affected us through our work in the Foreign Service.

PLANE CRASH 1969

The first of those events that had a profound impact on us was the plane crash in Maracaibo, Venezuela that killed over 150 people. It was, at that time, the worst air disaster in history. All eighty-four people on the Viasa DC9 died. The other victims were on the streets or in the fourteen destroyed homes.

Ray and Alba had invited us for brunch that Sunday in March. Ray was a businessman with a keen interest in HAM radio communication. He and Art were up on the roof installing an antenna when they spotted a huge column of black smoke coming from the direction of the airport. We turned on the radio—and heard the dreadful news. An airplane had crashed and burned just after take-off from Grano del Oro, Maracaibo's international airport.

When we learned that this was one of Viasa Airlines' regular flights originating in Caracas and bound for Miami, Florida, we knew that there would be American citizens on board. There were in fact forty-five, as we confirmed later in the day. The consul, Bart Moon, along with Art and Elijah, the vice-consuls, immediately set into motion the procedures and tasks required of consulates all over the world in such circumstances: coming to the aid of American citizens in a foreign country. And dealing with a tragedy of that magnitude has to be one of the most horrendous duties of any consular officer.

Because the bodies were too numerous for the morgue, the university's medical school laboratory became a makeshift facility. In order to be on the scene, Art suggested using a classroom for a temporary consular office. And there my husband and the others worked during the difficult days that followed—long long days.

As soon as the wire services in the United States had the story of the plane crash, long-distance calls started coming in from families who had relatives or friends on the plane. The airport produced a manifest of sorts. Written in pencil, it was smudged and wrinkled and difficult to read. But with the help of Ricardo, the consular assistant and invaluable translator, the list was eventually usable. Families who lived in Maracaibo came immediately to identify their loved ones. Identification was difficult, however, and often impossible. The crash itself dismembered many of the passengers and the fire disfigured and in some cases destroyed what was left of the bodies. Numerous family members made the difficult trip from the States. Confirmation of death was necessary not only for emotional release and for the grieving process to begin, but also for the legalities of insurance and inheritance.

Art has a vivid memory of bodies crowded side by side on long tables and finally on the floor lining the walls around the room. Remains were numbered and tagged. Isolated pieces of jewelry and personal items were sealed in plastic bags and these also had numbers. He remembers how bits of flesh and hair would fall away from a piece of jewelry each time a bag was opened. He wishes he could forget the shape of a young child, unrecognizable, and the baseball glove he saw, knowing how a child likes to carry a favorite plaything on a trip.

Art said, "No chance—that child had no chance to become an adult."

An American woman who came to identify her father said that he was a dentist whose hobby was making jewelry. She recognized a unique piece of jewelry that she knew he had made. She was one of the "lucky" ones—she had the means to identify her father. In the end the authorities were convinced that a few next-of-kin made improbable identifications solely for the importance of having a body, either for religious or for emotional reasons.

Sometime during the third day, it became necessary to bury the remains that had not been identified or claimed. Heat was a major factor in that decision: the temperature recorded on the day of the crash was 89.4 degrees Fahrenheit. Some bodies were later disinterred at the request of relatives who wanted to take the victims home. Other families wanted only confirmation of the death and the consoling reassurance that their loved one had had a religious burial. At the consulate telephone conversations and meetings with family members continued for several weeks, as did the processing of documents.

My memories of those days are sensory: the feeling of quiet bereavement in the community; the look of desolation on Art's face; and the heavy odor of fire and formaldehyde that clung to his body. When he came home at night, he undressed on the front porch and went immediately into the shower. I carried his clothes around to the back patio and hung the suit outside, hoping that a breeze would blow away some of the awful smells before we took it to the dry cleaners. The shirt and other washables went into the washing machine with hot water and bleach and there they soaked all night.

The death toll remained approximate. We knew how many people were on the plane but the number of deaths on the ground was impossible to confirm. The DC-9 crashed onto street number 58 that divided the suburb into two contrasting economic areas: white-collar low-income housing on one side, and on the other, a no-income slum. The latter, called a *barrio,* consisted of cardboard lean-tos and sheet-metal huts. Families on that side of the street were loosely structured and nomadic. Although the consulate was concerned, officially, only with Americans involved in the tragedy, in my mind for a long time were thoughts that there might be a missing Maracucho, a relative, an unmourned death.

The consulate received commendations from the Department of State for its skilled and competent handling of the situation. More importantly, many, many families sent letters expressing their appreciation for the care, support, and the human touch of the consular people that helped them deal with their losses.

Our friend Hal and others in the American business community told Art how impressed they were with the compassion and the efficiency with which their American government representatives dealt with the tragedy. Some people had mistakenly thought that all Foreign Service Officers were stuffed-shirt bureaucrats.

KIDNAPPING 1993

Haynes Mahoney wasn't the first foreigner who was kidnapped in or around Sanaa, Yemen, nor was he the last, but he was the first American embassy officer to suffer that fate. He was the Public Affairs Officer in charge of the United States Information Service and his captivity affected us professionally—and personally. Haynes and his family were our friends.

It happened on Thanksgiving. Americans associated with the embassy, as well as a few visitors, came for a potluck family dinner at the ambassador's residence (our home from 1991 to 1994). There were over eighty of us. We had stuffed and roasted two turkeys and baked some pumpkin pies. Sossi, Haynes' wife, had also cooked a large turkey. The other guests provided salads, appetizers, vegetables, desserts and bread. It was the most elegant potluck meal I had ever seen. The November day was warm and sunny and we ate outside on the patio.

Sossi and the children left around 4:30 p.m. They had come in two cars because he wanted to go to his office for a while before going home. Haynes went to the office—and then he intended to stop at a grocery store...

At ten o'clock that night Sossi called. "Is Haynes there with you?" No. "Has Art talked to him?" Again no.

Sossi told us they had planned to go to a party at eight o'clock but Haynes hadn't returned home and no one answered the telephone at his office. Eberhard, the host of the party and a mutual friend, became concerned and drove to the USIS building. Haynes' vehicle was not there and a guard reported that Mr. Mahoney had left hours ago.

Immediately after Sossi's phone call Art, in his capacity as ambassador, notified our Regional Security Officer. Mike alerted his people and began the usual procedures. They checked the hospitals and the police first. No sign of Haynes.

Art called Washington. "Haynes is missing and presumed kidnapped." The statement made my stomach swirl.

A report came in: from his upper window a Yemeni saw someone being pushed into a jeep. The witness thought he saw diplomatic license plates on a nearby vehicle. (The numbers on diplomats' plates were in red and easy to spot.) This sighting took place near a small supermarket.

The most convincing information was that a "Layla Alawi" had been spotted in various parts of the city during the evening with several men inside. Layla Alawi was the name of a popular female Egyptian singer with a sizable and curvaceous figure. Yemenis joked that the Toyota Landcruiser reminded them of her. Haynes had been driving a Landcruiser, which was now in the hands of the kidnappers.

Finally, police reported that a Toyota with Haynes' license plates was recorded in the logbook as the vehicle passed a Yemeni security checkpoint on the road east to Marib governate. (That piece of information confirmed to the embassy that the Yemenis did indeed watch the movements of diplomatic vehicles.)

Confirmation of the kidnapping came the next morning. The *kabili,* tribesmen, who were holding Haynes notified the Yemeni government of their demands. They wanted what the government had promised—and had not delivered: water wells, schools, and jobs, including reinstating army commissions for some of their men. Hearing such a list, one could have sympathy for the villagers. However, it was known that this tribe had been previously involved in sabotage, car theft and other illegal acts.

Kidnapping is a historic method by which Yemeni tribes put pressure on the government. A foreigner is considered a more useful hostage than a local—Yemenis don't put so much value on each other. Previous—and subsequent—taking of hostages involved mainly employees of foreign businesses, especially oil companies. Until Haynes, no foreign government official had been kidnapped. It is important to emphasize that the embassy, as the representative of the U.S. government, did no negotiating with the tribal leaders. Even though our man was in the middle, so to speak, his safety had to be mediated by representatives of the tribe and the Yemeni government. In fact, it was crucial that the kidnapping be kept "traditional," as Art put it, and not become a tribe/embassy matter.

Art conferred several times a day, by phone and in person, with the Interior Minister, Mr. Mutawakil, and he met with President Saleh and Foreign Minister Basindweh. As the American ambassador he insistently sought—and received—assurances that security forces would not launch any kind of attack on the offending tribe without his complete knowledge. Any storming of the village would be inherently dangerous for Haynes.

When Art and I arrived at the Mahoney home, Sossi was frightened and very angry but somewhat calmer after my husband explained what was being done. I had taken along an overnight bag—just in case—and I decided to stay. The phone was ringing constantly and visitors were streaming in and out. Sossi occupied herself serving coffee and tea; she wanted to keep busy but I thought she needed some help.

A Christmas Fair sponsored by the American Women's Group was to take place at the ambassador's residence a few days later. The question now was whether or not to cancel it. The Fair was intended to raise money for charity and also to be a festive event. But none of us was feeling at all festive. I thought of Scarlet O'Hara and I decided, "I'll think about it tomorrow."

Early on the third morning, I left for a committee meeting. The first group of visitors had already arrived, but Sossi was in good hands with our mutual friend Ruth, who had also spent the night. I stopped at home after the meeting to pick up some supplies: Kleenex and toilet paper that we might run short of; a bag of home-made cookies; and some rare salami that we had just acquired. I hurried back to the Mahoney's.

As I was unloading my bags in the kitchen, Sossi put her arms around me and began to cry. "With you, it's as if my mother were here," she said. She recovered quickly—she was not prone to tears for any reason. I thought she was unusually brave, considering what she was dealing with.

Don't be misled—we were not short of food, quite the opposite. Sossi always had a well-stocked larder and friends were bringing food every day. I discovered that during a crisis, we tend to do what we are accustomed to doing—and more so. Sossi was a giver. She liked to cook and she liked to feed people so every day she made one tasty concoction after another. She prepared several Armenian dishes and told us about her Armenian family background. We had to restrain her feeding impulses the day our friend, Harish, manager of the Taj Sheba Hotel called to say he was bringing over lunch for all of us.

Guests continued to arrive and the coffee maker was constantly bubbling. In the evening we served cold drinks and tea, along with all sorts of snacks—and we still had plenty of food. Jane, a USIS officer, called one afternoon and asked if she could bring anything. I told her the only thing we were out of was beer.

But underneath all this food-oriented busyness was the constant strain and worry about Haynes. How was he? How were the negotiations progressing? What if the government did something rash in spite of its promise? Full of anger and stress one evening, Sossi blurted out, "I'm going out to Marib. I'll find Haynes and bring him back!" (And she would have!) After some diplomatic mediating Art convinced her to at least wait a few days.

Somehow a letter arrived from Haynes. Art didn't tell me how it came about and I knew there was no point in asking. When Sossi went into her bedroom to read the message I realized that it was the only time she had wanted to be alone since the crisis began. When she came out, she handed me the letter to read while she got a bag ready. Her husband had asked her to send underwear, socks, and a book. I felt embarrassed looking at her private message but I realized—and Sossi knew, also—that embassy officials had already read it. Off went a driver with the bag and a note from Sossi to Haynes. I never found out how that was arranged.

Abdul Azziz, a friend of Haynes and editor of an English language weekly called *The Yemen Times*, found his way out to the village where the tribals were holding their hostage. The *kabili* permitted Abdul Azziz to interview Haynes and to take a photograph. He called Sossi that night and assured her that her husband was *well*.

What Abdul Azziz didn't tell her, however, was what he had said to Haynes. "I'm afraid the government is going to do something stupid." He had counted scores of government tanks along the road leading to the village.

At the Mahoney home we constantly had calls from the press; sometimes the same journalist phoned four or five times a day. Late one night the telephone woke us all up with an obscene call from a man speaking English with a heavy accent. I hung up quickly, but he called back later, and again the next night. What could I do? We had to answer the phone—there might be news of Haynes. A USIA press officer soon arrived in Sanaa, however, and took charge of issuing statements to the media. Thereafter we gave his number to all callers who had questions we couldn't or were not inclined to answer.

Several days after the kidnapping a journalist somehow received and believed a false report that Haynes was to be released imminently. He called the house repeatedly during the afternoon and evening asking for information. He didn't believe that we had no news. When he phoned again long after midnight, I lost my temper. "If you call here again I'll have you arrested for harassment!" Then I snarled, "This phone is tapped, you know." I hoped it was. But I regretted my impatience later when I found out that the journalist was a long-time friend of Haynes.

Sossi told their three daughters only that their daddy was away and she wasn't sure when he would be back. Coco was the youngest and she was at home with us. She wasn't yet a year old but she was beginning to toddle about on her own. Her antics and giggles brightened an otherwise bleak atmosphere. Karina and Dominique, who were in elementary school, spent their days at the homes of friends.

When a Yemeni tribe was involved in a difficult situation with the government, it was customary for a senior sheik from another tribe to act as an intermediary. This was generally self-serving since the go-between hoped for some reward. At the same time, the negotiations could be complicated by the relationships between the tribes. In this case a tribe of the Zaidi, which had kidnapped Haynes, became disenchanted with the Nehm who had possession of the Layla Alawi—and the Bakil became angry about the way the negotiations were finalized. But finalized they were...somehow. (To fully understand all of this tribal rivalry and its effect on Haynes' release, one would need to acquire the official report from the embassy—or hear the more entertaining version from the kidnappee himself.)

The *kabili* released Haynes, healthy and unharmed, eight days after he had been kidnapped. His homecoming was delayed, however, for twelve hours by the fore-mentioned tribal complications. The wait and the worry were over. A Yemeni military helicopter delivered the former hostage to the airport where Art and Sossi met him. They called on Minister Mutawakil and then President Saleh with whom the obligatory photos were taken. Haynes, who spoke Arabic, was dressed in tribal garb with a *kafiya*, an Arab scarf, around his neck. He wore no socks, much to the chagrin of his wife. He had a bandoleer of bullets over his shoulder and he carried a Mauser, previously owned by his guard. The ambassador diplomatically discouraged group pictures and the propensity to make light of the fact that Haynes Mahoney had been deprived of his liberty for a full week.

Word spread rapidly that Haynes was coming to the embassy after leaving the Yemeni president and we had just enough time to blow up some red, white and blue balloons and hang up bright streamers. Government employees and friends, Americans and Yemenis, rallied in front of the embassy. A great roar of welcome went up as the ambassador's car came through the gates bringing Haynes, Sossi and Art.

Haynes was deluged with hugs and handshakes, accompanied by a lot of whooping and laughing. Everyone felt a tremendous relief. I busily snapped photographs. When Dr. Scott, the embassy physician, took Haynes inside to be examined, I hurried home to finish the final details for the Christmas Fair. Happily, we hadn't canceled the event and we opened the doors an hour later. I took more photos.

At least, I thought I did. I discovered the next day that there was no film in my camera! So much for recording historical events.

CIVIL WAR 1994

I knew what tracers were because I had read a number of novels about war, but I had never seen them until that Thursday morning in May. I was mesmerized by the perfect path of sparkling lights that arced over the terrace outside our bedroom in Sanaa. The sparks had an odd beauty that fascinated me in spite of the horrendous noise that accompanied the antiaircraft artillery. Then we heard a plane—or planes.

"Get away from the window," shouted my husband and I dove for the floor. We knew abruptly that the peace, which already had cracks in it, had shattered.

After a long historic separation north and south Yemen united in 1990 and the northern city of Sanaa became the capital of the new Republic of Yemen. When we arrived sixteen months after unification, there was a great deal of optimism. In the presence of international observers, the first democratic elections in that country were peacefully concluded in 1993 and everyone continued to be hopeful. During the following months, however, the tiny fissures in the foundation of the government became widening crevices as political wrangling turned into serious struggles for power.

As the American ambassador my husband worked strenuously at gaining the confidence of Yemeni officials and politicians and maintaining a dialogue with both sides. He had a reputation for being open-minded and fair. In his efforts to keep unification from crumbling, he used diplomatic mortar to stress caution and talk peace.

But the military forces were never united, neither officially nor figuratively. When the two factions fired on each other early in the spring of 1994, "the troubles" began. Chris, our military attaché, was on a "listen and learn" trip when he found himself in the middle of the shooting only a few hours away from Sanaa. The embassy lost contact with Chris, but efforts to find him eventually produced a reassuring answer from a Yemeni government official: "We know where he is and he is safe." Art found out later, however, that the information had been false and the Yemeni military officers did *not* know where the major was. They were as worried as we were—they had "lost" an American officer.

Chris returned safely, however, with information about the status of forces. Each military group blamed the other for the provocation.

By this time embassy people, other American expatriates and foreign diplomats were forced to think about "what if?" Civil war? Evacuation? The embassy notified all Americans to meet in the garden of the residence. The political, military, and security officers gave briefings and Art answered questions about the local situation. Everyone was concerned and a few people were alarmed, but there was no sense of panic.

I knew what I had to do. I needed to have all my records up-to-date: representation files, residence expenses, staff records and salaries, and bills paid. I needed to make lots of lists: important papers and documents that I/we would hand-carry if we left the country suddenly; clothing and personal effects I could put into a suitcase quickly; and important items to have close at hand (passport, credit card, medications.) I made a list of emergency supplies for the house, such as bottled water and candles, in the event our generators failed. And because somehow I suspected that Art and I would not leave together, I needed to write memos for him. Never during all of this thinking, planning and list making did I believe that I would actually be *evacuated.*

For a short period diplomacy seemed to be working, but again the situation deteriorated. The evening of May fourth Art received an ominous phone call from a well-respected Yemeni cabinet minister.

"The inevitable has begun."

Art couldn't reach the Yemeni vice president, leader of the political opposition, who was in Aden. Nor was he able to talk to other members of that party to get information. In spite of all affirmations to the contrary, it appeared the south intended to secede.

And so it began. Phone calls came in all evening reporting troop movements in some areas and actual fighting in others. Around 8:30 Art reached two cabinet ministers in Aden—but the call was abruptly cut off. Someone phoned with the unexpected information that Lloyd's of London had canceled the insurance on any airliner that flew into Yemen. Since a Lufthansa flight was scheduled to arrive that night and leave the next day, we predicted that it would have no empty seats when it took off.

The most important call was between Art and Washington: if the situation didn't improve drastically by morning, the embassy would recommend the evacuation of all Americans from Yemen.

The antiaircraft artillery began at five o'clock the next morning. I thought at first it was gunfire, only louder. I crept out of bed, peeked around the curtain—and that's when I saw the tracers. After I dropped to the floor we "felt" a bomb hit—somewhere.

At 6:15 a call from Aden informed us that planes from the northern forces were making bombing runs over Aden airport. Crouched on the floor in our bedroom, Art called the State Department to report that war had started and to confirm that evacuation procedures would begin.

As soon as the AAA (antiaircraft artillery) diminished and we didn't hear any approaching planes, we checked on the well-being of our house guests. I went down to the kitchen and fried bacon while Abdul Hameed and Ali, our live-in Yemeni housekeepers, cut up fruit and made toast and coffee. They were nervous and apprehensive, but they diligently went about their work. We ate quickly, with the drapes shut, and discussed our next steps. (The bazooka attack two and a half years earlier had prodded FBO into sending us dining room drapes that *closed.*)

Our house guests were State Department officials, Assistant Secretary Pelletrau and also the deputy director for Arabian Peninsula affairs. Breakfast table conversation focused on efforts to get them out of the country quickly and safely. Fortunately, they were traveling in a U. S. Air Force plane and didn't need to rely on a commercial carrier. As the men were leaving for the embassy, Art cautioned me, "Keep the drapes closed and stay away from the windows." As it turned out, I spent the rest of the morning in the kitchen—where there were no windows at all.

The racket of AAA fire was sporadic as I frantically cooked. When Hassan, our cook, phoned, I told him to stay home with his family. Abdul Hameed and I carried breakfast next door to the embassy—there was no one there to operate the cafeteria. There were hungry Marines, plus communications officers and others who had courageously come in because essential work needed to be done. Members of the embassy's Emergency Action Committee met to formalize standard procedure. When other employees called in they were told to stay home and "keep your heads down."

Over the next forty-eight hours I wrote in my diary whenever I could. "Thursday afternoon: I have put two turkeys in the oven—stuffed. I know it was stupid but I thought those turkeys just had to have stuffing. We had planned a dinner party for 16 tonight—Yemeni ministers and politicians to meet the Assistant Secretary…We made sandwiches and packed a lunch for [visitors] Bob, Gerry, and their pilot and crew."

"Thursday evening: We fed turkey to about twenty people who came over from the embassy at intervals…I had only a few potatoes and they were finished quickly…We took them tuna sandwiches for lunch—I lost track of how many cans I opened."

That evening as I was dishing up turkey and stuffing for the first group of warriors, the phone rang—it was our daughter in New York. I went into the library to take the call. Just as I was telling Kathy that her dad and I were all right, anti-aircraft artillery began. The noise was horrible! I got down on the floor, facing away from the windows, and huddled against the sofa. It was difficult to hear Kathy so we quickly finished our conversation. I was too preoccupied with my chores to be frightened and only later did I realize how awful the situation must have sounded to our daughter on the other end of the line. I regretted not having called our children earlier to let them know we were safe.

Early Friday morning a message went out from the embassy: "If it is safe, all Americans should come to the residence at 10:00 a.m. for an information session." No planes had come over that morning and about a hundred people arrived to learn about evacuation procedures.

The embassy would draw down to only essential personnel as determined by the ambassador. (This decision is made on a case by case basis. Usually the chief of mission, the marines and a communications officer, at least, will remain once the level of safety is assessed.) The mission recommended that all Americans leave the country via U.S. government-arranged transportation. The embassy planned to get all Americans, including unofficial people who wanted to leave, out of Yemen by May 10th. (This goal would be accomplished—ahead of schedule.)

Since I considered myself "essential personnel," it didn't occur to me to think about leaving. As soon as the meeting was over, Abdul Hameed and Ali cleaned up the coffee and tea things and juice glasses while I started preparing lunch to take to the embassy. The adrenaline was up and running.

I wrote in my diary: "We thawed out several pounds of hot dogs—part of our supplies for the Fourth of July picnic—and sliced our last loaf of bread and that was lunch. We had pickles but no more fresh vegetables…"

Electricity was out in most parts of the city but the generators on our compound ran faithfully. That was especially fortunate because our stoves were electric and so were the water purifiers. And because I had forgotten to buy bottled water! Telephones were out in some areas but we continued to receive calls—hundreds of them, it seemed. At some point during that day, however, I discovered that we couldn't call out.

Lucy, the economics officer, who had spent the previous night in one of our guestrooms, went home for a change of clothes. When she came back she brought food that was in danger of spoiling in her refrigerator. The Marine Gunny delivered a thawing beef roast that I stowed in the refrigerator. Sossi arrived with the entire contents of a full-size freezer; her home had no electricity either. These food contributions plus supplies from our own freezers would be used during the following weeks to feed the remaining embassy staff.

Friday evening I jotted: "Along with the frozen food Sossi brought fresh fruit and vegies…Alan picked zucchini from his garden…scurvy and rickets have been avoided for another day…Hamburgers and buns are thawing, baked beans are in the oven…No one has shown up for dinner yet—so much to do." And for some reason, I felt the need to explain. "I realize that this is becoming very food-oriented, but everyone has a job to do and mine seems to be *feeding*."

Hassan, our cook, was able to get to the residence on Friday. He went to work baking bread and doing as much as he could before he had to return home by the 6:00 p.m. curfew. He told us he saw very few cars and almost no one on the streets. The stores were locked and shuttered and he couldn't find any of the little stands that normally sell fresh produce. He had been able to buy gas for his car the previous day but he had to wait in line for two hours.

Art phoned me in the afternoon. "Pat, you'll be leaving with the other evacuees in the morning." I begged to go with the very last flight—hoping he might change his mind and decide that I was "essential." I didn't want to leave and I was convinced I could be helpful to the embassy as well as to Art. But there was no way he could allow me to stay. In other words, no "special treatment" for the ambassador's wife.

At 10:12 p.m. I wrote: "Looking out the window toward the west is like looking into a black hole—there is no light anywhere. Last night there were a few dull glows, probably from generators. Tonight nothing. Looking east, I see an occasional car go by in front of the embassy." The quiet was somehow unsettling. My last diary entry that night was: "This is the pits! And it is much more difficult for families with children than it is for us."

Between midnight and 2:00 a.m. I packed a suitcase, paced the floor, watched CNN, and then I repacked the suitcase (with all the wrong things) and paced the floor again. CNN briefly and periodically carried a news bite about Yemen, but soon it became repetitious. Several people came to spend the night and I got cold drinks for them and made sure they had eaten.

Art came home very late. It was 4:00 a.m. by the time we finished discussing a myriad of details, including arrangements for the next day. The alarm clock rang at six. During the short night bursts of shelling—that sounded uncomfortably close—woke me twice. Art slept through the second round.

The American evacuees gathered at the Sheraton Hotel Saturday morning. Many families who were without electricity had chosen to spend the previous night at the hotel. The lobby and grounds were thronged with hundreds of people: men, women and children with "promised" seats on the first planes plus scores of others of varying nationalities who hoped to get seats. Husbands who were remaining in Sanaa said good-bye to tearful wives, fathers hugged crying children, friends met up to say brief farewells. There was a nervous hum in the atmosphere.

Acquaintances and people I had never met approached me and begged me to help them get seats on a plane for their children. All I could do was to empathize and direct them to Fred, the consul.

I felt especially proud that morning to be associated with the American Embassy. Our people did a superlative job organizing the evacuation and getting everyone out of Yemen who wanted to go. The United States Air Force, too, handled its task admirably. No USAF planes left with empty seats. Nearly 300 people departed that morning and another sizable group went out two days later. Yes, there are regulations dealing with evacuation and, yes, there are written instructions to refer to, but the likelihood of a Foreign Service Officer being involved in this type of crisis management more than once is slim. They can't practice. The majority of diplomats are fortunate not to ever be part of an evacuation.

Dr. Scott set up shop at the hotel. He made sure that anyone who needed medication got it. He conferred with mothers regarding their little ones. He gave advice on helping children cope with ear pain from changes in air pressure while flying. He was a calming and encouraging influence.

Our bags and suitcases, one per person except for handbags, were loaded onto trucks. When the signal came we headed for the buses. A monitor aboard each vehicle carried a two-way radio and stayed in communication with a security officer. We counted heads, then waited in or near our buses. By then it was midday and it was hot. Bottles of water circulated and most of us began to nibble on small snacks we had brought along. I had made the mistake of bringing cheese and crackers and my cheese had melted into an oily glob!

A voice finally crackled over the radios ordering the buses to "head on out." Three USAF C-130 airplanes were approaching the airport. Everyone was quiet during the twenty-minute ride to the airport, even the children. Unfamiliar feelings surfaced when I saw some Yemenis on the streets—a few waved to us, others just stared at the convoy of buses. Their country was at war, yet I was certain that most of the people I saw were more concerned with jobs, food and basic needs than with politics. I wondered for the first time how *they* felt. How long would the fighting last? How many Yemenis would die?

The buses parked a short distance from the tarmac and we saw the first plane land. I watched my husband going from bus to bus, shaking hands, smiling, giving hugs to some friends. When he reached my bus, he put his arm through the open window and squeezed my hand—and unleashed some tears that I hadn't wanted to part with just then. He was trying hard to keep up morale—telling everyone that the war wouldn't last long and we would be able to come back to our homes in Sanaa.

As soon as the plane began to taxi in our direction, we left the buses and claimed our suitcases from the truck. Speed was essential. Passengers had to board quickly so that the three planes could be in the air and away as fast as possible. Art materialized at my side. He took my hand, grabbed the suitcase and together we sprinted across the tarmac. The C-130 had opened at the back like a giant hatch and I felt the heat of the plane's exhaust as we hurriedly climbed up the ramp. Art found a place for my bag and then he hugged me.

"I'll see you soon." He hurried away, back to work.

The plane took off at 2:55 p.m. It had been 58 hours since the first Triple-A shocked us awake signaling civil war. And for the first time—I was afraid. Although I was surrounded—very closely—by nearly 100 people, more than half of whom I knew, I felt very much alone. The possibility of a nervous, or tired, or war-ready Yemeni soldier firing at our aircraft was very real. That thought pounded in my head along with the shriek of the engines as the plane gained altitude. Within seconds the vibration, the noise and the tremendous pressure in my ears supplanted all thought. Some of the children began to cry and the babies screamed with the pain in their ears. The fear left me and I felt enormous gratitude that my own children were grown up and safe in their own surroundings.

As we left the mountains surrounding Sanaa, the air pressure slowly stabilized. Our ears cleared, our muscles unclenched, and facial expressions began to relax. The roar of the engines continued to make conversation impossible, but I felt that everyone was thinking, "We're safe now, we're headed home."

Our temporary guardians, Air Force crewmembers, handed out rations: the same food that fed our troops during the Gulf war, the now-famous MRE or Meals Ready To Eat. The kids especially liked the peanut butter and crackers and the desserts. We began trading and passing around food, which further released the tension.

The plane made a refueling stop at an air base in Taif, Saudi Arabia and we had a welcome break. Friendly American soldiers offered soft drinks and juice and pointed the way to the restrooms—exactly what we needed at that juncture. (There were no toilets on the planes.) An hour and a half later we were in the air again. Except for a few airsick children, everyone seemed in good spirits.

At the international airport in Riyadh, Saudi Arabia, we were glad to leave the C-130 behind us. We had left Sanaa almost six hours earlier and we were ready for the next chapter in this saga. David Welch, chargé d'affaires of our embassy in Riyadh, with his wife, Gretchen, who was the consul general, met our plane. What a comfort to see familiar smiling faces. As our bedraggled group entered the airport, a wonderful crew of embassy people applauded and gave us a happy welcome. It was truly a "lump-in-your-throat" moment.

In addition to consular and administrative people, there were many, many volunteers who had plunged in on short notice to prepare for us. An entire section of the airport was set aside for use by the embassy. Tables and chairs were ready for processing paperwork. There was a diaper-changing area and a play space for the children. For all of us there was a long table laden with sandwiches, fruit, milk and soft drinks. The embassy doctor and two nurses were available in a private corner for anyone who needed them. The entire layout was impressively organized.

We ate first, tried to unwind a bit, and then it was time to ask questions, check documents, fill out forms, and acquire plane tickets. We would fly to the United States aboard a Saudi airliner later that night—and it would be a long night.

Sometime between the eating and the paper processing, a pleasant woman approached me and inquired, "Would you like to send a telegram?" I asked the obvious questions and she told me that through the courtesy of an international organization, I could send a telegram free of charge. I realized abruptly that our family didn't know I was on my way home! When the evacuation plans were finalized, we weren't able to make any phone calls. Grateful to the organization that had offered this service, I wrote a brief message to my daughter telling her the approximate time of my arrival in Washington, DC. I felt a great sense of relief. The telegram arrived two weeks later!

After several hours we boarded the aircraft—and waited another two hours before take-off. I walked around the plane locating the embassy families and inquiring if everyone was all right. Barbara, whose husband was the head of Yemen-Hunt Oil Company, was also circling, checking on the welfare of the Hunt group. With only two exceptions, one being a Foreign Service spouse who was whining like a child, everyone seemed in good fettle. Tummies were full, the seats were comfortable, the plane was quiet and the prospect of sleep raised our morale considerably.

We were in flight almost fourteen hours. As we began to anticipate our arrival, the loudspeaker told us that the plane needed to make a fuel stop in Bangor, Maine. We landed—we waited—and we heard the worst news a travel-weary group of evacuees could possibly hear. The plane had a mechanical problem possibly requiring a special technician from New York to repair it. A collective groan was heard as we deplaned and headed for the small airport.

Though our body clocks were dysfunctional, we soon discovered that it was a sunny Sunday in Maine—and it was Mother's Day. Children were happy to stretch their legs and run but many parents with little ones were feeling over-stretched. I had great admiration for a young father who patiently looked after his baby and toddler. His wife, a communications officer, had stayed at the embassy in Sanaa. He remained in good humor the entire trip.

A convivial group of friends soon discovered that "the bar was open" and we headed in that direction for a cold glass of beer. Before I got there, however, I discovered there was a complication. Several of the mothers felt too exhausted to continue the trip—and who could blame them? They wanted to go to a hotel. Unfortunately the Bangor airport did not have a customs official on duty that morning. Therefore, no one from the plane was allowed to leave, nor could any luggage be removed from the plane. I decided to call the State Department Operations Center.

Every pay phone was in use and there were long lines of people waiting with quarters in their hands. Sossi and I located the airport manager who kindly agreed to let us use his office and telephone. After several panicky and failed attempts I reached someone at the OPS Center. (Where are those important telephone numbers when you need them!) I told the officer where we were and explained that we had several worn-out mothers who wanted to take another flight the following day.

"Is there anything you can do to assist these people in making some alternate arrangements?" I was assertive and demanding and the officer probably thought I was quite hysterical. He must have thought even worse when my voice suddenly changed and I giggled! The manager had just interrupted to say that the aircraft was repaired and they were ready to load passengers. I don't know whether I was laughing or weeping when I went back to the phone and asked my State Department contact to please check back with the airport in an hour or so to be certain that we had indeed taken off. After being levelheaded and calm since the beginning of the crisis, I had suddenly turned into an emotional airhead!

When we emerged from the manager's office, an angry woman assailed me. She claimed that I was interested only in the well-being of the government families and had no regard for "the others," including her. Her accusations were ludicrous—I had made no such distinction during my plea for help from the State Department. In fact, the mothers about whom we were concerned were not embassy people. I wondered if her anger was prompted by the fact that I had used the manager's office while she stood waiting for a pay phone. I gritted my teeth and then blurted, "I don't like your attitude!" As I walked away, I realized how fatigue and stress were adversely effecting people—myself included.

Foreign Service Requisite: thick skin!

We re-boarded the aircraft and Barbara reported that all of the Yemen-Hunt families had agreed to continue on. Our next stop was New York's John F. Kennedy Airport where several people said good-bye and left the plane. I found out later that I could have deplaned also. When we made arrangements for our plane tickets in Riyadh, I was under the mistaken impression that I was required to go to Washington in order to finalize my ongoing travel plans. Maybe I also felt some sub-conscious obligation to go "all the way" with my compatriots.

And all the way I went, at least to Dulles Airport outside of Washington, DC. When we boarded the mobile lounge that took us from our plane to the gate, an announcement came over the loudspeaker: "The people with Yemen-Hunt Oil Company are asked to gather inside the gate where someone will meet them." A great cheer went up. "Someone" knew we had arrived! Later inside, a colleague of Art's, a deputy assistant secretary, gave me a huge bouquet of spring flowers to welcome all of us home. It was a lovely gesture.

We had been in transit for over 36 hours but the adrenaline once again revved up. We gathered our handbags, babies and children, claimed our luggage, passed quickly through customs, and outside to waiting buses. The State Department had arranged hotels for the embassy evacuees and we were to attend an orientation meeting the next morning. Afterwards we would go on to our individual "safe havens," places that we had previously designated.

Suddenly, I wanted desperately to see my children. Perhaps because it was Mother's Day, I revolted at the thought of spending the night alone in a hotel. As soon as the last people were settled in the buses, I told the representatives from the Family Liaison Office who had met us that I had decided to take the train to New York. Toni, who had brought the flowers, said immediately, "I'll take you to the train station."

When I called Kathy to tell her that I was on my way, I learned that she and her fiancé had spent nearly eight hours at Kennedy airport. They had found out through the Operations Center that our plane would land first in New York and they had waited there for me. (Where was that damn telegram?) I traveled another four hours and arrived at my daughter's apartment Sunday night, New York time.

A week later when I was telling my son about the long trip home, he asked a very intelligent question: "Mother, since you were at Dulles Airport, why didn't you *fly* to New York?"

I stared at Alex for a long minute and then I had to admit, "It never occurred to me!" I had traveled by train to New York City many times before—perhaps because I was weary and not a little stressed, I automatically did what was familiar. Perhaps.

After a shower and a full night's sleep, I felt whole again, albeit homeless. Art called to say that the evacuation was complete and he was certain that all who had wanted to leave Yemen had flown out. He sounded relieved and tired. A few more embassy officers had left on the last plane and only a small staff including the Marines remained. He reported that the French and German Embassies also had successfully evacuated their people along with other diplomatic families.

From the beginning Art thought that the war would last only a few weeks—unless Yemen's neighbor to the north, Saudi Arabia, involved itself on the part of the seceding southerners. Fortunately, the latter did not happen—Washington made it clear that the U.S. would oppose any such action. The fighting came to a slow finish after nine weeks. Most of the war damage took place in the south, particularly around Aden. Deaths and injuries occurred in many areas.

Two SCUDS (surface to surface short-range ballistic missiles) hit Sanaa during the war. I was terrified when I read about the first SCUD in the newspaper. I didn't know *where* it had landed. I worried constantly about Art and the safety of the embassy people and our friends in Sanaa. Art reached me several days later and reported that one SCUD hit less than a mile from the embassy compound. He not only heard it, he felt it—and it was more deafening than the bombs that had exploded next to our wall before the war. Another SCUD landed further away and in both cases many Yemenis were killed and scores injured.

After I was evacuated I felt an emotion that I had only briefly experienced in the past: "fear of the unknown." It was with me constantly like a deep nagging ache. The Yemeni telephone lines were unreliable and sometimes a week went by before I spoke to Art. I knew that every day he was in his car on the streets of Sanaa or meeting with officials in government buildings. At any time a SCUD or bomb could hit!

I searched the newspapers daily and I watched every news program on television. After the first week there was only an occasional article or sound bite about Yemen and much of it was inaccurate. There was a story, for instance, that one of the presidential palaces had been bombed. Art reported that it hadn't happened. A newspaper in my hometown published an article about the war. The journalist not only misquoted my mother, but also made several false statements.

Our daughter had a special reason for her high level of anxiety about Art. She and Jeff were to be married the end of July and she didn't want the wedding to take place without her daddy. If the war continued, he would have no means of transport out of Yemen.

In addition to the thousands of Yemeni military casualties and the many civilians who were killed in the SCUD attacks, there were other disasters. Somali refugees were reportedly caught in the shelling from offshore boats and over one hundred died in a camp near Aden. Another fifty-plus Somalis drowned when their boat sank in the Gulf of Aden. Having initially fled their own country because of the famine, they then attempted to return home to escape the fighting in Yemen.

Several of our embassy people had been "evicted" from previous posts (a more appropriate term than evacuated, my sister said.) Most of them kept their sense of humor through this latest uprooting. Jane said she was going to "get it right" this time. We all teased Lucy about her next assignment. We wanted early notice so we could avoid being posted with her. Lucy had been "evicted" twice before!

When the war ended in the middle of July, the fear and tension also came to an end—at least for our family and for other evacuees, expatriates and diplomats who had made Yemen their home temporarily. Thanks to a Hunt Oil Company airplane, Art flew out of Yemen and arrived in New York in time for Kathy and Jeff's wedding. My war time was spent visiting and re-visiting family in three states who were willing to put me up—and put up with me and my fragmented nerves. I was fortunate and very grateful. A week after the nuptials and three months after the civil war started, Art and I flew back to Yemen—together.

16

MR. AMBASSADOR

My emotions were skittering aimlessly as we departed Israel and returned to our home in Bethesda after a nine-year absence. Instead of planning dinners and receptions and taking guests to see the Western Wall in Jerusalem, we were sanding and painting and scrubbing away the wear and tear of tenants. Instead of watching our backs and monitoring our radios, we were whacking weeds and trying to salvage what was left of our garden. It was good to be home.

Embassy Tel Aviv was behind us. The crises, however, were not. My husband immediately jumped into the pool of events that were threatening peace and stability in the Middle East. Assigned to the Pentagon as the Deputy Assistant Secretary of Defense for Near East/South Asia International Security Affairs, he dealt with twenty-five countries in the Gulf, the Middle East and the Magreb. After Iraq brazenly invaded Kuwait in 1990 Art traveled so frequently that his suitcase never resettled up in the attic. Trips to the region with Secretary of Defense Dick Cheney called on Art's expertise and his familiarity with the players. We didn't plan family trips or buy season tickets for the opera during that period—his schedule was unpredictable.

At the Pentagon he took part in meetings with Cheney, General Norman Schwarzkopf and General Colin Powell, Chairman of the Joint Chiefs, as the U.S. planned and prepared its answering salvo to the Iraqi aggression. On one occasion, Cheney sent Art on a mission to Saudi Arabia and gave him a private plane to get him there and back quickly. The mission was accomplished. I didn't like it when Art was in the air at the same time SCUDs were flying. I was nervous and anxious when he went to the region but no more so than the military families who were concerned for their soldiers during Desert Shield and Desert Storm.

Art liked working with the military and he found the job enormously satisfying. At the end of his assignment Secretary Cheney awarded him the DOD Civilian Meritorious Service Medal, which was presented by his immediate boss, Paul Wolfowitz.

Meanwhile our next assignment was creeping onto the radar screen. The State Department included Art's name on several potential ambassador lists, including the one that read "Ambassador to the Republic of Yemen." Each step of the nomination process seemed to take longer than the one before and we were in a continual holding pattern. Waiting for THE committee to rank the candidates and send the short list to the Secretary of State. Waiting for the Secretary to sign his name to the list before sending it to the White House. Waiting for the announcement from the White House. Waiting for the Yemeni government to give *agrément*, accepting Art's appointment. And—finally—waiting for confirmation by the Senate. All Presidential appointees endure the same procedure, which is shorter for some and longer for others. And for a few, the nomination falls through for any number of reasons.

From the time Art's name went forward until the White House announced his nomination, seven months had passed. Long slow months during which we dithered about if and when we could put our house on the rental market. We couldn't even think about vacation and travel plans. What if the Senate went out for summer recess and Art's hearings were delayed until the fall? And what if the confirmation were stymied along the way? What if Senator Jesse Helms got a bee in his bonnet? Many an appointment was thwarted on the whim of that gentleman from South Carolina.

While we waited we studied about Yemen, took Arabic lessons and made countless lists of what we had to do before and *if* we went to Yemen. The State Department enrolled us in the Ambassadorial Seminar, which had been fondly nicknamed "charm school" by some of its earlier participants. No one approached the course with frivolity, however; the sessions were serious and informative and we benefited immensely from the training.

Spouses (all female in this case) weren't included in some of the classes; we were left out of defensive driving and we were not invited to visit the CIA. There were secrets to which we were not privy. But we had the enviable pleasure of going to the White House when the First Lady invited us for tea. Mrs. Bush remembered when she was "the wife of" at our embassy in China and later at the United Nations.

Except for the grandeur of the Yellow Room and the knowledge that our hostess was now "the wife of *the President*," we could have been having coffee with a neighbor—such was the informality, the easy conversation and the comfortable warmth of Mrs. Bush. When the visit was over, the group walked, musing, down the hallway. No one spoke. After the elevator doors closed someone expelled a grand satisfied sigh that made us all smile. As we climbed into the van to return to the State Department one of the women said reflectively, "It's too bad Mrs. Bush isn't President."

When Alan, our friend from Holland days, was sworn in as ambassador to Swaziland, he spoke about the preparations required of prospective Chiefs of Mission: briefings, conferences, visits, and the seminar. "Most of it was heady stuff," Alan said with a grin.

Then came the day his group of nominees (including one former congressman) went to the CIA for their briefing. They arrived in a government van and pulled up at the first security post. The driver cranked down the window. "I got another load from the State Department," he hollered to the guard. "Where do you want 'em?"

"Reality check," said Alan.

When the final t's were dotted and the eyes were crossed—that was the way it was by the end of the process—Art was ready for the penultimate but most important rite of passage on his way to becoming an ambassador.

In a plain ordinary room in the United States Capitol Art's confirmation hearings took place. He was rightfully nervous, but confident, as he faced the Senate Foreign Relations Committee. We were pleased that James Exxon, senator from Nebraska, was there to introduce Art. Senator Jesse Helms was absent. Members of the committee asked the candidate appropriate and sensible questions in an atmosphere that was non-threatening and almost relaxed. They evidently approved of his answers and accepted his knowledge about Yemen. The committee recommended his appointment, the Senate voted—and Art was confirmed.

The Benjamin Franklin Room on the eighth floor of the State Department with its Federal Period tasseled drapes, plush carpeting and ornate decor is an appropriately beautiful setting for ceremonies and special occasions of all kinds. We chose the room for Art's swearing-in, as had many other ambassadors-designate before us.

In addition to Alex, Kathy and me, twelve members of our family from Nebraska and Virginia plus friends and colleagues were present as Art took the oath of office. He promised to represent the President as he carried out his duties as ambassador to Yemen. Thomas Pickering, then ambassador to the United Nations, came from New York, introduced Art and addressed the guests. The ceremony was impressive and exciting and moving—all at the same time. Art's

Foreign Service career of twenty-six years reached a pinnacle with his ambassadorship. He would spend six more years as a Foreign Service Officer.

After the champagne toast, the hugs and the handshakes, we quickly gathered up the family. We had to hustle or, in addition to the room rent, the Department would charge us a late fee for keeping the elevator up after hours. We lined up the cars and headed home to Bethesda for a celebration.

While Kathy and I organized some appetizers—there wasn't room for anyone else in our tiny kitchen—I asked my husband to please empty the wastebasket. A member of the family, camera in hand, spotted Art coming back into the house with his mission accomplished and quipped, "Was that your first duty as ambassador—emptying the trash?"

Mr. Ambassador's next duty was one he had looked forward to for eight years. Early that morning he had unwrapped the special bottle of red wine that Jorgen Werner had given him before we left Copenhagen. This was the grand celebration—now was the moment to drink the wine. Art opened the bottle and poured—he tasted the wine—and the look of disappointment on his face was disheartening. The wine was not a good traveler—it had spoiled. We drank champagne instead—and it *was* a grand celebration.

I was again invited to the White House—this time to meet the President. It was Ambassador Hughes's invitation, of course, but he was encouraged to take his family along. Kathy, who had never met the Bushes—or any American President—went with us.

A cheerful George H.W. Bush, taller than I had remembered, was waiting for us in the Oval Office along with Brent Scowcroft, the National Security Advisor. We shook hands, we sat down, we chatted. And the White House photographer snapped pictures. The President talked about his visit to Yemen when he was Vice President and then he asked Art to give the Yemeni president a message. "Tell Saleh what he needs to do to establish good relations with the U.S….and how to repair things…" and Bush referred to Yemen's questionable position during the Gulf War.

That was it. That was all there was to it—fifteen memorable minutes. A discreet signal indicated that our time was up. The President wished us well in Yemen and the escort showed us out.

Thus Kathy, at age 25, moved ahead in the sibling "royal rivalry." A few months earlier she had stood next to Queen Elizabeth and today she visited the President of the United States. Add Queen Margrethe of Denmark—and her game piece was well across the board. Alex was behind with only one Queen and a vice president. But he was grown up and married and he and Mary were expecting twins. I think the parenting game had overtaken the game of "Royal Monopoly."

One of the photographs taken that day at the White House stood proudly on Kathy and Jeff's mantel for many years. In the picture were Art and I and Kathy with President Bush—and another man. Friends who saw the photo assumed the other man was someone famous, although they couldn't place him.

He wasn't famous; he was Bruce, a friend of Art's who was assigned to the National Security Council staff, doing escort duty that day. When Art told him that visitors to our daughter's New York apartment wanted to know his name, he replied that he was infamous to a few dignitaries. While still new at his assignment in the White House, Bruce opened the wrong door and escorted the guests into Bush's private bathroom—instead of the exit.

17

ARABIA FELIX

We arrived in Sanaa at night. The road from the airport was dark and we could see nothing of the countryside. The city, however, was illuminated by decorative colored lights that had shone on Yemen's national day festivities a few days before. A bright warm welcome, I thought.

Jet-lagged and body-weary after a trip of nearly thirty hours from Nebraska, we were nevertheless wide-awake. We wandered around the ambassador's residence and poked into every room of our new home. We discovered two stoves, three refrigerators and two freezers in the kitchen. Impressive. Our private quarters upstairs provided a cozy sitting room, dinette and small office. The master bedroom was pleasantly large and pretty—except for the mismatched and ill-fitting drapes. But, never mind, the house was only one year old and these things take time.

The following morning Art's first day of duty—and mine, too—began with a tour of the embassy where the DCM introduced us to the staff: Americans, Yemenis and third country nationals. We later drove to a different part of the city to meet the people of AID (Agency for International Development) and USIS (United States Information Service), whose offices were in other buildings.

As I peered through the car window I heard an echo from twenty-three years before. "What am I *doing* here?" I saw pile after pile of trash. A few dumpsters, yes, but they were surrounded by garbage. I watched a woman and child, each carrying bags of trash, approach a dumpster and drop their burdens several feet away. There was an occasional tree, a few scattered patches of brown grass, but not a flower in sight. Just dust. What are we *going* to do here?

We entered the USIS compound, the gates closed behind us, and there we saw green bushes, healthy grass and bright pretty flowers—like the gardens I had barely had time to glimpse at our residence that morning. I soon became accustomed to the dusty, dingy and colorless areas of the city. I knew that behind many walls and gates were lovely yards and pleasant homes.

Although we had seen pictures of Sanaa's unique appearance, we were completely awed when we saw a panoramic view of the city for the first time. The buildings, some stone and others of baked mud, were decorated—"frosted" it seemed—with sculpted whitewashed gypsum around the cornices and roofs. Windows composed of artful colored glass panes were also outlined in white. The fairy tale effect of the city has prompted many people to liken it to a Christmas gingerbread town. Many office and apartment buildings were as high as seven or eight stories and several hundred years old. Homes were multi-level squares or rectangles, no sprawling ranch-styles or split-levels in Sanaa. The newer buildings imitated the older shapes but some lacked the gypsum decoration. Instead, their beauty came from the stone itself, colorful pinks and pale greens.

By contrast, slums dotted every corner and edge of the city. Sanaa's poor and jobless huddled in whatever shelter they could find or scrape together. A holey piece of tarp over a few branches or paint and oilcans stacked to break the wind or shadow the sun. The poor were dirt poor.

The phone call came in the evening. Gazzim, the chief of protocol, told Art that he should appear before President Saleh the next morning to present his ambassadorial credentials. The Yemenis did things on short notice. But Art was ready; we had been in the country for three weeks.

Two dark and shiny BMW's arrived at the residence at 8:30 that October morning in 1991 along with an escort of three motorcycles. Art climbed into the first automobile with his Yemeni military escort and Bruce, the DCM. The other officers whom Art had invited to accompany him—the Public Affairs Officer, the director of AID and the defense attaché—rode in the second car. I stood on the sidewalk snapping photographs of the motorcade—and wishing I had been invited.

Several ambassadors presented credentials that day, Art reported. As each envoy arrived, a military band played the national anthem of his country. Inside, after exchanging pleasantries they sat together, wordless, waiting to be called. The Iraqi ambassador sat next to Art. When his turn came, Art spent twenty minutes with President Saleh and after the formalities, he delivered President Bush's message.

Since women weren't allowed at the ceremony, I called the spouses of the officers who were accompanying Art and invited them to join us for a celebration at the residence. Our cook, Hassan, made some fancy canapés and we chilled orange juice and a bottle of champagne. When the men returned, we toasted the new ambassador to Yemen—Art was now official. As life goes in the Foreign Service, that day was one of the most special. There were no striped pants and top hats, but there were a lot of smiling faces.

(I was the only American-born spouse that morning—two were Syrian and the other Armenian. By 1990 more than half the Foreign Service wives were foreign-born.)

Observing a long-standing diplomatic custom, Art paid courtesy calls on the other foreign envoys. Those with wives invited both of us to call on them in their homes. I remembered Francie telling me about making calls—so many of them—when her husband was ambassador to the Netherlands. But after one ambassador began to doze off over his teacup, Francie said "no more" and left the rest of the visits to Jerry. Fortunately the only downside to our courtesy calls in Sanaa was the increase in calorie intake. Our colleagues displayed overabundant hospitality by serving enormous samplings of their native dishes—in the middle of the morning.

And by the way, after Art and I had completed calling on the ambassadors and their spouses, they paid us back by making "return courtesy calls"—another diplomatic tradition.

Penny, the British ambassador's wife, referred to the other spouses by the name of their country: Mrs. China, Mrs. Denmark, Mrs. Lebanon. I didn't know if that was for my benefit—to initially help me identify the women—or because she couldn't remember their real names. Or her sense of humor?

Yemeni women are acclaimed for their beautiful eyes—and that was the only part of them a foreigner usually saw. In Sanaa nearly all females over the age of twelve hid their faces and hair. They covered their bodies with flowing full-length garments, some made of a colorful red print, but most were black. A few modern-thinking women did not veil their faces but they kept their hair carefully concealed. Underneath the coverings, dark heavy mascara, lipstick, nail polish and especially gold jewelry were common among those women who could afford luxuries.

A Yemeni family with whom we became friends had returned to Yemen after living in America for several years. Their four-year-old daughter had never been in Yemen. Observing so many black-clad figures at the Sanaa airport, she tugged at her mother's sleeve and whispered, "Ninjas, Mommy! Why are there so many Ninjas?"

Skin painting is a tradition among Yemeni women. Skilled experts etch designs onto the hands and ankles using a reddish-brown dye made from the dried ground leaves of the henna plant or a fragrant black dye made from *khithab* berries. Some women were always painted, others indulged only at weddings and other parties as a form of entertainment. The designs would last two or three weeks—depending on how many children the woman had to bathe.

Clothing for men appeared peculiar, at least to a westerner's eye. Traditionally Yemeni males dressed in one-piece white long-sleeved "dresses." Underneath—I was told—they wore baggy knee-length boxer shorts. The dresses were topped with western style sport coats that often carried the maker's label—still stitched to the outside of the sleeve. For casual occasions, especially at home, men wore long wrap-around skirts with long-sleeved shirts. Conversely, government officials usually dressed in suits and ties for the office.

I was flabbergasted the first time I saw Yemeni women disrobe. Invited to a coffee one morning, I approached the front door at the same time as several black-robed veiled women. Once we were inside they removed their headdresses, pulled their long garments up over their heads—and there they were in western-style brightly colored calf-length dresses! After I had become familiar with the customs, I hosted an afternoon tea. Again the Yemeni guests arrived completely covered, but when they came inside my home most of them shed layers of clothing—as well as formality. I had assured them that no males would be present that afternoon because I knew they would remain covered—and be uncomfortable—in front of our male staff. Some would refuse to come at all if there were men present.

In three years time only three Yemeni women came to our home for dinner. It wasn't personal—it was cultural. Women in Sanaa didn't attend mixed-gender social functions with their husbands, even though women were legally free to do whatever men did. They could drive an automobile, work in a business and study at the university. In fact during the 1990's there were more female medical students than male. A woman doctor told me, however, that she never had a male patient and building a clientele was difficult. A factory supervisor said he preferred women employees because they worked harder and were more reliable. But few women worked in factories or offices because fathers and/or husbands wouldn't allow them to. In Aden and its environs in the south gender separation was not as customary. Aden was a former British colony that became Marxist and continues to be more socially emancipated than the north.

Our residence employed three Yemeni men: a cook and two housekeepers. Abdul Hameed and Ali lived in the house, returning to their far-off village only for vacation and the two Moslem feasts. Hassan lived in the city with his family, but had a room in our staff quarters where he occasionally spent the night.

"I wouldn't want a man washing out *my* dainties," my mother commented. I didn't either, but I got used to it.

I was grateful, in fact, to have an experienced staff, people who were accustomed to working together. Never mind that they bickered regularly and each blamed the other when something went amiss—I got used to that, too. Never mind that Ali laundered black socks with white placemats—I would teach him. And never mind that he couldn't iron my dresses properly—he could practice. Abdul Hameed was well trained and took excellent care of us. Ali was elderly, and although he was slow and almost illiterate, he did his work willingly. Between them they knew how to set the table properly and they mixed drinks and served dinners in an accomplished fashion. And, just as important, they were cheerful and pleasant.

Hassan, however, was a challenge to my patience. He rejected the idea of a woman in "his" kitchen and, more to the point, a woman as the boss. Although I tried to be culturally sensitive, I was responsible for the house, including the kitchen, and I had to establish my authority. We were eventually able to work together peacefully, but it took time.

One of our new friends, an American businessman, complimented me effusively after dinner with us one evening. He had been invited several times by our predecessor and Hassan repeatedly served the same meal. "Always fish—and some kind of fruit cocktail cake for dessert," Bob told me, amused. This time, however, with me looking over his shoulder, Hassan had used quite a bit more creativity in his menu planning.

Lest I appear to be disparaging of the previous ambassador, a friend and able diplomat, I want to point out that for several years there was no full-time ambassador's spouse—no *female*—in the residence. (Sexist? Yes.) This situation suited Hassan. He wasn't challenged and he became lazy, which was fine with him. When I arrived I made him work, and eventually I discovered that Hassan was an excellent cook.

Bab al Yemen, the Gate to Yemen, was a fitting name for the souk in Sanaa. Behind the gates one could see and sense Yemeni life. Merchants sold everything from gold jewelry to silver antiques, from spices and dried beans to imported powdered milk. Fabric and clothing, aluminum pans and traditional stoneware pots, coffee husks and animal feed were available in the open-air market.

Traditional Yemeni justice was exemplified on the gates now and then. Several severed hands were hanging gruesomely from atop the entrance the first time I visited the souk. A few days earlier the authorities had carried out executions and had punished several thieves—publicly.

Qat (generally pronounced "gat") sellers squatted on every corner in the souk with their huge bundles of leafy branches. Usually they wrapped the qat in plastic to keep it from drying and losing its potency. Sometimes the dusty leaves glistened temporarily with a sprinkle of water.

Qat (also transliterated khat or gat) is an addictive plant, a bush that can grow to the size of a small tree. Its effect on the body resembles that of heavy-duty caffeine or a mild amphetamine. Yemenis chewed the leaves one by one, extracting and swallowing the juice. They collected the residue in their mouths and their cheeks gradually expanded to unbelievable sizes—especially if the chewing went on for many hours, as it usually did. When the ball of masticated leaves became unmanageable—or when the party was over—the chewer spat it out.

The "qat chew" was traditional throughout Yemen. After men consumed their lunch, they settled down together on comfortable cushions in the *muffrage,* a living room where the seating faced the windows. (*Muffrage* comes from an Arabic word that means "to look out.") Qat causes thirst so the men drank water and sometimes tea while they chewed. There was usually a water pipe available, a *medah* (also called a *hookah* or *hubble-bubble* in other countries). They discussed business and politics and shared local gossip during the long afternoons. For those who could afford it chewing was a daily activity.

Women also enjoyed qat, but they indulged less frequently and in fewer numbers than men. They were likely to chew at their weekly tea parties. Women who didn't chew simply enjoyed the sweets, the tea, the dancing and maybe the *hookah.*

In a 1997 Washington Post article, John Lancaster quoted Foreign Minister Dr. al Iryani on the subject of qat: "It is the most profitable cash crop in the country." The minister said he did a good deal of official work at qat chews. But what he didn't say in the interview was that the plant requires an enormous quantity of often-scarce water, and it has supplanted coffee, which Yemen previously exported in large quantities.

Some educated Yemenis, particularly women, said that the qat-chewing custom had become a financial drain on families. The average per capita income was less than $350. Our friend, Ms. Amat Sosowa, told me, "Qat chewing is becoming a social sickness." She was one of the few high-ranking women in the government.

In the U.S. qat is on the list of controlled substances, called a "schedule four" drug. Nevertheless it shows up, particularly in Detroit and New York, where there are large Yemeni communities.

Historically, the 1300-year-old Grand Mosque is one of the greatest treasures of Sanaa and in 1971, it yielded a treasure of its own. After heavy rains damaged the roof, repairmen made a major discovery in a small space between the ceiling and the roof: nearly 40,000 manuscript fragments on parchment and paper, most of them with Koranic texts.

When funds (mostly foreign) became available for restoration of the ancient manuscripts, Austrian Ursula Dreibholz, a book and paper conservator, established the *Dar al Makhtootat*, House of Manuscripts. She began by restoring the oldest pieces of parchment, those dating from the first three centuries of Islam. A very small number of the fragments were not religious texts, but letters, ownership deeds and writings concerned with health and science. A few of the latter were in Hebrew.

Ursula and her assistants restored and pieced together many almost-complete Koranic parchments with colored illumination. Their clarity and beauty astounded us. According to Ursula the parchments have great significance "for research into the development of Arabic script...and forms of decoration to embellish the beautiful calligraphy."

Initially Ursula had modern equipment to work with but when it broke down, there was no one in Yemen who could repair it. "I had to resort to using old, almost ancient, drying methods," which she demonstrated to us. "There is never enough money." Every year Ursula applies for grants and aid to keep the project going.

Our first official trip outside Sanaa was southwards, down out of the mountains to Taiz, Jibla and Ibb, an entirely different region of Yemen. George, director of the Agency for International Development, had asked Art to address the opening ceremony of a women's training program funded by AID in Taiz. The facility was impressive, as was the enthusiasm of the women who were learning how to find jobs, how to start small businesses and add to the family income. Many foreign aid projects were helping to emancipate Yemeni women.

A restaurant meal in Taiz, hosted by the governor, was an eye-opening experience for me, the only woman at the table. As the waiters brought out huge platters of food, our host showed his hospitality by serving me with the largest piece of goat—a haunch that was bigger than my plate! I didn't know what to do with it. There was no way to anchor the meat to my plate and no polite way to cut it up with a knife. It was a skinny goat and finally I followed the Yemeni's example and pulled away the stringy pieces with my fork and my fingers. After a waiter relieved me of my burden the governor quickly heaped copious mounds of rice and tasty vegetables onto my plate. I knew that in spite of his urging, I didn't have to eat it all.

The Area Studies Course at FSI had taught me that a host will personally serve the guests with the choicest pieces of food. If you finish everything on your plate, he will feel obligated to fill it again. Mister Peter, the class instructor, was renowned in the State Department for his knowledge of Arabic customs and traditions and his classes went far beyond geography, history and politics. Thanks to him many of us avoided embarrassing ourselves in our host countries.

Yemeni food was delicious—most of it. Although, as Art warned: "When your host started cracking open the skull of a sheep or goat, the best thing to do was become intensely involved in anything but making eye contact with said host—and to acquire a sudden case of deafness." If the guest showed an interest in what was being extracted from the skull, he would soon receive it as a gift.

At home Yemenis ate without plates. They sat at a tablecloth or piece of plastic spread over the carpet or floor. The men ate first and the women and children came in to finish what was left or they ate in another room. There were no courses; all the food was laid out at once, except maybe the dessert. There was no silverware, although sometimes they offered a large spoon to their guests. They ate solids with their right hand and drank soups and other liquids from bowls.

I liked goat when it was roasted and crispy—and when I had a manageable piece. Mutton on the other hand was often boiled and had a strong gamey taste. Yemenis ate various varieties of vegetables, stewed or roasted or sometimes stuffed, and great amounts of rice. Occasionally they served potatoes and even French fries, although I wondered if the latter were for the benefit of the foreigners whom they invited.

Sorghum, millet and other grains were predominant in the diet. The breads were wonderful, especially when eaten hot from the oven. In the absence of utensils, pieces of flat bread became scoopers and dippers. *Bint al sahn,* "daughter of the dish," was a baked layered pastry rich in eggs and ghee. This national dish was usually eaten at the beginning of the meal, although a few times our hosts served it as a dessert drizzled liberally with honey.

Dark, thick and somewhat scarce—and therefore expensive—Yemeni honey was often the main feature at meals to which we were invited. Honey covered the porridge alongside the meat and vegetables. We dipped bananas in the amber syrup and then we ate honeyed *bint al sahn*. All of which produced some very sticky fingers and chins.

There were no napkins. Instead, boxes of tissues were positioned here and there around the dining area. The first time I attempted to wipe away the honey residue with a tissue, it left its own white bits of residue clinging to my sticky skin. But our host soon led the way to a sink where diners took turns washing up. Afterward, in another room we had sweet tea or *qishr*, a hot drink made from steeped coffee husks flavored with cardamom and maybe cinnamon.

Yemenis were fast eaters, possibly because they were in a hurry to move on to the qat chewing or maybe, as Art remarked, "Their legs were begging for mercy." We weren't accustomed to sitting on the floor to eat and it was a relief to relax in the *muffrage* after the meal and stretch our legs out. But we had to be careful that the soles of our feet weren't looking at anyone. In Arab culture, the lookee would have been insulted.

Art went frequently to Yemeni lunches and he told me afterward how many "dinner partners" he had had. "People came and went throughout the meal!" Sometimes he was still eating when the drivers sat down or the children. Art liked to eat slowly and enjoy every bite. Not so his hosts.

Before entering the dining room or *muffrage* it was customary to remove your shoes and deposit them in the entry hall where they often ended up, unpaired, in a big pile. And occasionally, shoes disappeared. Art came home one day in his stocking feet—his shoes had been stolen during lunch! After that he wore old shoes when he went to a local event. I later discovered that many of my friends carried an extra pair of shoes in their handbags when they went to a lunch.

The Arabs as a people pride themselves on their hospitality and they have every right to be proud of their fine manner of welcoming and entertaining their guests. In the middle of a desert the host in a Bedouin tent will offer his visitor whatever refreshment he has available, especially tea. Even the shortest visit to a Yemeni home or office will begin with tea or coffee, and polite small talk will proceed any business discussions.

I wonder if this grand hospitality can sometimes be taken too far, however. Many times in Sanaa we went to National Day receptions given by countries that were among the poorest in the world—and they offered enormous quantities and varieties of food and drink.

At home we served our guests food from a variety of sources. Fresh fish, shrimp and small lobsters were available intermittently. They arrived early in the morning on trucks that drove up directly from the fishing boats on the coasts. Occasionally we were able to buy South American beef from an importer. We ordered ground beef and pork products for our own consumption—chops and sausages from England and bacon from Hungary. Sometimes Hassan cooked Yemeni food for us. Locally we were limited to whole chickens and the occasional piece of veal.

I declined to go to the meat markets with Hassan after I saw a sweet calf tied up outside a shop—soon to become someone's dinner. Aging was not on the butcher's agenda. Neither were veal steaks, chops, or scaloppini on his menu, unless you cut them yourself at home—and assuming the butcher gave you the right part of the animal. You paid the set price per kilo and the man gave you a piece of meat—along with some scraps, bones and innards. There was no picking and choosing.

Hassan suggested serving roast veal for our first dinner party and he went early to the butcher's. I came down to the kitchen after breakfast and discovered a huge hunk of red dripping meat on the counter. The veal was warm and still thumping and quivering, an unpleasant phenomenon I had previously only read about. No meat for me that evening.

Two extra guests showed up at that first dinner. One Yemeni brought his cousin and another insisted that his bodyguard join the meal. Fortunately we were able to squeeze them in at the table. After that unexpected experience I always allowed extra space when we invited Yemenis whom we didn't know well.

Another unexpected "guest" turned up at our New Year's Day reception. While people were filling their plates at the buffet table, Kathy came to me and whispered, "Who is that man in the green overalls?" He was one of the gardeners! He had been working in the rose beds when he heard Art inviting the guests, who were having drinks on the terrace, to come inside and eat. We assume there was a misunderstanding—somewhere.

"How hot is it?" people at home asked. Most didn't realize that the capital of Yemen nestles in the mountains at about 7200 feet, the same altitude as Santa Fe, New Mexico. The moderate climate with low humidity and constant sunshine was one of the most enjoyable of the places we lived. Summers were pleasantly warm and winters were mild with no snow or frost.

Dust devils played about the open spaces on a daily basis during the dry seasons. Sometimes huge swirls of sand and dirt, resembling tornadoes, clouded the sun. A fine powdery dust was ever present in the air and it settled into closets and drawers and sifted through clothing. The security-conscious folks who planned and built the residence gave us windows that didn't open and assumed that the air conditioner would be in constant use. We seldom needed air conditioning, but we needed fresh air. We therefore kept the doors open to the outside terraces and balconies—inviting in the dust as well as the fresh air. The closet doors in all the bedrooms had gaps of several inches at the tops to ensure that lots of dust settled onto our clothing.

More and more I wondered—as I had at other posts—who was watching over the Pertinent People at FBO (the Foreign Buildings Office) in Washington? It was obvious that the designers, architects and builders of this residence had carried out little or no research prior to the planning. Hadn't anyone studied the climate or the position of the property in relation to the sun and the elements? There was a lovely terrace with plants and flower boxes but we could use it only when necessary for large parties. The house was situated on a slight rise and the terrace had no protection from the wind—and dust!—that swished through regularly. There was no roofing or overhang to protect potential lunch guests from the piercing sun. (Although there was a covered bar, complete with sink.) The climate was ideal for outdoor entertaining—if only the area had been designed properly.

The laundry room was minuscule with no hanging space. Someone had assumed that all clothing, including lingerie and delicates, went into the dryer. And there was no sink in the laundry room—we had to order one. Someone also assumed that dainties would be washed in the kitchen sink! I'm convinced the architect was male.

The FBO *artiste* in charge of the décor was neither practical nor sensible. She may have been artistic but she obviously didn't ask for advice from Foreign Service people who had been there and done that. The living room and dining room furniture was faux Italian Renaissance/modern. We had claw-footed chairs and fake Corinthian capitols holding up the coffee tables. We had several enormous—and enormously heavy—square iron lamp tables that frequently had to be moved around to accommodate various numbers of guests. It took two people and a lot of muscle just to lift them. There were no drawers in the living room, no place to stow cocktail napkins or coasters or even a pencil. Nowhere to keep playing cards or a bottle opener. Perhaps the occupants weren't supposed to live in those rooms. The only drawers available in the representational areas were in a dining room buffet that had barely enough space to store a few every-day linens. The dining tables were poorly designed—and my wish is that whoever created them will be doomed to sit and bash their shins on those table legs for perpetuity.

The "powder rooms" in the front hall were equipped with electric hand dryers and—unbelievably—a urinal in the MEN's. They reminded me of the facilities in a train station! There were no amenities: no curtains on the windows, no throw rugs on the floors, no color whatsoever—just gray marble. We removed the hand dryers and put up towel bars immediately, but it took longer to arrange for curtains. My plea to the Pertinent People in Washington for rugs and guest towels was answered: "We have no sources for those supplies." And I did? (These were the same bureaucrats who had told us: "If you need anything, just let us know.") When we went on home leave, I had a lengthy shopping list just for the house. Of course, after acquiring the towels, there was no place to store them—or the extra toilet paper. No drawers, no shelves. Where was the *artiste* when the aforementioned Man was designing the powder rooms?

The walls in the representational areas were adorned with images of Yemen. There were several attractive prints by an American woman—but not a single piece of artwork represented the United States. Whose embassy was this?

The arrival of six paintings we had borrowed through the Art in Embassies Program partially ameliorated the situation. This Program (administered through FBO) accepts loans and donations of American art for display in ambassadors' residences abroad. To quote from the State Department's Foreign Affairs Manual (6 FAM—778.1): "The program is intended to enhance the communication of American values and cultural diversity through the display of American art." The department also owns an art collection from which works can be borrowed.

Art and I had chosen American landscapes and our borrowed paintings included scenes from Maryland, New York, New Mexico and California. We loved each one and most importantly, they added a charming American presence to the home. While embassies and chanceries may benefit from some assimilation of the culture and art of the host country, in our opinion the interior emphasis should be American.

We placed the largest painting in the front hall, a New York street scene complete with yellow taxicabs and spring tulips. It nicely balanced the picture on the opposite wall: an impressive skyline of Sanaa, painted by a Turkish artist.

"I've looked everywhere," Debbie told me facetiously, "And there are no Texaco stations in Yemen!" She was right—there were no gasoline stations along the roads with restrooms for travelers. And there were seldom any bushes large enough to provide privacy for a woman to relieve herself. Art had a driver and a (U.S. government-required) bodyguard—both Yemeni and both male. That fact, combined with the lack of privies, made traveling a challenge for this ambassador's wife.

Arabia Felix, happy or fortunate Arabia, was the name that first the Romans and later European geographers and cartographers used for the enormous area that included what is now Yemen. One of the oldest civilizations in the Near East, Yemen was once part of the Kingdom of Sheba, an important trade link between Africa and India. Legendary sought-after frankincense seeped from its trees. I saw it dripping and glistening in Marib governate, where we also watched herds of camels roaming peacefully across a gravely plain. They approached us, curious and unafraid.

Many of Yemen's nearly thirteen million Moslem inhabitants live in the few cities: Aden, Marib, Hodeidah, Mocca, Taiz and Ibb, with 1.2 million in Sanaa. The others, most of whom are tribal, are scattered among the tiny villages in the mountains, the plains and along the coasts. Bedouins still herd their animals through the deserts. Yemenis are a poor people who have remained relatively isolated in their different areas and who rely mainly on agriculture for their existence.

The discovery of oil in the 1980's brought a small improvement in the nation's economy, although less than was hoped for. Nevertheless, the 300,000-plus barrels per day (in the 1990's) added considerably to the country's coffers.

"Listen!" said an American oilman, cocking his ear. He was showing us around the Yemen-Hunt Oil Company's facilities near Marib. (Hunt discovered the first oil deposits in Yemen.) "Listen!" We did—and we heard the chuga-chuga of the pumping equipment. "The sound of money!" he said, grinning all over himself.

With the oil boom came foreigners and with the oil people came vehicles. Ergo—the car theft business boomed also. Vehicles disappeared from outlying oil camps and from city streets. Many were repainted, altered and sold—sometimes back to the oil companies—or the thieves drove the stolen vehicles across the desert of the Empty Quarter to sell in Saudi Arabia.

Hijacking came next. Vehicles, especially four-wheel drive, were robbed out from under their drivers unless they were part of an armed and heavily guarded convoy. Some of the Bedouins wanted cars for their own use. Carjacking became widespread and blatant with the perpetrators attacking in Sanaa in broad daylight. Who was going to argue when the hijacker pointed his Kalashnikov in your face? Several of our friends, women included, lost their vehicles that way.

Kidnappings were a routine method for disgruntled Yemeni tribesmen to put pressure on the government. Hostages were foreigners, almost always employees of oil companies or oil-related businesses. That is, until Haynes Mahoney—the first diplomat who was kidnapped. Later on, tourist nabbing became increasingly popular with those who had a grudge.

Two angry Yemenis waving AK47's hijacked a Yemen-Hunt mini-bus one early morning and held the six occupants hostage for the better part of a long day. The kidnappers were brothers who intended to coerce the government into releasing another brother from jail. One of them took over the driving and sped recklessly down the road. His brother, provoked by an oil company helicopter that was pursuing them in the air, shot out the vehicle's back window—unconcernedly firing over the heads of the hostages!

Increasingly angered by the presence of the helicopter, the same kidnapper brought out a hand grenade, held it up for everyone to see and began to twirl it menacingly on his finger. Tom, who wrote an eyewitness account of the day, included this remark: "I couldn't help but think that this is not the way you treat a live hand grenade!"

Suddenly the grenade went flying across the bus. There was a mad scramble in all directions until someone retrieved it—with the pin still in place. That incident prompted George, director of Yemen-Hunt and one of the hostages, to send the helicopter a radio message: "Stay away!"

When they arrived at a village, the kidnappers allowed the hostages to mill about the yard in front of a stone block building. It appeared to be a jail because of its thick walls and barred windows, but they discovered it was the captors' home. George hung around a big rock next to a depression in the ground, which he later described as the closest thing to a foxhole he could see.

"Foxholes were relatively rare in that yard," Tom observed.

Negotiators arrived and the kidnappers ordered their charges into the building. The army also arrived and Tom could see them on a hill across the way. "I found myself evaluating my position in case of trouble." He remembered what actor William Bendix once said on a television show: "What a revolting development this is!"

Deliberations proceeded outside. A sheik would intermittently approach the house and speak to the kidnappers through the window. If irked, the brothers responded by slamming their gun butts on the floor and banging on the window frames. In the middle of the afternoon a negotiating team entered the house for direct talks with the perpetrators. When the shouting suddenly escalated and the Yemenis began waving their *jambias* (curved daggers), Tom feared the talks had broken down. But one of the mediators motioned for the captives to leave the building. It was all over! Villagers promptly came to shake hands with the oilmen and thereby to show that they had had no part in the ordeal.

Tom said it was "only slightly amusing" when he found out later that the third brother was in jail for hijacking.

"Kidnapping in Yemen is hospitality," said the speaker of the Yemeni parliament in a Washington Post article by John Lancaster in 1997. The speaker continued: "Kidnapping is part of tourism; it's an adventure for the tourist…"

Perhaps it depends on your point of view. Haynes Mahoney (after *his* ordeal) said the hostage is "treated as a 'compulsory guest.'"

A man bearing an automatic rifle didn't necessarily have a sinister deed in mind. Weapons were synonymous with manhood—and boyhood, it appeared to me. The most common male accessory was the *jambia*, worn in a sheath on a belt around the waist. Some were plain; others (for ceremonial occasions) were elaborately decorated with intricate silver work. In Sanaa the *jambia* was an integral part of a man's daily attire.

Rifles were carried about nonchalantly. At wedding lunches Art sat next to many a young groom outfitted in white and gold finery, who had his AK47 close at his side. Gunshots in the middle of the night, though unsettling during our first weeks in the country, usually meant a family was announcing the birth of a son.

While on a country outing one day we heard a burst of gunfire and looked anxiously at Ali, the guard, who was sitting in the front seat of the car with our driver. "A wedding," he said nonchalantly. Art asked him how he knew and Ali's reply was merely, "I can tell."

Guns, rifles, grenades, all sorts of ammunition and even rocket launchers were widely available, especially at "gun souks." We visited a popular ordinance market in a small village about an hour from Sanaa. It was another world. Men strolled through the souk flashing great wads of money. Buyers and sellers were negotiating prices—their wide smiles exhibiting green qat-stained teeth. Every few minutes we heard the blast of a weapon that someone was testing.

Our first Fourth of July reception was an awesome challenge, requiring months of planning. The embassy staff took care of the guest list, invitations, and logistics such as parking and security, but the food was up to me. I had experienced many National Day events at previous posts, so I certainly knew how it was supposed to be done. But knowing and doing don't necessarily follow, especially in Yemen. I balked at doing it the easy (expensive) way with caterers and insisted that all the food (for over three hundred people!) be prepared at home. A case of foolish optimism.

Many embassies liked to serve their native foods if they could acquire the ingredients. When our German friends Heike and Helmut were in Botswana, for example, their embassy prepared a special German buffet for Constitution Day. As Heike was filling her plate with sauerkraut and smoked pork, she heard two local women whispering.

The first asked her friend, "Now what do you think that is?"

"I think it is cabbage," replied the other, "But don't you think it looks rather old?"

Sauerkraut would have been easy, but American native food wasn't. What *is* typical American food? We have borrowed dishes from all over the world. Turkey and cranberries? That would require mashed potatoes and gravy and we weren't offering a sit-down dinner. Fried chicken? Not feasible for so many people. BBQ? We didn't have the equipment or the personnel capable of accomplishing that. American picnic food seemed to be the answer and I had seen it work well at other posts.

We were unable to get hamburger, but eventually we were successful in acquiring beef hot dogs. After some exasperation and downright panic on my part, we found beef and turkey—typical American food, but unfortunately labor intensive. Hassan had to make rolls and buns the week before and freeze them. The beef and turkey had to be roasted, sliced and made into open-face sandwiches—finger food. At a stand-up party one couldn't possibly manipulate a knife *and* fork.

I cooked six pounds of dried beans and mixed them with two cases—48 cans—of prepared vegetarian baked beans. I added brown sugar, ketchup, dry mustard and chopped onions and we baked them in huge roasting pans. Hassan did an admirable job with the potato salad, which took an entire day to accomplish. Between us we made other salads and vegetables, shrimp and fish dishes and cheese spreads. Weeks ahead of time we baked star-shaped cookies decorated with red, white and blue sugars and those, too, went into the freezer.

We found flags, banners, streamers and balloons in the storage room. Art and the GSO staff hung, strung, fastened and spread them here and there until the terrace was festooned with red, white and blue decorations. I unpacked our Christmas tree lights and the crew wove them into the tree branches in the garden. They not only looked festive, but they brightened an otherwise dark area. Sossi happily volunteered to arrange the red roses and carnations for the tables—there was no florist to do that sort of thing in Sanaa. Ultimately, the garden and the tables were beautiful!

We composed a seating area for the dignitaries with small tables and chairs over a small carpet. It was customary for the ambassador to "sit a spell" with the Grand Mufti and the government representatives who weren't culturally adapted to stand-up diplomatic cocktail parties.

An hour before the guests arrived, I gathered together our staff and the hired waiters and I explained their duties. I had drawn maps of the garden highlighting the food tables: "fish and cheese" and "hot dogs, buns, condiments," as well as "canapés and salads," etc. I had also made charts and lists that I color-coded with the maps. Each waiter was assigned to a predetermined area or number of tables. Hassan was to oversee and to refill platters and dishes as necessary. I felt nervous but confident as I raced upstairs to shower and dress.

After the receiving line dissolved, I made the mistake of going out to the garden "to check on things." I discovered that no one had lit the Sterno fire under the chafing dishes—the baked beans and hot dogs were cold. The dishes of mustard and ketchup had long since been scraped clean and serving utensils were in short supply. The bartenders were running out of glasses and no one appeared eager to wash any. Hassan had forgotten to turn on the dishwasher, which was large and fast, but needed half an hour to heat its water. Abdul Hameed and Ali were doing their best, but they couldn't keep up. Marlene, Art's secretary, kindly offered to help and she went to work cutting and serving the cakes that were gifts from the major hotels. I spent the remainder of the party in and out of the kitchen, issuing orders and directing traffic.

After the 350 guests departed and I had supervised the stowing of the leftover food, I limped upstairs where I moaned and groaned about the many things that had gone wrong with the party. I was disappointed and frustrated. Art, weary of my complaints—and just plain weary from the day—tried to mollify me.

"Everyone had a good time and no one went away hungry. Those are the important things to remember." (It wasn't the first time he had said those words to me, nor would it be the last.) He was right. We were especially gratified that several members of the government came, including the Foreign Minister. Colleagues had told us that one government representative was assigned to attend a National Day function and no matter how many others an embassy invited, they wouldn't turn up. But they did.

My feet ached, keeping me from sleep that night. I lay in bed reliving all the problems of the evening and making a mental list of things I would do differently next year. I couldn't wear shoes for two days. Foreign Service Requisite—repeated: Sturdy Feet.

Just in time for the next Fourth of July, an American transport plane happened to be coming our way and it brought hamburgers, hot dogs *and* buns from the commissary in Riyadh. I improved and enlarged my maps and charts and I hired more waiters plus two chefs from a hotel to grill the hamburgers. I simplified the menu for Independence Day 1993 and I had great expectations.

Hassan and I again prepared the accompanying food. Since the menu was not complicated—no canapés—I decided to make homemade vanilla ice cream—seven gallons of it. Labor intensive? Well, yes. I had to make the custard and since cream wasn't available in Sanaa, we made our own, using butter and milk, a sort of reverse process. Abdul Hameed and Ali took turns chopping up ice cubes and I baby-sat the blessedly electric ice cream maker—adding salt and ice every few minutes. Labor intensive? Well, yes, but the ice cream cones were delicious and they prompted a lot of happy faces.

On the night of the reception I vowed to remain calm and enjoy my guests no matter what small problems arose. I was determined to stay out of the kitchen. We were still receiving guests when an American woman whispered in my ear. "Are there supposed to be rolls to go with the hot dogs?" Forgetting my vows, I dashed into the kitchen where I found the boxes of buns on the counter—still in their plastic bags unopened.

Much to my dismay, many of the mistakes of the previous year repeated themselves. After the party Art tried again to assuage my disappointment. "You shouldn't expect Yemenis to think about buns when they have never eaten a hot dog. And why should they remember serving utensils when they eat with their hands?"

Dan's words came back to me then. Our brother-in-law had recently written from Indonesia: "How can we expect people to build good highways when they have never driven a car? And why do we expect someone to be a good waiter if he has never eaten in a restaurant?"

I felt safe in Sanaa. The residence was part of a newly built compound that included the embassy, consulate, Marine House, storage facilities, motor pool, community swimming pool, tennis courts—even a horseshoe pit that we enjoyed with our guests on several occasions. Green lawns, rose gardens and flower patches graced the extensive surrounding spaces. High stone security walls circled the perimeter, relatively isolating us.

But the bazooka that introduced us, just after our arrival, to the Yemenis' predilection for ordnance was portentous. A bomb targeted the compound eleven months later and another bomb exploded the following year.

I saw the first bomb detonate: a stunningly white flash of light followed by a deafening explosion! I was looking out an upstairs window when the shock and concussion propelled me out of my chair. I dropped to the floor and crawled into the adjacent family room that faced the direction of the explosion. On my hands and knees I reached up, closed the balcony door and pulled shut the heavy drapes. The windows were made of bulletproof polycarbonate and were not likely to shatter and the walls were built to withstand a certain amount of concussion. But I didn't know what might be coming at us next.

Nothing came next. The perpetrators evidently didn't intend to hurt anyone with their "political bomb." They had planted the explosive *outside* the wall of the compound and detonated it from a distance. The explosion spewed dirt and rock over the wall and stones flew against our windows. The perimeter wall was damaged on the outside but not broken through. Nearby houses suffered a few broken windows but there was no other damage.

"The bomb left a crater two-and-a-half feet deep and nearly four feet in diameter," the RSO reported that evening. What a puny hole for such an enormous noise.

The German Embassy suffered severe damage from a bomb a month later (their second hit) and the Turkish Embassy required extensive repair work following an explosion outside its building. The bombs exploded in the evenings—after office hours.

Nazzim, our Turkish friend, needled the British ambassador, "Mark is disappointed because he's been left out—no bomb." Some time later, however, an explosive was detonated outside the British Embassy.

Foreign governments weren't the only bomb recipients in 1992 and 1993. Yemeni politicians were more frequent prey. We were having drinks on the terrace of a soon-to-depart American when a bomb blast sent the guests scrambling—some for cover and others for the sidewalk to see what was going on. The target that evening was a Yemeni politician who lived nearby. The only injuries were on our side of the street—a few bumps and bruises caused by colliding bodies.

The shooting of the Minister of Justice by an unknown gunman was a much more serious matter. The embassy arranged for emergency treatment at a USAF Hospital in Germany and the minister survived. But others weren't so fortunate. The following month there were two political assassinations. It wasn't clear how much of the violence had to do with upcoming elections—an effort to create instability—or foreign influences or private hostilities.

"May you live in interesting times," say the Chinese. There was certainly no lack of interesting times in Yemen. Bazookas, bombs—and a civil war. Prior to the war, however, Yemen held its first-ever democratic elections in 1993.

International observers arrived in the spring to monitor procedures before and during the elections. For the most part, they were successful in keeping the peace and preventing irregularities. Male voters had to hand in their AK47s, but not their *jambias*, before entering the polling stations. 2.7 million Yemenis voted, including a half million women. Fifty of those women were parliamentary candidates and several succeeded in winning seats.

It was a fair and free election, but the outcome was predictable. President Saleh's party gained a plurality and remained in power. But most important was the election itself, not only Yemen's first, but the first multi-party election on the Arabian Peninsula. Interesting times.

Yemeni women gave birth to an average of eight babies each and the mortality rate reduced the family size to about seven. Eighty percent of the women were illiterate. How were they to overcome poverty? Only an estimated four percent had used contraceptives, usually secretly, without the husband's knowledge. A USAID project funded a remarkable training facility that taught (the equivalent of) female nurses' aides to teach women about gynecology and obstetrics, including birth control using inter-uterine devices. Although the Pill was available in Yemen, it was difficult to obtain in rural areas and many uneducated women didn't understand its concept.

Opportunities for community service were innumerable. Foreign women in Sanaa reached out—with their hands, their wallets and their hearts. The newly established American Women's Group, the International Club of Sanaa, the Yemen-Hunt women, as well as other groups and individuals, raised funds through bazaars and similar events. They donated money and time to clinics, schools and other needy institutions.

Volunteerism is not a familiar concept in the Arab world where help and aid are traditionally provided through the extended family structure. But a handful of Yemeni women recognized the importance of helping the disadvantaged in their community. Basma, a single working woman, started a Women's Training Center where needy women learned basket weaving and sewing. They were ultimately able to create products at home to sell at the Center. As the project expanded and more volunteers joined the effort, trainees learned to market and sell their work. Within a few years, the Center owned twelve sewing machines and the women were producing and selling school uniforms.

A poster with the following quote hung on the wall of the Center: "If you educate a man, you educate a person, but if you educate a woman, you educate a family." (Ruby Manikan, India.)

Another Yemeni woman established a small school for disadvantaged children who were mentally and physically handicapped. She taught them cleanliness, basic manners and how to eat properly, as well as music, art and handicrafts.

Harish, manager of the Taj Sheba Hotel, lent his support to our charity projects. His staff saved bed sheets that had holes and were no longer usable for hotel guests. When a quantity accumulated, we picked them up and a volunteer cut and machine-hemmed the usable pieces to make sheets for the small beds at the Mother Teresa Home. The hotel also collected used—but still usable—pieces of soap from the guests' rooms and we distributed them to several places that would otherwise have had no soap at all. For poor people, soap was a luxury.

A small group of Yemeni women somehow discovered that female inmates in the local prison were being poorly treated and underfed. Several small children were incarcerated with their mothers and there was no milk, let alone fruits or vegetables. The concerned women asked the AWG for support and—following a great deal of bureaucratic nonsense from the prison officials—they arranged permission for several of us to visit. The warden was skeptical of foreign women "interfering."

We were shocked by what we saw at the prison! Living conditions for the women and children were abominable. At least two of the inmates were pregnant although they had been incarcerated for several years. One woman was clearly insane. Occasionally a nurse visited them, but there were few medical supplies available for even minor first aid. The prisoners subsisted mainly on rice.

Subsequently, the AWG along with the Yemeni women made several deliveries of food and some basic medicines to the women's section. We took fresh vegetables that didn't need cooking, melon and grapes, fruit juices and long-life milk. The inmates were overjoyed. Many of them talked to us about conditions in the prison and about their personal situations. I think some were happy just to have visitors.

An appalling incident at the prison caused us to question our aid priorities. When the warden abruptly said, "no more visits," we nevertheless wanted to continue providing food. One of the Yemeni volunteers, who was married to a man of some influence, pestered and prodded until the official agreed. One afternoon two women from the AWG took food supplies into the prison office and left them to be distributed. Afterwards, they were sitting in their vehicle across the road from the prison, discussing the next purchases.

"Look!" one of the women whispered, pointing toward the prison door. A female employee had just exited carrying two cases of orange juice—"presumably" the very ones that our volunteers had just delivered. She put the juice in a nearby car and drove away!

I came by—I won't say how—a purloined list of the women who were imprisoned, the dates and reasons for their sentences. Almost all had been arrested for prostitution or theft or both. The purloiner of the paper, as well as others, told me (reliably) that the main reason these women turned to crime was so they could eat! Forced into arranged marriages or sold by their parents, they ultimately ran away—for any number of reasons. They had nowhere to go, no home, no food. Their families would have nothing to do with them.

Prison sentences for even small crimes amounted to several years. And when their time was up many women remained. The authorities wouldn't release them unless there was someone "responsible" to release them to. Otherwise "they might commit another crime." Many women told us they were afraid to leave the prison.

I had little patience with some of the diplomatic spouses who complained that Sanaa was boring—nothing to do but go to the souk or play bridge. There were few cultural events, it's true, maybe two or three a year, and only one small museum to visit. Otherwise, it was teas, coffees, dinners, receptions—party party party. And so many poor people in need of help.

Eighty-plus Peace Corps volunteers worked successfully throughout the country, initiating and/or sustaining many needed projects. Because it was important for them to establish relationships with the local people, the volunteers preferred generally to disassociate themselves from the American Embassy so as not to be seen as "political" or "government." Nevertheless most of them came to our home at least once a year for a Christmas party and I met many of the women through volunteer projects. One of them, June, was a sixty-ish widow with grown-up children. She told me she had joined the Peace Corps because she wanted "to give something back" to society.

Since we hadn't had any direct contact with the Peace Corps since our tour in Venezuela in the late 1960's, I was surprised to discover that the members were no longer mostly young people. Many were middle-aged or older, retired from careers, with worthy experience and expertise to share. Some of the men and women taught English in Sanaa, others helped with city management or were medical technicians outside the capital.

There were a mere three traffic signals in all of Sanaa when we arrived, but two or three more eventually appeared. Drivers *did* pause for the red lights but stop signs were generally ignored by the populace. Yemenis drove crazily, but at moderate speeds so you could usually get out of the way in time. They made U-turns anywhere and everywhere and they never signaled their intention to turn or stop. One-way streets were seldom one-way in reality and it was commonplace to come upon a car parked in the middle of the street. A familiar sight was a battered pickup truck with several men crammed into the front. (Yemenis were small people.) The women, clutching their veils and headdresses, were relegated to the truck bed along with their children and the kids—the animal kind.

Driving in the mountains was a scary adventure. From my place in the back seat of a four-wheel drive Toyota I could look over the precipice to the depths beyond. There were no white lines to divide the narrow lanes and no barriers to protect vehicles from going over the edge. Neither were there any reflectors to warn night travelers. And many cars didn't have functioning headlights.

When former President Jimmy Carter and his wife Rosalyn came to Yemen, it was evident they had done their homework and they exhibited a genuine interest in the country. Mr. Carter discussed Yemen's agriculture and water issues with the Yemenis and in turn told them about peanut farming in Georgia. His wife asked pertinent questions about education and women's opportunities. The Carters expressed their concern for health issues and discussed their projects in other developing countries, such as working toward the eradication of guinea worm in parts of Africa.

Well known as a peacemaker and international statesman, President Carter impressed a receptive audience at Sanaa University, and in between meetings and visits the Yemenis feted the two at (gender separate) lunches and dinners. Art and I welcomed them together at a reception in our home. We had difficulty deciding on a reasonably-sized guest list. Everyone wanted to meet the Carters—Yemenis, embassy officials and other expatriate Americans. Our telephone rang repeatedly with people pleading for invitations.

Lunch at the presidential palace for Mrs. Carter was a typically Yemeni experience—in many ways. Art wangled invitations for all the embassy spouses and female officers, which wasn't difficult as those events normally included a cast of thousands. It was probably the only opportunity any of us would have to meet the hostesses, President Saleh's wives.

He had two wives—each tall, slim, dark-haired and beautiful. They were dressed elegantly in street-length white dresses, no veils, no head-coverings. I thought they looked very much alike. Both women were cordial and friendly hostesses and I wished—again—that I could speak enough Arabic to have a conversation with them.

Before eating we drank juice and soft drinks in a large colorful room, crowded with garish over-stuffed furniture. The only thing atypical about the lunch was that we sat at tables on comfortable chairs rather than on the floor. Otherwise, the food was traditional for a household of means—delicious and abundant.

After the meal and during tea in another salon, we asked to use the ladies' room. The American guests were led to a different part of the house where we entered a small undecorated bathroom with two stalls. The first two women took their turns—and came out to tell us that neither of the toilets functioned. One tank put forth a trickle of water, but there was not enough pressure to thoroughly flush. The other commode had a broken handle and was nearly overflowing. Those in urgent need relieved themselves, but the rest of us decided to forego the pleasure. The sink worked and we were able to wash our hands—and dry them with Kleenex tissues. There were no towels.

According to the laws of Islam, a Moslem man may have up to four wives as long as he treats each of them equally. Generally, this is not economically feasible, but in Sanaa I had the opportunity of meeting a few "multiple" wives. Not being accustomed to the custom, I was surprised by the direction of the conversation when I first met Soumaya.

"I'm the mayor's third wife, you know." The statement was an eye-opener. "My husband's daughter with his first wife is getting married next week. I'll send you an invitation."

Our German friend, Dagmar, thought it might be beneficial if her husband Awni had another wife. He was an Iraqi who worked for the United Nations in Sanaa and because of his job, they had moved many times during their marriage. She was becoming fed up with cleaning, washing and ironing, in between packing and unpacking.

"So one day I told Awni," she related with a sly smile, "Please tell your father to get you a second wife because I need a wife to help me!" Awni reacted to her tale with good humor—he had probably heard it many times before.

Wedding celebrations were huge, grand events that sometimes continued for several days. The women gathered at the bride's home and the groom's family hosted the male guests. We never saw the bride and groom together, nor did we witness a marriage ceremony. Guest lists were not pondered over and inviolable as they are in the United States. Like Soumaya, family members felt free to invite even the newest acquaintances. I was sometimes invited verbally to a wedding feast taking place the next day. Yemenis were friendly and hospitable people.

I showed up at my first wedding lunch at 11:45 even though the invitation read eleven; old-timers had advised me to arrive "late." Only two women preceded me, ambassadors' wives who were new to Sanaa. The room was enormous, furnished with little else than floor cushions and an occasional armrest around the periphery, leaving the center of the room open and bare. After a few more foreigners arrived, someone offered us glasses of juice. It was well after one o'clock before we saw any Yemeni guests, but gradually the room filled. Local women greeted each other and showed off their fancy dresses—and vied for cushion space. Several of us non-Yemenis had to stand up and wiggle a few times to encourage circulation in our legs.

A pretty cousin of the bride, whose shaky English far surpassed my few words of Arabic, told us that the bride would be arriving "soon." The sound of a drum brought a buzz of anticipation and excitement around the room. Three women came in—the drummer and two others who lit a good-sized incense burner. The aroma rapidly filled the air. It was 2:30.

And "soon" there she was—the smiling bride, crowned with a shining gold headdress. Her long gown was a satiny bottle green trimmed in gold. She began to circle the room along with the drummer who was beating a constant cadence. Close friends and family members gradually made a train and they circled with the bride. And they circled. And the smell of smoldering incense also circled through the closed room.

The beat of the drum began to pound inside my head—louder and louder—and I knew I had to get away from the incense and the noise. I said my good-byes and headed out into the fresh air. I was sorry to leave the party (and even sorrier to miss the food) but the unfortunate combination of incense and empty stomach propelled me out to the car. It was 3:30.

The burning of aromatic wood was traditional in Yemen. One could detect the scent almost everywhere, in shops, in homes, and frequently on peoples' clothing. A women's party was not a party without incense. When Kathy and I accompanied Art on a business trip to Marib, the mayor's wife invited us to an afternoon party.

When the wood was burning nicely and smoke was pervading the room, one woman lifted her skirt and straddled the burner. While gyrating her hips she waved her hand to direct the smoke upward. Another guest explained with a lascivious grin that men liked their wives to smell of incense. Our hostess carried a smaller ornate incense burner around the room, waving the smoke into the hair of each guest, all of whom appeared delighted. Except for Kathy and me. We found the unfamiliar custom downright smelly.

There was another custom that involved the olfactory sense. This ritual came at the end of a party or a lunch or almost any social celebration. When the goodbye handshaking and kissing began, out came the atomizer. Hosts and hostesses alike (separately, of course) sprayed the guests' hands until they were saturated with perfume or cologne. I always tried to say a quick thank you to my hostess and sneak out the door before the spraying began. Art never managed to avoid it—he came home from wedding lunches smelling like the proverbial French whorehouse.

Although I avoided the incense and the perfume whenever possible, I found those Yemeni customs to be endearing—though perhaps too enduring.

Dancing was another integral part of women's parties. Not everyone danced, only those who felt in the mood. The dancing was individualized, usually an undulating erotic movement or a belly dance. Though several people would dance at the same time, they didn't touch one other. Basma, a large woman with a chubby, pretty face amazed us with her graceful and sexy belly dance. In spite of her size and layers of clothing, her movements were mesmerizing.

The party in Marib included all the elements of a typical Yemeni women's gathering: incense, tea, a *medah,* conversation, qat, dancing—and a movie showing on the TV. On the other hand, Art and I observed that even at parties, Yemeni men and women could be quite content sitting together and not saying a word.

The consular section had uncovered a visa fraud a few months before we arrived and a thorough overhaul was in progress. Local authorities had dealt with the perpetrators, none of whom were Americans, but the embassy had to reckon with its negligence in not spotting the scam earlier. The situation grimly reminded me of the sneak thieves among our local GSO staff in Tel Aviv. It's dismaying to find out that employees and colleagues aren't trustworthy.

But what happened at the British Embassy was disastrous. One of their own defrauded Her Majesty's government in a money-changing scheme. A second secretary was illegally exchanging embassy pounds for Yemeni *rials* on the black market and pocketing a tidy profit. With the discovery of the crime, accusations of bribery and other misuse of funds also surfaced. By that time the perpetrator was back in London on routine transfer. After his arrest (and subsequent release on bail) the London Daily Mail reported that the investigation involved "the disappearance of a sum believed to be more than half a million pounds."

Fallout from the Foreign Service Officer's nefarious activities permeated the entire British embassy. The investigation of currency profiteering, combined with allegations of mismanagement and ineffectiveness in other areas, may have hastened the retirement of the two ambassadors who served in Sanaa in the early 90's. We were shocked to hear that the accused second secretary (whom we had met on several occasions) committed suicide at the end of 1994.

Outside observers and interested foreigners, including us, thought that the relative success of the 1993 elections was a positive sign for Yemen's three-year-old reunification. Less than a year later, however, the unity government fell apart and the South attempted to secede. The civil war exploded—and cooled down after nine weeks. The healing process for Yemen took much longer.

After an absence of more than three months the embassy evacuees returned to Sanaa—a different Sanaa than we had last seen when the war began. Art and I invited small groups of returnees to the residence for Happy Hour to welcome everyone back. During one of the get-togethers several planes flew fast, low and loudly over the compound. Conversation stopped and everyone stared in obvious discomfort toward the windows. When the planes and noise had passed us, the group inevitably began talking about the first days of the war. Everyone had an experience to relay. Some had seen looting; others had witnessed arson—homes of the opposition. We heard about the group of Americans who watched from a rooftop as Yemenis stormed a home. They carried out a heavy rolled-up carpet that the witnesses believed contained a body.

Other diplomats, too, had war stories—some had remained in the country throughout. Mirella laughed about the change in dining habits. "Lunch at two and dinner at six!" The government had imposed an evening curfew.

While I was languishing, homeless, in the States, Art organized the American Independence Day reception in spite of the war. There were fewer guests, about one hundred, but I heard it was a welcome distraction and a much-appreciated event. And Art and the staff managed it without the spouse of the house.

"I have just received a video from the State Department," Art announced one morning at the staff meeting. "It's part of a new Foreign Service recruiting pro-

gram and the Director General would like some feedback." Having gotten everyone's attention he pushed the PLAY button.

"Are you stuck in a go-nowhere, do-nothing job?" the narrator began. "This is
your chance to start an exciting career in the world of international diplomacy.

Ambassadors live in luxury, get to mingle with glamorous celebrities, royalty
and the social elite. And—they don't have to pick up after themselves!"

Confusion registered first on a few faces and then incredulity as the voice continued. "Ambassadors put in long hours without working hard and they are often
the center of attention. And the food—fantastic! Ambassadors dine on the finest
gourmet food." As scenes of liveried horse-drawn carriages and sumptuous buffets brightened the screen, everyone began to laugh.

"At the Ambassador Training Institute you will learn how to accept gifts graciously, how to propose toasts, learn phrases like 'delighted to see you again,' and
'pass the sweet and sour shrimp.'"

The "recruiting" film ended with information regarding where to send
$300,000 to buy your ambassadorship (somewhere in Mexico). When the laugh-
ter died down, Art confessed that Alex had sent us the video—a sketch he had
taped from an NBC television show, *Saturday Night*.

I will add another Foreign Service Requisite: Enjoy yourself!

For three years and three months I was "Mrs. Ambassador." The title was
improper for a spouse—I was merely Mrs. Hughes—but I heard the title often
and I gladly answered to it. The job was hard work but the rewards were immea-
surable. Bilquis, the Queen of Sheba, preceded us in the fascinating land of
Yemen. If her legend is true, I am sorry I missed her—another royal in a grand
procession of events, places and especially people that enriched my life during
thirty-two years with my husband in the Foreign Service.

REFERENCES

Ewert-Biggs, Jane. *Pay, Pack, and Follow.* Academy Chicago Publishers, 1986

Freifeld, Sidney. *Undiplomatic Notes.* Canada, Hounslow Press, 1990

Hughes, Katherine L. *The Accidental Diplomat: Dilemmas of the Trailing Spouse.* Putnam Valley NY, Aletheia Publications, 1999

Oldfield, Barney. *Never a Shot in Anger.* New York, Van Rees Press, 1956

Portner, Paul. *Sheer Madness.* (Adapted by Bruce Jordon and Marilyn Abrams)

Russell, Beatrice. *Living in State.* New York, David McKay Co., Inc., 1959

GLOSSARY

AAA Antiaircraft artillery

AID (also USAID) Agency for International Development

AEWG American Embassy Women's Group

APO Army Post Office

AWG American Women's Group

CLO Community Liaison Office or Officer

COM Chief of Mission

DAS Deputy Assistant Secretary

DCM Deputy Chief of Mission

DCR Deputy Chief's Residence

DOD Department of Defense

DS Diplomatic Security

ECON Economic Office

FAS Foreign Agriculture Service

FBO Foreign Buildings Office

FCS Foreign Commercial Service

FMO Facilities Management Office or Officer

FS Foreign Service

FSI Foreign Service Institute

FSN Foreign Service National

GSO General Services Office or Officer

Gunny Marine Gunnery Sergeant

HHE Household Effects

IRS Internal Revenue Service

MED Medical Division

PER Personnel Office or Officer

POL Political Office

R&R Rest and Relaxation or Rest and Recuperation

RMO Regional Medical Officer

RSO Regional Security Office or Officer

SALT Strategic Arms Limitation Treaty

SecDef Secretary of Defense

UN United Nations

USAF United States Air Force

USG United States Government

USIA United States Information Agency

USIS United States Information Service

0-595-31496-1